Descriptive and Comparative Linguistics

The Latin Language
Mycenaeans and Minoans:
Aegean Prehistory in the Light of the Linear B Tablets
A New Guide to the Palace of Knossos

STUDIES IN GENERAL LINGUISTICS

edited by L. R. Palmer and G. C. Lepschy

Elements of General Linguistics
ANDRÉ MARTINET
English Phonetic Texts
DAVID ABERCROMBIE
A Survey of Structural Linguistics
GIULIO C. LEPSCHY

Plate I. Sound spectrogram of the sentence *This seed should make good feed*

Descriptive and Comparative Linguistics

A CRITICAL INTRODUCTION

BY

Leonard R. Palmer

FABER & FABER
3 QUEEN SQUARE, LONDON

FIRST PUBLISHED 1972
BY FABER AND FABER LIMITED
3 QUEEN SQUARE LONDON WC1

PRINTED IN GREAT BRITAIN BY
WILLIAM CLOWES & SONS, LIMITED
LONDON, BECCLES AND COLCHESTER

ISBN 0 571 09940 8

Contents

Illustrations

Acknowledgements

Figure 2 is reproduced from *Physics* (Second Edition) by Marshall, Pounder and Stewart, published by Macmillan Company of Canada in 1967.

Figure 14 is reproduced from *Elements of General Linguistics* by André Martinet, published by Faber and Faber Ltd.

Figure 47, 'British River Names', is reproduced from *Language and History in Early Britain* by K. Jackson, published by Edinburgh University Press.

Figures 37, 38, 39, 40, 43 and 44 have been reproduced from *An Introduction to Modern Linguistics*, published in 1936, in which acknowledgement was made to Professors K. Jaberg, A. Bach, E. Gamillscheg and A. Dauzat.

Plate 1: the spectrogram was recorded at the Studio für Experimentallinguistik (Director Professor F. Zaic), University of Salzburg.

Phonetic chart after *The Principles of the International Phonetic Association*, Hertford, 1961.

Preface

In a letter addressed to the publishers of the present work and printed as a preface to his *Aspects of Language* (1953) W. J. Entwistle referred to the endless flow of new literature by linguists and philosophers on the topic of language. Since then the flow has increased to a flood, and it has included many excellent introductions to linguistics. This might prompt the question 'Why another such *Introduction*?' The simplest answer would be that the publishers have received repeated requests for a reissue of the earlier book *An Introduction to Modern Linguistics*. The fact that this first book took shape in 1931–32, when the great revolution in linguistics was only in its beginnings, will suffice to explain why a simple reissue was unthinkable. It also explains why the requests were made: the main emphasis of the book was on comparative and historical linguistics, and most university linguists today are 'philologists', who pursue their studies in the schools of ancient and modern languages, centred on texts as sources of information about particular societies and civilizations. Languages are sited in their social worlds. Such scholars, both senior and junior, are apt to find the abstract and formal approaches of modern descriptive linguistics dry and barren. Yet without descriptions there can be no comparison, and linguistic history emerges from the comparison of descriptions. This ineluctable truth prescribed the form of the new book. An account of descriptive linguistics precedes the part on comparative ('diachronic') linguistics.

Like Entwistle, I found that one of the problems was to keep pace with the flow of new publications. In linguistics this is a peculiarly formidable difficulty, for over the years the emphasis has changed with great rapidity as one charismatic figure has followed another. The book was virtually finished when transformational generative grammar made its impact and the decipherment of the Linear B script concentrated my main attention on Aegean studies. Now, fourteen years after the publication of *Syntactic Structures*, the doctrines of N. Chomsky can be seen in better focus. In 1970 a disciple wrote,[1] 'Chomsky's position is not only unique within linguistics at the present time, but is probably unprecedented in the whole history of the subject.' Almost simultaneously an article in *Language*[2] began 'It has become clear over the past five years that transformational generative grammar is nowhere near being an adequate theory of human language.'

Still more impressive was the recantation of a master of modern linguistics, C. F. Hockett, who has written one of the best introductions to the subject and who, in a presidential address, referred to Chomsky's doctrines as one of the major break-throughs in the history of linguistics. More recently, in his book *The State of the Art*, Hockett not only submits these doctrines to a profound and devastating analysis, but delivers a no less radical judgment on much of his own work and that of the modern American school in general: '. . . we must set aside not only Chomsky's theories but also much of the rest of the theorizing we have done in the last three decades, returning with very minor emendation, to our heritage of scientific linguistics as largely channeled to us through Bloomfield. . . . It is, of course, frustrating to realize that we have spent so much time and energy exploring blind alleys, but this is the sort of frustration a scientist must be prepared to accept from time to time.'

In this counter-revolutionary situation the writer of an introductory manual has a delicate task. Where there is no *communis opinio*, he cannot be otherwise than critical. This explains what may be regarded as a deplorable feature of such an elementary

1. J. Lyons, *Chomsky* (1970), p. 9.
2. G. Lakoff, 'Global Rules', *Language*, 46 (1970), 627.

work: the introduction of new technical terms. This was made necessary by my conviction that certain protracted and vexed discussions were largely due to the ambiguity of the terms used. The endless wrangle over the 'phoneme' is an instance of this. Another is the use of the term 'sentence' in the new syntactic doctrines. The book, after an Introduction on the nature of speech, first covers the main departments of descriptive linguistics. The second part goes over the same ground as the earlier book, but little has remained unaltered.

Inevitably, a short manual of this character involves selection and simplification. This requires schematization, and not all scholars in the tumultuous linguistic world of today will be wholly pleased with the inevitable distortions and omissions. The latter include the whole of the mathematical linguistics and machine translation, because I have principally in mind the 'philologists', who make up the vast majority of linguists in our schools and universities. Fortunately, a clear account of these branches is available in another work published in this series: G. C. Lepschy, *A Survey of Structural Linguistics* (1970), 139–150. Apart from that, it is a consolation that schematization by its very imperfections may stimulate fruitful discussion, and the recommended reading list will help to remedy onesidedness.

The co-editor of this series, Mr. G. C. Lepschy, read the proofs with great skill and care, removed many errors and made suggestions for the improvement of the exposition. The same debt of gratitude is owed to Professor E. Henderson, who kindly agreed to look through Chapters 2–4. My wife took an active interest in the book throughout its composition, as she did with its predecessor of 1936. She typed the manuscript and compiled the Index. I thank them all. Without their help the book would have had even more blemishes.

Sistrans, February 1972.   L. R. PALMER

1

Introduction

The student of linguistics must first pose the question what is the object of his studies. He might be tempted to answer at once 'linguistics is the scientific study of language'. But with this apparently simple and straightforward answer he would have involved himself in one of the most keenly discussed problems of modern linguistics, namely the relationship between 'speech' and 'language'. It will be later argued that this is one of the complex pseudo-problems arising out of the special language which linguists devise to describe phenomena with which they are peculiarly concerned. To avoid such pseudo-problems we must from the outset render an accurate account of each technical term we need to coin as the investigation proceeds.

We begin again and ask what phenomena are observed by the linguist. When we enter a foreign country, the first thing that strikes us is the fact that the inhabitants make strange noises with their mouths, and that their social behaviour is in some way influenced by the perception of these noises. This phenomenon is the object of our study: the production of vocal sounds by human beings in order to influence the behaviour of their fellows, and conversely, the interpretation by the hearer of such sounds in order to understand what is in the mind of the speaker. Such vocal behaviour is perhaps the most characteristically human activity. No human community has been observed which functions without this peculiar mode of social behaviour. To designate it we use the first of our technical terms: this socially determined vocal activity we shall call 'speech'. The term 'language' will be reserved for a more technical application (p. 81).

The question at once arises why it should be necessary for human societies to use such a device. The necessity arises from the fact that direct communication between minds is impossible. We cannot (the doubtful evidence for extrasensory perception being ignored) implant our thoughts and intentions directly in the mind of a person to whom we wish to convey a message. In order to do so, I can either wear a flower, affix a postage stamp in a peculiar way, make facial contortions and gestures, or produce vocal sounds. In the case of Helen Keller, who became both blind and deaf in infancy, the teacher had recourse to the sense of touch. She invented a system of taps on the hand, and in this way communication was established between the two personalities. But for this the miracle of Helen Keller's education could never have been accomplished. For it is only by affecting the organs of sense perception in some way or other that we can convey a message to a recipient mind. The way in which this communication between minds is established constitutes the fundamental problem of speech. But before dealing with the specific question of human speech it will be necessary to consider the general nature of signs.

The statement has been made that we can only know other persons' mental processes by making inferences from observations of their behaviour. Thus if I blush, the observer will assume that I am ashamed or embarrassed; if my eyes twitch, he will conclude I am nervous. He is enabled to make such deductions because of his experience of his own feelings and their accompanying physical manifestations. That is to say, he infers from certain observations a state of mind similar to his own under similar circumstances. There is, however, a considerable difference between a blush and speech. A blush is usually involuntary. It is the effect of some disturbance in the nervous system; so that there is a cause and effect relation between the psychological state and the physical sign (a blush). But when we utter the sound complex 'I am ashamed', this is an action which lies under the control of the will, and the connexion between this sound complex and the mental state is wholly arbitrary. A Frenchman would use quite a different

set of sounds and a German another set again, though both
Frenchmen and Germans blush in the same way as ourselves. This
enables us to draw a distinction between symptom and symbol.
A blush, the natural unwilled result of the mental state, is a
symptom of that mental state, while the sound complex 'embarrassment' is something quite arbitrary which we produce deliberately in order that a hearer may interpret it and thus learn
indirectly of our mental state. This is what we call a symbol. Thus
smoke may be a symptom of fire, while the sound complex [faɪə]¹
is the symbol for it. This insistence on the arbitrary nature of the
linguistic symbol is of fundamental importance for our science,
and we shall obtain a clearer understanding of this essential fact
if we compare language with systems of communication used by
creatures other than human beings.

The German scientist K. v. Frisch² has made a number of
interesting observations on the social life of bees and their mode
of communication. A piece of paper was smeared with honey and
placed somewhere in the neighbourhood of the hive. Often several
hours or even days passed before the paper was discovered by the
bees. But then things happened rapidly. The bee would take its
load back to the hive and return as quickly as possible to the place
where it had made the find. But it did not return alone; before
long hundreds of bees were clustered around the honey. It was
obvious that in some way the first bee had 'informed' its fellows
of the find. How does this act of 'communication' take place?
Close observation revealed that a most interesting ceremony is
performed in the hive after the return of the discoverer. After it
has been relieved of its burden, the returned bee begins a complicated dance which attracts and excites other members of the
colony. They gather round and touch the performer with their
feelers. Suddenly it stops and flies away. Now v. Frisch observed
that the other bees do not simply *follow* it; but in due course they
find their own way to the proper place even if the honey has been
removed in the meantime and a cup of sugar water substituted.

---

1. For an explanation of these phonetic symbols see Chapter 3.
2. K. v. Frisch, *Bees: Their Vision, Chemical Senses and Language*, Ithaca,
1950.

How do the bees know? How has the information been communi-
cated to them? Von Frisch has established conclusively by a
series of experiments that when a bee enters a flower some of the
perfume clings to the body. This is smelled by the others who go
out in search of a similar scent. The bees, however, are just as
successful in their search even when the find consists of a bowl of
sugar water which has no perfume. By further experiment v.
Frisch discovered that the bees can mark their finds by use of a
natural perfume contained in a gland of their bodies. The bowl of
sugar water is sprayed with this perfume and attracts the bees
from a wide area. In yet another series of experiments v. Frisch
was able to establish that by varying the details of the dance the
returned explorer was able to indicate the direction and distance
of his find.

This is a crude symbolism compared with human speech. Its
limitations and drawbacks are obvious at first glance. The perfume
'symbol' is taken from the same sphere; it is made of the same stuff
as the thing symbolized. Consequently it can only be applied to
material objects of comparatively simple structure. For the
complicated purposes of human communication we need something more elastic and less cumbersome. We cannot always carry
around with us samples of all the physical objects to which we
have occasion to refer, to say nothing of abstract ideas like love,
honour and obedience. We are, however, almost always in a
position to make noises with our vocal organs. The utilization of
this possibility to form symbols is what mainly distinguishes man
from the animal world. The immense advantages of our system
are obvious. In speech the symbol is de-materialized; it dispenses
with any resemblance to, or imitation of, the thing represented.
The connexion between them is of a quite different kind. We say
that there is an arbitrary allocation of certain mental contents
to certain sound groups. We must now examine this peculiar
relationship; that is to say, the connexion between word and
'thing'. How does this connexion arise, how is it possible?

The experiments of the Russian physiologist Pavlov throw
considerable light on the development of linguistic symbolism in
the child. In his experiments with dogs Pavlov, when giving food
to the animal, used to blow a whistle of a certain pitch. This was

repeated at each meal. Eventually he observed that even when the whistle was blown without offering food the dog showed all the signs of food expectancy, such as salivation, etc. This pheno-menon is known to psychologists as a 'conditioned response'. The response, salivation, is 'conditioned' by the blowing of a whistle of a particular pitch.

Such 'conditioning' is observable among other animals, even quite humble ones. A remarkable and grotesque case of condition-ing is reported by K. Z. Lorenz in his book *King Solomon's Ring*.[1] Von Frisch, whose investigations into the habits of bees we have just mentioned, possessed a parakeet. Naturally, in the interests of his furniture, the scientist would let the bird out of its cage only after he had seen it evacuate its bowels. The parakeet thus learned to associate the pleasure of free flight round the room with this natural act and would try to produce something, regardless of necessity, every time von Frisch came near the cage. Its strainings were such that it simply had to be let out of its cage every time its owner came near the cage. Quite briefly we may say that such modifications of behaviour by training or conditioning imply memory, the power to store up experiences in some way so as to modify later reactions. Very interesting work has been done on octopods in this respect, while even an earthworm has been taught to turn right rather than left after experiencing electric shocks in the left arm of a T-tube. What governs the difference in behaviour of an unconditioned worm which turns indiscriminately and one which turns right is the stored previous experience of the electric shock.

Now let us observe a child in the process of learning its mother tongue. It sees an object, say a spoon, and hears from its mother a certain sound complex *spoon*. This happens repeatedly. It hears phrases like 'this is a *spoon*', 'where is the *spoon*?', 'all gone *spoon*'. Eventually this sound complex will evoke in it a certain mental image corresponding to the physical object spoon. This is a conditioned response similar to the response of Pavlov's dog to the whistle. We have been speaking, of course, of an English child. A French child would have a different 'conditioning', a differently

---

1. *King Solomon's Ring*, Chapter VIII. Methuen, 1952.

pitched whistle. It would hear [kʉijɛ:r].[1] A German child would
hear [lœf]]. Thus it is only as a result of a long and complex training
that a child comes to understand the sound symbols used in the
community into which it is born. There is nothing natural or
instinctive about it. No English-born child speaks English
naturally. If it were removed at birth to China, its Chinese would
be indistinguishable from that of the natives, and English would
be a foreign tongue to it. We conclude then that the relation
between the sound symbol and the thing symbolized is wholly
arbitrary and that there is no natural or necessary connexion
between them. By 'arbitrary connexion' we mean simply this:
there is nothing in the psycho-physical constitution of man which
makes him utter spontaneously a sound complex [spuwn], or any
other, on beholding this particular object. This is the essential
difference between human speech and the means of communication used among the social animals. Bees, it is clear, possess *innate*
instinctive modes of behaviour for giving the orientation of a rich
store of nectar at any time. The essence of the matter is clearly
stated by Lorenz,[2] and we summarize his chief points. Animals
have no language in the true sense of the term. Among the higher
vertebrates and the insects, it is true, the socially living species
make certain *innate* movements and sounds and also possess
corresponding *innate* ways of reacting to these sounds and movements on the part of the other members of their community.
Quite complex signals are produced and 'understood' without
previous learning or training. This is quite different from the
laborious learning process to which the human infant is subjected
before it can master the language of the community into which it
is born. Lorenz notes that the language of bird species, being
genetically fixed, is therefore also ubiquitous, and he records his
surprise at hearing the jackdaws of Northern Russia 'talk' in
exactly the same way as his own birds from Altenburg (Austria).

Absent, too, from such bird 'speech' is the element of conscious
intention. This is shown by the fact that birds kept singly produce
these signals and expressions when the right mood overtakes them.

---

1. The phonetic script used here will be explained in Chapter 3.
2. Op. cit.

It is the unconscious and automatic character of the 'speech behaviour' of birds which sharply distinguishes it from human speech. Another limitation is the incapacity of animals and birds to use human language elements actively even when they have been trained to respond passively to them. A talking bird which has the capacity to associate such sound-expressions with certain things and happenings nevertheless cannot use this capacity to achieve a purpose. Lorenz notes that Köhler, who had succeeded in teaching pigeons to count up to six, failed to teach his grey parrot to utter the word 'food' when hungry and 'water' when thirsty, even though the bird was quite capable of producing these vocables.

It may be thought that we have somewhat laboured this point of the arbitrary connexion between the linguistic symbol and the thing meant. Our excuse is that this is the fundamental axiom on which the whole of comparative linguistics rests. Since the above stated dogma is the keystone in the arch of the theory of comparative linguistics we must at once consider some minor modifications.

It is, of course, obvious that words like 'cuckoo' and 'ding-dong' are imitations of sounds perceived and as such they must be excepted from our dogma that the relationship between word and meaning is arbitrary. Yet certain scholars have gone further and asserted that every sound has a certain innate quality which renders it suitable to represent certain ideas. Thus Jakob Grimm, one of the founders of modern linguistics, remarked that each sound has a natural content that is founded in the organ that produces it. The Danish scholar Otto Jespersen has shown that many English words with the meaning small, delicate, unstable, etc., contain the vowel short *i*. Examples are *little, flimsy, brittle, fickle, fritter, niggling snigger, giggle, thin, kid, nipper*, etc. But however expressive such sounds may be, no general principle can be formulated. The arbitrary nature of language is evident from words like *big* and *thick*, which contain the short vowel *i*, while *small* has the same vowel as *broad*.

Some support for Jespersen's conception of language seems to be provided by the words for 'father' and 'mother', which have a similar form in the most widely diverse languages, the words for father containing *p* or *d* (*papa, dada*) and those for mother *m* or *n* (*mama*). This, however, does not prove any natural connexion between these sounds and the meaning expressed. There is nothing in these sounds that is expressive of the nature of fatherhood or motherhood. The coincidence must be explained in some other way. The lip sounds *m* and *p* are among the first sounds that every human child will make, the lips being strongly developed even at birth for the purpose of sucking. What is more natural than that the parents should make these first sounds refer to themselves? This is indeed the way in which most baby languages are evolved. The child makes a peculiar set of sounds in a particular situation either by accident or through an unsuccessful attempt to reproduce something it has heard. These sounds, these embryo words, are caught up by the persons of its environment and endowed by them with the meaning which they suppose the baby has intended to convey. In this way the nurse or parents themselves create the baby language and in fact actually teach it to their child, thus establishing early verbal communication.

Other scholars have put forward the thesis that language has evolved from primitive mouth gestures. Thus in certain languages of Central America the lips are pushed forward to indicate something distant and retracted to point to something near. This results in vowels of different quality (see Chapter 3). Such an alternation of sounds may actually be observed in the demonstrative pronouns of languages. English has *there*, *yon* and *here*; German *dies* and *das*, French *ceci* and *cela*, Malay *iki* and *ika*, etc. In other cases sounds may be used analogically to represent the ideas they mean. Thus the alternation of the vowels in *see-saw* represents the up-and-down motion. Another example of the kind is *zig-zag*. But however widespread such phenomena may be and however natural it is to enhance expressiveness by the use of sound symbolism, it will be noticed that such similarities between words of different speech are usually confined to one element in those words. Sound symbolism hardly ever results in the independent creation of *identical* words. *Bim-bam* says the German for the sound of the bells; we respond with *ding-dong*. A German cock cries *kikeriki*, his English cousin *cocka-doodle-do*.

One further objection. Most of those theories about the linguistic symbol have been put forward to account for the origin of speech. We must insist, however, that speculation about the origin of speech is not an essential part of linguistic science as we understand it, any more than the chemist feels called upon to theorize about the origin of matter. Linguistics is an empirical and positivist science. The proper object of its interest and study is the speech habits which we can directly observe or deduce from written records. Doubtless sound symbolism, in the sense we have just discussed, has played and will continue to play some part in the creation and growth of verbal communication. But it must be insisted that in the vast majority of cases no necessary connexion can be traced between sound and meaning. With this in mind we can now proceed to compare different systems of linguistic symbols.

On learning German the English student is struck by the number of common words that are identical or similar.

e.g.	Mann: man	Schwester: sister
	Weib: wife	Milch: milk
	Kalb: calf	Butter: butter
	Gras: grass	grün: green, etc.

How does this come about? The process of naming involves a process like sticking a label on an object. Suppose that we have two new recruits to a department store and they are given the task of labelling the various items of merchandise. As raw material they are provided with wire and beads of different shapes and colours. Their first task is to devise labels by stringing the beads together to form distinctive patterns; this done, they have to attach them *at random* to the different sorts of objects. What are the chances that they will devise the same patterns and arrive at identical allocations? A mathematician will inform us that the improbability is so great as to amount to an impossibility. Speech symbols offer an analogous, though more complicated, process. The vocal organs form sounds and strings of sounds that are allocated to certain 'things'. Different communities, may, of course, possess similar labels in the form of sound groups (e.g. Engl. *feel*, Germ. *viel* 'much', Engl. *reason*, Germ. *Riesen* 'giants'); but the chances that two sets of speakers will independently arrive at identical or parallel word-meaning allocations are extremely remote. Thus in the case of the above similarities between English and German where similar sound groups ('vocables') have the same meaning, we must have recourse to some other explanation. Since such far-going resemblances could not be accidental and due to independent invention, we must conclude that the two sets of speech-habits are somehow connected in origin. The facts that we are comparing are essentially forms of conventional social behaviour. The question we pose is how to account for these striking resemblances in the complex social behaviour of Englishmen and Germans. Each speaker, if challenged to account for his speech habits, will refer the interlocutor to his parents and the older members of the community. As an infant he had no alternative: he simply imitated his elders. Thus the acquisition of speech is essentially a mimetic activity. It is by such mimetic processes that speech habits are transmitted from speaker to hearer through time and space. The linguistic symbol, viewed in its historical aspect as a social acquisition by new members of the community, is deserving of a special technical term. In accordance with prevailing terminological custom, I propose the term 'mimeme'. Thus if we reject, as we must, the possibility that the English and Germans independently invented the sound symbols *hand*, *finger*, etc., we are driven to the conclusion that, if we trace the 'mimetic generations' back step by step, the two chains will eventually join up. Our linguistic ancestors were once *tête-à-tête* with those of present-day Germans. Here we have the definition of a term which has caused much trouble to linguists. This is 'relationship'. When we say that the English *hand* is related to German *Hand*, we simply mean that the arbitrary nature of the linguistic symbol compels us to rule out the possibility of independent invention and to conclude that the two resemblant sets of speech habits are connected by an unbroken chain of mimetic acts. But these acts are part of a mode of social behaviour so complex and peculiar that they may be used to define the societies in question: 'English' = 'English-speaking'. Thus to trace the transmission of linguistic symbols is to write in part the history of the community which uses them. To reconstruct the ancestral forms which account for the resemblances in the communities under observation is simultaneously to make some kind of assertion about an ancestral community. The matter will be discussed in detail below,[1] but we make the point at the outset since the concentration of modern linguistics on problems of description (see Chapter 2) has led some scholars to occasional outbursts against comparative and historical linguistics and to decry reconstructed ancestral languages as figments of the romantic imagination. We repeat, then, that observed resemblances between speech habits, given the empirical principle of arbitrariness, force us to the conclusion of historical connectedness by an unbroken chain of mimetic acts. This connectedness is what is understood by 'relationship'.

In order to establish the fact of such a relationship our evidence must not consist entirely of points of vocabulary. For, as we shall see below (see Chapter 13), words are often borrowed by one language from another as a result of cultural contact. Thus English has borrowed words like *algebra* from Arabic sources. No one on that account will assert that English is 'related' to the Semitic languages. What constitutes the most certain evidence of relationship is resemblance of grammatical structure, for languages retain their native structure even when their vocabularies have been swamped by foreign borrowing, such as has been the case for English and Hittite.

If we apply such criteria to our assertion about the relationship of German and English, we are immediately presented with conclusive evidence. English forms the past tense of a large number of verbs by adding a -*t* or -*d*, e.g. *learn: learnt, love: loved.* Now there is no intrinsic reason why the sound *d* or *t* should serve to indicate the past tense. Consequently the presence in German of a similar grammatical device (*sagen: sagte; fragen: fragte*) is important evidence for relationship of German with English.

In the foregoing paragraphs we have illustrated by brief and simple examples the principles underlying the comparative method practised by linguists. It is from this method that an important branch of linguistics derives its name 'Comparative philology'. The speech habits of different communities are compared with a

---

1. See Chapter 14.

view to discovering similarities. Once resemblances of structure
and vocabulary are established which preclude the possibility of
independent invention, we are forced to conclude that there is some
historical connexion between the two communities employing the
resemblant signalling systems.

This concept of relationship involves another fact which leads
us to formulate the second axiom of historical linguistics. If
speech habits are resemblant but different (e.g. English *foot*, Germ.
Fuss) and we postulate common ancestral forms, that involves the
notion of change. The modern Englishman requires considerable
help in order to read even Shakespeare; for Chaucer he needs a
grammar and a glossary, while Beowulf is a closed book. Yet Old
English was spoken by our direct ancestors here in England.
That form of speech, passed down from parent to child in a
direct line, has in thirty or so generations changed so much that
it has become to all intents and purposes a foreign language. If
the student turns to other countries, he is faced with the necessity
of learning not merely modern German, but Old High German
and all the other varieties and subspecies which exercise the
university student. All over the world we may observe the same
process; nowhere does language stand still. This is the second
axiom of linguistics. In language, at any rate, the Heraclitan tag
pánta rheî 'everything flows' holds good: the linguistic symbols,
in their spoken form at least, are all involved in a continuous
process of change. Corresponding to this second axiom we have
the second method which linguists employ—the historical method.
This consists in tracing the changes in any given language back
to its earliest records. Thus we may follow changes in English
back to the earliest Old English texts. In German, Old High
German will provide the ultimate goal of our textual studies.
Only when we have pushed the historical method to its ultimate
limit shall we have recourse to the comparative method discussed
above.

By the application of these methods linguists have been led to
the conclusion that widely different languages spoken over huge
areas of Europe and Asia, ranging from Irish in Western Europe
to the languages of Northern and Central India, are closely related
and descended from a common parent. The table of comparisons

below will show at a glance the truth of this statement. These
languages, which are called the Indo-European family, will be
listed below (Appendix A). But for the present we have to examine
such aspects of language as may be universally observed.

GREEK	LATIN	SANSKRIT	GOTHIC	GERMAN	ENGLISH
estí	est	asti	ist	ist	is
zugón	iugum	yugám	yuk	Joch	yoke
phérō	fero	bhárāmi	baíran	ge-bären	bear
oktő	octo	aṣṭāu	ahtau	acht	eight
agrós	ager	ajrás	akrs	Acker	acre
patér	pater	pitár-	fadar	Vater	father

In the preceding paragraph we used the word 'language', which
was expressly reserved for later definition in a more restricted
sense than it is used in everyday speech. The reason for this is
implicit in the preceding table: the terms of comparison are
'words' which have been extracted from the speech habits of
communities under observation. It will be evident that the infinitely
complex mouthings of widely scattered communities cannot be
directly compared with each other. The first step must be to reduce
each set of speech habits to an ordered description and, as will
appear later (Chapter 2), each such description will take the form
of lists of 'items' at different levels together with statements of
their combinations. Such a description will be judged adequate if
it accounts for the boundless productivity of human speech. It is to
such a description that we propose to restrict the term 'language'
(see further below, pp. 81f.).

Comparison of 'languages' is carried out by inspection of such
descriptions. We may compare item with item (e.g. the Latin,
Greek, Sanskrit, Gothic words for 'seven') or structure with
structure (e.g. Is there anything in Latin which matches the vowel
alternations observed in English *sing, sang, sung*?). But such
questions and their answers must be based on complete descriptions. It follows that the techniques of descriptive linguistics must
be our first concern, all the more so because of the concentration of

modern linguistics on the practical problems and the theory of
speech analysis and description, whereas up till about 1930
linguists were mainly concerned with the history of changes in
language. A phenomenon was regarded as 'explained' if its history
could be traced through time. Such was the 'diachronic' approach.
If we attempt a description of the speech habits of a given community at one particular time, this is the 'synchronic' approach.

Part I

Descriptive (Synchronic) Linguistics

2

The Analysis and Description of Speech

THE ITEM EXPERIENCE

The problems of speech analysis and description have absorbed a large part of linguistic effort over the last three or four decades. Techniques have become more and more sophisticated and definitions increasingly rigorous. Inevitably this has led to a great proliferation of technical terminology. This has proceeded so far that linguists of different schools find it difficult to communicate with one another. Since all scholars in the last resort are talking about the same object of investigation and the impressive progress achieved has resulted, as in all sciences, simply from the refinement of common sense, it will be well to begin with the plain man's 'intuitive' approach to an unknown language which he wishes to learn.

When we first take up residence in a foreign country, our ears are assailed by strings of unintelligible sounds emitted by the inhabitants who by this means coordinate their behaviour. We learn to operate this new signalling system by experimental imitation. As our ears become habituated, we gradually pick out recurrent sound patterns. Such 'recurrence' is an elemental experience often ignored in the highly self-conscious procedures of linguistic analysis. No speech habits can be acquired or described without first experiencing the 'that there' of the primary perception followed by the 'that there again' which identifies a given perception with some other stored in the memory. This 'that there *again*' experience is so fundamental to linguistic analysis that it deserves a special technical term. It will be conveniently designated by the Latin adverb *item* 'again': it will be called the '*item* experience'.

For the apprehension of the speech 'item' the procedure is more complex than with the recognition of the physical objects about us. In learning French, the 'that there again' of a perceived sound pattern, say *soupe*, has to be matched with an item in the recurrent situation. Hungrily we follow a hungry-looking Frenchman to a restaurant and observe the results produced by his utterance of the sound pattern [sup]. To 'learn the language' one of the first steps must be to match such vocal 'items' with 'items' of the total signalling situation until there jumps that vitalizing spark which transforms a concatenation of vocal sounds into the linguistic sign. This fundamental point must be made at the outset: the units of speech are sound complexes ('vocables') which are endowed with certain signalling properties. They are sound-meaning units. Henceforth they will be referred to as S-M items. Thus *hair* (S-M1) is a different item from *hare* (S-M2), though the 'vocable' is the same in both cases.

THE FIRST ARTICULATION: THE MONEME

It is thanks to the phenomenon of recurrence and repetitiveness that the linguist is enabled to fashion an orderly description of the speech habits of a given community, despite the fleeting nature of the speech act and despite the infinite inventiveness of the native speakers who constantly devise new utterances in response to fresh needs and novel situations. It may be said in advance that the speech flux can be broken down into a limited inventory of 'items' of different kinds which recur in different combinations. As the Danish scholar L. Hjelmslev has written, it should be possible to set up a general and exhaustive calculus of the possible combinations of the basic elements (our 'items').

In describing the speech habits of a given community the linguist will normally begin with an adequate sample, a 'corpus', consisting of a large number of gross items, i.e. speech events. Ideally this will take the form of complete dialogues between native speakers recorded in carefully observed situations. Like our rule-of-thumb learner, the describer will first observe that the natives emit strings of sounds in bursts marked off by the pauses of greater or lesser duration, such stretches of speech mostly being further characterized by variations of speed, loudness, pitch and pause. These universal features of human utterances are called 'prosodies'.[1] While such prosodic features are among the first to be noticed by the observer (and imitated by native infants in their process of speech acquisition), their description will be more conveniently treated at a later stage (see below, pp. 58ff.).

Such gross items of speech, whose completeness is marked off by pauses and further characterized by certain types of prosody peculiar to a given language, may be called 'utterances'. The first steps in acquiring a foreign language are normally the recognition of certain such gross items appropriate to stereotyped situations. *Good morning. How d'you do? Step this way. Passports, please. Thank you.* With growing experience we learn to pick out the recurring sub-items within the gross items: *please, you, this, good,* etc. Some of these sub-items may themselves recur as complete utterances emitted by a speech partner in the give-and-take of dialogue. This means that they function as complete 'sentences'.[2] *Do I turn left or right? Right. Who goes and gets it? You or I? You.* Analysis proceeds along these intuitive commonsense lines. Utterance is matched with utterance, their similarities and differences being correlated with similarities and differences in the situation. The items thus elicited become smaller and smaller until, after prolonged experience and experiment, all those items have been sorted out which have been observed to function as complete 'sentences', i.e. as completed contributions to the dialogue by one of the speech partners. If further experience shows that these minimal sentences cannot be further broken down into sub-items which are themselves capable of functioning as complete utterances, an important water-shed will have been reached. Such

---

1. From the Greek word *prosodia*. This originally meant 'a song sung to an instrumental accompaniment', but it was applied by ancient Greek theorists to accent and other features of speech which were not indicated by their alphabetic writing (see further p. 60, n. 1).

2. This word is used at present in its everyday sense. Below it will be given a more technical definition.

minimal sentences are called 'minimal free forms' and this has proved a convenient empirical criterion for the technical definition of the 'word'.

The term 'word' will have a narrower technical application than it has in everyday usage. The 'word' must be separately elicited and defined for each speech community under observation. For any given language the 'word' will be the minimal speech unit (S-M item) capable of functioning as a complete utterance. The definition is thus completely empirical. If we are asked whether *I* is a word in English, we shall simply invite the questioner to go out and make observations in the English speech community. If he can collect a reasonable number of authentic specimens of dialogue in which one of the participants has simply uttered the vocable *I* as a contribution to the dialogue, then *I* will be established as a word in English. The same test may be applied to the French item *je*. If no such specimens can be collected in the normal speech of Frenchmen, then word status will be denied to this speech unit in French. It will be a 'bound form', not a 'free form'. We should not be deterred by finding that English *I* is a word whereas its equivalent in French is not. The 'grammar' of each language must be allowed to reveal itself by intrinsic analysis and by empirical observation of natural speech acts[1] without reference to the grammatical schemata and categories found appropriate to another speech community. The scientific description of languages was long impeded by attempts to force speech material into the grammatical moulds which have proved useful in the description of the classical languages Greek and Latin.

Once we have assembled an inventory of words, as just defined, we may compare and contrast word with word and in this way pick out other similarities and differences. Such item analysis can be carried on beyond the word level until we reach the smallest S-M items which are not amenable to further subdivision into S-M components. Such sub-items have their own signal value and make a distinctive contribution to the whole utterance of which they form part. Thus the opposition of (*one*) *cat*: (*two*) *cats*; (*one*) *hat*:

---

1. That is authentic social events and not specimens concocted by the linguist.

(*two*) *hats* enables us to detect an item -*s* with a pluralizing function. On the other hand the opposition of two gross items like *a cat likes milk: cats like milk* reveals the existence of another -*s*, which is 'bound to' the verb *like*. It marks the 'singular' of the verb. Thus the analysis of the speech corpus into S-M units, when carried to its logical conclusion, will yield an inventory of irreducible S-M units such as *cat, hat, milk, s_1* 'plural of nouns', s_2 '3rd person singular of verbs'. Such an analysis has been called the first articulation.[1] The irreducible S-M items are called *monemes* and the complete inventory of such monemes elicited from a given corpus may be called the monematicon.

The monematicon of English will contain, besides irreducible words such as *cat, like, milk*, many 'bound forms' such as -s_1 'plural', -s_2 'third person singular', -*y* 'adjectival formant' (e.g. *milky*), -*ness* 'formant of abstract nouns' (e.g. *goodness*). It will be evident that the 'first articulation', culminating in the production of the monematicon, will present complex problems of analysis such as are enshrined in the terms of traditional grammar. These will be conveniently postponed until we have taken the next step in analysis, which has been called the 'second articulation'.[2] The object of the second articulation is to examine the S-aspect (the 'vocable') of the monemes (defined as irreducible S-M units) and to break down these complex vocables in their turn to irreducible basic components.

THE SECOND ARTICULATION: THE STOECHEUM

Here, too, analysis may begin with commonsense and common experience in using and learning a language. The following piece of dialogue will serve as an illustration. A married couple are out in the country for a walk. They find a field path and the following conversation takes place. W.: *Lovely day for a walk.* H.: *It's a bit muggy.* W.: *Never mind, we can keep to the path.* H. (after a moment's bewilderment): *I said* '**muggy**' *not* '**muddy**'. Here the man has commented on his previous signal and carried out a

---

1. See A. Martinet, *Elements of General Linguistics*, pp. 22f.
2. Martinet, op. cit., pp. 47ff.

piece of linguistic analysis, contrasting two different signalling units which are minimally distinguished by the two components (*d* and *g*) which he has emphasized in his repetition of this part of the message. It is evident that in the signalling system used by the partners ('the English language') *g* and *d* cannot be interchanged at will without causing confusion. The difference is alone sufficient to distinguish between two signals similar in all other respects but of different content or 'meaning'. This is what is known as the principle of semasiological relevance. In the eighth century B.C. the Greeks analysed their language along these commonsense lines, sorted out the basic sound units and created a notation for them—the alphabet.[1] They also at a later date theorized about their procedure and coined a technical term to designate the basic unit—the *stoikheion*. It was this term which in its Latin translation *elementum* was to become a key word of scientific terminology. Thanks to this development 'element' has become too diluted a term to serve for the narrowly defined endproducts of the second articulation, the minimally distinctive units to which the vocables of the monemes are reduced. A Latinized version of the Greek term, *stoecheum*, will serve our purpose better. We may define it much as the Greeks did in terms of semasiological relevance. A *d* is a different *stoecheum* from *g* because of a change of meaning resulting from the substitution of one for the other. We may say that the *stoechea* are the elements of the vocable.

Before the next step in the analysis is taken it will clarify later discussion and obviate certain pseudo-problems if the procedures leading to the emergence of what has been called the *stoecheum* are made explicit. The fundamental point is that meaning is relevant at all stages of the analysis. In the first place two gross items (sentences) of different signal value have been contrasted and the differences between them localized in the two words *muddy* and *muggy*. These are S-M items intuitively apprehended through the basic item experience. The vocables of these words are next broken down into irreducible basic components which are no less intuitively apprehended as 'items': *d* and *g* can be separately

---

1. See Chapter 11.

reproduced and 'quoted' by the speaker in his intuitive analysis. The reason for this insistence on the obvious is that 'intuitive' is a term of frequent use in linguistic theorizing and it needs definition. The basis of 'intuitive analysis' is the elemental item experience. This simply has to be accepted as a basic fact of consciousness itself. It is pointless to ask how we know that the *p* of *pill* is the same as the *p* of *pin*. The question itself could not be framed without the item experience. We could not even talk of *pin* and *pill*.

The complexity of the linguistic item experience, however, needs emphasizing. To sort out the difference between *d* and *g* in *muddy* and *muggy* the observer must know not only the different signal values of those two vocables; he must also observe *where* the difference lies. The two configurations are perceived as two strings ('chains') of stoechea with the decisive differences located in a given 'position'.[1] In this position the interchange[2] of *d* and *g* effects a difference in the message signalled: it is semasiologically relevant. In this position *d* and *g* are said to be in opposition. This analytical operation (which we might call 'stoecheosis'), is carried out until the whole set of such distinctive sound elements used in a given speech community is discovered. In a pair like *pie* and *buy*, *p* and *b* are opposed, and both are opposed to zero in the initial position when contrasted with the word *eye*. Further oppositions come to light when *fie*, *my*, *tie*, *die*, *thigh*, *nigh*, *guy*, *lie*, *rye*, *sigh*, *shy*, *high* are adduced. So far the procedure has been confined to the initial ante-vocalic position. The list of stoechea will not be completed until all syntagmatic positions have been scrutinized. Thus the stoecheum *h* of English occurs only before a vowel. Another unit comes to light only when post-vocalic positions are examined. Thus the *ng* sound of English is revealed

---

1. An ordered succession of elements which make up a linguistic item is called a 'syntagm', and the elements are said to be in 'syntagmatic relation'. When such items are compared and analysis carried out by the commutation process, the set of elements which may be interchanged in a given position constitute a 'paradigm'. The point must be stressed that syntagmatic and paradigmatic analysis are carried out simultaneously: *d* and *g* form a paradigm at a given syntagmatic position (inter-vocalically) in the words *muddy* and *muggy*.

2. The technical term for this interchange is 'commutation'.

by such oppositions as *sin: sing*, *thin: thing*. From this peculiarity of distribution it follows that *h* and *ng* are never directly opposed; but this does not affect their intuitive apprehension as separate and distinct stoechea.[1] Another stoecheum of English with a limited distribution is that which occupies a medial position in *pleasure* and the final position in *garage*.

THE DESCRIPTION OF THE STOECHEUM: THE PHONE

In analysing the speech material the stage has now been reached where we have an inventory of the basic sound units of the given signalling system. In the case of *muddy* and *muggy*, the vocables of the two words are seen as different combinations of the basic units *m*, *u*, *d*, *g*, *y*.[2] Each of these units has its unmistakable identity intuitively apprehended. The essence of the item experience is that we can say 'that and no other'. It is in virtue of this quality of 'discreteness' that we can recognize and distinguish speech signals. But we are still at a crude stage of analysis and description, in that by way of definition we can merely give samples of *d*, *g* and all other stoechea. Certainly, this aspect of 'quotability' is an important criterion (see p. 79), but for the scientific description we cannot be content with such 'ostensive definition'. We need a closer analysis and description. This can be implemented in two ways. The stoecheum, when quoted either in isolation or in a stretch of natural speech, can be treated as an acoustic phenomenon (i.e. as a disturbance of the air), or as a set of muscular actions on the part of the speaker (i.e. as an 'articulation'). Both these approaches to the description of speech sounds belong to the province of phonetics. The first task of the phonetician is to devise a description for each *stoecheum*. Once described, the stoecheum becomes a 'phone'.[3]

---

1. The point is made here to anticipate certain difficulties which have arisen over the definition of the phoneme, which is confused by some theoreticians with the stoecheum (see pp. 79f.).

2. At present we use the letters of standard orthography to stand for the stoechea.

3. For further discussion of this step-by-step procedure, see pp. 67ff.

3

Phonetics
From the Stoecheum to the Phone

THE PHYSICS OF SOUND

Perceptions of sound are caused by a rhythmical series of pressures on the ear drum, the pitch of sound heard depending on the rate at which these successive pressures are imparted.[1] If the pressures recur at about 16 per second, we experience the lowest tone perceptible by the human ear. With the gradual increase of rate the sound heard rises in pitch until at about 20,000 per second the highest perceptible tone is reached. These successive pressures on the ear drum are produced by disturbances of the air. The physicists tell us that if the air is agitated, a series of waves spread out from the centre of the disturbance in much the same way as ripples are caused by throwing a stone in a pond. The air is an elastic medium, and the waves spread out from their point of origin at a speed of about 1100 feet per second. The particles of air do not actually travel but vibrate to and fro in a direction parallel to that of the wave (unlike light waves, in which the particles of the medium oscillate at right angles to the direction in which the waves are moving). Sound waves can be created in various ways. Thus if a vibrating string agitates the air in its immediate vicinity, a series of waves is radiated which, impinging on the human ear, cause the ear drum to respond to the rapid changes of pressure and so produce by intricate means (which we need not go into) the perception of sound. A sound has three auditory characteristics

---

1. This is true for singable sounds called 'tones'. For 'noises', see p. 39.

(the so-called parameters of sound): pitch, loudness and quality (timbre).

Three factors in the wave need to be distinguished to account for the auditory phenomena: (1) wavelength, (2) frequency and (3) intensity. The wavelength is simply the distance between the crests of successive waves. Frequency is measured as the number of waves that pass a given point in a stated time. This is expressed as cycles per second (c/s), a cycle being a complete oscillation (see Fig. 1). The frequency of a wave determines the perception of

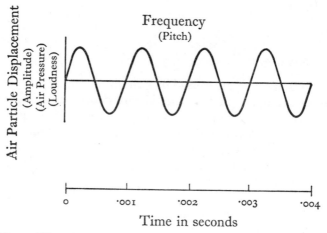

Fig. 1. Wave form of a pure tone with a frequency of 1000 c/s.

pitch. Given the constant speed of a sound wave, it follows that the longer the wavelength the lower the frequency. Intensity may be most simply visualized as the 'height' of the wave. In general terms, intensity is the maximum displacement of a vibrating body, such as a violin string. These vibrations are of a pendulum-like character, the position of the maximum displacement (i.e. in the case of the pendulum, the position furthest from the vertical) being called the amplitude. Both frequency and amplitude contribute to intensity, and it is intensity which is related to the auditory phenomenon of loudness. Two further concepts need elucidation. A wave of a given periodicity and amplitude produces a pure tone with a given pitch and degree of loudness. But a wave may be the product of interaction of two or more simple waves and have the more complex form shown in Fig. 2. If there are well-defined ratios between the component frequencies of the complex wave, the sound still has the quality of a singable 'tone'. But if the component sound waves are not regular and periodic and if the ratios between the components have no simple numerical relationships, in other words if there is a random combination of frequencies, the resultant sound is a 'noise' rather than a singable 'tone'.

To return to the example of the vibrating string, the speed of the vibration, and consequently the pitch of the tone produced, depends on (1) the length of the string, (2) its tension and (3) its mass. There are simple numerical relationships between these factors: the frequency can be halved by doubling the length of the string; the same effect is achieved by multiplying the mass by four or dividing the tension by four. The strings of the violin have different mass, and so a given length at a given tension will produce tones of different pitch. The violinist tunes the instrument by increasing or decreasing the tension. During performance the changes of length effected by different finger stoppings of the strings produce notes of different pitch, while the bow controls the amplitude and hence the loudness of tone. Another way of producing the sounds is to use a flexible material that can be caused to vibrate by a current of air. This is the principle embodied in the reed pipe, the clarinet and the oboe. The human voice is produced by similar means (see below).

Before proceeding to the discussion of speech sounds in particular there are two other general phenomena to be mentioned—resonance and overtones. Any cavity has the quality of what is known as resonance. It owes this property to the fact that if a cavity is agitated in any way, the surging of the air in and out of the orifice causes waves to be radiated, and this may give rise to the perception of sound. The frequency of the surgings, and consequently the pitch of the tone produced, depend chiefly on the volume of the cavity and the size of the orifice. Thus a large cavity with a small aperture makes for a low rate of vibration and a low tone. The pitch of the tone produced rises as the cavity is made smaller or the orifice larger.[1] A cavity has furthermore the

---

1. The resonant pitch of a cavity depends on the *relation* between the capa-

capability of responding to a tone of the same pitch as its natural frequency. Thus if over a mouth of a cavity with a natural pitch C a succession of notes A, B and C is whistled, when the note C is reached, the cavity will vibrate in sympathy.[1] This principle of resonance is applied in practically all musical instruments, which are provided with some sort of device to augment the sound. A

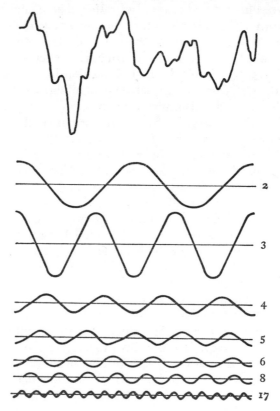

Fig. 2. One complete cycle of the wave form of a violin (top) and its harmonics (2 to 17), all plotted as displacement against time.

city of the cavity and the size of the orifice. This explains why men, women and children can make similar vowel sounds despite the difference in the size of the vocal organs (see below).

1. The musical note to which a cavity responds is called its resonant pitch.

violin string vibrating alone would give out a weak, thin sound; but when it is amplified by the resonance of the body, its tone is increased and made fuller. This leads to the consideration of the phenomenon called the timbre or quality of the tone.

A tone may be pure or complex. A pure tone is one which has a given frequency and no other. An example is the tone produced by a tuning fork. Differences of timbre come about by making a pure tone complex, that is by the interaction of two or more sound waves, each of a given frequency and intensity. It is easy to recognize the difference between a violin and a flute even when they are playing at the same pitch. In order to understand the cause of this difference in quality it will be necessary to consider other properties of a vibrating string. Suppose that a string of a given length is caused to vibrate so as to produce a basic note C. The string, however, vibrates not only as a whole but in its parts as well, and the vibrating fractions produce a series of higher tones, called overtones.[1] The presence of such overtones in varying proportions determines the quality or timbre of the tone given out by a string or a vibrating column of air. The clarinet differs from a violin playing at the same tone not in the frequency of the vibration that constitutes that tone but in the nature of the overtones combined with it (see Fig. 2). This consideration is of fundamental importance in dealing with those sounds we call vowels.[2]

VOWELS AND DIPHTHONGS

The human vocal apparatus is in principle the same as a wind instrument like a clarinet or an oboe; sound is produced in a column of air by means of a vibrating membrane. When we breathe out, the air is expelled from the lungs along the windpipe (see Fig. 3) and emerges from the mouth and nose. To set this column of air in vibration we have to make use of the so-called vocal cords or folds. These are two pieces of flexible membrane which in

---

1. The fundamental and the overtones together make up the 'partials' of a given tone. If the frequencies or the overtones stand in simple numerical relationship with the fundamental (2, 3, 4, etc.), they are called 'harmonics'.

2. For a discussion of the term vowel, see pp. 54f.

normal breathing are folded back against the sides of the larynx.[1]
They are provided with muscles by which they can be brought
together so as to obstruct the flow of air from the lungs. When the
air is forced between these vocal cords, they are caused to vibrate,
thus producing sound. As in the case of the violin string, the pitch
of the tone produced is influenced by the three factors of length,
tension and mass. The cords of the adult male are longer than those
of the female and also of greater mass; hence the different pitch
ranges of men and women. Within this inherent range tones of
different pitch are produced by varying the tension by muscular
action. But how are these sounds modified in such a way as to

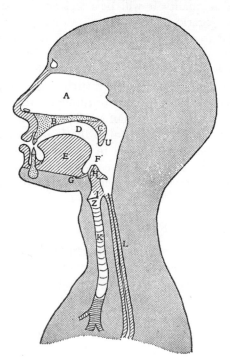

Fig. 3. A, nasal cavity; B, hard palate; C, velum; D, mouth cavity;
E, tongue; F, pharynx; G, hyoid bone; H, epiglottis; I, vocal cords;
K, trachea; L, oesophagus; U, uvula; Z, larynx.

---

1. The larynx is externally visible as the 'Adam's apple'.

produce such different vowel sounds as in the words, *fat, fate, fit, feet, foot*? It has been established that the different quality of vowels, like the different timbre of musical instruments, depends on varying combinations of overtones with the fundamental tone. These overtones are called the 'formants' of the particular vowel. The tables in Figs. 4 and 5 give the main formants of some of the most common vowels.

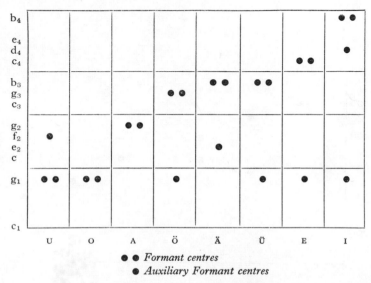

●● *Formant centres*
● *Auxiliary Formant centres*

Fig. 4. (after C. Stumpf).

The human vocal apparatus, as may be seen from Fig. 3, consists of a vibrating double reed like an oboe and resonating cavities formed by the throat, nose and mouth. The shape, and consequently the resonant pitches, of these cavities can be altered by pouting the lips ('rounding') or drawing them back ('retraction'), by opening and closing the mouth and, most of all, by changing the shape and position of the tongue, which is an extremely powerful muscle capable of being contracted and expanded in all directions. These resonating cavities, as has been observed above, have the property of selecting and amplifying overtones that correspond to their own resonant pitch. Thus if the mouth is opened wide and

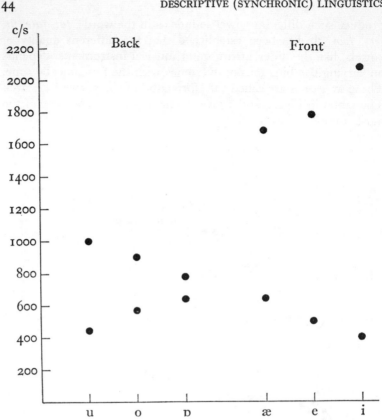

Fig. 5. Formants of the English front and back vowels. The lower formants correlate with the degree of tongue raising, the higher formants with backing and fronting of the tongue.

the tongue kept flat the vowel [a][1] is produced as in the German word *Mann*. The mouth cavity in this shape selects and amplifies the overtones that are the formants of the vowel [a]; that is the tones g_2 and d_3. If we modify the mouth cavity by gradually raising the tongue towards the front of the hard palate, we make a

---

1. Note that phonetic notation is included within square brackets, whereas italics are used for the stoechea. For the use of slants, e.g. /a/, to denote the phoneme, see Chapter 4.

series of vowels contained in the words *mat, met, mate, mit, meet,* in phonetic script [æ, ɛ, e, ı, i].[1] If, on the other hand, the tongue is progressively raised towards the back of the mouth, we hear the series of vowels contained in the words *sap, sop, soap, soup,* in phonetic script [æ, ɔ, o, u].[1]

The oral vowels thus owe their distinctive timbre to, and so may be described in terms of, three modes of articulation: (1) the movement of the tongue from back to front, (2) from low to high and (3) the rounding or retracting of the lips, the movement of the lower jaw being regarded as merely a concomitant feature. This enables us to map out the extreme articulatory positions within which all vowel sounds must lie. The quadrilateral of Fig. 6, the

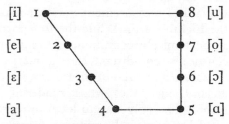

Fig. 6. The primary cardinal vowels.

so-called cardinal vowel figure, is a schematic representation of this 'vowel area' of the mouth, the periphery being the lines drawn between the four extreme positions of the tongue. At 1 the tongue is raised to the highest possible level at which a vowel can be produced. If it were raised higher, audible friction would be produced by the air hissing through the constricted passage between the tongue and the hard palate, and the result would be a consonant.[2] Similarly at 8 the tongue is raised to its highest position towards the soft palate, again stopping short of the position where audible friction would result. At 4 and 5 the tongue is flattened and occupies the lowest possible position; but to

---

1. The sounds contained in the words *mate, meet, soap, soup* are, strictly speaking, diphthongs, only the first element of which corresponds to the vowels notated above, see below, p. 47.

2. See below pp. 54f. for the terms vowel and consonant.

produce [a] it is pushed forward, while to produce [ɑ] it is pulled back as far as possible. Between the extreme closed positions 1 and 8 and the extreme open positions 4 and 5 respectively, we choose two intermediate positions half-close and half-open, such that the acoustic distance between the neighbouring vowels is equal. This gives us points 2 and 7 as half-close front and back respectively, and 3 and 6 as the corresponding half-open vowels. Thus we may describe [ɛ] as a half-open front vowel and [o] as a half-close back vowel.

The cardinal vowels are simply a device giving a system of fixed reference points which enables the phonetician to 'place' any vowel which he may encounter in the course of his observations on speech. While any given cardinal vowel has a fixed acoustic quality, the standard of measurement is rather like the length of King Henry the Eighth's arm. While the four extreme positions 1, 4, 5 and 8 are anatomically conditioned, the intermediate points, defined as acoustically equidistant, are a matter for personal judgment. The standard at present in use was introduced by the British phonetician Daniel Jones, whose rendering of the cardinal vowels is on record. The only way to learn to reproduce them is simply by careful listening and assiduous practice. This is one more of the 'item experiences' which the language learner in general must acquire.

The cardinal vowel figure omits the third factor concerned in the production of vowels. The reference points represent the different positions of the tongue as defined by the horizontal and vertical axes, but it takes no account of the activity of the lips. If the student makes the two series of English vowels [æ]–[i] and [ɑ]–[u], he will notice that with the first (front) series the lips are drawn further and further back, reaching the maximum retraction with [i]. In pronouncing the second (back) series the lips instead of being retracted are progressively rounded. Vowels of different quality are produced as a consequence of the changed shape of the resonating cavities. Thus if the sound [e] is pronounced with protruded lips, the vowel that is produced resembles that contained in the German word *schön* [ʃøn]. Again, if the tongue posture of the high front vowel [i] is accompanied by lip rounding, the vowel that results is like that in the German word *süss* [zys] or the French word *lune* [lyn]. A different series of vowels is produced if the lips are progressively retracted while the tongue postures characteristic of the back series [a] to [u] are assumed. The vowel of the Russian word сын, 'son', may serve as an example: it is an [u] pronounced with retracted lips and is written [ɯ]. This 'perverse' (from an Englishman's point of view) action of the lips gives us an additional eight vowel qualities which are sometimes referred to as the secondary cardinal vowels; they can be represented by a similar figure (Fig. 7).

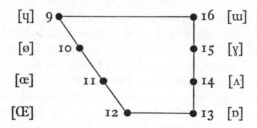

Fig. 7. The secondary cardinal vowels.

The vowels so far described have been sounds regarded as stable and constant over the duration of their emission. In many languages, however, unstable vowels are encountered, during the production of which the speech organs change their posture. An example is the vowel sound of *how* [haʊ] during which the organs move from the [a] posture to the [u] posture. Such a sound is described by naming the initial and final postures, hence the term diphthong ('two-sound'). In addition to [aʊ] the following diphthongs are to be heard in English: [aɪ] in *high*, [ɛə] in *hair*, [eɪ] in *hay*, [ɪə] in *here*, [ɔɪ] in *boy*, [oʊ] in *low* and [ʊə] in *poor*. The so-called long vowels of standard English (see page 71 for 'length') are in fact such unstable vowels. Thus the long [i:][1] is more accurately represented as [ij] and the long [u:], as in *hoot*, as [uw]. Some scholars regard even the vowel of *heard* as a diphthong.

We are now in a position to 'place' and describe the vowel

---

1. Note the use of the colon to denote 'length'.

sounds of any language whatsoever. Fig. 8 is an extract from the International Phonetic Alphabet, which locates some key vowels and gives their notations. By way of example, the vowels of English may now be more precisely located within the system of articulatory reference points. The cardinal vowel [i] does not occur as a simple vowel, but the closest approximation appears as the first element in the vocalic part of words like *feet* [fijt]. The vowel of *fit* lies between [i] and [e] and is written [ɩ]. Nor does the cardinal vowel [e] occur as a pure vowel, although it may be heard at the beginning of the diphthongal component of *fate* [feɩt]. The vowel of *fed* [fɛd] is not far from the half-open cardinal vowel, but the front-open [a] is not heard in standard British English, for the vowel of *fad* [fæd] lies between [a] and [ɛ] (see Fig. 8).

In the back series, the close vowel forms the first component of the diphthongal sound of words like *food* [fuwd]. The vowel of *foot* lies lower than [u] and is written [ɷ]. This sound also occurs as the second component in the vocalic part of *road*, in which the first element approximates to the half-close vowel of the back series: [oɷ]. The vowel of *rod* is often written with the symbol for the half-open cardinal vowel [ɔ], but in fact it lies rather lower and is more accurately represented as [ɒ] (see Fig. 8). The vowel

	FRONT		CENTRAL	BACK	
	Spread	Rounded		Spread	Rounded
Close	i	y	iʉ	ɯ	u
	ɩ				ɷ
Half-close	e	ø		ɤ	o
			ə		
Half-open	ɛ	œ		ʌ	ɔ
	æ				
Open	a			ɑ	ɒ

Fig. 8.

of *bud* is close in position to that of *rod* but the lips are more spread. This vowel receives the notation [ʌ] (see Fig. 8). The open vowel of the back series does not occur as a short vowel in English, but it is heard as the long of *hard* [ɑ:], which some scholars analyse as a diphthong. One important vocalic sound of English remains to mention: this is the vowel heard only in unaccented syllables, such as the first syllable of *about*. The sound also occurs as the second element of diphthongs as in *fear* [ɪə], *fair* [ɛə], *poor* [ʊə]. For this vowel the position of the highest point of the tongue on the horizontal axis is neither back nor front, but central, and this gives us a new category of 'central vowels' (see Fig. 8). One of these is the long vowel heard in words like *bird*, which is described as central, half-open and spread. The symbol used is a reversed form of the notation for the half-open front vowel [ɛ] – [ɜ]. This may also be regarded simply as a lengthened [ə], but some scholars analyse it as a diphthong.

A further modification of vowel production must now be investigated. The speaker is able to shut off the nasal cavity altogether by raising the little tongue which can be seen at the back of the throat when the mouth is opened wide. In producing the vowels so far discussed, the uvula, as it is called (see U in Fig. 3), is raised and shuts off the nasal passage, so that the whole of the air passes through the mouth. Such vowels are therefore called oral vowels. But if we allow the uvula to relax, this will open up the nasal cavity, and its resonance brings a new set of overtones into play, giving the vowels the peculiar quality that we call nasalization. The French phrase *en bon point* contains three such nasalized vowels. The first is a nasalization of [a], written [ã], the second is [õ] corresponding to [o] and the third is [ɛ̃] corresponding to [ɛ]. Yet another nasalized vowel of French is that we hear in *un*, the oral correspondent of which is the half-open rounded front vowel [œ].

CONSONANTS

In the sounds hitherto discussed the primary source of sound has been the vocal cords, and the sounds have been 'tones', i.e. sounds characterized by regular and periodic waves. Such 'singable' sounds are called vowels.[1] But human speech makes use of other

1. For the terms 'vowel' and 'consonant' and their application to sounds like [r], [l], [m] and [n], see below p. 54f.

possibilities. If the vocal cords are folded back against the walls of the larynx, the air is allowed to pass without interference through the glottis (the space between the cords) into the mouth; but we can obstruct the supraglottal air stream in various ways. Thus by placing the tip of the tongue against the upper teeth the air can be made to hiss through the narrow channel thus made. The sound produced by such constriction of the air passage is called a fricative. Such sounds which involve another agency in place of, or in addition to, the vocal cords, are called consonants.[1] Acoustically speaking, the waves thus produced are not regular and periodic, and the sounds caused by such agency, which are not 'singable' because no definite pitch can be assigned to them, are described as 'noises'. These 'rubbing sounds' can be produced by constriction of the air passage at different points, and they are classified accordingly. The lips can be pursed and the air made to hiss through them. This sound is called a bilabial fricative [ɸ]. This is a rare sound, however, and we usually find a slight modification, the lower lip being placed against the upper teeth, as in the first sound of the English *five* [faɪv]. This is the labio-dental fricative. When the tip of the tongue is placed against the upper teeth, the first sound of the English *thing* is heard—the dental fricative [θ]. Constriction of the air passage can be made further back. Thus the tongue can be raised still higher than the position necessary for the vowel [i] and a narrow passage made with the tongue humped near the hard palate. The palatal fricative [ç] is produced in this position and is the sound contained in the German *Licht* and *Gicht*. The tongue can also be raised at the back and brought near the soft palate (the velum, see Fig. 3), thus producing the velar fricative, the scraping, throat-clearing sound heard in the Welsh *bach* and the German *Dach* [x].

We now come to the so-called aspirate [h], which must be also classified as a fricative consonant. In this sound, however, the friction is produced in the larynx itself, the vocal cords being brought together so as to leave only a small aperture through which

---

1. See previous note.

the air hisses.[1] This sound is called a glottal or laryngeal fricative (glottis being the name for the space between the vocal cords, see above).

During the production of the sounds just discussed the vocal cords are inactive. But it is possible to let them vibrate at the same time as these fricative sounds are made. The series thus produced are called voiced fricatives, as contrasted with the voiceless fricatives described in the last paragraph.

Voiced Labio-Dental Fricative [v]: Engl. *very*, Germ. *Wetter*, Fr. *vin*

Voiced Dental Fricative [ð]: Engl. *there, this*, Welsh, *ddim*

Voiced Palatal Fricative [j]: Engl. *yes, jung*.

Voiced Velar Fricative [ɣ]: Germ. (Berlin dialect) *Wagen*; Russ. (*slava*) *bogu*

Voiced Bilabial Fricative (with lips rounded)[2] [w]: Engl. *will*; Fr. *oui*

Yet another series of speech sounds is produced if, instead of merely constricting the air-stream by narrowing the aperture, it is shut off altogether for a moment and the pent-up air is allowed to escape with a pop. Such sounds, produced by a maximum constriction of the air passage, are called stops or plosives, and they too may be voiced or voiceless. Like the fricatives, they are classified according to the place where the stopping is made. By pressing the lips together and then releasing the pent-up air pressure, the voiceless labial plosive is produced; it is the first sound of the English *pat* [p]. The air can also be shut off by pressing the

---

1. This is the basis of whispered speech, during which the resonating cavities are energized by turbulent air, the characteristic resonances being set up in much the same way as we can produce a sound of distinct pitch by blowing across the mouth of a bottle. Since all glottal fricatives must be accompanied by some sort of resonance, it follows that there are as many varieties of [h] as there are vowel qualities.

2. The corresponding voiceless variety (written [ʍ]), occurs in some pronunciations of *which, where*, etc. The French sound heard in *lui* is often identified by English speakers with their [w]. It is, in fact, a consonantal version of [y]: that is the tongue is raised beyond the front high position to produce [j] and the lips are tightly rounded. The notation of this sound is [ɥ].

tip of the tongue against the teeth. This results in the dental plosive, the first sound of the French *thé* [t].[1] The palatal plosive is made by raising the front of the tongue against the hard palate. This sound occurs in Hungarian; its phonetic notation is [c]. For the velar plosive [k] the tongue is raised against the soft palate as in *coo*. The corresponding voiced plosives are exemplified in the initial sounds of the following examples:

Voiced Labial Plosive [b]: *bat*
Voiced Dental Plosive [d]: *dog*
Voiced Palatial Plosive [j]: Hungarian *Magyar*
Voiced Velar Plosive [g]: Engl. *goose*; Germ. *gut*

All these plosive sounds involve the creation of a slight air pressure in the mouth and its subsequent release, and it is essential that there should be no leakage. Consequently in the production of all plosive sounds the uvula must shut off the nasal passage (see Fig. 3). This suggests another variation: the passage of air through the mouth can be stopped and the vocal cords set in vibration; but now the air is allowed to pass through the nose. The sounds produced in this way are called nasal consonants. Thus when the lips are pressed together as for the plosive [b], the vocal cords set in vibration and the uvula relaxed, we make the first sound of *man*, the labial nasal [m]. Similarly, to the dental plosives [t/d] there corresponds the dental nasal [n] as in *not*. The palatal nasal [ɲ] is exemplified in the second consonant of the French *mignon* and the Spanish *cañon*, while the velar nasal [ŋ] is the last sound of the English words *sing*, *ring*, *thing*, etc.

There remains to be mentioned a group of fricatives known as sibilants. Their conditions of production are complicated, and they are consequently more difficult to describe and designate. They are exemplified respectively in the initial sounds of the

---

1. The first sound of the English *tin* is produced slightly further back, the *tip* of the tongue making the closure against the teeth ridge, the technical name being alveolar plosive. Another difference between French and English voiceless stops deserves mention at this point. The English stops, especially in the initial position before vowels, are strongly aspirated, that is a glottal fricative is perceptible after the release of the stop before the onset of the following vowel (see further, p. 68).

following words: (1) *sink*, (2) *zinc*, (3) *ship* (4) (French) *jour*. In English the first of these sounds [s] is made by raising the edges of the blade of the tongue against the teeth ridge so as to form a gulley in the middle along which the air streams. The tip is in a neutral position or points towards the lower teeth, while the front of the tongue is raised slightly towards the hard palate. It has been described as a voiceless blade-alveolar[1] fricative. [z] is the corresponding voiced sound, as in *zinc*, heard also in the North German *See* and in the French *zéro*. The English *sh* sound [ʃ] is pronounced with the tip and blade of the tongue behind the teeth ridge, the rest of the tongue being raised close to the palate. The lips are simultaneously pouted. It may be described as a voiceless, rounded, palato-alveolar fricative. The voiced variety of this sound does not occur in English in an initial position, but is found medially in words like *leisure* [lɛʒə], and finally in French loanwords like *garage* [gærɑ:ʒ].

More complex fricatives are the sounds known as affricates. In the production of these a complete constriction of the air passage is first made, producing a plosive; but after the release of the closure the air passage remains constricted so that a following fricative sound is audible. An example is the first and final sound of *church* which represents an alveolar voiceless plosive [t] followed by [ʃ]. The corresponding voiced affricate can be heard in *judge* [dʒʌdʒ]. Other affricates combine plosives with other sibilants or fricatives. The initial sound in German *Pferd* starts with a voiceless labial plosive which merges into a voiceless labio-dental fricative [pf]. The first sound of German *Zeit* consists of the voiceless dental plosive followed by an [s]: [ts]. The corresponding voiced sound is heard in the medial consonant of the Italian *azzuro* [dz].

Other additions to the rich variety of sounds at our command are produced by the rapid vibration of various flexible parts of the vocal apparatus. We can make the lips vibrate and produce the sound we make when we are cold: *brrr*! This is not used in any European language; but the trill made with the tip of the tongue [r] is extremely common. It is the sound which marks off the

---

1. Also 'lamino-alveolar' (Latin *lamina* 'blade').

(stage) Scot from the speaker of southern English. The first sound of *red* in standard English is not a trill but a voiced fricative, written [ɹ]. Another trill can be produced by vibrating the uvula (see Fig. 3, U), a sound frequent in French (e.g. *rouge*) and many dialects of German (e.g. *Rad*, *rot*). It is also heard in the Northumberland dialect of English. This is the uvular trill: [ʀ]. The corresponding non-trilled fricative is often heard in Parisian French. This sound is written [ʁ]. Another variety of the trill is the so-called flap [ɾ], which is made by flicking the tip of the tongue against the teeth ridge whence it rebounds after making a brief contact. Such is the sound heard in the Spanish *pero* 'but' as opposed to *perro* 'dog'.

One English sound remains to be discussed. This is the sound heard in words like *leaf* and *full*. It is articulated by making a complete closure with the tip of the tongue against the teeth ridge. The air, however, is allowed to escape by the side or sides of the tongue; hence its name 'lateral consonant': [l]. It may be voiced or voiceless. English has two main varieties of voiced lateral consonant, 'light' and 'dark'. In *leaf* and *please* the tongue is in the required position, but the front is raised towards the hard palate. In words like *field*, however, the tongue is raised at the back, giving the sound its 'dark' quality. In a more scientific terminology they are called palatalized and velarized laterals written [l] and [ɫ] respectively. The voiceless lateral [l̥] does not occur in English, but it is frequent in Welsh. It may be heard in names like *Llanelly*, etc., where English speakers tend to hear and pronounce [θl]. It occurs also in French after a voiceless stop, as in the word *cercle* [sɛʁkl̩] or *peuple* [pœpl̩]. A true palatal lateral [ʎ] is heard in Italian words like *gli*, *figlio*. This sound is articulated by raising the front of the tongue against the hard palate. For the velarized lateral [ɫ] the back of the tongue is raised towards the soft palate or velum.

THE SYLLABLE: VOWELS AND CONSONANTS

In the above phonetic analysis and description of the stoechea elicited from the corpus the terms 'vowel' and 'consonant' have been freely used. The identity of a given vocable as a 'Gestalt' or

configuration results not merely from the concatenation of a
given set of stoechea but often also from the prominence given
to one or more of the elements (see below, pp. 58ff). Suppose we
were set the task of devising labels consisting of beads strung
together on wire. To increase the number of possible combinations
some of the differently coloured beads could be of larger size (this
might correspond to vowels of different length); prominence could
also be achieved by bending the wire so that some beads were
higher than others. Such an effect is achieved in speech by 'accent'.
But this important concept of 'prominence' cannot be profitably
discussed without prior consideration of the syllable.

Speakers have an intuitive awareness of this unit of speech when
they execute a 'song and dance' or write verse. Many early
writing systems were also based on the syllable. Long before the
invention of the alphabet the Bronze Age Greeks had used such a
syllabary (Linear B) for recording simple transactions in their
language (see p. 260). Yet, despite the plain man's awareness of
this unit, linguists have been unable to agree on a satisfactory
definition of the syllable.

Since our descriptions of speech sounds have been couched in
articulatory terms, in the interest of purism preference should
perhaps be given to a similar account of the syllable. Such a
theory has been put forward, but in the absence of experimental
verification it remains purely speculative. This is the chest-pulse
theory of the syllable, put forward by the American phonetician
R. H. Stetson, who claimed to have observed a correlation between
syllabification and the action of the respiratory muscles. These
muscles, by rapid contraction and relaxation, produce a succession
of small puffs of breath, and it is these emissions of air which
supposedly provide the energy for the peaks of prominence which
we perceive as 'syllables'.

Another widely accepted account of the syllable has an acoustic
basis in that it resolves round the concept of sonority. The
sonority of a sound depends on the volume of air made to vibrate.
The large pipes of an organ, for instance, are more sonorous than
the small ones. Since no two speech sounds are of exactly the same
sonority, it is possible to arrange them in a series in which the
voiceless consonants, which are least sonorous, occupy one end

of the scale and the vowels the other. Jespersen distinguishes eight
different grades as follows:

(1) Voiceless   (a) Plosives
                (b) Fricatives
(2) Voiced Plosives
(3) Voiced Fricatives
(4) Voiced   (a) Nasals
             (b) Laterals
(5) Voiced r-sounds
(6) Close vowels
(7) Mid Vowels
(8) Open vowels

We shall see that this quality provides us with a criterion for the
division of syllables if we represent in a diagram (Fig. 9) the

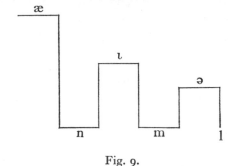

Fig. 9.

respective sonorities of a word like *animal*: [ænɩməl]. We may
now venture on an acoustic definition of a syllable. A syllabic
sound is one which represents a peak of sonority. Thus the above
word contains three syllables. This account of the syllable also
clears up the position of those sounds called sonants, e.g. [m], [n],
[r], [l], which are sometimes syllabic and sometimes not. In the
word *button* [bʌtn̩], for instance, the ear distinguishes two syllables.
If we draw a diagram representing the sound sonorities, the reason
for this is clear (Fig. 10). The [n] represents here a peak in the
sonority curve as contrasted with that of the previous word, where
the vowels enclosing the [n] were of greater sonority. Thus we

may say that a sound will make a syllabic peak if it occurs in an environment of lesser sonority.

This, however, is not completely satisfactory, for it has often been pointed out that German words like *haben* and *sieben* are sometimes pronounced [ha:m̩], [zi:m̩], in which [m̩], though not a peak of sonority, constitutes a distinct syllable. What characterizes this syllabification is an extra strong pronunciation of this sound.[1] A more serious difficulty is that, according to Jespersen's own table, a word like *stinks* should have three syllables, since the two [s] sounds are of greater sonority than the neighbouring voiceless plosives [t] and [k].

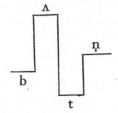

Fig. 10.

An articulatory version of this theory links sonority with the degree of opening. Thus the flat tongue results in a larger resonant cavity and hence greater sonority, and the cavity reduces progressively as the tongue is raised towards the roof of the mouth, reaching its minimum with the stops. The graph of any stretch of speech which represents the successive phases of raising and lowering of the active articulator will show peaks and valleys. The sound produced at a peak, i.e. at a point of least constriction, forms the 'nucleus' of a syllable, and within such a theory of the syllable we should define 'vowels' as such syllabic nuclei. The

---

1. The difficulties in these words may be resolved by postulating a glottal stop. This certainly occurs in the author's pronunciation of words like *fatten* [fæʔn̩], where a distinct glottal release is felt before the final nasal. But what we have here is a combination of two factors: the inherent sonority of this sound and the force of expiration, that is its loudness. A definition of the syllabic peak which took account of both factors would describe it as 'a peak of audibility'.

marginal sounds assigned to the syllable which occur before and after the nucleus, as in *stinks*, are called 'consonants', i.e. those 'sounded with a vowel'. Thus the terms 'vowel' and 'consonant' apply strictly only when considering the relations of phones in the spoken chain. They are syntagmatic[1] terms. If the corresponding phones are considered in isolation for the purposes of phonetic description (both acoustic and articulatory), they are sometimes dubbed 'vocoids' and 'contoids'.

It is often important in linguistic studies to distinguish types of syllables and the various positions of the components of a syllable. The explosive position is occupied by the consonant or cluster which precedes the nucleus, while the post-nuclear sounds are said to be in the implosive[2] position. Other authors use the terms 'release', 'vowel', 'arrest' for the three phases of the syllable; others again prefer 'onset', 'peak' and 'coda'. Either marginal position or both may in fact be occupied by zero as in *on*, *no* and *Oh*! Thus in principle syllables are of four main types—CVC, VC, CV and V, where C stands for one or more consonants and V for the vocalic nucleus. A syllable of the CV type is said to be open, as opposed to the closed syllable of the (C)VC type. Languages vary widely in their preference for syllabic types and in the number of consonants admitted as clusters in the release and arrest positions.

PROSODIES

In the series of syllables of which words and sentences are composed some may be given prominence over others. This can be done in two ways. We may pronounce them more loudly; that is to say, a stronger breath impulse is devoted to the production of these favoured syllables, or rather to the vocalic nucleus which forms the peak in each case. This is what is known as 'stress accent'.[3] In the word *penitent*, for instance, greatest force and

---

1. For this term, see p. 35 (note 1).

2. 'Implosive' is also used in phonetics for a sound made with the closed glottis by means of an ingressive air stream.

3. Other terms are expiratory and dynamic accent.

prominence is given to the first syllable [pˈɛnɪtənt], whereas in *penitentiary* the stress falls on the ante-penultimate (one before the last but one) syllable [pɛnɪtˈɛnʃərɪ]. Such stress accent is a feature of most modern European languages, e.g. English, German, Russian, etc. Prominence may also be given to a sound or syllable, however, by pronouncing it at a higher pitch than the neighbouring sounds. In classical Greek, words like *lógos* bore such an accent on the first syllable. The ancient grammarians inform us that the vowel of this syllable was pronounced a musical interval of a fifth above the adjacent vowels. The high-pitched vowel (e.g. in *lógos*) was called *oxys* ('sharp') and the low-pitched vowel *barys* ('heavy'). The translations of these terms by Roman grammarians as *acūtus* and *gravis* have given us the familiar modern terms 'acute' and 'grave'. Further, in pronouncing a long vowel the voice might rise and fall, this intonation being marked by the so-called circumflex accent: *polîtôn*. Among European languages, Lithuanian, Swedish, Norwegian and Serbo-Croatian are characterized by such pitch or musical accents.

In Chinese pitch is of particular importance; in this language, which consists to a great extent entirely of monosyllables, homophonic words like *chu* are often distinguished from one another only by their accent, just as classical Greek distinguished between *én* 'behold' and *ên* 'I said'. The Mandarin dialect possesses a system of four tones: (1) the even tone ‾, which starts at a fairly high pitch, is maintained for a while and broken off sharply; (2) the quickly rising tone ´, which also starts fairly high and jumps about a third higher; (3) the slowly rising tone ˇ, which starts at a low pitch and is sustained for a while before rising about a fifth at the end; (4) the falling tone ˋ, which starts in the middle register and falls suddenly at the end. Thus, if a Pekinese says *chu‾*, it means 'pig'; if he says *chu´*, it means 'bamboo'; '*chuˇ* is 'master, god'; and '*chuˋ* is 'to dwell'.[1]

The point has just been made that the identity of the vocable as a 'Gestalt' or configuration depends not merely on the string of sounds but also on ordering relations between them, such as accent. Such distinctive syntagmatic relations are called 'pro-

---

1. B. Karlgren, *Sound and Symbol in Chinese*, p. 21.

sodies'.[1] Thus the distinction between (1) *green house* and (2) *green-house* is marked mainly by their different prosodic features (intonations).[2] In writing, the hyphen is often used to indicate that the components (e.g. *green* and *house*) are to be taken 'as one' (this is the meaning of the Greek word 'hyphen'). Thus the hyphen may be regarded as a prosodic notation. It is an indication of intonation.

The phenomenon known as 'juncture' is another syntagmatic relation which may be classified as a prosody. It may be illustrated by the sentence *Why choose white shoes?*; this falls into two nearly identical halves, (1) [waɪ|tʃuwz] and (2) [waɪt|ʃuwz]. But in (1) there is closer juncture between [t] and [ʃ] than in (2). The difference also manifests itself in the subtle play of vowel quantity; the [aɪ] of *why* is distinctly longer than the corresponding sound of *white*. Another often quoted example of close and open juncture is *nitrate* as opposed to *night rate*. Here, too, there is a secondary phenomenon which helps the hearer: the onset of the [ɹ] of *nitrate* is devoiced: that is, there is some lag in starting the vibration of the vocal cords after the release of the voiceless stop [t] whereas the first sound of *rate* is fully voiced. The symbol # is used to indicate such 'open juncture' between [t] and [ɹ]: [naɪt#ɹeɪt]. A similar but more complex set of articulations distinguishes *free*

---

1. In their linguistic analyses the Greeks used the term *prosōdiā* in addition to the *stoikheion*. *Prosōdiā* was the noun corresponding to the verb *prosāidein* 'sing in tune with an accompanying instrument'. The term originally applied to the accentuation of syllables as well as the intonation of the whole sentence. Later it was extended to include all phenomena not indicated by the stoechea, such as breathing, quantity, and even what we call punctuation, including apostrophe, hyphen and comma. This was a striking anticipation of modern views. We may say that for the adequate representation of speech we need, in addition to a succession of written characters for the strings of the stoechea, indications of their various interrelationships, such as length, stress, pitch, melody (intonation), variations of speed, modes of joining, and so on. The Greeks used the term 'prosody' not only for the phenomena but also for their different notations.

2. Note that in *green house* there are two equal accents; with each of the two syllable nuclei the voice starts high and then falls: \\. In the case of *green-house* there is only one accent, and the second syllabic nucleus is produced at the same low pitch as the final stage of the first: ⌐.

quarters [fɹij#kwɔ:təz] from *freak waters* [fɹijk#wɔ:təz]. In the first phrase /kw/, with close juncture, is pronounced with the onset of the /w/ breathed rather than voiced. Moreover, the /k/ is pronounced with the lips already rounded, while the point of constriction is further back in the mouth than the /k/ of the second phrase. In *quarters* /kw/ is, in fact, a labio-velar [kʷ]. In the second phrase, with open juncture between [k] and [w], the lips still persist in the retraction of [ij] when the final /k/ is being pronounced and the following initial /w/ is fully voiced. The distinction between the unitary labio-velar sound /kʷ/ and the consonant cluster /kw/ is important in Indo-European studies.

One of the most important prosodies of speech is sentence melody or 'intonation'. Children acquire these characteristic tunes before they start to speak, and it is perhaps the most difficult phonetic feature of a foreign language for an adult to learn. For English, two main sentence tunes have been distinguished: these may be exemplified in the two sentences (1) *I'm going to town tomorrow*, (2) *Will you be back late?* (Fig. 11). In (1) the melody

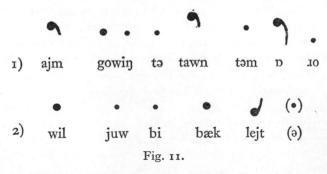

1)   ajm   gowiŋ   tə   tawn   təm   ɒ   ɹo

2)   wil   juw   bi   bæk   lejt   (ə)

Fig. 11.

reaches its highest pitch with the word *town*. But what essentially gives the sense group its 'statement' value is the intonation of the last stressed syllable (the second of *tomorrow*). During the pronunciation of this vowel the voice slides down to a low pitch, which still persists during the last unaccented vowel. This last stressed vowel, the intonation of which gives the 'cue' to the hearer, is called the 'nucleus' and what follows is the 'tail'. Contrast the nuclear intonation of the second type of tune: here the voice slides upwards on the vowel of *late* to a higher pitch. This higher pitch may be maintained even if the accented vowel is followed by one or more unaccented (or relatively unaccented) vowels, for instance if for *late* we substitute *later*.

GLIDES, ASSIMILATION, DISSIMILATION

Under the heading of syntagmatic phenomena, i.e. the relationships of sounds in the spoken chain, it will be convenient to discuss some points which, strictly speaking, go beyond linguistic description and belong partly to diachronic linguistics, that is the study of the historical changes in language. To produce strings of sounds in rapid succession the speech organs must move with great rapidity from one posture to another. To effect these different postures the active articulators must pass through a series of intermediate positions, and in so doing they may involuntarily produce fleeting sounds. Such sounds are called 'glide sounds'. The vulgar pronunciation of the name *Henry* illustrates this phenomenon. When the alveolar nasal [n] is pronounced, the mouth passage is closed at the teeth ridge (alveoli) and the uvula is lowered to allow the nasal cavity to resonate while the air escapes through the nasal fossae. But to pronounce the immediately following [r], while the tongue remains in the same position, the uvula must be raised to prevent the passage of air through the nose in order to build up pressure necessary for making the alveolar trill [r] (or fricative [ɹ] according to dialect). But these are precisely the conditions which are necessary for producing the alveolar plosive [d]. If there is a slight lack of coordination and the vibration of the tongue tip is delayed, a [d] will be actually heard: *Endry*. This difficult cluster of consonants may be avoided in another way, by 'anaptyxis', i.e. by inserting a vowel: *Enery* [ɛnərɪ]. Both these types of glide sounds are frequently encountered in linguistic description and comparison. Thus the Greek noun *anér* 'man' once made its genitive **anrós*,[1] but this appears in Attic as *andrós*—the *Endry* phenomenon. Homer, however, also has the *Enery*-form: *anéros* (genitive sing.). The same glide type appears in French *cendre* (our *cinder*), which goes back to the Latin *cinerem* (accusative of *cinis* 'ash') or rather

---

1. Reconstructed forms are asterisked.

cinrem with syncope of the medial vowel. Similarly *camera*, via *camra*, gave rise to *chambre* (our *chamber*), with the development of the corresponding labial plosive after the labial nasal.

This glide is also seen in the word *ambrosia*, the beverage of the Greek gods. This is an abstract noun from the Greek adjective meaning 'immortal', *ámrotos*, which was changed to *ámbrotos* by the insertion of the glide. A *t*-glide developed in Germanic (and in Slavonic) in the cluster *sr*. Thus English *stream*, *sister* and *Easter* all go back to forms exhibiting *sr*: Indo-European *sreu 'flow', *swesr- 'sister' and *ausro-* 'bright'.[1]

The vulgar *chimbley* for *chimney* also exhibits a glide [b] that developed between *m* and *l*, and this finds a parallel in *humble* from the Latin *hum(i)lem*. But this explanation presupposes a prior change of *chimney* to *chimley*. Such a change of *-mn-* (two nasals) to *-ml-* (a nasal and a lateral) is known as 'dissimilation', and is another syntagmatic phenomenon which may be considered together with what is apparently its opposite, 'assimilation'. Both these phenomena are in fact different facets of the general human tendency towards economy of effort, and they both arise from the difficulties encountered in pronouncing a series of sounds in rapid succession.

Assimilation is defined as 'the process of replacing a sound by another sound under the influence of a third sound which is near to it in the word or sentence'. It is accounted for by the speaker's tendency to simplify articulatory movements. In this way a sound may be modified by approximation of its articulation either to a following or a preceding sound. For instance, in the Latin *octo* 'eight' two voiceless plosives had to be pronounced in succession. In Italian, however, the dental closure of the second consonant has been anticipated so that we find *otto*. The [k] is said to be assimilated to the following [t]. We may represent the change thus $k \leftarrow t$, where the arrow shows the direction of the influence from the dominant sound. This is an example of 'regressive assimilation'. In classical Latin there are many examples: *ad-fero* > *affero* 'carry to', *ad-cēdo* > *accēdo* 'proceed to', *sub-cēdo* > *succēdo* '(literally) proceed', *ad-tango* > *attingo* (literally) 'touch

---

1. On *Easter*, see p. 354.

against', etc. In colloquial English examples are heard constantly: e.g. [bɹɛmbʌtə] for *bread and butter*. Similarly, *blind me*! is run together as [blaɪmɪ]. The contrast of spelling and pronunciation in words like *cupboard, blackguard* and *raspberry* provides further examples. Similarly in German, *bleiben* may be rendered as [blaim̩]. In sentences like *Man muss das Leben eben nehmen wie es ist*, the pronunciation [lem̩, em̩, nem̩][1] may be heard.

Assimilation is not confined to adjacent sounds. Regressive assimilation is held responsible for the form of Latin *quinque* 'five'. The parent form was *$penq^we$ (to which Greek *pente* is also traceable); but in Italic, as well as in Celtic, this Indo-European word became *q^wenq^we by a regressive assimilation which we may symbolize thus $p \leftarrow q^w$.

If a sound exerts an influence over the following sound resulting in assimilation, this is represented as $1 \rightarrow 2$ and is called 'progressive'. This type is rarer. In colloquial English *halfpenny* is sometimes pronounced [heɪpmɪ], where the alveolar nasal is changed to a labial under the influence of the preceding [p]. The Latin infinitives *ferre* 'to bear' and *velle* 'to be willing' come from unassimilated forms *fer-se and *vel-se, where -*se* is the infinitive ending.

The term *sandhi* (a Sanskrit word meaning 'putting together') is applied to changes affecting adjacent words in the utterance. A frequent example in English is the assimilation of the final consonant of the verb in such phrases as *is she*? [ɪʒʃɪ], *does she*? [dʌʒʃɪ], in which the [z] is normally assimilated to the hushing sound of the pronoun. Conversely, the [j] of *you* is devoiced in the pronunciation of *don't you*? as [doʊntʃu]. In the Greek phrase *eis tēn polin* 'to the city' the final [n] of the definite article was assimilated to the initial labial plosive of the noun, and this plosive in its turn was later voiced by regressive assimilation. The resulting Greek phrase [istimboli] gave rise to the Turkish name for Constantinople—Istanbul.

Daniel Jones would extend the term assimilation to cases where the two sounds in question merge and produce a single new sound different from either. This he calls 'coalescent assimilation'.

---

1. [m] denotes syllabic [m]; see p. 56f.

Below (p. 73) this notion will be used to eliminate [ŋ] from the inventory of English phonemes and to regard it as a coalescence of two adjacent phonemes [n] and [g]. Complex assimilations are heard in a pronunciation of a word like *mountain* as [mãʊ̃ʔn̩], in which the first nasal coalesces with the diphthong which is nasalized, while the [t] coalesces with the second [n], which is pronounced with glottal stop and release. Similar are pronunciations of *shorten* as [ʃɔ:ʔn̩] as distinguished from [ʃɔ:n] (*shorn*).

A particularly frequent form of assimilation is the approximation of consonants to the articulatory posture of neighbouring vowels. An instance of this general tendency is the so-called palatalization, the fronting of consonants under the influence of a front vowel.[1] In most Romance languages the Latin dorsal plosives were thus palatalized. The Italian descendants of Latin words like *cinis*, *centum* are pronounced with an initial affricate [tʃ], whereas *casa*, *colle* still preserve the plosive unchanged before low and back vowels. The same phenomenon appears in the English *chin*, *church* and *edge*, the original plosives being exemplified in the German counterparts *Kinn*, *Kirche* und *Ecke*. Palatalization also accounts for the [ʒ] in words like *leisure* [lɛʒə], *pleasure* [plɛʒə] and the [tʃ] of *nature* [neɪtʃə], while [dʒ] occurs in the substandard pronunciation of words like *idiot* as [ɪdʒət]. A similar phenomenon appears in Italian *giorno* [dʒɔrno] from Latin *diurnus*.

The processes just discussed owe their genesis to a natural human tendency towards economy of effort. But while the speaker tends to move his speech organs only as much as is necessary to make himself understood, there is one factor which seems to produce exactly the opposite result. It is difficult for human muscles to execute a rapid series of identical movements. The beginner at the piano finds it difficult to execute a rapid series of chords and finds his wrists become as stiff as a poker. This is a physiological state known as tetanus. A similar difficulty in speaking leads to the invention of those feats of vocal gymnastics known as tongue-twisters: *She sells sea-shells on the sea-shore.* In normal speech there is a tendency to avoid the difficulty by altering one of the two identical sounds, like the piano player who changes his

---

1. Palatalization caused by [j] is called 'yodization' (see p. 224).

fingers when playing a rapid series of identical notes. *Chimney*, as we have seen, is a case in point: the second of the two nasals in the cluster [mn] is changed to a lateral [-ml-] with a subsequent insertion of the glide [-b-]. The fate of Latin *hominem* in Spanish illustrates much the same processes. After the syncope of the medial vowel *homnem* became *homre* and this, by insertion of a glide, *hombre*. Here the second nasal was dissimilated to the corresponding trill. Another example of this type of dissimilation is held responsible for the different forms of the Germanic words for 'heaven'. Gothic *himins* with two nasals is regarded as the closest to the original consonantal skeleton of the word. In Old Saxon and Old English the labial nasal is replaced by the corresponding fricative (OE *heofen*, OS *hevan*).

Old High German *himil* exemplifies the 'chimley' phenomenon, in which the alveolar nasal was dissimilated to the corresponding lateral. Thus English *heaven* exemplifies a regressive dissimilation in which the second consonant is dominant: $v \leftarrow n$; German *Himmel* is due to a progressive dissimilation: $m \rightarrow l$. A frequent type of dissimilation is that which leads to the loss of one of the similar sounds rather like the failure to execute one of the notes in a difficult passage on the piano. Illustrations of such dissimilatory loss ('haplology') may be found in substandard pronunciations such as [sɛkətɹɪ] for *secretary* and [ɹɛkənaɪz] for *recognize*. In the first example there is a loss of the first of the two *r* sounds; in the second there is loss of the second dorsal plosive.

4

Phonemics

From the Phone to the Phoneme

The stoechea, the units of the first intuitive analysis (Chapter 2), have been submitted to technical analysis and description (Chapter 3). For the crude ostensive 'definition' of a *d* or a *g*, extracted from the opposed items *muddy* and *muggy*, an articulatory description can now be substituted: the voiced alveolar plosive and the voiced dorsal plosive. Such a description of a stoecheum we call a phone. But the phonetician's exact scrutiny brings surprise. It turns out that a given stoecheum which is apprehended by the native speaker as a single discrete unit may, in fact, embrace a number of different phones. In the series of words *kit, cat, cot, coot* meticulous observation distinguishes four different varieties of dorsal plosive, the point of closure against the roof of the mouth being made progressively farther back.[1] What is of importance is that these phonetic distinctions (k_1, k_2, k_3, k_4) are not made use of in the signalling system of English. There is no word k_4it different in meaning from k_1it. That is to say, the slight phonetic differences are semasiologically irrelevant. This is presumably why the normal speaker of English remains unaware of the differences between these varieties of *k*. They are unimportant for the purpose of communication, and we are, as it were, to this extent phonetically 'colour-blind'. On the other hand a speaker of a language in which

---

1. This is an instance of 'similitude', that is the approximation of the consonant articulation to the tongue position necessary for producing the following vowel.

differences between palatal and velar closure are semasiologically
relevant (as in certain languages of the Caucasus), can easily distinguish them in English. Again, different varieties of plosive
consonants are detected by the phonetician. The [p] of *pin* is
aspirated, whereas that of *spin* and *pepper* is not. D. Jones quotes
(p. 37) the example of a speaker of Urmian Syriac who 'once observed to me that the t's in *ten* and *letter* struck him as being quite
different; it afterwards transpired that in his native language
aspirated and unaspirated [t] occur as separate phonemes, so that
the (to me slight) difference in the amount of aspiration between
the English stressed and unstressed [t] was very apparent to him'.
The reverse is also true.   A foreigner is often blind to distinctions
which do not occur in his own speech. Thus Germans are often
insensitive to the difference between *man* and *men* ([mæn] and
[mɛn]) and *so* and *though* ([soʊ] and [ðoʊ]). Austrians tend to con-
fuse voiced and voiceless plosives, and they also have difficulties in
distinguishing [ʌ] and [a]. As a consequence constant confusion
once arose in ascribing minor nuisances, as reported by our
children's nurse, to the neighbour's dog *Bud* or the child *Pat*.[1]

Jones, in the passage just quoted, used the key term 'phoneme'.
There has been keen debate about the definition of this term (see
pp. 79ff), and it will be best to consider the matter operationally.
That is we shall follow the course of investigation and observe at
what stage of analysis the new term becomes necessary. The
stoecheum, under the scrutiny of the phonetician, has dissolved
into a group of similar phones. But it is noted that the aspirated [t]
occurs initially before the stressed vowel (as in *ten*), whereas the
unaspirated [t] of *letter* occurs medially before an unstressed
vowel. The unaspirated [t] is also heard in the initial cluster of
steal. Thus each of the phones corresponding to the intuitive
stoecheum *t* occurs in a set of exclusive syntagmatic positions:
[tʰ] and [t] each has a territory from which the other is excluded.

---

1. In fact the situation was rather more complex. In south German the
voiceless (breathed) plosives are pronounced with little or no aspiration (such
sounds, called 'mediae', are represented as [b̥], [d̥], etc.). This absence of
aspiration made it difficult for me to distinguish this type of plosive from
voiced [b], [d], which in English also have absence of aspiration as a concomitant
feature of their voicing.

The two phones are said to be in 'complementary distribution'. Such a family of mutually exclusive phones constitutes a phoneme. The phones of the group are said to be 'allophones' of the phoneme. Each phoneme will have its description, no less than each phone. What is of importance is that those features of the phones will be omitted from the description of the phoneme which are merely positional variants, such as the aspiration of the voiceless plosives. In other words, the phonetic description of the phoneme will be the highest phonetic factor common to the whole family of phones which constitute that phoneme. The English phoneme /t/,[1] despite the keen hearing of the Syrian, will be described as a voiceless, alveolar plosive without mention of the presence or absence of aspiration.

By thus grouping the phones into closely related families two things are achieved. The first is economy and simplicity of the description. A phonemic representation of the sounds of a language will evidently be less complex than one which seeks to devise notations for the whole variety of allophones.[2] This is of importance for the invention of scripts for unwritten languages. Further, by eliminating the irrelevant differentia of the allophones, the describer finds in the phoneme a unit corresponding to the intuitive unity of the stoecheum. We may say that the phoneme represents an important aspect of the native speaker's 'competence'. His 'performance', that is the particular ways in which he 'realises' a phoneme in different environments, can be described by 'performance rules', such as that relating to the presence of absence of aspiration in the /t/.

THE PHONEME INVENTORY: ECONOMY AND SIMPLICITY

The problem presented by the English phoneme /t/ is comparatively straightforward, for the phones concerned are few and their distribution is clear cut. More difficult and complicated is the

---

1. The character denoting the phoneme is placed between slant lines. Italics are used for the stoecheum and square brackets for the phone.

2. The allophonic transcription is said to be 'narrow' as contrasted with the 'broad' phonemic transcription.

task of determining the English vowel phonemes from the rich inventory of vocalic phones as set forth in Fig. 12. The same method of simplification will be pursued: resemblant phones in complementary distribution will be grouped together and regarded as allophones of a phoneme. It will be clear that [ɪ] (as in *hit*) and [i] are in complementary distribution since the latter occurs in the diphthong [ij] (as in *heat*). We might then regard both these phones as allophones of the phoneme /i/. There is a similar relationship between [ɛ] and [e] for the latter occurs only in the

FRONT	CENTRAL	BACK
iː or ij		uː or uw
ɪ		ʊ
eː or ej	ɜː	oː or oʊ
ɛ	ə	ɔː
	ʌ	ɒ
æ		ɑː

Fig. 12. The English vowels.

diphthong [ej] (e.g. *late* as opposed to *let*). Each of these phones, in view of their complementary distribution, will be assigned as allophones to the phoneme /e/, and performance rules will give guidance to appropriate realizations of the notation.

The series of back phones shows similar relationships, and they are susceptible to the same phonemic arrangement. [u] (as in *fool*) occurs only in the diphthong [uw], and it may be grouped with the somewhat lower vowel [ʊ] (as in *full*) as allophones of the /u/ phoneme. Similarly, [o] (as in *coat*) occurs only as the first element of a diphthong [oʊ] and will partner [ɒ] (as in *cot*) as allophones of the /o/ phoneme.

In the most open position English also offers two phones in complementary distribution, for the back open vowel [ɑ], as opposed to the fronted and slightly raised [æ], occurs only as a long vowel [ɑː]. The rigid application of the principle of complementary distribution prescribes the grouping of these two phones as allophones of the /a/ phoneme. But if *cad* and *card* are phonemically represented as /kad/, /ka:d/, what is the phonemic status of the lengthener ':'? It would be a neat solution and bring the relation of this pair of allophones into line with the others if we could regard ':' as the second element of a diphthong which has the effect in performance of lowering and backing the /a/. This solution would, however, involve the addition of the 'lengthener' to the inventory of phonemes, and it would be difficult to frame its description in articulatory terms, as has been done for the other phonemes.

A sophisticated descriptive device would identify the lengthener with another phoneme of limited distribution. Above it has been pointed out that [h] is encountered only in the position before a vowel. It is thus open to us to describe the phoneme [ɑ:] as the performance of the phoneme cluster /ah/. We then append a 'performance rule' to the notation to the effect that the /h/ backs and lengthens the /a/ but is itself not otherwise 'realized' or manifested. The same phoneme could be utilized to account for the vowel qualities in words like *nought* [nɔ:t] as opposed to *not* [nɒt]. These have been accounted for (1) by positing two phonemes of different quality /ɔ/ and /ɒ/ or (2) a quantitative distinction /ɔ:/ and /ɔ/. In the first solution a performance rule must be added to ensure its realization as a long vowel; in the second a different rule is required to secure the change of vowel quality. The 'lengthener' could be dispensed with in the phoneme inventory if *not, note* and *nought* were phonemically described as /not/, /nowt/ and /noht/. Here, too, the requisite performance rules would have to be appended to the notations to secure the correct 'realizations': [nɒt], [noot], [nɔ:t].

The phoneme /ə/, as we saw, is confined to unaccented syllables. Its nearest phonetic counterpart in the accented position is the long vowel which occurs in *hurt* [ɜ:]. Consequently, in many treatments of English a phoneme /ə:/ is found. This grouping with /ə/ has the disadvantage that [ə] is the realization of many vowel phonemes in an unaccented position. It also leaves us with the difficult problem of the phonemic status and phonetic description of the lengthener. The vowel of *hurt* [ɜ:] might alternatively be brought into partnership with the phonetically not too dissimilar vowel [ʌ] of *hut*; the long vowel could then be regarded as the realization of a diphthong /ʌh/. Here, too, the description would need appropriate performance rules about the effect of /h/ on the quality and length of the first component. These are, of course, no different in status from the performance rules concerning the clusters of vowel plus /r/ as in *there*. In such words the /r/ persists before a following initial vowel as in *there is*, but in absolute final position the /e/ of *there* is lowered and lengthened with disappearance of the /r/. Phonemic transcriptions such as /ɛə/ cling too closely to the notation of the phones. The notation /ðer/ has the advantage of indicating the /r/ which is actually heard in such phrases as *there is*, *there are*, etc.[1]

By such analyses and devices the rich variety of vowel phones detected in English speech can be ascribed to an inventory of phonemes with the articulatory positions indicated in Fig. 13 and their diphthongal combinations with the three phonemes /j/, /w/ and /h/.

/i/   /u/

/e/   /o/

/ʌ/

/a/

Fig. 13. The English vowel phonemes.

By this means /h/ is also released from its solitary confinement to the initial antevocalic position. Another device will rid the inventory of the phoneme /ŋ/, which occurs solely in the post-

---

1. Another consideration should be borne in mind. Phonology is not an 'autonomous discipline', despite academic compartmentalism. A linguistic description forms a single whole, and a phonemic transcription must be chosen with an eye on the other parts of the description, e.g. the lexicon and the grammar. Thus there are good grounds for choosing the phonemic notation /ðer/ for *there* instead of /ðɛə/. Any notation is devised for interpretation by the performer, and it is easier to devise a rule for the 'omission' of the /r/ from the first notation than a rule for the insertion of the /r/ in the second. All descriptions are devised for use; all are in fact 'prescriptive'. This is particularly important in constructing models to account for the relationship of 'competence' to 'performance', where we imagine the speaker as obeying a set of 'instructions' (see pp. 161ff).

vocalic position as in *sting* /stiŋ/. Just as it was proposed to eliminate /ɜː/ by regarding it as the realization of the cluster /ʌh/, so we
can dispense with /ŋ/ by interpreting it as the realization of the
cluster /ng/, which occurs only postvocalically. This notation will
likewise require a 'performance rule' to the effect that the alveolar
/n/ is assimilated to the following dorsal plosive, which then disappears. Such an analysis will remove /ŋ/ from the inventory of
English phonemes. In the phonetic description of English, [ŋ] will
be grouped with other assimilations of /n/ as in *stink* [stiŋk], where
the [ŋ] is correctly interpreted simply as a positional allophone of
the phoneme /n/.[1]

In setting up the phone classes called phonemes, alternative
systems sometimes present themselves. German for instance has
(1) a phone [h] (as in *hart* 'hard'), (2) a palatal fricative [ç] (as in
Licht 'light') and (3) a velar fricative [x] (as in *lacht* 'laughs').
(2) and (3) are in complementary distribution in the overwhelming
majority of instances; consequently they are usually grouped together as allophones of a single dorsal fricative phoneme, in which
the precise position of the constriction is irrelevant. A case has,
however, been made out for grouping the velar variety with [h],
which is confined, as in English, to the antevocalic position, and
regarding the palatal fricative as a separate phoneme. The reason
for this is that it makes semantic distinctions in opposition to /h/ in
identical environments. However, here, too, the claims of other
parts of the description influence the choice. Grammar and lexicon
resist the separation of *Buch* from *Bücher* (plural), for both are
forms of the stem /bux-/, the difference between the velar and
palatal fricatives being a matter of 'performance' in different
environments. If the alternative solution were chosen, we should

---

1. This proposal in effect regards [ŋ] as an instance of 'coalescent assimilation' (see p. 64). Some difficulties arise. In comparatives like *longer* there is close
cohesion between *long* and the comparative suffix *-er* with the result that the [g]
is heard: [loŋgə]. Contrast this with *singer* where the agent suffix *-er* is added to
the pausal form: [siŋə]. The distinction appears to rest on the unconscious
morphological analysis: it is a problem of 'morphophonemics'. Phonemic status
for /ŋ/ has been urged by citing the opposition of *longer* (adjective): *longer* (agent
noun from 'to long'). The contrived nature of the example strengthens the case
for elimination of /ŋ/ as a separate phoneme in the description of English.

have in grammar and lexicon two different phonemic transcriptions of the 'stem': /bux-, byç-/.

THE SYSTEMIZATION OF THE PHONEME INVENTORY: PHONEMIC STRUCTURE, DISTINCTIVE FEATURES

By 'stoecheosis', phonetic description and observation of the distribution of phones, the sound 'elements' used in a given speech community are reduced to a limited number of phonemes. The number devised for any particular form of speech will naturally vary according to the decision of the describer (e.g. the acceptance or rejection of a phoneme /ŋ/ in English); but all languages of the world so far examined can be described with a phoneme inventory amounting only to a few dozens, a favourite number being about thirty. In principle it would be possible simply to number the phonemes P_1, P_2, P_3, etc., but for many reasons it is advisable to present the inventory in an ordered form, such an arrangement representing the phonemic structure of the language in question.

The structure emerges if we arrange the phonemes in tabular form in such a way that neighbours are minimally distinctive. This is done simply by examining the phonetic description of the phonemes. These descriptions, it may be recalled, are the highest common factors of the groups of phones which constitute the phonemes (see further p. 79). As a preliminary, the principles involved in the description and naming of speech sounds may be reviewed. Above consonants were described in articulatory terms (1) by the nature of the stricture (stops and fricatives, etc.) and (2) by the place of this stricture (labial, dental, etc.), each such 'manner-place' description being further differentiated by the criterion of voice versus breath: e.g. [b] as stop, labial, voiced.

As regards place, certain of the descriptions (e.g. labio-dental fricative) mention two articulators, the active articulator, the lower lip, and the passive articulator, the upper teeth. This mode of description can be extended to all consonantal phones. The chief articulator is the tongue, and it is useful for purposes of reference to divide the tongue into different zones (see Fig. 14). First we have the tip or apex, while the part of the upper surface adjacent to it is called the blade. The rest of the upper surface is called the dorsum,

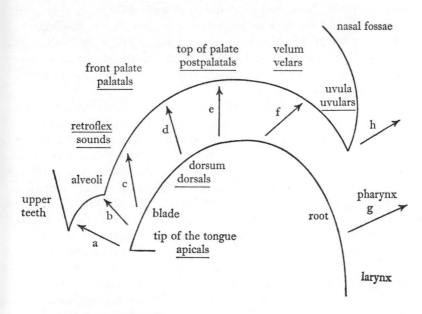

a: apico-dental articulation
b: alveolar articulation
c: retroflex articulation
d: palatal articulation
e: postpalatal and velar articulations
f: uvular articulation
g: pharyngal articulation
h: raising of velum (oral articulations)

Fig. 14.

DIAGRAM OF INTRA-ORAL ARTICULATIONS

(Organs playing no part in phonation are not indicated)

(See A. Martinet: *Elements of General Linguistics*, p. 58).

which is subdivided into the front (opposite the hard palate when
the tongue is at rest), the back (opposite the soft palate or velum),
and the root (facing the pharynx). A 'posture' of the vocal organs

for any particular sound can now be described by specifying both the active and the passive articulator concerned in its production. Thus [t] will be an apico-alveolar stop, and an [s] a blade-alveolar fricative. In addition to this we must specify the state of the glottis, i.e. whether the cords are kept apart or brought together to produce voice.

Given such descriptions of the phonemes, classification of the inventory takes place in the usual way by progressive differentiation. We keep adding specifications until we arrive at a description which gives each phoneme its 'identity'. Thus a primary division by the criterion of 'manner' will yield the classes stops, fricatives, nasals, laterals, etc. This will be followed by further differentiation according to 'place' (labial, dental, etc.). Finally, for English it will suffice to add the criterion of voice. Such a bundle of criteria will enable us to distinguish any consonantal phoneme of English from all other members of the inventory, and so establish its 'identity'. Each such criterion is called a 'distinctive feature', and a phoneme as thus described is a bundle of distinctive features. For example, /t/ belongs to the class of stops as distinguished from fricatives, etc.; it belongs to the class of alveolars as distinguished from labials and dorsals; finally, it belongs to the class of voiceless (or 'breathed') sounds as opposed to voiced. Again, a /d/ is minimally distinguished from /n/ by being a plosive rather than a nasal, the articulatory feature which corresponds to this being velic closure as opposed to velic relaxation.

Such a description, which enables us to arrange the items of the phoneme inventory in a systematic way, is called a 'taxonomic' description. Fig. 15[1] gives a tabular representation of the structure of English consonantal phonemes which brings out the distinctive features by arranging the phonemes in such a way that neighbours are minimally distinguished. All the phonemes produced at a given articulatory place constitute an 'order'. These are shown in the columns of Fig. 15. All phonemes which share a common feature (e.g. voice) constitute a 'series'. These are seen in the rows of Fig. 15. Two parallel series distinguished by a single feature

---

1. On a plane surface only two featural dimensions can be represented. The distinction of voice (e.g. as between [p] and [b]) should be imagined in depth.

		LABIAL	DENTAL	ALVEOLAR	ALVEO-PALATAL	DORSAL	GLOTTAL
Stops	Voiceless	p		t		k	
	Voiced	b		d		g	
Affricates	Voiceless				tʃ		
	Voiced				ʤ		
Fricatives	Voiceless	ʍ f	θ	s	ʃ		h
	Voiced	w v	ð	z	ʒ		
Trill				r[1]			
Lateral				l			
Nasals		m		n		ŋ[2]	

Fig. 15.

1. This phoneme, in RP, is not a trill but a frictionless voiced continuant given the phonetic notation [ɹ].
2. If not eliminated.

form a 'correlation', and the feature in question is called the 'mark'.

The steps which lead to the structural description of the speech sounds of a given community may now be reviewed. Intuitive analysis of meaningful sound complexes first yields the stoechea as distinguishing units. These, when submitted to phonetic description, turn into phones. Phones are grouped into families by the criterion of complementary distribution, each such family being a phoneme. Each phoneme has a phonetic description consisting of the highest common factor (HCF) of the family of phones. Finally the describer devises a structural representation of the phoneme inventory on the lines just described. This structure is part of the phonological system of the language, the other parts being the rules for the siting and combination of the phonemes and the prosodic or supra-segmental phenomena (see pp. 58ff).

EXPLOITATION OF THE INVENTORY: FUNCTIONAL LOAD, NEUTRALIZATION

No language makes absolutely uniform use of the phonemes in its inventory. Some phonemes are more frequent than others and are said to bear a heavier 'functional load'. Others have favourite positions and also positions from which they are excluded. The limited distribution of /h/ and /ŋ/ in certain descriptions of English has already been mentioned: one is confined to the position before stressed vowels and the other to the postvocalic position (for our solution, see pp. 71ff.).

In German no voiced stop occurs at the end of a word: the word *Rad* 'wheel' (plural *Räder*) is pronounced [ʀat] and so is indistinguishable from *Rat* 'council', 'advice'. A similar treatment of the phoneme /b/ emerges from the comparison of the phrase *ich liebe* [liːbə] *dich* and *ich habe dich lieb* [liːp], while the pair of words *betrügen* 'deceive' [bətrygən], *Betrug* [bətruk] shows a parallel alternation of [g] and [k]. This means, in general terms, that in German there is no utilization of the phonemic opposition between voice and breath in this position. The opposition is said to be 'neutralized'. If we have regard for the morphological patterning, the voiceless plosives will in the given cases simply be regarded as positional allophones of the corresponding voiced stops. A positional statement of the phonemes would omit /d/ and /t/ in the inventory of word-final phonemes and substitute an 'archiphoneme', which will be described as having the phonemic features common to voiced and voiceless dental plosives; that is to say that in this position the inventory will contain an archiphoneme (with the notation /T/), which will simply be described as a dental plosive, the 'neutralized' feature being omitted. In Greek the plosives do not occur in the word-final position. The word for 'honey' in the oblique cases has the stem *melit-*, whereas the nominative appears as *meli*. Again, *galakt-* 'milk' has the nominative *gala*. Here we have the theoretically interesting point that zero [Ø] may be regarded as a common allophone of all the Greek plosives, just as the English vowels have a common reduced form [ə]. The utility of the archiphoneme as a descriptive device has been questioned, and no reference is found to it in many standard works. If we insist on the unity of overall description, in the case of Greek, grammar and lexicon will be best served if the stem forms of the above words are given the phonemic transcriptions /melit-/, /galakt-/ with appended 'performance rules' for the ante -#- position (# being the symbol for open juncture in the word-final position).

DEFINITIONS OF THE PHONEME

There has been much discussion about the definition of the phoneme. The differences have arisen in the main from the different emphasis given to one or the other of the successive operations by which the analyst arrives at his descriptive units. The definitions may be classified by reference to these successive steps: (1) the intuitive stoecheum, with the criterion of semasiological relevance, (2) the phone families in complementary distribution, (3) the description of the phoneme as the HCF of the allophones, (4) the structurizing of the phoneme inventory using the criterion of minimal distinctive features.

What we have called the 'item experience', which underlies the analysis into stoechea, was stressed by the pioneer of the phoneme theory, Baudouin de Courtenay: for him the phoneme is the psychological equivalent of a sound in language. This evidently refers to the speaker's intuition.[1] The crux in this definition is 'a sound in language'. This is what concerns the linguist, who must set up his own concepts and definitions without reference to psychology.

Still further from objective data are the definitions which refer to a supra-psychological entity: the phonemes of a language form a category of linguistic elements which exist in the mind of all members of a linguistic community. Such definitions have been rightly criticized because they postulate entities inaccessible to the scientific procedures of linguistics.

L. Bloomfield's formulation of 'a minimum unit of distinctive sound-feature' is also actually a definition of the stoecheum, as emerges clearly from his exposition of the analytical steps which lead up to an inventory of 'replaceable parts'.

The stoecheum also enters into the definition offered by the leader of the Prague School, N. Troubetzkoy, although he uses the psychological term 'phonic image'. Thus the *p* of *pin* is a phonic image. Troubetzkoy combines this with step 3: each such image

---

1. D. Jones notes (*Phoneme*[3], 253): '. . . people possess what the eminent American linguistician Edward Sapir (1884–1939) called "phonemic intuitions" . . .'. This concept corresponds to our 'stoecheum'.

comports certain phonological features, some of which are semasiologically relevant, and others which are not. The phoneme is thus the sum of the relevant phonological features present in the phonic image.

This definition appears in a new guise in Martinet's formulation: a phoneme is a simultaneous bundle of distinctive features, where 'distinctive' means 'semasiologically relevant'. What is meant is that the phonemes, which emerge on the familiar lines, may be *described* as combinations of phonetic features.

Daniel Jones offers a phonetician's definition and stops at step 2: a phoneme is a family of sounds in a given language which are related in character and are used in such a way that no member ever occurs in a word in the same phonetic context as any other member. Jones insisted that the fact that phonemes are capable of distinguishing words is not part of the definition of the phoneme. The unit, elicited by this criterion, as we have seen, is once again the stoecheum.

O. Jespersen added to Jones' definition the criterion of distinctiveness: a phoneme is a family of sounds which from an objective point of view may be regarded as distinct, but which are felt naturally by speakers of a certain language as identical because they are not used to keep words apart. This resembles the definition of Bloch and Trager, who also regard the phoneme as a class of phonetically similar sounds but add the proviso that it must contrast and be mutually exclusive with all similar classes in the language. By contrast and exclusiveness they mean semasiological relevance. This, again, is the criterion for the stoecheum. So in effect these definitions embrace the units of steps 1 and 2.

C. F. Hockett's definition relates to step 4: the phonemes of a language are the elements which stand in contrast with each other in the phonological system of the language. A phoneme is defined only in terms of its differences from other phonemes of the same language. Hockett's exposition however, resembles others in beginning with intuitive analysis into '*p*-sound' and '*b*-sound' and the like. These contrasting units can be described by progressive differentiation on the lines outlined above. What is meant by the definition is that the intuitive stoechea can be described phonetically; that the phonemes which emerge in step 2 can be described

by specifying their differentia, as in step 3; and can be systematized
by reference to these descriptions as in step 4.

Many scholars feel the necessity to stress the phonetic similarity of phones which enter a given family group making up a
phoneme. Such insistence has been prompted by the difficulties
which arise in applying the criterion of complementary distribution in order to determine the phones to be assigned to a given
phoneme. Thus [h] [ŋ] occur in mutually exclusive positions; but it
would be patently absurd to group these together as allophones of
one and the same phoneme. The difficulties disappear if the prior
establishment of the stoecheum is made explicit. It was the
phonetic description of the 'itemized' stoecheum which dissolved
the intuitive unity; this unity was restored simply by omitting the
differentia of the phones that emerged from a given stoecheum.
The *description* of a particular phoneme as the HCF of such a set
of phones leads to an absurdity when applied to the supposed
allophones [h] and [ŋ]. For what is the HCF of 'glottal fricative'
and 'velar nasal'?

In conclusion, in view of the protracted discussion of these
problems in the scholarly literature, the operational origin of the
phoneme concept may once again be stressed. Since so many
scholars have used the word 'language' in their definitions, as
though this term were a 'prime' not requiring explanation, the
notion of 'language' fundamental to the present work may be
briefly stated. 'Speech' is the name for the object of enquiry—a
universal form of human social behaviour. By different techniques
the linguist arrives at a description of this activity in terms of
items at different 'levels' (i.e. stages of the enquiry) and their interrelationships. Such a description is called the 'language' of the
speech community in question. In this sense the phoneme, as
part of the description, is a fact of 'language'. The arrrangement
of the phoneme inventory in the way described above is an aspect
of the 'phonological system' of that 'language'. It conjures up a
pseudo-problem to ask whether the 'structure' is 'in the phenomena' or 'in the mind of the observer'. Viewing the scientific
scene as an outside observer, one may simply state that speech
activity lends itself to description in terms of items and their
interrelationships. A phenomenon so describable is said to be

'structured', and only in this sense can we say that speech has a 'structure'. If 'language' is the scientific name for the description of the speech behaviour of a community and all such descriptions turn out to be 'structured', then the adjective in the phrase 'structural linguistics' is otiose.

DISTINCTIVE FEATURES: ACOUSTIC ANALYSIS

Each phone corresponding to an intuitive stoecheum can be scrutinized not merely as the product of the speaker's articulatory movements, i.e. as a motor event, but also as an acoustic event. For this purpose technical means have been devised to procure visual representations of the complex sound waves which lie behind the perception of each individual speech sound, whether vowel or consonant. The factors which need such visual recording are (see pp. 37ff) (1) the component frequencies and (2) their respective amplitudes. The apparatus which produces such visual records of the factorial analysis of a given complex wave is called a sound spectrograph and the record itself is a sound spectrogram (see Fig. 16a and Pl. I).

What the instrument does is to measure the amplitudes of a group of frequencies lying within a given zone or 'band'. If the amplitude of each frequency band is represented by a column of the

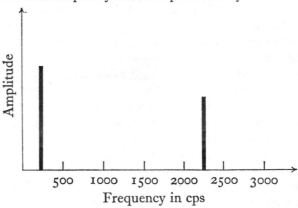

Fig. 16a. Spectrum showing the relative amplitudes of the component frequencies of the vowel [iː] as in *seed*.

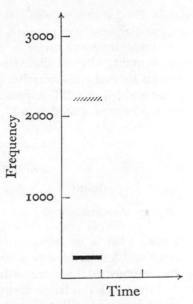

Fig. 16b. Sound spectrogram of the vowel [iː] as in *seed*. The horizontal scale shows the succession of the sounds in the spoken chain; the vertical scale records the component frequencies, the relative amplitudes being visible in the different shades of the inking.

appropriate height, then the tops of the columns will show peaks of greatest amplitude and these represent the 'formants' which give each sound its peculiar timbre. This is true not only of vowels (see pp. 43ff), but also of consonants, as can be readily heard if a hissing sound [s] is followed by a hushing sound [ʃ], the former having a higher inherent pitch than the latter (see Pl. I).

Since the physical event, thus acoustically analysed, is the effect of a motor event, i.e., the speaker's articulations, it should be possible to relate the two directly, and so to classify the articulations by reference to the acoustic data. Consider the case of the consonants. They have been classified (according to 'place') as (1) labials, (2) dentals, (3) palatals and (4) velars. The proposal has also been made to reclassify the consonants by acoustic criteria. Labials and velars are grouped together as 'grave' because of the low pitch of their characteristic formants as contrasted with the 'acute' nature of dentals and palatals. Next a cross-classification is achieved by using the criterion 'compactness' (as opposed to 'diffuseness'). Compact sounds are those in which there is a single centrally located predominant formant, whereas diffuse sounds have their predominant frequencies located non-centrally. [k] is an example of a compact consonant and [p] of a diffuse consonant. These two pairs of 'oppositions' can be represented as in Fig. 17

k	c	Compact
p	t	Diffuse
Grave	Acute	

Fig. 17. Acoustic oppositions.

In articulatory terms, what is common to labials and velars ([p] and [k]) is a larger and less divided oral cavity, the point of constriction lying respectively at the extreme front and the extreme back of the vocal tract. It is this larger cavity which generates the lower lying resonant frequencies that give the acoustic quality called in intuitive terms 'grave'. Conversely, both dentals and palatals divide the oral cavity by a more centrally placed constriction. The resulting smaller cavities have higher resonant frequencies, hence the 'acute' quality of these sounds.

Within these two major classes the distinction between 'diffuse' and 'compact' comes from the ratio between the cavities in front of the point of constriction and behind it. In velars, the point being far back in the mouth, this means that the forward cavity is much larger than the back cavity, while the reverse is true of the labials, in which the point of constriction lies at the very front of the vocal tract.

By such acoustic distinctions Jakobson and Halle[1] have listed twelve acoustic 'oppositions'. These represent the whole gamut of articulatory movements of which the human vocal apparatus is capable in producing significant distinctions of sound. These elemental features constitute the basic acoustic-articulatory stock from which each language makes its particular selection in forming

---

1. *Fundamentals of Language*, pp. 29ff.

its phonemes. Thus for the plosives at each 'place' English utilizes
only the opposition voice/breath to make phonemic distinctions;
but Classical Greek also made use of aspiration. Thus English has
a binary opposition in the plosives, whereas Greek has a triple
opposition:

$$
\begin{array}{ccc}
\text{t} & & \text{t} \\
\text{d} & \text{t}^{\text{h}} & \text{d}
\end{array}
$$

Jakobson and Halle divide the twelve binary oppositions into
(A) sonority features and (B) tonality features. (A) comprises
vocalic/non-vocalic, consonantal/non-consonantal, compact/
diffuse, tense/lax, voiced/voiceless, nasal/oral, discontinuous/con-
tinuant, strident/mellow, checked/unchecked; and (B) includes
grave/acute, flat/plain, and sharp/plain.

Much remains to be done in this field of study, and there is room
for criticism. For instance, it is doubtful whether the concepts of
vowel and consonant belong to the category of inherent features
forming part of the 'simultaneous bundle' that makes up the
phoneme. As argued above, these are syntagmatic phenomena and
statable as relations between the phonemes, not as features of the
phonemes.

We shall not discuss the psycholinguistic applications of this
theory in detail. This assigns to the mental furniture of speaker and
hearer a 'code' corresponding to the set of binary oppositions
chosen from the universal stock. The hearer is sensitized to these
distinctions and not to those neglected in his language. An example
quoted above is the insensitivity of the Englishman to the distinction between the 'hard and soft p'.

The hearer faced with the incoming message 'identifies' each
phoneme by a kind of scanning device which poses a series of yes–
no questions corresponding to the acoustic 'oppositions' relevant
to his language: vowel or consonant?, compact or diffuse?, and so
on. Such a scanning assumes, of course, the prior segmentation,
since the scanner moves from one 'position' to the next.

In transformation theory, too (see Chapter 7), the phonetic
representations are regarded as sequences of feature bundles
('feature matrices'), such features belonging to a restricted set of
universal phonetic features, which in the last resort are determined

by the capacities of the human vocal apparatus. What is new is the psycholinguistic hypothesis that such representations are 'mentally constructed' by the speaker–hearer.

Finally, the notion that 'any one language code has a finite set of distinctive features and a finite set of rules for grouping them into phonemes and also for grouping the latter into sequences', this multiple set being what is called the 'phonemic pattern' of the language in question, will be discussed below apropos of the relationship between the terms 'speech' and 'language' (see above p. 81 for a preliminary statement). If the hypothetical psycholinguistic 'code' is deleted from this formulation, it corresponds in the main to the exposition favoured in this chapter.

5

The First Articulation

From the Utterance to the Moneme

The second articulation was considered first for practical reasons: for a written discussion of speech it is necessary to devise a notation for the speech signals. Nevertheless the segmentation of the vocal expression presupposed the dismemberment of utterances into the ultimate sound-meaning units (S–M units) called 'monemes' by Martinet (see p. 30ff). The stoechea *d* and *g* were elicited by contrasting *muddy* with *muggy*, these being apprehended as two different S–M units: S_1–M_1, S_2–M_2. Meaning evidently cannot be disregarded in phonemic analysis, and it is not scientifically more 'rigorous' to attempt to do so. The first articulation is completed when the given speech corpus, taken as adequately representative of the speech habits of a given community, has been reduced to the meaningful elements, i.e. S–M units, which are not further reducible to still smaller S–M units. *Muddy*, for instance, compared with *mud* yields a moneme *-y*, which also emerges from pairs like *dirty*, *dirt*, etc.[1] By applying this commonsense method of analysis, relying on our basic and unchallengeable 'item experiences', the

---

1. The analysis of *muggy* presents a problem which has been much discussed. The removal of the *-y* leaves a moneme *mug-* to which no meaning can be attached in standard English that will give a satisfactory explanation of the meaning of the resultant word. *Rasp-berry* is often quoted in this connexion, for what is the meaning of the constituent *rasp-*? Often these monemes are ancient S–M items surviving only in such compounded forms. For instance, *mug* survives in dialect in the sense 'mist, drizzle'. A term is needed for such linguistic husks.

corpus is seen simply as combinations of these linguistic atoms. The complete inventory of the monemes thus elicited from the speech of the community under examination may be called the 'monematicon'.

Before proceeding further, certain distinctions essential to the concept 'moneme' must be made. The S-side consists of one or more phonemes, e.g./mʌd/, /i/. This may be called the 'keneme', a term coined by the Danish scholar L. Hjelmslev on the basis of the Greek word *kenos* 'empty'. The content of the keneme, what we have called the M-side, may be called the 'plereme', from the Greek word *plērēs* 'full'. Thus the moneme is a combination of a keneme with a plereme. When analysed in this way the moneme would have the full notation {/mʌd/ ~ 'MUD'}. This may be abbreviated by the use of brackets with conventional ortho-graphy: {*mud*} stands for the moneme.

The monematicon will differ from the lexicon in that it will contain not only full words like *mud, dirt, mess, fun,* but also such 'word-partials' as *-y, -ness* (*messiness*), *-al* (*arrival*), *-en* (*shorten*), etc. Difficulties may arise in assigning a sufficiently defined M to the given S. In the case of *-y* the ODEE (*Oxford Dictionary of English Etymology*) defines it as 'a suffix of adjectives denoting "having the character of . . .", "inclined to . . .", "full or consisting of . . ."'. The definition thus requires the grammatical concept 'adjective'. Again, from the utterances *A cat likes a bird* and *Cats like birds* two monemes can be extracted which are homonymous. -S_1 is defined as forming the 'plural' of the 'noun' *cat* and -s_2 as forming the 'singular' of the verb *like*. But a fundamental dif-ference is concealed by the use of the grammatical terms 'singular' and 'plural' for these separate phenomena. The meaning of -s_1 is established by studying the use of the noun *cats* 'referentially'. It is observed that this form occurs with reference to 'more than one' cat in the situation referred to by the utterance, although we shall also be helped by noting such syntagmatic clues as the use of *cats* after the numerals *two, three, four,* etc. Still, since the meaning of these clue-giving words is also arrived at by examining the situa-tion, it will be true to say that the definition of the moneme -s_1 is 'world-orientated'.

Quite different is the case of -s_2 in *likes*. In the monematicon this will be defined as the formant of 'the third person singular present indicative active of certain verbs'. This complex and sophisticated 'meaning' will be discussed below. For the moment we concentrate on the term 'singular'. This grammatical term, like the corresponding term 'plural', has quite a different significance when applied to a verb. To establish the function of -s_2 in *likes* as opposed to the 'zero' ending of *like* in *cats like*, we do not examine the situation to detect correlations with one or more acts of 'liking'. The singular and plural monemes of the verb are not 'world orientated'. The presence or absence of -s_2 is determined by other constituents of the utterance. That is, this particular moneme is syntagmatically orientated, not situationally. Thus the grammatical terms 'plural' and 'singular', when applied to both nouns and verbs, conceal essential differences of fact and analytical operations.

The same point may be made of the so-called personal pronouns. The 'meaning' of *I* and *you* is established situationally. They are in fact 'pointing' (deictic) words. *I* points to the person speaking and *you* to the person addressed. *He*, *she* and *it* are, however, not meaningful in this direct deictic way.[1] In normal use *he*, *she* and *it* (and the corresponding plural *they*) refer to individuals already mentioned in the dialogue: *I saw John yesterday. He was looking very fit.* The third personal pronouns are not deictic but anaphoric.[2]

These brief discussions will have brought out the immense complexity of the task facing the scholar who attempts to compile a monematicon. In the dismemberment of utterances he will compare utterances partially alike and will seize on the recurrent partials of the expression and try to divine what contribution such forms make to a given utterance. In practice this will be a matter of trial and error, and the experiments will include the deletion and addition of the particular moneme or its substitution by others.

---

1. We could, of course, use *he* when pointing to an unknown person, e.g. when informing a policeman: '*he* did it'. But here it is the deictic gesture which identifies and not *he*; this is quite unlike *I* and *you* which are intrinsically deictic.

2. From the Greek word *anaphora*, literally 'carrying back'; the verb *anaphérō* corresponds to the Latin *refero*.

Space precludes the detailed consideration of these field techniques. What will have already become clear is that the elucidation of the total moneme stock from which the corpus can be regarded as constituted will involve not only situational analyses and the determination of correlations between situational components and certain 'world-orientated' monemes such as *cat, like, bird, two,* etc., but also complex syntagmatic relations between the members of the utterance. A definition such as 'third person singular present indicative active of the verb . . .' presupposes much of what is called formal grammar and in particular the doctrine of the 'parts of speech' (see below pp. 91ff., 142).

IMMEDIATE CONSTITUENTS

In the reduction of utterances to their minimal 'working parts', the monemes, we attempt to pull them apart at the joints. The detection of these joints (*articuli*, hence 'articulation') is the first task of the analyst. Such analysis was pioneered by the Greeks, and it was they who gradually evolved the concepts of the *mérē toû lógou*, a phrase literally translated into Latin as *partes orationis* and then, no less literally, into English as 'the parts of speech'. A better term would be 'the members of the utterance'. In such 'dismemberment' grammarians start with simple utterances the analysis of which is self-evident and attempt to fit more complex phenomena into the structural frames devised for the description of the simpler instances. In this task the structural frames will be kept as few and as simple as is compatible with an adequate description, i.e. one which 'accounts for' the given speech habits as represented in the available corpus.

Two such useful frames have been devised for the description of utterances: the types (1) *Cats chase birds* and (2) *Cats climb well*. In both two constituents can be detected: both focus on and 'name' a certain 'thing' and say something about it. This simple dichotomy is a powerful aid in the dismemberment of utterances, and it gives us the two most important 'parts of speech'. The Greeks coined the terms for the two structural parts: the focal item which is named they called *onoma* (Latin *nōmen*, English *noun*); for 'what is said' they used the 'result noun' from the verb 'to say'—*rhêma* (Latin *verbum*). If we carry out this simple dicho-tomy on the two utterances now under examination by asking 'What is focally named?' and 'What is said about it?', the pro-ducts of such an analytical operation are said to be the immediate constituents (abbreviated ICs). The utterances may be pro-gressively reduced to smaller and smaller constituents by further operations which yield ICs at each step.

The onoma–rhema distinction which we owe to the Greeks enables us to divide a large number of utterances into two structural parts. Let us call them 'functional sites'. It is now proposed to carry out further analysis on those parts of the utterances which occupy these sites.

In the utterances (1) and (2) the onoma remains constant, but the rhema constituents have a different structure. The rhema of (1) *chase birds* has two constituents and so has (2) *climb well*. But there is an important difference of relation between the two con-stituents. Common to both is a constituent which has a form re-sponsive to the 'singular' or 'plural' of the onoma: *chase(s)*, *climb(s)*. We thus have two criteria for this constituent which it is necessary to distinguish. It occurs in a functional site and it ex-hibits certain formal features. In our terminology it will be advis-able to make a corresponding distinction. To the site we give a Greek name: it is 'rhematic'. The unit which occupies this site and exhibits certain formal features (such as indications of syntag-matic connexion with singular and plural 'subjects') will be called by a derivative from the corresponding Latin word: a 'verb'.

The rhemas of (1) and (2) are both more complex than, for instance, that of (*cats*) *hunt*, and they may be regarded as 'expan-sions' of this simpler form. The verb is the essential component of the rhema; it is said to be the 'head' of the rhematic construc-tion. The other rhematic constituents which depend structurally on the verb will be called 'epirrhematic'. To distinguish the epirrhe-matic constituents of (1) and (2) we can first use a formal criterion. In (1) *birds* exhibits the 'world orientated' plural moneme $-s_1$ which also figures in the 'noun' that occupies the onoma site, whereas this is not the case with *well*. To this formal distinction we may add another culled from the situation. In (1) the activity denoted by the verb is directed towards another entity whereas this is not the case with (2). Grammarians use the term 'transitive construction' for the rhematic expressions which contain such a 'goal', and 'intransitive' for those which do not. The immediate constituents of an utterance which emerge in response to the questions *onoma?*, *rhema?* are called 'subject' and 'predicate' respectively. We need these functional names in order to state the syntagmatic relations which hold between *cat(s)* and *like(s)*: the verb of the predicate agrees in 'number' with the noun of the subject.

Noun-like expressions which figure in the 'goal' site of the rhema are said to be the 'object' of the verb. Other epirrhematic constituents like *well* in (2) or *better*, and *at night* (as in *Black cats chase birds better at night*) are called 'adverbs' (from *adverbium*, the Latin equivalent of Greek *epirrhēma*). They give answers to such questions as how? when? where?, etc., relating to the verbal event.

The onoma may also have a complex form. The noun is the essential 'head'; its structurally dependent constituents may be labelled functionally, with reference to their 'site', as 'eponomatic': *black* (*cats*), *the big black* (*cat*) *with one ear over there*. Among such eponomatic site-occupants we may single out the 'articles': *the* and *a(n)* form an opposing pair whose main function is to particularize or not. The traditional names are the definite article (*the*) and the indefinite article (*a(n)*).

Constituents like *black* are established not merely by their structural ('eponomatic') site and their semantic function (giving answers to questions like *qualis* 'of what kind') but also by certain formal features, what we might call their morphological behaviour. Thus, negatively, they do not display (in English at any rate) the overt markers of singular and plural; positively, they have the peculiarity of combining with the monemes *-er*, *-est*, which serve as marks for the 'degrees of comparison'. Such multiple characterization—functional 'site', semantic function, and morphological behaviour—justifies the setting up of a separate class of 'adjectives' (from the Latin *adiectīvum* = Greek *epitheton*) among the eponomatic constituents.

The point about multiple characterization is an important one because needless difficulties have arisen through demands for consistency of criteria in defining the parts of speech. It is right, of course, to reject purely semantic definitions, such as that of the noun as 'the name of a person, place or thing', or that of the verb as 'a word which stands for action or being acted upon'. But 'consistency of criteria' has in practice often meant singleness of criterion.

Many scholars have favoured the method of 'substitution in frames' as a means of arriving at the word classes of a given language. Thus, if we take as the starting point a simple utterance like *The weather was good*, we can draw up a list of English words which can be substituted for *weather* 'with no change of structural meaning'. It is regarded as more scientific to call these 'Class 1 words' rather than 'nouns'. Similarly, in another type of sentence such as *John forgot his keys* all the words which can be substituted for *forgot* without change of structural meaning form a class which can be called 'Class 2 words'. The crux here is the question-begging phrase 'without change of structural meaning'. It is obvious that this cannot be established until all the sentences used in setting up the class have been independently analysed to establish their structure. Only then can we know whether the structure has changed or not. This is tacitly taken for granted. It is implicit in the term 'frame'. In fact, the frames within which the substitutions are made are much the same as the functional sites used by the Greeks. If this implication were eliminated from the frame method as expounded, then Class I words would mean nothing but 'words like *weather*', and it would be an empty concept until the structural function of *weather* had been made explicit. If then (1) it is common practice to take the structure of simple sentences as the model for the analysis of more complex sentences and (2) to group words into constituents when it is possible to substitute a single word for the group without changing the structure, this evidently implies the prior establishment of the structure of simple sentences in terms of functional sites and such structural relations as subject and predicate. Expressions which occupy a given syntactic site constitute a 'form class'. Complex expressions which occupy a site are called 'expansions', and the several members of such an expansion are said to exhibit cohesion in virtue of their collective ability to fill a given site.

To recapitulate, the 'parts of speech' are classes of words grouped according to the part they play in the structure of the utterances in which they occur. The structure emerges in response to certain functional questions posed by the analyst in broad semantic terms: What is named? What is said about it? The statement of functional sites gives the syntactical structure of a given sentence.

Morphology, the study of the ways and means by which the occupants of functional sites indicate syntactical relationships, comes later. Morphology is secondary to syntax. It has been rightly claimed that 'the definition of a class, and its membership, can only arise from the criteria used to establish it in the first place' (Robins). The word classes emerge step by step as the utterances are reduced by various analytical operations, beginning with the first dichotomy into onoma and rhema. Since there is progressive reduction from complex structures to simpler constituents (e.g. the analysis of the complex onomatic *the black cats* into its 'head' *cats* and the two eponomatic constituents, the article *the* and the epithet (adjective) *black*), it follows that each part of the speech is defined by the role it plays in the structure of the 'member' next above it in the 'scale' (literally 'ladder') of operations.

A final point must be made. The 'parts of speech' are not universal. The analyst faced with a new body of material will set up only those word classes which his analytical operations will suggest as useful for the purposes of description. He will not bring to his task ready-made sets of word classes such as those made familiar by the grammars of Greek and Latin.

The point has been made that morphology is secondary to syntax. It is the study of the overt marks which indicate syntactical function. Yet it is these overt marks which appear in the monematicon. It will now be clear why such grammatical concepts as the 'parts of speech' must appear in the monematicon as parts of the 'meaning' of certain monemes.

THE WAY UP AND THE WAY DOWN: FROM UTTERANCE TO SENTENCE

The successive dismembering operations performed on an utterance until its final dissolution into irreducible monemes can be given a schematic representation in the form of a branching tree (see Fig. 18). Contrary to the usual practice, our figure shows an upwards branching tree since in effect we rise from the ground of observed fact (the utterance U) to the ultimate units, the monemes, from which all utterances in the last resort are put together. This process of analysis whereby we rise from the firm earth of the speech phenomena to the highest linguistic abstractions may be called the 'Way Up'. It is distinguished from the 'Way Down', that is the set of operations which 'generates' utterances by employing the units, the concepts, and the definitions evolved on the 'Way Up'. This distinction is necessary for the clarification of a central term in linguistics. A finished product of the 'Way Down', the result of applying the descriptive devices evolved on the 'Way Up', will be given the technical name 'logos'. Thus we start with the observed phenomena, the utterances, and devise descriptions along the lines just adumbrated, by functional and formal analysis, such as is represented in Fig. 18. The concepts and units which emerge progressively with each step of the 'Way Up' will be defined operationally at this stage. When the given sample (the corpus) has been satisfactorily described by these means, concepts and definitions will be logically examined, purified and organized into a theory. The adequacy of the theory in 'accounting for' the speech habits of the community under examination will be tested in the usual way by applications. If the products generated by the theory pass muster by native speakers (i.e. are found 'acceptable'), in so far the theory will be found adequate. If exception is taken to the 'logos' so produced then the theory will have to be revised. It will avoid confusion if we insist that a 'logos' is a result of the application of the theory, certain parts of the theory being called the 'grammar' (see p. 108). The relationship of the Way Up to the Way Down and of utterance to sentence is shown in Fig. 19.

One important point must be made in preparation for the discussion of transformational generative grammar (Chapter 7). The grammar generates a limited number of 'site-structures' into which we can fit monemes and moneme combinations appropriate to our intention. It is these abstract schemata that we propose to call 'sentences'. This corresponds to everyday usage, as when we say that a given form of words 'is not a sentence'. The moneme-filled site-structures will be called 'logoi'. Thus the description will generate an infinite number of logoi which fit into the small number of 'sentences' generated by the grammar. It causes much confusion of thought if the term grammar is used for the whole description. Our usage again conforms to normal use. When we say that a form of words used in an utterance is not 'grammatical', we mean that they do not fit into one of the abstract schemata of site-structures generated by the grammar.

From this it follows that there can be no 'ungrammatical sentences'. What are so called are in fact either products of inadequate descriptions or of descriptions culled from utterances branded as 'social misfits', such as *I don't know nothing*.

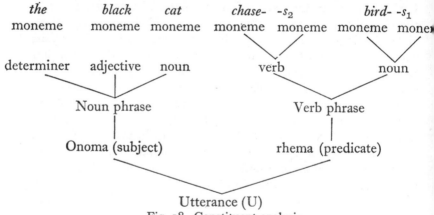

Fig. 18. Constituent analysis.

Note: Some scholars favour a mode of dismemberment which takes the form of a simple dichotomy at each step: e.g. *the + black cat > the + black + cat*, and their 'trees' would mirror such a procedure.

THE DEFINITION OF THE SENTENCE

Linguists have wrestled with, and wrangled over, the definition of the sentence since the beginning of linguistic science with the

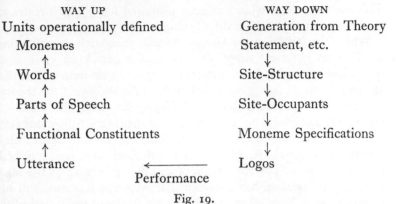

Fig. 19.

Greeks. Over two hundred definitions were listed in a thorough German publication entitled *Was ist ein Satz?* ('What is a sentence?'). It must be insisted at the outset that a satisfactory definition must be a linguistic one and not rely on, or appeal to, concepts and criteria which lie outside the competence of the linguist *qua* linguist. This defect afflicts the ancient definition of the sentence as a group of words expressing a complete thought, for this puts the onus on the logician, who may be presumed to know what a 'complete thought' is. It is no improvement to substitute other 'mentalistic' concepts, like the 'intention of the speaker' as is done in the proposal by A. H. Gardiner: 'A sentence is an utterance which makes just as long a communication as the speaker intended to make before giving himself a rest.' The attempt is particularly instructive because it brings out so clearly the confusion between utterance, sentence and logos. What is meant by 'giving himself a rest' is, of course, the final cadence and pause which are among the prosodic symptoms of the completed utterance (see p. 61).

A clear distinction between utterance and sentence will help to obviate difficulties which afflict another recent proposal which equates the sentence with the potentially complete utterance and defines it phonologically as 'a stretch of speech that may be uttered with a prepausal intonation tune'. This is, of course, again the utterance. On the other hand, it is said that the sentence is the longest structure within which a full grammatical analysis is possible and that a sentence is by definition grammatically complete.

This comes close to what has been proposed here, which restricts the term sentence to the products of grammatical generation.

With this definition we simply do not pose such questions as whether an elliptical utterance like *Got a match on you?* is a 'complete sentence'. It is certainly a complete utterance. But the sentence finds its definition simply within the theory. If the theory provides for optional deletion of *Have you*, then this form of words will be a complete sentence. A sentence is a formula that sets forth the interrelations of monemes and other grammatical elements, using certain functional-morphological schemata, couched in 'parts of speech' terms, which form the 'grammar of the language'. The relationship between grammar and sentence will be taken up again later when we discuss the limits of grammaticality (p. 145).

SPEECH AND LANGUAGE

The distinction between utterance and sentence is part of the distinction between speech and language. A. H. Gardiner regarded the sentence as the unit of speech, whereas the word is the unit of language. In fact, the unit of speech is the utterance. The 'language', on the other hand, may be defined as the completed description of the speech habits of the community under investigation. It will comprise phonology, grammar (morphology and syntax) and lexicon. In a broader sense the 'language' of a given speech community may also be regarded as the sum total of all conceivable logoi generated by applying the description. If the description, with its moneme inventory, and its rules of combination, is found to be empirically adequate, it may be used by students of speech psychology (psycholinguists) to construct a sort of 'black box' to account for the speaker's ability to form utterances adequate to the manifold social demands which confront him (his 'competence'). Doubtless the speaker is endowed with the capacity to store the lexicon and the monematicon and to manipulate the rules formulated in the grammar, but these are matters which lie beyond the limits of linguistics proper.

Much effort has gone into exploring and defining relations between speech and language. In some expositions the terms are partially synonymous, and this is implicit in the definition of linguistics as the study of language. Modern theory, however, makes a distinction which goes back to the French–Swiss scholar Ferdinand de Saussure. He called the speech utterances we actually observe *parole*, whereas *langue* he regarded as something supra-individual, the common possession of all those who regard themselves as 'speaking the same language'. De Sassure thought of *langue* as somehow stored in the collective consciousness of all members of the community. It is a social phenomenon, yet a concrete object no less than *parole*.

Most modern scholars, however, would reject this view of the relationship of speech and language and agree in regarding *langue* as the system of regularities underlying the shifting phenomena of speech. Yet the term 'underlying' is a crude and question-begging metaphor. We may make the relationship clear by stating at which stage in our descriptive operations we find it necessary to coin the term 'language'. We start with speech and examine an indefinitely large sample. Eventually we attain to an adequate description couched in terms of items at different levels and statements of their interrelationships. It is to this completed description that we may apply the term 'language'. As for the relationship between speech and language, *qua* linguists we do not need to pose questions which are the province of the psycholinguist; nor need we wonder how the 'system' comes to be stored in the brains of the speakers. Nor again do we need to pose metaphysical questions which remind one of the difficulties raised by the relation of the Platonic ideas to the objects of the sensory world: language is the immutable reality which lies behind the imperfections of speech. If a linguist is asked about the connexion of speech with language, he will reply 'I am'. The relation between the abstractions of the 'language' in this sense and the observed phenomena is called 'realization'. Thus the 'phones', the observables of speech, are the realizations of the phonemes, the abstract units which are devised by the linguist for the description and so form part of the *langue*.

If we posit the storage in the mind of the speaker of an entity corresponding to the linguistic description, then his utterances can be regarded as resulting from a succession of choices from among the devices duly set forth in the linguist's description of his speech habits. It remains true to say that the only way we can attain to knowledge of the 'language' in this psycholinguistic sense is through analysis of speech. Thus the linguist in effect adds nothing to his description by positing psycho-linguistic mechanisms and asserting that by ascribing a 'knowledge of the language' to speakers he thus accounts for their 'competence'. (See further pp. 167, 179.)

PHRASE STRUCTURE GRAMMARS

The procedures of analysis that break an utterance down into its ultimate meaningful constituents and define the relations that hold between them, as illustrated in Fig. 18, can be formalized as a set of 'rewrite rules'. This will facilitate comparison with transformational grammar. The first step, the dichotomy into onoma and rhema in the traditional theory, is formalized thus:

(1) S(entence) $\longrightarrow$ NP (noun phrase) + VP (verb phrase).

Here the labels are taken from the traditional 'parts of speech' (see below). Note also that it gives no explicit expression to the prior functional dichotomy into onoma and rhema, although it is this relationship which determines the structure. Our second and third divisions follow on:

(2) VP $\longrightarrow$ V + Adv

(3) NP $\longrightarrow$ A + N

Such a system of rewrite rules will assign an unambiguous constituent structure to a sentence such as *black cats hunt better*. A grammar which uses this device for assigning constituent structures to sentences is called a phrase-structure grammar, and the particular set of rewrite rules is a phrase-marker (PM). After all the rewrite rules have been carried out, the end-product appears as a structure couched in terms of elements familiar to us as the 'parts of speech'. These elements which appear in the final analysis, N(oun), V(erb), A(djective), Adv(erb), etc., are called the terminal symbols. Their modes of combination, which characterize the whole structure, can be represented not only in the form of a branching tree (as in Fig. 18) but also by means of 'labelled brackets':

$$S\{NP (A + N) + VP (V + Adv)\}$$

Such bracketed strings of terminal symbols are called for short 'terminal strings'. They represent the syntactic structure of all utterances made by substituting lexical items of the appropriate word class (parts of speech) for the class symbols: e.g., *red dragons hiss terribly, green ideas propagate remarkably*. Common to all such utterances is an 'underlying string' of terminal symbols.

An important point must be made here in anticipation of later discussion of Chomsky's proposals. When we give substance to an abstract syntactic structure in the sense that we put monemic and lexical flesh on the structural skeleton, we make use of the S–M elements listed in the monematicon. This means that we simultaneously carry out a phonological and a semantic 'interpretation' of the underlying abstract structure. It is this structure, which is couched in the general 'parts of speech' terminology, that belongs to grammar. Grammar ends when we proceed to substitute actual monemes and moneme combinations (lexical items) for general terms (e.g. *red dragons* for $A + N$). The choice of the particular words so substituted is, of course, motivated by the requirements of the situation. Here the lexicon takes over from grammar.

The phrase structure grammars of the simple type so far used by way of example can handle expansions such as are symbolized by the rewrite rule $NP \rightarrow A + N$. It can also, in traditional practice, cope with more complex syntactical problems like the embedding of a whole sentence in the onomatic and rhematic sites. Take the two sentences (1) *John wants a new car* (2) *I know that*. To form a single sentence (1) must be embedded in (2). This procedure can be formalized by substituting the symbol S'(entence) at the appropriate place in the phrase-marker of (2) (see Fig. 20).

The possibility of introducing the initial symbol S at appropriate points of the phrase-marker (that is of inserting sentences in functional sites) enables us to introduce a 'recursive' device into the rules, and this makes it possible to expand indefinitely the simple basic structures so as to generate without theoretical limit 'complex sentences'. In traditional grammar such an embedded sentence was called a 'clause'. The device of embedding was always implicit in the clausal analysis of a complex sentence into main clauses, adverbial clauses, and so on. There is nothing new here except the notation. A phrase-marker which contains one or more

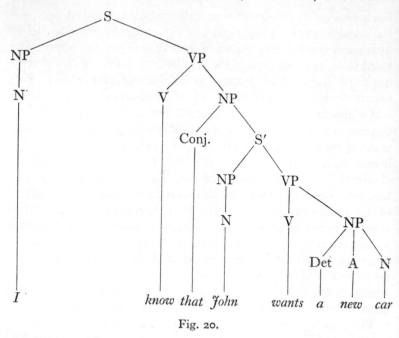

Fig. 20.

symbols S after the initial one is called a 'a generalized phrase-marker'.

THE SYSTEMATIZATION OF THE MONEMATICON

The monematicon, once the operations delineated above are completed, will consist of a vast inventory of minimal S–M units. In this crude form it will be simply a list arranged for convenience of reference in alphabetical order. We are in much the same position as we were when the inventory of phonemes had been established before this was systematized. However, this task of analysis was merely the preliminary necessary to describe the corpus, which is seen as the product of manifold combinations of certain recurrent items, the monemes. What we need to know are the rules for the combinations; for without explicit statement of the powers of combination of the monemes we cannot formulate instructions for reassembly. We are in the position of a man who has taken a watch to pieces, has labelled the parts and now wants to put it together again so that it works. In essence, to start the linguistic watch working we want to know which part goes immediately together with which and what the functions of each such successive 'constitute' are within the whole mechanism as it is built up.

An essential distinction in the structural specification of the monemes may be exemplified by the sentences *A weakness in the structure was responsible*, *Weaknesses in the structure were responsible*. Both -*ness* and -s_1 figure in the monematicon, but there is a fundamental difference in their function. In traditional terms, s_1 is an inflection of the word *weakness*, which is an abstract noun formed by the suffix -*ness* from the adjective *weak*. English exhibits few such inflections, and the point may be better illustrated from Latin. The noun *dictātōr*- indicates its syntactic function in the sentence by adding different monemes: -*em* (accusative), -*is* (genitive), -*ī* (dative), -*e* (ablative) (all these being in the singular). If we remove these inflections the truncated 'word' is called the stem:[1] *dictātōr*-. This stem is built on the 'root' *dīc*- 'say' by an accumulation of stem-forming suffixes. A frequentative suffix -*t*- is added to form the verb stem *dictā*- (cf. *cantāre* from *can*-), and from this stem an agent noun is formed by the suffix -*tōr*-. The monematic analysis of *dictatorem* is thus *dic-tā-tōr- em*. The last, the one which indicates the relationship of the 'word' *dictator*- to the other components of the sentence, i.e. the index of the syntactical function, is set apart from the merely stem-forming monemes. For such syntactic monemes the term 'functional monemes' has been proposed. It will be seen that the example chosen from English does not illustrate this type of moneme. Better would have been the *architect's weakness*, for here the moneme -s_3 indicates the relationship of the word *architect* to *weakness*. The -s_1 of *weaknesses* does not indicate the relation ('subject') of *weakness* to the rest of the sentence.

As we have said above, the 'plural' moneme -s_1 is world-orientated or 'referential'[2] unlike the singular moneme -s_2 of the

---

1. The nominative case of this class of nouns has the inflection zero, *dictātōr* being realized with a short final vowel *dictătŏr*.

2. For the semantic relation 'reference', see p. 174.

verb, which is syntagmatically orientated. In Latin this 'referential' indication has no separate moneme. The 'plural' has a separate set of monemes which indicate both syntactic function and plural: *dictātōr-ēs* (nominative), *dictātōr-ēs* (accusative), *dictātōr-um* (genitive) *dictātōr-ibus* (dative and ablative). This phenomenon has been described as 'amalgamation' between the expressions of the 'plural moneme' and the particular 'case moneme'. Similarly with the 'plural' of the verb, which is a truly syntactic phenomenon, the expression for this does double duty: in *dictātōrēs bellum gerunt* 'dictators wage war', the *-nt* of the verb indicates not only the agreement with the plural subject but also the third 'person' (see below). The terms 'plural moneme' and 'case moneme' are, however, unfortunate and certain terminological distinctions must now be made.

MONEME, MORPHEME, ALLOMORPH

The term 'morpheme' is used in a variety of ways in the scholarly literature. Most often it is applied to what is here called the moneme, i.e. the ultimate S–M unit. Other authors use morpheme in a more restricted sense for what has here been called 'functional monemes'. We need, however, a term for a group of monemes which have an identical function. Thus in the phrase *senātus populusque Rōmānus* the genitive is *senātūs populīque Rōmānī*, the dative *senātūī populōque Rōmānō*, and the ablative *senātū populōque Rōmānō*. The identity of the syntactic function of the coordinated components of the phrase is self-evident, but it is signalled by different functional monemes: the words *senatus* and *populus* belong to different inflexional classes, what are called paradigms (see below). Such a family of synonymous monemes may be called a 'morpheme'. A morpheme so defined will be labelled by naming the function common to the member morphemes. We shall speak of a 'genitive morpheme', which comprises a number of synonymous monemes. The monemes in such a family are called the 'allomorphs' of the (genitive) morpheme. The parallelism with the relationship between the phones and the phonemes is evident. Care should be taken not to speak of the 'genitive moneme', for a moneme is a given S–M unit, such as the {-ī} of *populī*.

Unfortunately the term allomorph is also widely applied to a totally different phenomenon. Often used in illustration are the English plural monemes: in (*cat*)-*s* and (*ox*)-*en*. {-*s*} and {-*en*} certainly may be grouped as allomorphs of the plural morpheme, for they have an identical reference. But with the -*s* of *cats* scholars group the -*z* of *dogs* [dɔgz] and the -*iz* of *lashes* [læʃɪz]. That all belong together as 'realizations' of one moneme is clear from their complementary distribution: -*iz* occurs only after hissing and hushing sounds, -*z* after vowels and voiced consonants, and -*s* after voiceless consonants. The distribution may be described thus: the canonical form is {-*iz*}, which loses its vowel after all sounds except the hissing and hushing consonants, while this syncopated form [-*z*] is devoiced after voiceless consonants. In the monematicon {-iz} will be listed for the moneme expression (the keneme) and appropriate performance rules will be given. What is necessary to stress is that the moneme identification has to be stated in the requisite S–M form, the rule about the 'alloforms' being simply a matter of performance of the S, which is governed by the phonemic pattern of the 'stem'. The distribution of {-*iz*} and {-*en*}, on the other hand, requires a monematic statement: we must list the words which require this or that inflection. That is to say, the statement of the distribution is in S–M terms, not simply S terms. It is, therefore, confusing to say that -*iz*, -*z*, and -*s* are 'allomorphs'. Since they are 'alloforms' of a moneme, to make a clear terminological distinction between the two different phenomena, they might be called 'allomons', as opposed to the allomorphs {-*iz*}, {-*en*}. Alternatively, since the variants simply concern the expression aspect of the moneme (what we have called the 'keneme'), /iz/, /-z/, /-s/ might be called 'allokens' of the keneme /ɪz/.

ONOMATIC MONEMES: DECLENSION

Since (1) the object of the monematicon is to provide the basic items for the reassembly of utterances and (2) a favourite type of utterance shows a structural dichotomy into *onoma* and *rhema*, it will be useful to consider in turn the monemes which appear in the onomatic and rhematic sites.

For the onomatic word-classes the category 'case' is of paramount importance. The origin of the technical term is obscure. It goes back to the Greek word *ptōsis*, literally 'falling', which was translated into Latin as *cāsus*, the abstract noun from *cado* 'fall'. But what image the Greek inventor of the term had in mind when he coined the term is a matter for speculation. One plausible theory is that the word was conceived of as a dice which showed different facets as it was cast down in the game of speech. One side was considered as the norm and this was called the 'upright' (*orthē*) case, while the others were 'sideways' (*plagiai*). The Romans translated *orthē* and *plagiā* as *rectus* and *obliquus*, and this is why we speak of 'oblique cases'.

The chief function of a case of a noun as the head of the onomatic constituent is to mark its relation to the rhematic part of the utterance. The main structural use of the nominative is to indicate that the noun is the subject of the verb. The 'semantic' definitions which assert that the noun names the 'actor' as the performer of the verbal 'action' fit only a small part of the nominative functions: *the dictator kills his opponents* comes under the definition, but *the dictator needs money* and *the dictator is admired by all* do not. Semantically, the widest definition would be to say that the nominative names the focus of the predication. Formally, the function of the nominative as marking the 'subject' is made clear in a language like English and Latin by the verbal concord: the verb agrees in number with that of the noun which is its subject (see above).

The accusative[1] in the Indo–European languages has a variety of functions. The main one is to indicate that the noun is the 'object' of the verb. It denotes the 'goal' of the verbal activity, whether the noun in question refers to the 'sufferer' of the action (*dictātor cīvēs amat* 'the dictator loves the citizens') or the result or content of the action (*dictātor bellum gerit* 'the dictator wages war' cf. *he hit the ball, he hit a six*). In Latin the accusative may also de-

---

1. This curious term originated in a mistranslation of the Greek word *aitiātikē*, case of the *aitiā* 'cause', the case being understood as 'what is caused'. The Roman translator, however, brought it into connexion with the verb *aitiāomai* 'to accuse': hence *accusativus*.

note the physical goal as in *Roman īre* 'to go to Rome'. The accusative function may be symbolized as →|, where the arrow stands for the verbal event.

The genitive case in essence turns a noun into an adjective modifying another noun. The 'possessive' function is merely one common application of such an 'adnominal noun', for *the black hat* delimits *hat* in much the same way as the *boy's hat*. *Poenōrum bellum* 'the Carthaginians' war' indicates a war that has to do with the Carthaginians whether fought by them (the subjective genitive) or against them (the objective genitive). It can just as well be described adjectivally as *bellum Pūnicum*. Since the essential function of the genitive is to delimit another noun it might be symbolized: ⊙ .

The dative is named semantically from one of its common functions: its name indicates the person to whom something is given. But this is merely one application of a much wider usage. The noun in this case form indicates the person interested or concerned in the verbal event: e.g. *vobis arābitur ager* 'the field will be ploughed for you'. There are many semantically distinguished varieties: datives of advantage and disadvantage, ethic datives, sympathetic datives, etc. The function may best be symbolized thus: ⇢, where the dot indicates the involvement of the noun in the field of the verbal event without being the 'direct object'. This is what is implied by the traditional term 'indirect object'.

The ablative, as its name implies ('carrying away') indicates the point of departure of the verbal event and thus contrasts directly with the accusative as the goal of action: *ab urbe proficīscitur* 'he sets out from the city'. There are a variety of transferred uses (agent, comparison, etc.) but the essential function of these constructions may be symbolized thus: ↦.

Other case forms and functions are known. For instance, place 'where' is indicated by the locative (e.g. Latin *domī* 'at home'). Symbolically it may be represented thus: ⊥ . The sociative (or comitative) is the 'together with' case which might be represented thus: →←. The function of the instrumental is sufficiently indicated by its name. In Latin, a single case form, named the ablative from one of its chief uses, has also taken over the functions of the locative and instrumental, which once had separate monemes. This phenomenon is an example of what is known as the 'syncretism of the cases'. In Greek the genitive combines the genitival and the ablatival functions, while the dative and locative share for the most part a single moneme in the various declensions.

The vocative is the case of the person addressed. Such an address, which merely alerts the attention of the hearer, has no functional relationship with the utterance concerned with the verbal action, and this is why the vocative in some declensions consists of the bare stem, that is its moneme is zero, signifying 'no relationship'.

SOLIDARITY OF MONEMES: PARADIGMS

The different case monemes form groups with internal solidarity, in the sense that if a stem has the genitive form, say -*ae* as in *puellae* ('of the girl'), the ablative form will be -*ā*. A similar exclusive group has genitive -*ī*, ablative -*ō*, and another with genitive -*ūs*, ablative -*ū*. Such a group of monemes with internal solidarity and stem 'loyalties' form what is known as a 'paradigm'—a declension of a noun and a conjugation of a verb. This fact enables us to simplify the monematicon. All we need to do is to number such groups (first declension, etc.) and to put this reference after the stem form, the general statements of the paradigm being transferred to a separate part of the description, the morphology. Such general statements made with a view to simplifying the monematicon form part of the 'grammar'. The grammar will be completed when all such general statements ('rules') have been made. What is left over, the residue of the monematicon which is not amenable to statements of 'rule', in other words the 'non-regular' which simply has to be stated *ad hoc* item by item, is what is known as the lexicon (see further below for discussion of the relation of grammar to lexicon).

THE CATEGORY OF CASE

With the cases we can clearly see the difficulties which beset the grammarian in the definition of the items which he isolates as elements in his description. Certain of the cases are clearly 'world-orientated'. For some uses of the accusative it is the progress of some person or thing towards a physical (or temporal) goal in the situation which gives the clue to the 'meaning' of the form. The same is true of some uses of the genitive, for here 'space (or time) within which' is an adequate description of the function. The ablative and locative are no less spatial or local in reference. Instrumental and comitative uses are likewise determined by aspects of the situation, and this is no less true of the 'to whom given' uses of the dative. Distinct from these 'concrete' case functions are the purely grammatical cases—the nominative (subject), accusative (direct object), and dative (indirect object). Not surprisingly, scholars have been tempted to posit that these purely grammatical functions have arisen as a consequence of a step-by-step extension of purely local references. According to this theory the 'direct object' is merely an abstract description of a network of usages which ultimately go back to the function of the accusative case to denote the physical goal of the action. Such is the localistic theory of cases.

The category of case as a part of a linguistic description is dictated by the necessity to account for certain dependent (functional) monemes. That is to say it is an inflectional category. If we had to do only with nouns and adjectives, case need not figure in the description of English, for the possessive moneme could be accommodated under word formation as a means of making an adjective from a noun parallel with -*y* (as in *muddy*), -*ly* (as in *manly*), -*ish* (as in *sheepish*), etc. What impels the grammarian to introduce the category of case into the description of English is the morphology of the 'pronouns'. *I/me, thou/thee, he/him, she/her, we/us, they/them, who/whom.* In the noun the case function of the Latin 'grammatical cases', nominative and accusative, are indicated by a fixed word order: subject–verb–object. The contrast in meaning between *cats fear dogs* and *dogs fear cats* requires the grammarian of English to treat linear position as structurally significant, unlike Latin and other inflected languages, where the word order is free and may be varied for stylistic reasons because the grammatical function is for the most part adequately signalled by the functional moneme, no matter where the word is placed in the utterance, i.e. *cīvēs amat dictātor, amat cīvēs dictātor, dictātor cīvēs amat.* The indirect object and the more concrete case functions of Latin are expressed in English by noun phrases of the type *to the boy, for the boy, to the school, from the school, with a friend, with a stick* (instrumental), *in the school, at the school.* A language which thus uses independent words and/or linear position to express grammatical relations is distinguished as an 'analytic language' from those which use dependent monemes. The latter languages are of two main types. Where there is functional amalgamation or fusion, i.e. where the case has more than one function (e.g. accusative and plural) as in Latin and other Indo–European languages, they are called inflectional languages. Where there is greater morphological transparency in that each function is separately signalled by a particular moneme each of which is attached in regular ways, we speak of agglutinative languages. Such a language is Turkish, where the moneme of the plural is *-ler/lar* and the case monemes are *-i* (accusative), *-in* (genitive), *-e* (dative), *-de* (locative), and *-den* (ablative). These monemes are attached in a perfectly regular way to the noun stems so that the student, once he has learnt the rules governing the 'realization' of the monemes,[1] is not burdened with the task of learning a cumbrous morphology, as is the case with the Indo–European languages. Given a noun stem like *ev-* 'house', the declension of the singular (with zero moneme) may be confidently put together as *ev* (with zero moneme of the nominative) *ev-i, ev-in, ev-e, ev-de, ev-den*, the same case monemes being added to the plural stem: *ev-ler, ev-ler-i, ev-ler-in, ev-ler-e, ev-ler-de, ev-ler-den.*

PREPOSITIONS

The invariable monemes constructed with nouns to signal such grammatical and spatio-temporal relations are called prepositions (even though they may be placed after the noun). Such parts of speech are also present in the inflectional languages like Latin, where they reinforce and give closer orientational precision to the general case function with which they are constructed: e.g. *ab*

---

1. The vowel of the endings harmonize with that of the word to which it is appended: the ablative has the 'allokens' *-den/-dan* (see p. 105).

'away from' and *ex* 'from inside' are both constructed with ('govern') the ablative. In the course of history, since the orientational functions were adequately signalled by the prepositions, the case endings became dispensable; and this is how English and French came to discard so much of the inflexional resources which they had inherited from their distant Indo–European ancestors.

The task of the linguist is, however, to describe English speech habits as they are today (the synchronic approach) and not to be distracted from, or influenced by, historical considerations (the diachronic approach). Modern linguistic literature contains many satirical references to those old-fashioned grammarians who tried to force English into the mould of Latin grammar and solemnly drew up noun declensions of the type *of the boy, to* or *from the boy*. If case is considered as an inflectional category, such rejection is justified. Again, if the grammar is considered (as in this book) as the means whereby the monematicon is simplified, the prepositions remain in the lexicon as items of brute memorization. The only grammatical index they need in the residual 'lexicon' is 'preposition', and this only because we need to know that they 'govern' the accusative of the pronouns: *for me, to her, from him*, etc. They will also figure as a class in that part of the syntax relating to word order: *the school he went to*, etc.

GENDER

In Latin and other Indo–European languages adjectives also have case inflections. But the adjective as a separate and eponomatic part of speech has to be set up because of certain syntactical phenomena which cannot be wholly accounted for with the concepts devised for the noun. Examples are *le beau garçon, la belle fille, ein schöner Knabe, ein schönes Mädchen, pulcher puer, pulchra puella* ('a beautiful boy, a beautiful girl'). The genders are named (1) masculine, (2) feminine, (3) neuter ('neither') because of the preponderance of males, females and inanimate objects among the referents of nouns that enter into these different gender classes. In principle, however, grammatical gender has nothing to do with sex. Gender is a concept devised to account for a syntactic phenomenon —the changing forms of the adjective that qualifies the noun.

Since the English adjective shows no such concord with the noun, the category of gender would be superfluous in a grammar of English. What makes it a necessary part of English grammar is a phenomenon of 'anaphora'. Above it was stated that the personal pronouns of the third person differ from the first and second in being anaphoric and not deictic, that is they refer to, and substitute for, a noun already used in the context. In the singular the speaker is obliged to choose between *he, she, it*, and this choice must be ascribed to the gender of the noun. It is true, of course, that in the overwhelming majority of nouns such gender is world-orientated, i.e. determined by the sex (or its absence) of the entities referred to by the nouns in question.

The adjective is also required as a separate part of speech for a different type of grammatical statement: the attachment of the monemes which indicate the 'degree of comparison' (see above p. 92).

PRONOUN

Among the onomatic constituents it remains to consider the pronouns. The name suggests that this part of speech comprises words which 'stand for' nouns. That this is not wholly true is evident from the discussion of *I* and *you*, which are fully semantic in their own right since they refer directly to components of the utterance situation. As such they are not properly called pronouns. They are deictic nouns.

In the plural of the first person some languages distinguish between the inclusive and the exclusive 'we', i.e. between 'I and you' and 'I and some other(s)'.

The category of 'person' is required not because of the *semantic* difference between person speaking, person addressed, and person referred to, but because of the syntactic determination in some languages of the form of the verb by the 'person' of the subject. This means that if English presented the forms *I be, you be, he be* instead of *I am, you are, he is*, and *he go* instead of *he goes*, then 'person' would not be required for its grammatical description, since the difference between *I, you, he, she, it*, etc., would be purely lexical. Operationally considered, these items would first

figure in the monematicon; and if no general rule could be formulated apart from the *ad hoc* statement of their meanings, then they
would remain as part of the residue of the monematicon not
amenable to 'regular' statement, such non-regular residue being
called the 'lexicon'. This means that 'person' is a grammatical
category required for the description of the verb and not the pronoun. The pronoun merely requires a distinction between 'deictic'
(demonstrative) and 'anaphoric'.

With this approach we may contrast a transformationist view of
the category of person in the verb. According to this, person, like
number, is only 'secondarily and derivatively a category of the
verb' (Lyons). The observed facts, it may be remarked, are common to both accounts. In English the pronoun subject of the verb
is obligatory in statements like *I say* (cf. French *je dis*, where *je*,
despite its spacing as a separate orthographic word, is a bound
moneme prefixed to the verb). In Latin, by contrast, the person is
normally signalled by a bound moneme (*dīc-o, dīc-is, dīc-it*), a
personal pronoun being used only exceptionally for purposes of
emphasis, contrast and the like. Such are the observed facts which
have to be accounted for in the grammatical description. For the
transformationist the differences between Latin and English are
simply a matter of 'surface structure', which is a 'realization' of an
underlying abstract 'deep structure'. In terms of the deep structure there is little difference, they argue, between Latin and English. To this deep structure a pronominal element is ascribed, and
it is this which controls the rules 'governing the phonological
realization of the verb in surface structure'. The rule is that the
verb in its form reflects the number and person of the subject.
Once the abstract pronominal element has done its work in the
generation of the correct verbal form (the 'phonological interpretation') in the Latin sentence, it undergoes the operation 'delete'
as opposed to English, for which there is a rule of 'phonological
realization' to rewrite as *I*, etc.

The key concept here is 'realization', which has already been
discussed apropos of the relations between phoneme and phone,
and in a more general way between language and speech. The
relation of 'realization' is that of description to phenomena; it
arises on the 'Way Down' (see p. 95). The question of the re-

lationship of deep to surface structure will be taken up again in Chapter 7.

The second person singular *thou, thee* has largely gone out of use (though it survives in dialect use). In many European languages the corresponding forms survive but with a purely social restriction: for instance in German *Du* is used among members of a family, intimate friends, and towards animals. The plural form *Sie* is the normal equivalent of 'you' outside this intimate circle. Such a social description of the 'use of the forms' is not grammatical; it forms a part of 'sociolinguistics'. Of the same type are the 'honorific' modes of address, the choice of which is determined by conventions peculiar to certain speech communities such as the Japanese.

The distinctions between the demonstrative pronouns *this, that,* etc., are also a lexical matter rather than a grammatical one. Such differences are stated in the lexicon typically as 'indicating object or person present or near the speaker' and '. . . not near the speaker'. These distinction of proximity are the matter of the pre-linguistic articulation of the speaker's world. Some dialects of English have three planes of proximity: *this, that* and *yon*. Similar are the distinctions between the Latin pronouns with the added specification that the three planes are linked with the three persons: *hīc* (vicinity of speaker), *iste* (vicinity of the person addressed) and *ille*. *is* is not a demonstrative pronoun at all since its function is not deictic but anaphoric: it refers to a noun already used in the context.

RHEMATIC CONSTITUENTS AND MONEMES

For the description of the verb as the 'head' of the rhema the categories found necessary with the Indo–European languages are person, number, tense, mood, voice and aspect. The first two have already been dealt with apropos of the moneme $-s_2$, which was defined as the ending of the third person singular present indicative active of certain verbs. The category of tense is required to account for a number of phenomena. In the first place $-s_2$ does not appear in (*he*) *liked*, though it is also a third person singular form of the verb. This opposition, taken together with *I like, I liked* isolates a moneme -*d*, which cannot be accounted for as 'third person' or as 'singular'. It signals 'past' as opposed to 'present'; further in forms so marked as 'past' there are no verbal distinctions of person and number. The category of tense is thus defined semantically, but temporal references to past, present and future do not alone justify setting up tense as a grammatical category of the verb. If English signalled such references by utterances like *I eat now*, *I no eat yesterday*, *I eat much tomorrow*, *I have eat enough*, the description would have to remain on the purely lexical level. It is only if time references are signalled by linguistic means admitting of 'regular' formulation that the description becomes 'grammatical'.

In English the major tense opposition is between present and past (*he likes/he liked*, *he writes/he wrote*). The future stands apart in that it is expressed by phrases which combine an 'auxiliary' verb with the infinitive: *I shall write*, *he will write*. The auxiliaries are thus verbal monemes (as is especially clear in the spoken forms *I'll come*, etc., which might be described as constructed with a prefixed bound moneme {*l-*}), which once had a fuller meaning than mere reference to time. *Shall* once meant 'obligation' and *will* 'desire'. The development of future forms from one-time modal expressions is widespread. It seems that the parent Indo–European language had no 'future indicative'. This is not surprising since there is no such thing as a 'future fact'. What the speaker expresses is an attitude to the future—confident expectation (the 'prospective'), will (the 'voluntative'), wish (the 'optative'), contingency (the 'potential'), and so on. It is from such modal expressions (subjunctive, optative, desiderative, etc.) that the various individual languages have created their future indicative forms.

In Latin the tense system is organized not merely with reference to time of speaking and what precedes and follows but also with respect to a stipulated moment of the past and the future, as in English *at that moment he had gone too far for retreat* (pluperfect), *by then he will have realized* (future perfect). This is merely one of the ways in which speakers may structure their temporal references, or to put it another way, may 'articulate' their temporal world.

ASPECT

English, apart from its three tenses, present, past and future, makes fine distinctions in presenting verbal events. In the present tense the simple verb is used for general statements and habitual occurrence (*we take guests, I write books*, etc.) while the peri-phrastic forms made up of the verb *to be* and the present participle refer to action in progress (*I am writing a book*). This distinction between 'progressive' (also called the 'durative' or 'continuative') and non-progressive is made in all three tenses: e.g. *Next week we shall be leaving for New York; this time last year we were praying for rain*. These different ways of presenting a verbal event are called the 'aspects' of the verb. The choice of aspect has nothing to do with the actual duration of the event. One and the same happening can be represented either as an historical unit or as an event in progress. Different is the so-called perfect, which refers to a state resulting from an action: *he has resigned*.

These three aspects of the verb, which in essence go back to the Indo–European parent language, were still maintained in ancient Greek, where the verb appears with three 'tense' stems whose function it was to make aspectual distinctions: e.g. the three stem forms of the verb 'to leave', *leip-* the present stem, *lip-* the 'aorist' (a term which means 'undefined'), and *le-loip-* the perfect.

In Latin this triple opposition of the aspects was transformed into a binary system by the combination of the ancient aorist and perfect into a 'perfect', which in fact expressed both the unitary event and the state resulting. On the basis of these two opposed aspectual stems (e.g. *dīc-/dīx-*) a system of tenses was created: *dīc-it*, present, *dīc-et* future, *dīc-ēbat* imperfect; *dīx-it* perfect, *dīx-erit* future perfect, *dīx-erat* pluperfect.

In the Slavonic languages, too, the verb exhibits a thorough-going binary aspectual opposition between perfective and imper-fective: *pisal* 'I was writing'/*na-pisal* 'I wrote'. The perfective 'present' in fact refers to the future: *zavtra ja pročitaju knigu* 'tomorrow I shall read through (i.e. finish reading) the book'. It will be noticed that in *na-pisal* the verb is perfectivized by adding a verbal prefix. This was an old Indo–European device which is still reflected in English idiom: *read through, eat up, finish off*, etc.

MOOD

Our specification of the verbal moneme -s_2 included a reference to 'indicative mood'. This was because of the opposition *God save the Queen/God saves the Queen*. *Save* is third person singular present, yet it lacks the moneme. The distinction between the two is one of mood, for the one without the -s_2 expresses a wish, whereas the other makes a statement. These are examples of the opposition between the subjunctive and indicative moods. If the attitudes of the speaker to what he is saying over and above the simple declaration are signalled by grammatical means, these devices are ascribed to 'moods'. Apropos of the future tense we have referred to the speaker's expectation ('prospective'), his will ('voluntative'), and wish ('optative'). All these are modal expressions. We may add the 'contingent': e.g. *Things would come right if we were given time*. This usage is an example of the 'potential' mood.

The Indo–European parent language possessed two distinct sets of forms for subjunctive and optative. Both these survived in ancient Greek, the usages of the subjunctive being divided into prospective and voluntative, and those of the optative into potential and optative (the wish function giving its name to the mood). In Latin, syncretism of the two sets of modal forms had taken place and the 'subjunctive' (which gets its name from the fact that the mood figures so largely in subordinate clauses) carries the load of both Indo–European moods. Its morphology, too, shows clear traces of this double origin: e.g. the Old Latin subjunctive form *siem* (Classical form *sim*) goes back to the optative *syēm, which also underlies the Sanskrit *syām*.

In English there are few subjunctive forms, and even these may be replaced by periphrases: *Heaven help us/May heaven help us*. Expressions like *If I were you* are increasingly replaced by *If I was you*. The latter is an example of the modal use of the past tense.

Non-declarative, and hence also a mood, is the imperative. This verbal form of direct command resembles the vocative case in being often represented by the bare stem: *Domine, parce nobis* 'Lord, spare us'. It has been suggested (Lyons) that questions are also non-declarative and as such ought to be classified as modal. If, however, we regard grammar as the means whereby the monematicon is simplified (see above p. 108), then we would set up an interrogative mood only if there were a set of overt forms which could be extracted from the monematicon and made the subject of a 'rule'. In English questions are framed by inverting the word order (*Is she at home?*), a dummy verb being employed in most instances (*Does she go to work?*), and by special types of intonation (see p. 61). Both these are in the widest sense 'prosodic' devices and so do not figure in the monematicon, which consists of indivisible S–M items. It is true that Latin has such monemes: an enclitic *-ne* is attached to the first word of the sentence for neutral questions, *nōnne* introduces questions expecting an affirmative answer, and *num* those expecting a negative answer. These items certainly figure in the monematicon, but they have a purely lexical description and so do not justify setting up an interrogative mood as a verbal category.

VOICE

In a situation involving (1) an actor, (2) an action and (3) the 'sufferer' of the action the speaker may choose to centre his utterance round (1), (2) or (3). To take (2) first, he might say *a fierce defence was put up* and so suppress a reference to the participants. In Latin in similar circumstances the 'impersonal' form of the verb could be used: *acriter pugnātur*. This use of the 'impersonal passive' (as in *sīc ītur ad astra*, literally 'thus it is gone to the stars', i.e. 'this is the way to the stars') goes back to an impersonal form of the verb which was originally distinct from the passive. In choice (1), where the doer is made the focus of the utterance (its 'subject'), we have the familiar active construction: *the townsfolk routed the besiegers*. With choice (3) where the focus is on the 'suffering' besiegers the construction is in the 'passive' (a derivative from the Latin *patior* 'I suffer'): *The besiegers were routed by the townsfolk*, where Latin uses the ablative of the agent preceded by *ab*, *ab oppidānīs*.

In English the passive is expressed by periphrastic forms in which the verb *to be* is combined with the passive participle: *English is spoken here*. This is also true of the Latin perfect passive

(*interfectus est* 'he was killed'), but in the durative tenses a
r-moneme appears: *rogātur* (present), *rogābitur* (future), *rogābātur*
(imperfect) of *rogo* 'I ask'. This *r*-passive was confined to a small
part of the Indo–European territory, and for the most part we find
a non-active voice which served two functions—middle and
passive.

Those uses are called 'middle' in which the verbal forms express the 'subject-centred' nature of the verbal action. Greek
active *louō* means 'I wash (others)', whereas middle *louomai*
means 'I wash myself' or 'I wash something for myself'. A
peculiarity of Greek is that so many verbs have their future tense
in the middle form. This is due to the fact that the futures go back
to 'desideratives' which are of their nature 'self-centred'. The
concentration of the verbal action on the subject was, in the
opinion of most grammarians, the original function of the middle
forms, the few exclusively passive forms of the Greek verb being
late developments. Where there is no formal distinction of voice
the use of the description 'passive' is justified only where there
is explicit expression of the 'agent'.

The transformational relations between active and passive will
be discussed in Chapter 7.

ADVERBS

The constituents that depend on the verbal 'head' of the rhema
have been called epirrhematic, or, to use the corresponding Latin
expression, 'adverbial'. Such constituents give greater precision
and specification to what is conveyed by the verb; they give information elicited by the questions when?, where?, why? and the like.
In addition to the comparatively limited number of single-word
adverbs like *slowly, fast, often, again, then,* a vast number of
adverbial expressions can be created by means of prepositional
phrases such as *by the middle of next week, in the far corner, for
unknown reasons.*

The Latinized term 'adverb' is to some extent a misnomer
since such expressions modify not only verbs but also adjectives:
an extremely able scholar. It is true that the ancient term *rhema*
comprised both verbs and adjectives, but since in our theory the

parts of speech are distinguished primarily by their functions as
onomatic and rhematic, it cannot be denied that the 'adverb'
figures on both sides of this fundamental dividing line. The point
is no more abstruse, however, than the use of a noun to modify
another noun as in *forest clearing*. When we say that here a noun
is used as an adjective, this is merely an abbreviation of the correct
formulation that a given lexeme, which for the most part functions
as head of the onoma, may at other times serve as an eponomatic
constituent. A given lexeme is not *per se* 'a part of speech'. It only
becomes so when it forms part of an utterance (*oratio*), and it
receives its classification from instance to instance according to its
functional site in the given utterance. Certain lexemes classified
in the lexicon as 'adverbs' in virtue of their predominant function
may modify not only adjectives, which are eponomatic, so that their
function is 'ad-nominal', but even nouns (e.g. *the then bishop*). The
fact is that words have different combinatorial potentialities, for
which we might utilize the chemical term 'valencies', by which the
combinatorial potentialities of atoms are measured. Adverbs stand
alone among the parts of speech in being able to modify another
word of the same class: *he ran a mile incredibly fast*.

Certain adverbs are characterized by special monemes. The
-ly of *incredibly* is a case in point. This moneme is used in English
to make adverbs of 'manner' (answering the question 'how?')
from adjectives (*incredible*). This is not the only stem-forming
function of *-ly*: in *manly* and *friendly* it forms adjectives from the
nouns *man* and *friend*, whereas in *goodly* it creates another adjective from an adjective *good*.

Adverbs resemble adjectives in admitting the 'degrees of comparison', which are expressed either by the monemes *-er* and *-est*
(*faster, fastest*) or, periphrastically, by combinations of the basic
adverb with *more* and *most*.

It has been argued that adverbs of manner are transformationally
related to the corresponding adjectives. This appears to mean no
more than that *He is a graceful runner* is semantically equivalent to
He runs gracefully and that, given the structural analysis of each of
these utterances, we can transform one into the other by a series
of 'rewrite rules'. That each of the utterances thus equated on
semantic grounds reflects a common 'deep structure' which is

converted by separate set of rules into different surface structures (which will include the attachment of the 'adverbial suffix -*ly*') is a mode of grammatical thinking which will be discussed in Chapter 7.

SUMMARY

The reduction of a corpus, taken as an adequate sample of the speech of a given community, to its ultimate discrete S-M units, the monemes, involves complex analytical procedures of the type called 'grammatical'. The complete inventory of the monemes is called the monematicon. This will contain all the material of the corpus, which will be regarded as the product of the combinatorial potentialities of the monemes. From this it follows that each moneme in the monematicon will have an indication of its 'valencies', that is its possibilities of combining with other monemes. Fundamental is the distinction between the 'lexeme' (the stem) and the functional moneme which indicates the syntactic function of the lexeme in the utterance.

When the functional monemes have been picked out as 'kenemes' (the S-side) and their contributions to the utterances (their 'pleremes') have been determined, the monematicon is simplified by systematization. That is, general statements are made about the combinatorial possibilities of the monemes and their solidarities. It is at this stage that the linguist sets up his paradigms, the declensional and conjugational models which group the lexemes according to their morphological behaviour. Traditional grammars usually list the form classes under the heading morphology before going on to discuss the 'use of the forms' under the heading syntax. But syntax is prior to morphology; an entry like 'accusative' alongside the form *dictatorem* in the morphology is in effect a condensed syntactical statement.

Once the monematicon has been thus simplified, the set of general statements made about it will form the grammar. The residue not thus amenable to 'rule' will be a series of *ad hoc* semantic statements made necessary by the arbitrary nature of the connexion between the vocable and the meaning. Each such entry in what will now be called the lexicon will carry a reference to the grammar. In this sense the lexicon is also the index to the grammar.

One final point must be reiterated which is of importance to the discussion of transformational grammar in Chapter 7. The analysis of utterances starts with a functional dichotomy into onoma and rhema which is essentially syntactic. In using a 'part of speech' term like 'noun' we imply the prior term onoma, which is functional and syntactic. Any representation of logos generation must make explicit the priority of the dichotomy into onoma and rhema, that is, functionally speaking, subject and predicate, before introducing the terms noun (phrase) and verb (phrase).

6

The Assembly of Sentences
Some Grammatical Models

The previous chapter was concerned with the analysis of utterances and their reduction to their minimal meaningful units. In
such an analysis we are in the position of a hearer grappling with
an incoming message or with a learner doing an unseen in a
foreign language. We might conceive of him as first scanning the
utterance, noting the monemes, their combinations and sites, and
then looking them up in the monematicon 'code', which records
not only the S-M units but also their modes of combination, what
we have called their 'valencies'. This corresponds to the Way Up.

In the assembly of logoi from the description we act much like
the speaker who has to form the utterance in response to a situational conjuncture and is prompted by an intention[1] to influence
his hearer(s). Alternatively, we might compare the task of a learner
doing a piece of 'composition', that is translation into a foreign
language, or a foreigner trying to piece together an intelligible
utterance. This corresponds to the Way Down from the items and
abstractions of the description to the firm earth of speech.

The process of assembly might take the form of a series of
instructions. First there are quite general instructions: e.g. make a
statement, question, command, etc.; this will consist of a subject
and predicate; for the subject choose an onomatic expression, and
for the predicate a rhematic expression, and so on. Once the

---

1. Later, in the chapter on Semantics, the Greek term *dianoia* will be used
for the speaker's intention.

abstract form of the 'sentence'[1] is complete, the particular moneme combinations which will signal the speaker's intention will be chosen from the lexicon and inserted in their appropriate 'sites'.

There are theoretically two ways in which we can proceed from the monematicon and its adjunct, the grammar, to the assembly of logoi. One of these is to go by the direct route from the moneme to the logos without any intermediate stages. The other is to do the job in two phases: first to assemble the 'parts of speech' as the working parts of sentences, and from this basis to proceed by a second stage to the completion of logoi.

The latter method has been the traditional one in descriptive grammar, and that this preferable is suggested by the consideration that the 'Way Down' from description to logos should retrace the steps of the 'Way Up' from utterance to description. The diagram of the 'Way Up' (Fig. 19, p. 97) shows that the monemes emerge in the final resort from the analysis of words as 'parts of speech'. It would, consequently, appear reasonable to assemble the logos from those constituents which by definition are its structural parts. Thus once the preliminary general instructions about the type of sentence (statements, etc.) and its basic structure (subject–predicate) have been given, the first step towards putting the flesh of speech on the structural skeleton will be to insert in the *onoma* and *rhema* sites the 'parts of speech', i.e. the stems (lexemes) appropriate to the intended message and then provide them with the set of markers that signal their syntactic function. This information will be stored in the parts of the grammar called 'morphology', which tells the would-be speaker what modifications the lexemes chosen as appropriate to his intended signal must undergo in order to play their proper part in the structure of the whole logos. The morphology sets forth the word paradigms. Hence this method and model of logos generation is called the Word and Paradigm model (abbreviated to WP).

What has chiefly characterized modern descriptive linguistics, especially in America, has been a reaction against the traditional model of logos generation. Instead, attempts have been made to

---

1. It will be recalled that the 'sentence' is an abstract structure of functional sites (see p. 96).

devise techniques for proceeding directly from morpheme to utterance (in our terminology 'from moneme to logos'). The method (or 'model') has taken two main forms: Item and Arrangement (IA) and Item and Process (IP).

To a great extent the differences between the two are terminological. 'Process' is not intended to imply progress from one state to another in an historical sense, but is meant as a model of grammatical description: e.g. 'the plural of nouns is made by adding an -s to the singular form'. Thus affixation, reduplication, vowel substitution (*geese* for *goose*), etc., are all describable as 'processes' in so far as they are conceived as operations which change one form into another. However, because of the diachronic implications of the term 'process' purists have preferred the term 'arrangement'. This also avoids giving (say) *goose* a kind of priority over *geese*, which is felt to be undesirable because both forms coexist with equal status in the language. Again, objection is taken to personalizing the 'language' in such formulations as 'Greek forms the past tense by means of the augment'.

IA simply assumes that every utterance under examination consists of grammatically relevant 'morphemes' (our 'monemes'), and that it can be completely accounted for as an arrangement of these 'morphemes', which are selected from the total stock of monemes available in the language in question.

What should be noted here is the stipulation that all 'morphemes' are 'grammatically relevant', for this implies that in the inventory of 'morphemes' each entry must include in its description a statement of its grammatical relevance, whatever that may mean. According to this view, once we have the total stock of 'morphemes' and have stated their modes of combination, we have 'the pattern of the whole language'. In fact, this statement applies equally well to the other model, WP, which also assembles sentences (our logoi) by combining monemes but finds it preferable to present the assembly with the 'word' as an intermediate stage: moneme—word (i.e. appropriately formed lexeme)—logos.

Practitioners of WP may also equally subscribe to the programme of those structuralists who claim that IA gives a quasi-mathematical rigour to linguistic description in that it operates exclusively with a set of elements (the monemes) for which certain relations are defined. A review of the chief concepts of IA will bring out the similarities and differences between the two models of description (IA and WP).

Both models include the notion of analysability, without which there could be no description, for it will be recalled that the infinite variety of speech is amenable to description only because it can be seen as the result of manifold modes of combination of a finite number of recurrent items. Analysis in terms of meaningful units (the first articulation) is pushed to the ultimate limit which defines the 'simple' forms, the 'morphemes' ('monemes' in our terminology).[1] In such an analysis the form analysed is by definition a 'constitute', and the products of the analysis are its 'constituents'. Each such constitute is a 'construction', that is each of its constituents occupies a given position (what we have called a 'site'). Some of the positions in a construction have overt 'markers'. What is called the 'tactical pattern' of a language emerges if we list the constructions, and then for each position record the morphemes (monemes) occurring there. We also need a list of the composite forms, that is expansions of the simple forms which may occupy a given constructional position. Thus, in simple terms, the 'tactical pattern' is a statement of which morpheme (moneme) goes where.

So far there is nothing but terminological differences between the two models. In both models (IA/IP and WP) we also find the confusions between 'allomorph' and 'allomon', on which we have already commented (pp. 104f). But what is new in IA is 'morphophonemics'. This is defined thus: the morphophonemic pattern of a language is the statement of the conditions governing the alternation of the allomorphs. This pattern, together with the tactical patterns, makes up the 'grammatical pattern' of the language.

Morphophonemics is dismissed by most English textbooks in a few lines. American textbooks, on the other hand, devote considerable space to the subject, and since it creates vexed problems with proposed solutions which from the viewpoint of traditional WP appear strange and baffling, if not downright pointless, a discussion cannot be avoided.

---

1. For our definition of the 'morpheme', see p. 79.

Under morphophonemics is included the description of the S-side of the S-M unit, the moneme; that is the 'expression', what we have proposed to call the 'keneme'. It is here that the necessity for a clear terminology makes itself apparent. C. F. Hockett lists the five words *bought, went, paid, sold* and *sang* and states that they all consist of two 'morphemes'. One of these morphemes is a verb stem (*buy, go, pay, sell, sing*) while the other, common to all examples, is the 'past tense morpheme'. Such is the morphemic analysis. This task achieved, next comes the turn of morphophonemics, which examines the 'phonetic shapes which represent the morphemes'.

This formulation of the relation between the sound configuration (the keneme) and the 'morpheme' as 'representation' persists throughout the exposition. '*Pay*' is represented by /péj/ in *pays, paid, paying* . . . . But the 'past tense morpheme' is represented by a suffixed /d/ in *paid*; in *sold* it is represented by the same /d/ combined with an infixed /ow/. As for the morpheme *sell*, this is sometimes represented by /sél/, but when it is accompanied by the past tense morpheme it is represented by a discontinuous /s . . . l-/, so that /s . . . l-/ is combined with a discontinuous /. . . ow . . .-d/ to yield *sold*. Again, the past tense *sang* is accounted for on similar lines. The morpheme usually has the phonemic shape /siŋ/, but at other times (as in *sang, sung, song*) it is represented by /s . . . ŋ/, which forms a kind of frame into which 'representations of' certain inflectional morphemes are 'infixed'. Given such a mode of analysis, morphophonemics has two main tasks: to determine (1) which 'shapes' (i.e. sound configurations) are to be taken as 'representations of' which morphemes; and (2) the different types of relationships between 'representations'.

The key word in this exposition is 'representation', and since it is this which leads to the strange solutions proposed, the term must be scrutinized. Representation is a relation between two terms, the phonemic shape and the 'morpheme'. The first is clear: the phonemic shape is the vocable, the keneme, e.g. /boj/ (*boy*). The other term needs elucidation.

Consider the statement '. . . the morpheme *boy* is represented by the phonemic shape /boj/ in all environments'. From this it appears that what is called the morpheme is a *meaningful* configuration of sound, an S-M unit, what we have called the moneme. In the present instance let us symbolize this as {/boj/~ BOY}, the capitalized word standing for the 'content' (in our terminology the 'plereme') and ~ for the relationship 'signalling'. It would be correct to say that /boj/ 'represents' BOY. Such is, in fact, the definition of this and any other moneme. But it is confusing to say that /boj/ is a representation of {/boj/~ BOY}.[1]

Still more complex is the term 'past tense morpheme'. This has already been discussed (p. 104), but the point needs restatement in the present connexion. The morpheme in question comprises a group (i.e. one or more) of monemes identical in content; it is the common content (plereme) that defines the 'morpheme' (e.g. 'accusative morpheme', etc.). *Sell, boy*, etc., are monemes when considered as indivisible S-M units; they are 'words' when considered as elements in the syntactical structure of a sentence. Thus there is no combination of a 'morpheme' *sell* with a morpheme 'past tense'. The two units are on different levels of description: one is defined as an S-M unit, a moneme, and the other as an M-unit, a group of monemes each with the given M.

Much the same IA/IP approach characterizes another American textbook. A. A. Hill (1958) includes the vocalic alternations of the strong verbs under 'morphophonemics'. In the past tense *drove* he isolates a 'morpheme' {ow} and classes it with the suffixes. To distinguish it from suffixes in the usual sense he devises the notation {OW}, and his notation for the whole form is '{drajv} {OW} which equals /drówv/'. To pursue the matter further, if /ow/ is extracted from *drove* as the 'past tense morpheme', then we are left with the discontinuous expression /dr . . . v/, which must figure in this guise in the monematicon along with the /aj/ of the present tense *drive*, and we need yet another discontinuous

---

1. Scholars who use 'morpheme' for the ultimate S-M unit apply the term 'morph' to what we call the keneme. Thus *sweetest* can have its vocable analysed into two morphs /swijt/ and /ist/. The statement that each morph (keneme) 'represents a particular morpheme' makes sense only if 'morpheme' refers to the contentual aspect: 'the morph /swijt/ represents SWEET'. It is confusing to state that /swijt/ represents (or 'is the exponent of') {/swijt/~ SWEET}.

expression /i . . . en/, the attachment of which to the verbal morpheme yields the past participle *driven*.

Such solutions stem from the fundamental tenet of IA that all utterances must be broken down into morphemes (in the double sense elucidated above), which have a discrete 'representation'. The position of IA/IP vis-à-vis WP will be clarified by a scrutiny of the various solutions proposed for an analogous problem, the 'past tense' *took* as contrasted with *baked*.

(1) '*Took* is a single morpheme'. It is here that we see most clearly the unfortunate consequences of a confusion in terminology. *Took* is a single moneme, but its M side is complex. The vocable (keneme) signals simultaneously the content TAKE and a reference to PAST. This formulation is, in essence, no different from the commonsense '*took* is the past tense of *take*' and, theoretically, it offers no more difficulty than the double function of kenemes signalling both 'accusative' and 'singular' (e.g. Latin *-is* as a genitive singular moneme). If, however, the distinction between moneme and morpheme is not made, then the apparent 'mono-morphemical status' has to be rejected because of the 'tactic parallelism' between *took* and *baked*. By 'tactic parallelism' is meant identity of syntactic function and reference to past tense. Consequently, two 'morphemes' and two 'morpheme representations' have to be found in *took* as in *sold*, etc. These difficulties do not arise in WP. In the 'grammar' (as the set of statements generalizing as much as possible of the monematicon), under the heading 'past tense' it will be found convenient, after stating the 'regularities', to append a list of the forms which fulfil the same function but are not amenable to rule. These may be grouped together in classes, say 'verbs showing vocalic alternation' (the Ablaut verbs); others admit no descriptive statement except an *ad hoc* one, e.g. that *went* is the past tense of *go*. Such is the practice of traditional grammars. It is neither more 'rigorous' nor more 'practical' to adopt the IA practice of devising such notations as '{drajv} {OW} which equals /drowv/', for when the appropriate instructions are given for the 'performance' of this notation, it says no more than that the past tense of *drive* is *drove*, which is what will appear in the WP description.

(2) '*Took* is a fusion of the two morpheme sequences /take/ and

/ed/.' Here much the same criticism applies: /ed/ is not a morpheme represented in '*took*' but a moneme which forms no part of *took*. In fact, strictly speaking, /-ed/ is the keneme of the moneme {/ed/~PAST}. What we observe is a referential, contextual, and 'tactical' parallelism between *took* and *baked* (e.g. *I took some dough and baked it*). The functional opposition *take/took* is paralleled by *bake/baked*, and this opposition is statable as 'present'/'past'. But it creates a pseudo-problem to say that the 'morpheme' /-ed/ is 'represented' in *took*. If the term morpheme is used at all, it should be described as 'preterite' or 'past'. The formulation that the morpheme is 'represented in . . .' raises philosophical problems like those concerning the relation of the Platonic ideas to the things of the senses.[1]

(3) '*Took* is an allomorph of the morpheme which appears elsewhere as *take*, plus a zero allomorph of /ed/'. From our point of view, the 'zero allomorph of the morpheme /ed/' is yet another of the ghost problems raised by the confusion between 'morpheme' and 'moneme'. The keneme /ed/ assumes different phonemic shapes according to the phonemic structure of the verb. To put it in a different way, the keneme of the suffix is adapted to the keneme of the stem: in our terminology, the allokens of /ed/ are [id] (*waited*), [d] (*heard*) and [t] (*felt*). In some verbs, e.g. *put*, *hit*, etc., the keneme coalesces with final phoneme of the stem. Here it would be quite in order to say that there was zero representation, and we might legitimately speak of a 'zero alloken'. We can also posit zero among English plural monemes which collectively make up the 'plural morpheme'; to the monematic classes *cats*, *oxen* we can add *sheep*. Here the absence of an overt plural mark cannot be ascribed to phonetic conditions and so cannot be assigned to any of the plural monemes as an 'alloken'. Here the mark of the

---

1. An analogous proposal (J. Lyons) would regard *went* as a combination of two morphemes {go} and {ed}, where the latter is presumably merely a symbol for PAST, while *went* 'realizes', or 'represents' or 'is the exponent of' the combined morphemes. In plain language, *went* functions as the past tense of *go*, a fact which will be duly listed in the monematicon in the first place. It will reappear for convenience in the grammar as an *ad hoc* statement appended to the section which states the rules for past tense formation—it will be one of our old friends, the 'irregular' formations.

plural is indeed zero, and it would be legitimate to say that the keneme is zero. Given this analysis, represented as {ʃijp-Ø}, zero would qualify as a true 'allomorph' of the plural morpheme.

(4) '*Took* is a discontinuous allomorph /t . . . k/ of *take*, and an infixed allomorph /u/ of /ed/'. This is regarded as the most attractive solution within the IA framework. But then we should also have to analyse *take* as consisting of /t . . . k/ and an infixed allomorph /ej/. Again the solution suffers from the same defective terminological discrimination. No /u/ would have to figure as an S-M unit in the list of 'monemes' on a par with /ed/; and no reason is given for choosing /ed/ as the 'past morpheme' par excellence, reducing /u/ to one of its allomorphs. If this solution is chosen, then there would have to be similar entries for /saw/see, sang/sing, rode/ride, etc. Somewhere we should have to list in the inventory of 'morphemes' (which is presupposed by IA) /ɔ:/ 'past', /a/ 'past', /oʊ/ 'past', and so on. In any case, /ed/ in this preliminary list would have to have equal rank and status with the others, and it would not be permissible to say that such 'monemes' (in our terminology) are 'allomorphs of the morpheme /ed/'. They would all be independent S-M units, including /ed/, and all rank as allomorphs of the 'past tense morpheme'. In the IA grammar there would have to be a separate statement about the distribution of the alleged allomorphs, and whatever the notation devised, it would boil down to the commonsense statement that the past tense of *see* is *saw*.

(5) '*Took* is *take* plus a replacive morph /u/ → /ey/ (read "/u/ replaces /ey/")'. It is rightly objected that this calls an allomorph something which does not come within the definition of the term. So it is not valid within the IA framework. Each morph[1] which represents a morpheme in a given instance is an expression consisting wholly of phonemic material. In our terms, it does not conform to the S-M definition of the moneme. The confusion is caused by substantivizing a process or an instruction: 'to form the past tense of *take* replace /ej/ by /u/'. What replaces is called a

---

1. Morph is defined as any particular representation of a morpheme: e.g. /sel/ and /s . . . l/ are both morphs which 'represent the morpheme *sell*' (see above p. 128).

'replacive', which is now said to 'occur' as a class 'represented by' /u/. The further point is made that in other instances we should have to speak of 'subtractives'. Thus in descriptions of the French gender forms of adjectives it is more convenient to take the feminine forms as a base from which the masculine are formed: the masculine of *mauvaise* /movɛz/ is made by subtracting the final consonant. The opposition feminine/masculine is manifested in the expression by consonant/zero.

Under morphophonemics, as the study of the S side of the S-M unit, are also included the 'canonical forms', that is the syllabic structure of the moneme in terms, V, VC, CV, CVC, etc. (see above p. 58). Another topic included under this head is the various types of change to which the 'keneme' is subjected in the spoken chain: assimilation, dissimilation, sandhi, etc. (see pp. 63ff). Yet another treats of the various ways in which the expression is affected by the function it has to fulfil, that is the effects of the M side on the S side and vice versa (see Chapter 10).

While recognizing the important contributions to descriptive techniques, the formalization of the procedures, and the logical purging of terminology by linguistic scholars over the past three or four decades, no cogent reasons have been given for abandoning the traditional WP model of grammatical description. C. F. Hockett himself acknowledges this when he writes: 'As yet we have no completely adequate model: WP deserves the same consideration given to IP and IA'. The difference between the two may be brought out by an analogy. In chemistry and physics the nature of the physical world is accounted for by theoretical constructs ranging from the electron to the atom and the molecule. In our linguistic constructs it makes needless complications if we attempt to eliminate the word as the molecule and to explain all constructions on the basis of the 'atom', i.e. the morpheme (moneme).

THE WORD

Since our preferred model is centred on the 'word', the definition of this key unit must now be reconsidered. It is a fact that native speakers have an intuitive awareness of some such stable unit of speech. This is made plain by early systems of writing. In the Linear B script of the Aegean Bronze Age, for instance, words are divided by a vertical line (which is also used occasionally to separate the components of compound words). Such instinctive apprehension of the word unit is doubtless to be ascribed to language learning in infancy, for the child is taught by minimal utterances repeated with infinite patience. From this acquisitive point of view the word might be considered as the unit of 'dosage'. This would accord with the above definition of the word as 'the smallest S-M item which can function as a complete utterance'.

Such commonsense observations yield the 'word' in the first place as a unit of speech. We can proceed further in this empirical way and note that most of these 'utterance-words', e.g. *apples*, also occur as components of larger utterances, e.g. *What fruit would you like? Apples. Apples are rather scarce now. I like an apple for breakfast. Red apples look more appetizing.* The 'item' shifts its position within the utterance and may serve different syntactical functions (e.g. *apple market, apple cheeked*), but it retains its 'Gestalt' quality in the sense of a stable configuration which does not permit the insertion of other phonemic or monemic material. At this stage of analysis we are relying on the crude 'item experience'. We are in much the same position with regard to the 'word' as we were with the stoecheum (pp. 33ff) as the first step in phonological analysis and description.

Other empirical observations could be added to justify the establishment of such a unit. To state the incidence of prosodic features like accent it is necessary to delimit the word as a unit within the utterance. The Latin accent, for instance, falls on the last syllable but one of the word if that syllable is long, but otherwise on the antepenultimate syllable. Again, the word end may be signalled by phonological phenomena like neutralization (see p. 78): e.g. the pronunciation of the final stem phoneme /d/ as [t] at the end of the word in German. An extreme case of neutralization is the loss of the plosive consonants in Greek at the end of the word, e.g. *melit* # > *meli*. Again, vowel harmony in languages like Turkish and Hungarian is also statable with reference to the word as unit.

In the last paragraph we have left behind the crude intuition of

the 'item experience' and have been engaged in the task of describing the perceived phenomenon. The word is here set up as a
unit for devising descriptive formulae relating to certain aspects of
the S-side of the S-M phenomena. We should, therefore, now
speak of the 'phonological word' as a unit of 'language'. In
this connexion care must be taken with the terminology, in particular with the terms used for the units set up by the linguist for
his descriptive purposes. 'Phonological word'[1] is clear enough, but
it must be insisted once again that 'phonology' belongs to the
'second articulation' and that utterance analysis in S-M terms
comes first. This leads to the consideration of 'grammatical words'.

On the level of syntax the reality of the 'word' is revealed by the
technique of substitution. Other S-M units can be exchanged for
apples without altering the structure of the sentence, but merely
its 'reference' (for this term see p. 103): e.g. *oranges, bananas
grapes*, etc. For *fruit* we can substitute *vegetables* or items of
similar syntactic status from remoter semantic fields like *tickets,
hair-style, car, university*, etc. Such operations bring to light the
'syntactic word'.

On the level of morphology (inseparable from syntax, see p. 121),
in many languages the phenomenon of inflection brings out the
'morphological word' as a unit composed of stem and inflection.
Such 'variable words' are entered in the lexicon as stems (e.g.
melit- 'honey') with the appropriate declensional index to that
part of the grammar where the inflexions are set forth as paradigms.
'Lexeme' is a modern term for the abstract stem which underlies
the 'accidence' of the inflected forms. The combination of syntactical and morphological criteria defines the 'grammatical
word', grammar being that part of the description which general-
izes as far as possible the data of the monematicon.

The example of Greek *melit-* may be taken once again as an
illustration: within different utterances *meli, melitos, meliti* (all
referable to a stem or 'lexeme' *melit-*) may all function as 'grammatical words'. In the nominative-accusative form *meli* there is the

---

1. In everyday usage 'word' sometimes is equivalent to the 'vocable'
(keneme): e.g. 'the word *reason* [rijzən] means something different in German
(*Riesen* "giants")'. Or again, '*Confabulation* is rather a long word'.

additional phonological pointer of the neutralization of the final -*t* as zero. Thus there are three converging criteria which determine *meli* as a unit which we may call a 'word': (1) its function (apart from its semantic 'reference') as the occupant of a syntactic site (as subject, object, etc.); (2) its composition as stem plus inflection; (3) the phonological mark of delimitation. Such a convergence of criteria in determining a linguistic unit (i.e. a unit set up for the purposes of description) is what is known as the 'congruence of levels'.

Thus the 'word' as an intuitive 'item' on the level of the stoecheum, i.e. as a unit of speech, should be distinguished from the 'word' as a convenient unit set up for the *description* of speech phenomena, where it is on a par with the phoneme. The much discussed 'marginal cases' like the English definite and indefinite articles and the French personal pronouns *je, tu, il, elle*, etc. are not words according to the first intuitive definition. Except in a 'quotative' metalinguistic situation (e.g. *Did you say 'the' or 'a'? The.*) the article would not be observed as a complete utterance. Whether they are to be considered as 'phonological words' or 'grammatical words' depends on the choice and convenience of the linguist who is devising what he considers the most adequate description and in so doing gives a formal expression to the criteria for awarding or denying 'word' status to his chosen building blocks. One final point. The linguist devises his constructs for convenience of description. It may well be that with some speech communities the 'word' will not be a useful construct.

Much ink has been spilled over the status of the English possessive -*s* which can be attached to phrases like (*the length of*) *King Henry the Eighth's arm.* Some linguists propose to confer word status on -*s* because of its detachment from *Henry*. If such instances are regarded as exceptional and the possessive -*s* is taken as an inflection or suffix (like the plural -*s*), then *King-Henry-the-Eighth* must be regarded as a stem, and the possibility of such stem formation should be stated in the grammar where -*s* is discussed. A related phenomenon on the morphological level is the attachment of an adjective-forming suffix -*ed* to phrases like *many-headed, bone-headed, foul-tempered*. A similar syntactical phenomenon is the single-word treatment of phrases and even sentences, e.g. a '*take-it-or-leave-it* attitude', 'the popularity of the *do-it-yourself movement*'.

As for the terminological relationships between the 'words' on the different levels of description, a recent textbook makes the following distinctions: (1) a 'grammatical word' is 'realized by' a group or complex of elements belonging to the expression (this is the 'phonological word'); (2) these elements of expression in their turn are 'realized by' particular sounds. The 'expression complexes' appear to correspond to our kenemes; in plain language, the vocable side of the S-M units. Thus the relationship of the S to the M (which includes, of course, its grammatical function) is one of 'signalling'. The analysis of S into 'expression elements' set up to account for the observed sounds gives a relationship of 'sounds' to 'phonemes' and 'prosodies'. If we reverse this relationship, then the sounds and prosodies appear as 'realizations' of the abstract entities of description. But it may give rise to confusion if we use 'realization' for the wholly different 'signalling' relationship. We recall what was said above about /boj/ 'representing' {/boj/ ~ BOY}. On the vexed question of 'realization' (and similar metaphorical expressions) which forms part of the larger question of the relationship of *parole* and *langue*, see p. 99.

7

Transformational Grammar

THE SPEAKER AND 'THE USE OF LANGUAGE'

Thus far attention has been concentrated on observed speech situations. What has been the object of analysis has been what the cartoonist puts inside the 'bubbles' issuing from the mouths of his characters. The data subjected to analysis have been acts of speech. In devising notations for the various elements and combinations we have repeatedly been led to formulate 'performance' rules, e.g. that /ng/, a string of two elements (phonemes), is performed as [ŋ]. In particular, an utterance is the result of a 'performance' of the notation which includes rules for the combination of elements at different levels.[1] In all this no thought has been given to the nature of man as a speaker. That the members of the society under observation have this gift of speech, possess this competence, has been taken for granted. It is an empirical observation that speech is a phenomenon found in all natural human communities and that it is *sui generis*, a capacity which sets man apart from the rest of the animal world. In each community which comes under examination by the linguist he will first seek to establish 'normality' by filtering the material, by eliminating false starts, hesitations, stammering, spoonerisms and so on. Every member of the speech community may be deemed to approximate

---

1. For the important distinction between the grammatical level and the lexical level see below. Any given utterance may be regarded from the descriptive-generative point of view as the performance of a *logos* (see Fig. 19, p. 97).

to a norm which is in the last resort statistical, and in establishing this norm the investigator will often be helped by the 'operator's chat' which speakers engage in to comment on and correct their signals. Such work on the raw corpus is a preliminary step to description. The competence of the native speaker is taken as given.

In recent years this capacity has been the focus of a new school of linguists whose aim is to devise 'transformational generative grammars'. Whereas the linguists whose work has been discussed in previous chapters rigidly exclude mentalistic explanations and shrink from the stigma of 'psychologism', transformationists seek to reintegrate linguistics into the 'mental and moral sciences', and they regard the study of language as part of human psychology. Noam Chomsky has described his work as 'an attempt to construct a theory of mental processes'. Further, he makes the explicit claim that the new approach is largely a return to the doctrines of traditional grammar which were rejected or ignored by 'modern linguistics'. Yet he goes beyond traditional grammar in attempting to clarify the general properties of any grammar ('system of rules') that underlies human language. Briefly, the ultimate aim of transformational grammar is to provide an analysis of the universal human faculty of speech.

Despite intensive work over the last decade and a half, only fragments of such grammars have been propounded, and fundamental changes are being made in its doctrines. Moreover (to quote a recent article of late 1970) 'it has become clear over the past five years that transformational generative grammar is nowhere near being an adequate theory of human language'. Yet some account of the movement and its tenets is called for, all the more because of the widespread interest in transformational grammar (TG) outside the ranks of professional linguists.

THE FORM OF A TRANSFORMATIONAL GRAMMAR

The claim has been made that TG excels all other types of grammar in both describing human language and explaining its structure. In so doing it provides other disciplines such as philosophy, psychology and social anthropology with a scientific answer to the question 'What is language?'

These claims can best be assessed against the background of what was achieved by traditional grammar. 'Language' is defined by transformationists along lines that conform to the approach preferred in this work. It is regarded as a set of 'sentences', each having a phonetic (we should say phonological) aspect and a semantic one. We, too, while defining language as the description of the data in terms of items and their combinations, would give substantial fullness to the concept 'language' by extending the term to cover all the 'sentences'[1] generated by applying the rules of the description, such 'sentences' being indefinitely many. Seeing that all such sentences by definition consist of S-M items, the rules provide us with directions for framing and understanding meaningful signals. In this sense there is nothing new in the claim that any generative grammar takes the form of a system of rules and principles that determines sound-meaning connexions for an infinite set of sentences. This programme is equivalent to our 'Way Down' as set forth in Chapter 5. The S-M connexions are of two kinds: (1) the more general syntactic relations which are specified in functional-categorial ('parts of speech') terms and (2) the specific contents signalled by the monemes and the stems into which they enter at a lower level of the 'Way Down'.

The description of the first component takes the form of a phrase-structure grammar (PS), while the information relating to (2) is listed in the lexicon, that is the processed monematicon. The entries in the lexicon are provided with grammatical indexes which provide information on 'site-occupancy'. This two-stage treatment of the sound-meaning connexions within the generated sentence as a whole and between its several parts differs fundamentally from that propounded in TG. The new school of thought holds that a PS type of grammar, while necessary,[2] does not suffice for the generation of an infinite number of 'sentences' such

---

1. Throughout this chapter it should be borne in mind that 'sentence' in Chomsky's terminology corresponds to our 'logos', which is the product obtained by lexical filling of the 'sentence', defined as an abstract structure of functional sites (see above p. 96). 'Logoi' thus generated are indefinitely many, whereas 'sentences' are comparatively few.

2. For Chomsky's formalization of phrase structure grammar as a sequence of 'rewrite rules' see Chapter 5.

as is required of an adequate grammar. Nor does it account for the structural connexions between 'sentences' which are intuitively apprehended by the native speaker. This defect is remedied by using the PS component as a 'base' which generates structures on which the transformational rules operate to generate derived structures. The base structures are called 'deep structures', and it is they which are subjected to semantic interpretation and specify those structural relationships which are important in determining the overall meaning of a 'sentence'. The transformational rules result in a 'surface structure', and it is on this that the phonological interpretation operates to determine the S-side of a sentence. Thus the overall plan of a TG can be represented diagrammatically as in Fig. 21a.

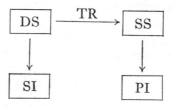

Fig. 21a.

DS = Deep structure, SS = Surface Structure, SI = Semantic Interpretation, PI = Phonological Interpretation.

These fundamental concepts must now be given concrete illustrations. It will underline the extent and nature of the innovations proposed if the examples used by Chomsky in his exposition are first worked in the traditional way and then set against the new mode. It will also help us to pass judgment on Chomsky's claim that this type of grammar is a return to traditional (i.e. pre-Bloomfieldian) ways of thinking and that the differences between his and old-time grammar are largely notational—a claim which has dismayed some of his disciples.

THE PASSIVE TRANSFORMATION

An example which figures largely both in his own work and in popular expositions is the passive transformation. It is claimed that phrase structure grammar fails to account for the intuition of the native speaker that 'the same thing is said'[1] by two sentences such as

(1)   *The bad boy spilled the hot water.*

(2)   *The hot water was spilled by the bad boy.*

Traditional grammar accounts for the structural (and semantic) relationship by a formula which is couched in terms of 'structural sites'. A sentence with the structure

(Subject (N_1) + Predicate (Verb Transitive + direct object (N_2)))

can be transformed into the passive by putting N_2 in the subject site, turning the verb into the passive form, and giving N_1 an agentive form (in English by prefixing the preposition *by*). Similarly in Latin by the same formula

Rōmānī Gallōs vīcērunt   'The Romans conquered the Gauls'.

is transformed into

Gallī ā Rōmānīs victī sunt   'The Gauls were conquered by the Romans'.

If we give the base form (the active) its structural description in PS terms:

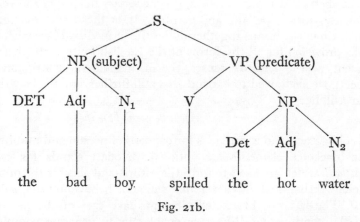

Fig. 21b.

and formulate the passive transformation as

$$N_1 + V + N_2 \longrightarrow N_2 + V + by + N_1$$

---

1. Cf. Lyons, *Introduction*, p. 254.

it will be obvious that the passive transformation formula is couched in the high-level terms that form the 'nodes' of the tree. But more important is that our rule uses *functional* terms, because the apparent use of purely categorial[1] terms N_1 and N_2 masks the fact that the subscript distinction is in fact a functional one— subject and direct object.

Chomsky's own formulation of the passive transformation turns out to be virtually identical with that of old-time grammars. Its puzzling features on closer inspection can be seen to be purely notational. He assigns the active construction exemplified in

(3) *Jack kissed Jill*

to the base component and gives it the now familiar structural analysis (SA) on immediate constituent (IC) lines: $NP_1 + Aux + V + NP_2$. This is transformed to $NP_2 + Aux + be + en + V + by + NP_1$. The structural change (SC) is formulated thus:

$$\text{SC: } x_1 + x_2 + x_3 + x_4 \longrightarrow x_4 + x_2 + be + en + x_3 + by + x_1$$

The element *Aux* first requires comment. In order to generate the terminal string by what we call moneme insertion or 'cladding' of the abstract structure of sites, it is necessary to specify the verb by tense, mood, person and number. It is these specifications which Chomsky lumps together under the term *Aux*. If we wish to make provision for all the forms of the English finite verb (that is present, past and future tenses, the moods and the continuative aspect), we shall need to expand *Aux* still further, and the 'rewrite rule' will be:

$$Aux \longrightarrow C(M)(have + en)(be + ing)$$

C is obligatory, and it provides for concord of person and number. The bracketed elements are optional. *M*(odal) stands for *will* and *shall*, which are used to form the future, and also for the other 'modal' verbs which have a similar syntactic behaviour: *can*, *may*, *must*. The last two bracketed elements take care of the perfect and the continuative. The rule enables us to generate complex

---

1. The distinction between 'functional' and 'categorial' is vital. 'Categorial' is here used with reference to the 'parts of speech' which may occupy the several functional sites.

forms like *he will have been taking drugs*. Note that *–en* is simply the notation for the past participles, which in traditional grammar is called PPP (perfect participle passive). In the formula *–en* precedes the verb to which it is attached (e.g. *en + kiss → kissed*).

Thus to generate the elements *was kissed* at the terminal stage we need *Past + be + en + V*. It is clear that these are simply morphological instructions on how to form the passive of the verb in English, and they are strictly speaking not of a syntactical nature. Much the same is true of the insertion of *by* before NP, for this is nothing more than an instruction on how to form the agentive. As for the notation X_1, etc., the subscript numerals have meaning only in so far as they refer to functional sites, e.g. *subject* and *predicate*, the latter with two sub-sites *verb* and *direct object*.

We may now turn to the points which have been emphasized by exponents of Chomsky's doctrines. First, whereas the PS rules rewrite only a single element at a time, the T-rules operate on a whole string and bring about a change in its structure, e.g. the interchange ('permutation' is the technical term used) of the two NPs in passive transformation. Traditional modes of thinking are also reflected in the concept 'analysability', which is stressed as 'the basic predicate in terms of which transformational grammar developed'. The T-rule requires as its input (the left hand part of the rule) that a string be analysed in a particular way represented either as a labelled bracketing or a 'tree'.[1] To satisfy ourselves that a given T-rule applies, we scan the phrase-marker to establish whether the symbols occurring in the SA of the T-rule is present. An additional point, which again characterizes traditional grammar (see above), is also insisted on by TG exponents. The rule is couched not in terms of the low-level constants (e.g. *Jack*, or *the boy with the pail*), but must contain at least one higher-level term, a 'variable', like *NP*, that is a 'nodal' term which 'dominates' sub-strings. It is by the use of such high-level terms that a simple general grammatical statement can be made to cover a large variety of actual utterances. Thus the same formula will apply to *The brave little boy with blue trousers who had been carrying a pail may possibly have kissed the pretty girl with the golden curls*

---

1. See Chapter 5.

at the top of the hill. The derivational tree of this sentence at its higher level will show the structure $NP_1 + VP(V + NP_2)$. The further analysis assigning the elements of the sub-strings to their eponomatic and epirrhematic sub-sites is irrelevant to the rule. Such a formula with a wide range of application is said to be more 'powerful' than one which covers a narrower range of phenomena. A transformational rule applies to strings in which analysis has detected a given structure. This is all that 'analysability' means, and it is implicit in the traditional rule about the interchange of subject and direct object.

SURFACE STRUCTURE (OLD STYLE)

Chomsky claims that the syntactic doctrines of structural (taxonomic) linguistics are based on the confusion of deep and surface structures. Herein lies the chief distinctiveness of transformational grammar. Its central idea is that deep and surface structures are separate and that the relationship between them is expressed by transformational rules. This being so, an example of such a taxonomic analysis may first be given. It relates to the sentence

(4)   *We examined transformational grammar*

The analysis of this sentence is presented in the form of a tree in Fig. 22, but this has been given the modified form of a genealogical tree which shows the functional bracketing of the constituents at the different levels of analysis, starting with the first dichotomy into *onoma* and *rhema* and ending with the insertion of the monemes (e.g. *trans, form, ation, al,* etc.). We again underline the point that the categorial terms Noun, Verb, etc., are meaningless without reference to the prior distinction of functional sites. The syntactical unit is taken as the word, and these elements are 'boxed' in the diagram. If the diagram is read upwards, the analysis first assigns each minimal meaningful unit to its place in the structure of the word, which is then assigned its function in the syntax of the sentence. Thus *-al* is an adjective-forming affix attached to a noun, which is formed by the affix *-ation* added to the verb *transform,* which consists of the prefix *trans* plus the root *form.* The diagram when read downwards represents the generation of the sentence first by syntactical specification down to the word

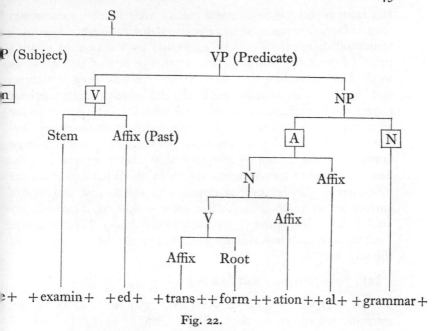

Fig. 22.

limit, and then by morphological operations down to the moneme limit. The whole tree represents the structure of the string of lexical elements; each element is uniquely assigned to its place in the whole structure. It is this analysis and representation which Chomsky presumably regards as defective. One final point must be made again. The limit of grammaticality is reached before we insert the actual monemes and moneme configurations which signal a given content (i.e. the 'purport' of the sentence, see p. 173). If we make this final *ad hoc* operation a part of the 'grammar', we shall be faced with a number of vexatious pseudo-problems which have prompted complex elaborations of theory and practice (see below on the ambiguity of *flying planes can be dangerous*).

DEEP STRUCTURE

In fact Chomsky, while maintaining that a PS grammar is inadequate, agrees that the sort of grammatical information contained in the above analysis and its diagrammatical representation is correct.

His main concern is to devise a means whereby this information 'can be formally presented in a structural description and how such structural descriptions can be generated by a system of explicit rules' (*Aspects*, 64). It was to this end that he devised the two-stage method of generating first basic structures (the deep structure) and then applying transformational rules which change the base phrase-marker(s) into a derived phrase-marker. The nature of the resulting surface structures will emerge more clearly from examination of a few examples of deep structures and the transformations applied to them. It will be seen that deep structure represents the heart and core of transformationist thinking. What prompted the invention of this theoretical device was the alleged inability of surface structure to indicate the grammatical relations that are vital to the understanding ('semantic interpretation') of a sentence.

Chomsky illustrates this alleged inadequacy by an analysis of the sentence

(5) *John persuaded Bill to leave*

To his way of thinking this sentence requires for its correct semantic interpretation that Bill be specified as the 'Subject-of' *leave*, which itself functions as the 'Complement-of' the verb *persuade*, and he holds that a PS grammar is incapable of doing this. Thus 'deep structure' is here devised as a means of accounting for Chomsky's prior analysis in the *functional* terms of traditional grammar, Subject and Predicate, the latter being divided into verb, direct object and complement. According to his 'parsing', *Bill* functions both as the direct object of the verb *persuade* and also as the subject of the verbal complement *to leave*. The last relation is, however, dubious in terms of traditional grammar. When *Bill* is said to be the 'grammatical subject' of *leave*, what is presumably meant is that in the situation referred to BILL LEFT (small capitals are used to indicate situational elements). But this is a situational analysis and not a grammatical analysis.

Quite a different purely grammatical analysis could legitimately be made which would not designate the relation between *Bill* and *to leave* as subject-predicate. The prefixed form of the verb *to-leave* is a verbal noun (e.g. *to leave is cowardly* cf. *leaving would be cowardly*), and in the present instance this noun functions as the 'internal object' of *persuade*, which also has an 'external object' *Bill*. Thus *persuade to-leave* is syntactically on all fours with *ask a question* or *hit a six*. The transformational quandary thus arises simply from an erroneous grammatical analysis in traditional terms which makes Bill both the 'object of' *persuade* and the 'grammatical subject' of the verb *leave*. If we examine the situation referred to by the sentence, we should say in old-fashioned terms that BILL is the 'logical subject' of LEAVE, and this purely situational analysis would be our 'deep structure'. But the given situation could be described in many different forms of words and it is these which must be examined for their intrinsic grammar, i.e. their surface structure, e.g. *On John's advice Bill left*.

What is important to note in Chomsky's analysis is the use of the functional terms like subject, predicate, object. As was expounded above, the functional dichotomy of the utterance is operationally and logically prior to the emergence of the categorial terms 'noun phrase' and 'verb phrase'. If we do not give explicit expression to the functional sites of such categorial terms, then a string, however bracketed, gives no representation of grammatical structure. Yet in the schematic representation of phrase structure in TG the functional step is suppressed. Indeed, Chomsky holds that it would be a mistake to insert such a step in the structural 'tree'. He goes further and reverses the steps of the analysis by defining 'subject' as the relation between the *NP* of a sentence with the form *NP Aux VP* and the whole sentence. But this leaves undiscussed the definition of the terms *NP*, etc.,[1] which, as was shown above, are 'parts of speech' occurring in different functional sites, though often having ancillary morphological indicators that facilitate their identification and definition.

Chomsky supports his contention that functional and categorial terms should be kept separate by an analysis of the sentence:

(6) *What disturbed John was being regarded as incompetent*

---

1. He concedes that 'general significance of the [said definition] depends on the assumption that the symbols *S*, *NP*, *VP*, *N* and *V* have been characterized as grammatical universals'. But grammatical universals can only be established by the study of grammars, in each of which *NP* is preceded by the functional analysis.

John he regards as (a) the Object-of *disturbed*; (b) Object-of *regard* (*as incompetent*), and (c) Subject-of the predication *as incompetent*. Having analysed the functional relations in this way, he then points to the impossibility of giving a categorial interpretation to these functional notions. Such analyses, he maintains, require the device of 'deep structure' by which these 'significant grammatical *functions*' will be taken care of. It was such prior analyses which prompted, and provided, the 'empirical justification for' the theory of transformational grammar.

We are thus in at the birth of TG and have an excellent exposition of the nature of the difficulties which made traditional grammar of the WP type appear so unsatisfactory and brought TG on the scene to provide a remedy. A preliminary point must be made at once. A sophisticated grammatical analysis of this kind is not, of course, an 'empirical justification'. A quite different analysis could be easily defended. It is one which is more easily apparent in another form of expression for the same content:

(7)   *It disturbed John to be regarded as incompetent*

Here *it* is the dummy subject,[1] which is given fuller content by the verbal noun-phrase *to be regarded* (*as incompetent*). Another expression of the same kind which can fill this particular syntactic site is *to be hated*, for which the other English verbal noun in *-ing* could also be substituted (*being hated*) or even the abstract noun *hatred*. There is no 'grammatical' functional relationship between *John* and *regard* in the sentence under examination or between *John* and *as incompetent*. We might, of course, choose to communicate the facts of the situation in a more piecemeal way:

(8)   *People regarded John as incompetent*
(9)   *This disturbed John*

In these sentences *John* figures first as the object of *regarded* and then of *disturbed*. Alternatively we could derive the complex sentence from the following:

---

1. *It* refers forward to a later expression. It is thus an anaphoric element like *he she, it*, etc., the only difference being that these have a backward reference to the noun previously used.

(10)   *What disturbed John?*
(11)   *It was this*
(12)   *People regarded him as incompetent*

The grammatical functions in these simple sentences are easily apparent. But the preliminary operations carried out on these base constituents so as to fit them into the functional sites of the complex target sentence (the one we shall construct to include all of them) result in formal transformations which make such functional relationships otiose,[1] so that the need of providing a categorial interpretation does not arise, whereas this is achieved without difficulty in the piecemeal signalling of the situational components. Within the theory and practice of the pre-TG grammar there is simply no place for Chomsky's analysis of the complete sentence as above, and so his dilemma does not arise.

We may at this point examine an example which has achieved classical status. The following sentences are deemed to have identical surface structure:

(13)   *John is eager to please*
(14)   *John is easy to please*

Chomsky maintains that in (13) *John* is the Subject-of *please* whereas in (14) *John* is the Object-of *please*. Since they are described in phrase structure grammar by identical strings of categorial terms, this fails to bring out the difference of structure. Once again, it is argued, this inadequacy necessitates the postulation of deep structures from which the apparently identical surface structures are derived by transformation.

It will be noted that Chomsky's diagnosis is again in terms of the grammatical *functions* 'Subject-of' and 'Object-of'. But this neglects the fact (obscured by orthography) that the linguistic form which figures as one element in the grammatical relations is *easy-to-please*. Another point is that in English this verbal noun ('infinitive') is often neutral as to voice (*This house is to let*; cf. *for*

---

1. For instance we could make the last sentence the subject of the complex sentence, in which case we shall have to make a 'nominal clause': *People's disregarding him*, or even *people's disregard of him*.

sale). As the result of historical developments (which are irrelevant for the description of modern English) compound adjectives of the type *ready-to-wear* (*suit*) can be made. To this class belongs both *eager-to-please* and *easy-to-please*. Thus both sentences (13, 14) fit naturally into the pattern of the phrase-structure

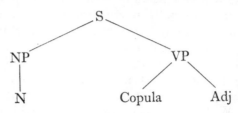

and the grammatical relation of *John* to *easy-to-please* is no different from that in *John is complacent* or *John is irascible* (*easy-to-anger*). Once again the deep structure is postulated in order to justify a *functional* analysis in traditional terms. It is true that if we simply represent the sentences as a simple string of categorial terms *Noun + copula + Adjective + 'to -form'* and call this 'surface structure', then both sentences have an identical description. But the problem is conjured up when Chomsky diagnoses a difference of structure in functional terms.

The functional relationships do not exist as grammatical relationships in the sentences as they stand. When it is said that in (13) *John* is the subject of *please*, what is really referred to is a situation in which JOHN PLEASES. Similarly, in the situation referred to by (14) JOHN is affected by a certain sentiment PLEASE. But these situational relationships are not the business of the grammatical analysis. The grammarian does not wrack his brains over whether *suit* is the 'Object-of' *wear* in the phrase *a ready-to-wear suit*. If he did, what would he do with *a do-it-yourself manual* or *a take-it-or-leave-it attitude*?

The need for deep structure also makes itself felt when the investigator who 'knows the language' is faced with the possibility of 'construing' a form of words in more than one way. Such an ambiguity may arise simply through the use of homonymous monemes. One such pair of homonymous monemes figures largely in transformationist expositions and creates pseudo-problems.

They are the two monemes $-ing_1$ and $-ing_2$, which once had distinct forms in English. (1) is used to form 'verbal nouns' ('gerunds') as in *seeing is believing* or *speaking is a difficult art*; (2), on the other hand, forms adjectives as in a *speaking likeness*.[1] By means of this homonymous pair TG theorists have devised sentences containing such *-ing* forms which can be construed in two ways.[2] Chomsky makes great use of the example

(15) *Flying planes can be dangerous*

If we take *flying* as an adjective, the *Noun Phrase* which figures as the subject of the sentence is to be analysed as $Adj + N$, in which case *planes* is the subject of the verb *can be*. Alternatively, *flying* may be taken as a verbal noun ('gerund') which, while being the subject of the sentence, can nevertheless take a direct object (*planes*). These analyses can be represented by different phrase-structure 'trees' (Fig. 23).

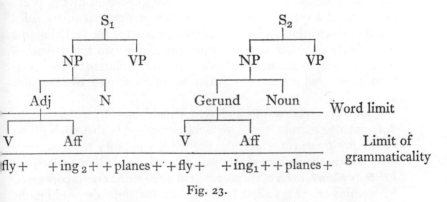

Fig. 23.

Two points must again be stressed: first the nature of the 'tree' structure and secondly the limit of 'grammaticality' at the stage before moneme insertion (see above). The tree simply uses

---

1. Lyons states that 'traditional statements about the "participle" and the "gerund" are transformational in nature'. Presumably the same is true of all derivations of word-stems from roots.

2. Chomsky would say 'It is intuitively obvious' that the utterance can be taken in two ways.

categorial terms ('parts of speech') and leaves the syntactic functional relations (e.g. that the gerund *flying* functions as subject of the sentence and that the noun *planes* is its direct object) without an overt indication. Yet (we repeat) the terms 'noun', 'verb', etc., have meaning only in so far as they classify occupants of functional sites. Moreover, the left-to-right order in the tree is to be read in a functional sense 'subject-predicate', etc. Further, as was pointed out above, the ambiguity only arises beyond the limit of grammaticality when the two different moneme strings *flying*$_1$ and *flying*$_2$ are inserted in their different structural sub-sites. It is only if we ignore these two crucial points of traditional grammatical theory that there appears to be an identical surface structure and the TG dilemma arises. It is simply not true that the two sentences are 'Phonemically and morphemically identical'. There are two phonemically identical forms *flying*, but they are made up of different monemes (morphemes). From this it emerges that the 'ambiguity' in this famous example arises at the post-grammatical level of generation. English grammar requires rules about the formation and modes of combination of the verbal nouns and adjectives. After that the problem of the two homonymous monemes *-ing* is no more abstruse (or the 'solution' more profound) than that posed by the existence of homonyms like *hair* and *hare*.

Chomsky explains the different construings by reference to different deep structures. One such structure is that underlying *Planes are flying* (in which the participle combines with the verb *to be* to form the present progressive) and the other that underlying *Pilots fly planes*. Each of these different deep structures is converted by a series of steps called 'transformations' into the ambiguous surface terminal string which was the starting point of the investigation. What must be stressed is that his 'intuitively obvious' different constructions form the first step of the exposition. The explicatory grammatical analysis follows after the intuitive semantic interpretations of the given signal. Unambiguous formulations are then devised to convey the same message. These are then given a grammatical analysis and the structures are further subjected to a series of grammatical processes which converge on the ambiguous string of monemes.

To this extent traditional grammar (as exemplified in our exposition) might claim to operate with 'deep structure' and 'transformations'. The difference is that our own exposition is represented as an example of the Way Up, which begins (like Chomsky) with intuitive semantic interpretations of the signal in the light of the given situation and progressively divides the utterance in functional syntactic terms, beginning with onoma and rhema and ending with the discovery of two different but homonymous monemes. If we retrace our steps and expound the syntactic structure (which thus emerges in the form of the Way Down), then 'semantic interpretation' comes last, but, let it again be stressed, simultaneously with 'phonological interpretation'. This is the post-grammatical stage when both for *Gerund + Noun* and *Adjective + Noun* we insert *flying planes*. We ourselves would of course make the monemic distinction clear by writing $fly + ing_1$ and $fly + ing_2$. If this precaution had been taken, the trivial nature of the 'problem' would have been recognized.

It will now be clear that in TG theory transformation is a relation between deep structure and surface structure, and that the former is required because, according to the transformationists, the surface structure in no way expresses the grammatical relations that are crucial for semantic interpretation.[1] As we have seen, this is only true in the sense that modern English now has two homonymous monemes *-ing*. It is the postulated deep structure together with its successive transformations which formalizes the way in which the surface structure is to be 'construed', and makes plain the way in which it is to be taken.

In this sense the theory holds that the deep structure makes an important contribution to the 'semantic interpretation'. The point could be put in a different way. It could be said that the different semantic interpretations of a given signal, carried out by those who 'know the language', may be explicated in ambiguous cases by unambiguous paraphrases, and it is these which are

---

1. 'The inability of surface structure to indicate semantically significant grammatical relations (i.e. to serve as deep structure) is one fundamental fact that motivated the development of transformational generative grammar. . . . that deep structures must in general be distinct from surface structures . . . is surely much too obvious to require elaborate defense' (*Topics*, 17–18).

formalized as 'deep structures'. In this way 'deep structure' would depend on the prior semantic interpretation of the utterance. The speaker would say 'I don't mean that planes are flying but that someone is flying the planes.' Such commonsense 'operator's chat' lies behind the traditional distinction in English grammar between gerund and participle.

While the notion of deep structure lies at the heart of transformational thinking, yet recent discussion shows that no very clear idea of what it is has emerged from authoritative expositions of TG theory. In a recent publication[1] Chomsky attempts to elucidate what he understands under deep structure by means of the sentence *Invisible God created the visible world*. The deep structure from which this surface structural sentence is generated by transformational processes consists of a system of three propositions: (1) *that God is invisible*, (2) *that he created the world* and (3) *that the world is visible*. The objection can immediately be made that propositions (to say nothing of systems of propositions) are not linguistic entities but logical ones. This means that in some way, which is not elucidated, certain processes transform a logical structure into a linguistic one, called the surface structure. Such an approach firmly bases grammar on logic and so effectively removes it from the control and competence of the linguist *qua* linguist. The point is not made clearer by the comment that the underlying propositions are not asserted in the generated sentence: 'rather these propositions enter into the complex ideas that are present to the mind, though rarely articulated in the signal, when the sentence is uttered'. The position now seems to be that the deep structures are 'certain complex ideas which are present to the mind'. The mind performs certain operations on these complex ideas and these result in the surface structure. The so-called 'grammatical' transformations are these 'certain mental operations'. Finally, Chomsky makes the point that it is inaccurate to say that one sentence is derived from another by transformation. More strictly what is meant is that 'the structure associated with the first sentence is derived from the structure underlying the second . . .'.

---

1. *Language and Mind*, 1968.

It is precisely this point which was made above by distinguishing the 'structure of sites' from the 'logos' (the latter being what Chomsky means by 'sentence'). A strictly linguistic grammar expounds the build-up of complex sentences from a system of simpler sentences. It analyses the structure of a given complex sentence and shows how the structure and forms of the constituent sentences are adapted to fit their new role. It is left to the logician to study the relation of such grammatical structures from a propositional point of view. Doubtless philosophers would wish to be heard on the subject of 'complex ideas present to the mind' and how these are formed into abstract structures. Finally, both philosophers and psychologists would claim a professional interest in the 'certain mental operations' performed on the said 'complex ideas'. The linguist's grammar will be independent of and prior to such considerations. When it is divested of its logical and psychological trappings, a grammar of the transformational-generative type is seen to be different only in its terminology from the traditional 'site and occupant' grammar with its rules for sentence formation.

Elsewhere Chomsky defines 'deep structure' as the aspect of syntactic description (SD) which determines its semantic interpretation. Yet, at the time of writing, 'semantic interpretation' remains a vague, if not empty, concept.[1] But whatever the theoretical status of 'semantic interpretation', the fact remains that the native English hearer (and one of these is the theoretician of 'deep structure') construes the ambiguous signal in one way or other using his experience, linguistic know-how, knowledge of the context and situation, and his general 'intelligence'.[2] Each construing yields for the describer intuitive groupings of forma-

---

1. 'The SD assigned to a signal must determine the semantic interpretation of the signal in some way which, in detail, remains unclear' (*Topics*, 16).
2. Chomsky makes much the same point when he writes: 'The hearer may use information that goes well beyond grammar to determine which of the potential interpretations was intended' (*Topics*, 29). From his experience of quasi-identical utterances such as (1) *Flying planes low is dangerous* and (2) *Low flying planes are dangerous* the hearer becomes aware of two different -*ing* forms, and he will opt for one or the other in a given utterance according as it 'makes sense' in a given context and situation.

tives within the utterance, and it is certain aspects of these groupings ('syntactic organization') which are formalized as 'significant grammatical relations'. We emphasized 'certain aspects' because some sources of ambiguity cannot be formalized as 'grammatical'. Such are the purely lexical ambiguities like the *-ing* forms.

TRANSFORMATIONAL RULES

Transformation (defined as a relation between surface structure and deep structure) takes the form of a series of transformational rules which, when applied, are said to 'map' the phrase-marker (PM) on to new 'derived' PMs. Thus each transformational rule requires a structural analysis of the PMs to which it applies. Such an analysis presents the terminal string (the string of formatives which is the end-product of the rewriting rules of the PM) as successive parts, each with its appropriate specification in categorial terms (see above).

A few illustrations may serve to clarify the obscurity of these abstractions. Take the utterance:

(16)   *I expected the student who neglected his work to be dismissed*

In traditional terms this would be analysed as a combination of three different simple sentences (base structures).

(17)   *I expected that:*
(18)   *the student will be dismissed:*
(19)   *the student neglected his work.*

To construct the single complex target sentence (16), sentence (17) is chosen as the main clause. In modern terms, this will be the 'matrix' sentence in which the others are inserted as 'constituent sentences' (subordinate clauses would be better since the matrix is also a constituent). The insertions take place in specified syntactic sites each with a given structural function. Obviously this will entail the prior analysis of the matrix (17) in the usual grammatical terms: Subject + Predicate (Verb + Object). First (19) is inserted in (18) by the use of the relative pronoun as an anaphoric device which is used when there is a repetition of the same noun in the base structures to be combined. Next (18) and (19), thus combined, are inserted in the epirrhematic site (with the function 'direct object') occupied by *that* in sentence (17). To fulfil this syntactical function and occupy the said site the finite verb *will be dismissed* must be nominalized by transforming it into the *to*-form (the 'infinitive'), while *that* in the main clause, which serves as a dummy indicating 'direct object' site, is deleted. These operations, when completed, yield the complex sentence in the form quoted. Figure 24a is a structural schema which shows (with the omission of irrelevant details) the relations of the base sentences (strings) to each other and to the complex sentence as a whole. The devices which adapt the base structures to fill their subordinate role in syntactic life are stated as commentary on this scheme. These in the new terminology, can be called transformations and labelled respectively T_{rel}, T_{to} and T_{del}.

After complicated and abortive experiments transformational analysis has returned to a position closely resembling the traditional ways of generating such complex sentences. It also devises much the same 'generalized phrase-markers' to show the structural relations of the embedded sentences. In our Fig. 24 the position of the embedded sentences has been indicated by inserting the symbol S (Sentence) in the appropriate syntactic site. Such a device is called in the new terminology a 'recursive operation'. The successive embeddings and necessary adaptations (transformations) are schematically indicated by a diagram (see Fig. 24b), which is called a transformation marker. This device is merely a scheme which is said to 'map' the reshaping operations familiar from traditional grammar as just expounded.

Here we can assent to Chomsky's claim that only the terminology is novel. The grammatical structures underlying the base sentences, couched in the familiar categorial terms (the phrase-markers) are called the base PMs. For short, the three BPMs will be symbolized B_1, B_2, B_3. Their relations within the whole complex sentence are shown in Fig. 24a by the generalized PM (GPM) dominated by S. The transformational operations necessary to adapt the base PMs for their new role within a single complex sentence are now applied to the GPM in a fixed order dictated by 'degrees of

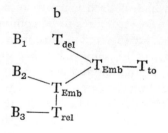

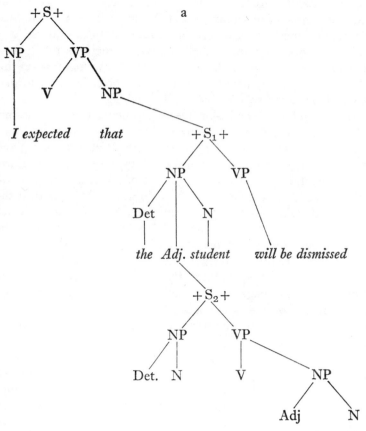

Fig. 24a. Generalized phrase-marker; b. Transformation marker.

embeddedness'. The most deeply embedded structure is that dominated by the S (S_2) lowest down in the derivational tree. Here the first transformation is applied (T_{rel}). We now proceed to the next highest structure dominated by an S; this is S_1, in which the 'transformed' S_2 is embedded. Here an *ad hoc* 'inversion rule' is required to situate this embedded sentence in the structural 'position' 'Adj.' after the noun. Now comes the turn of the next highest S, that is the initial one which dominates the whole phrase-marker. Here *that* is deleted and its place is taken by $S_1 + S_2$. This operation requires the nominalization transformation (T_{to}), which produces *to be dismissed*.

This account has omitted a complication introduced by transformational grammar; TG does not permit passive constructions in base sentences but derives them from active expressions by means of the passive transformation (T_{Pass}). If we choose as the base form of (18) *someone will dismiss the student*, then two operations are required to generate the target sentence: (a) T_{Pass} which produces *the student will be dismissed by someone* and (b) a deletion transformation (T_{Del}) which gets rid of the explicit agent expression. The structural places for these transformations are indicated in the phrase-marker by 'dummy symbols'. So in our generalized phrase-marker the structure dominated immediately by S_1 will be replaced by the following:

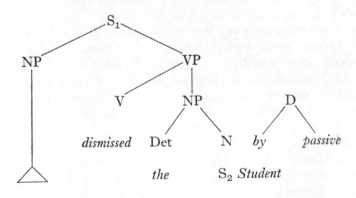

Fig. 25.

THE PHONOLOGICAL COMPONENT

The syntactical component of transformational grammar operating with base components and transformational rules generates a surface structure which takes the form of a string of elements called formatives. Such a string forms the input of the phonological component, which is said to assign to the string a representation as a string of phones. The nature of the formatives and of the rules applied to them which result in the string of phones are thus the objects of our scrutiny. But again it will be useful first to summarize the procedures of the kind of grammar which TG seeks to improve and replace.

The itemization of utterances contrasting in sound and meaning and their reduction to elements at the word and moneme levels was the necessary presupposition for phonemic analysis. In this four stages were detected (1) stoechea, (2) phones, (3) phonemes, (4) phonemic features. There can thus be no question of the 'autonomy of phonology'. Meaning is relevant at all stages of the analysis down to the stoecheum: *d* and *g* emerged as stoechea because of the identification of *muddy* and *muggy* as different meaningful elements of speech. Further, certain phonemic and phonic phenomena are describable only by bringing in morphological considerations such as moneme and word limits. Again, many prosodies require reference to the whole sentence as a semantic unit (e.g. 'interrogative sentences').

The stoecheum, as an 'item experience', can justly be regarded as having 'psychological reality'. The phone, the object of articulatory or acoustic phonetics, on the other hand, has physical reality. The phoneme is a logical construct which mediates between the stoecheum and phones and restores to the former the intuitive unity which was lost among the diversity of the phones. By this construct we can account for the speaker's 'intuition'. A phoneme is *described* as a bundle of the features common to all its allophones (their phonetic HCF). These features may be described in either articulatory or acoustic terms. The relationship of the phones to the phonemes is one of 'realization'. To put it in another way, if (with TG theorists) we regard a sentence as an object generated by the rules of the grammar and include phonology within such a 'grammar', we can say that the phones are the result of the application of 'performance rules' to the notations devised for the strings of phonemes and to the accompanying prosodies.

In the exposition of the analysis of utterances the priority of syntax has been amply demonstrated.[1] Yet the analysis of utterances and their description as sentences consisting of a structure of functional sites required all the time semantic considerations. Unless a given utterance were understood, we could not give an answer to the basic onoma–rhema question. Once the structural sites and sub-sites are established as general schemata, consideration can be given to their occupants on a given occasion. To repeat a fundamental point, there are two stages in the generation of logoi, and it is advisable to make a clear distinction between them. The first ends with the most detailed specification in abstract terms of the several occupants-to-be of the sites of the given structure. This represents the limit of grammaticality in our sense. Next comes the stage where we can make only *ad hoc* choices. This is represented in TG theory by such a rewrite rule:

$$\text{Noun} \longrightarrow dog, \ boy, \ cat, \ truth, \ size \dots$$

This simply says 'choose from the lexicon a word which has the grammatical index "Noun"'. Which particular (or moneme) is chosen depends, of course, on the message to be signalled. This is where the *dianoia* of the speaker intervenes, his intention to signal his reactions to the WORLD, or rather that relevant aspect of it we call the SITUATION. This is prelinguistically articulated, say as CAT, HUNT BIRD, which is a fragment of WORLD structure. It may well be that a given grammatical structure generated by applying the rules of the grammar may be common to a number of different languages. If it could be applied usefully to all languages, then we should have a universal structure, say NP + VP. In taking the next step, however, which would generate logoi due for testing, (say) in the speech communities of England, France and Germany, we cannot

---

1. This is true only of the Way Up, that is the emergence of the phoneme as the end-product of a sequence of 'discovery procedures'. In the theoretical generation or presentation of sentences (the Way Down) the phonemic structure is usually regarded as independent of the syntactic structure of a language.

circumvent the basic fact of human speech, that is the arbitrary connexion between sound and meaning. For CAT we shall have to insert *cat*, or *chat* or *Katze*. For HUNT either *hunt*, *chasser* or *jagen*. For BIRD, either *bird*, or *oiseau*, or *Vogel*.

Such insertion of arbitrary S-M units is beyond the scope of grammar. Here we have recourse to the lexicon which, it will be recalled, contains the residue of the monematicon not amenable to 'rule making'. But the moneme is by definition an S-M unit, and it is available as an occupant for a given site only if it has been given a description in phonological and semantic terms (and its proper grammatical indexes). To our way of thinking, then, the grammar ends at the stage when we must choose a situationally appropriate set of monemes for insertion in the syntactical schema. The representation of the vocable side as a string of phoneme symbols was a necessary part of the compilation of the monematicon. The phonemic symbol implies a set of performance rules which mirror the steps of the Way Up which led up to the phoneme from the physical phones of the act of speech which are the primary data of the observer. This is what we understand by the 'phonological' interpretation of the 'logos' represented by the terminal string of the grammar, whether this appears in standard orthography or in phonemic symbols.

The dispute which has arisen revolves largely around the proposal that a representation in terms of 'autonomous phonemics' is entirely superfluous and should be eliminated. All that is necessary is a representation in terms of 'systematic phonemics' which is 'mapped' by the application of rules to a phonetic representation. The two terms require exegesis.

By 'autonomous phonemics' (also called 'taxonomic phonemics') is understood the body of the doctrine which had won wide acceptance in the United States by 1945. What characterized this school of thought (see Chapter 4) was the insistence that phonological analysis should be based purely on phonic data. This doctrinal position became increasingly radical and reached a stage at which meaning, grammatical categories (e.g. Noun and Verb), morpheme boundaries (e.g. word end), and the like were regarded as irrelevant. The phonological description of a language must take place in total independence of syntactical and morphological information. The 'systematic phonemics' of the TG school is in effect a return to the position (also adopted in this book) of those scholars who insisted that there were 'grammatical prerequisites' to phonemic analysis. What is new and revolutionary is the suggestion that a representation on the level of autonomous phonemics is entirely superfluous and should be eliminated from linguistic description.

We may now turn to 'systematic phonemics', which in fact approximates to what has been called 'morphophonemics' (see pp. 126–132). What is called the level of 'systematic phonemics' is a certain representation in phonemic symbols of the terminal string generated by the syntactical component. But in the theory this stage is reached after the application of certain rules of the phonological component, such rules being ordered in a given sequence. As an example of such a terminal string, which becomes the input stage of the phonological component, we have:

(20) $+ the + cat + see + Past + the + bird$

Noteworthy is that the 'morpheme' *Past* (as in our definition, see p. 104) figures in the terminal string as a formative on the same level of synthesis ('generation') as the monemes (lexemes).[1] In the theory lexical and grammatical formatives are distinguished, and the rules prescribe first the replacement of the grammatical formatives. Chomsky writes (*Issues*, 68): 'Let us assume that at a certain stage in the application of the rules of the phonological component, all grammatical formatives except junctures [marks of word and moneme limits] will have been eliminated.... At this point, for example, English "saw", which at the input stage is /sī/ + *past*, might be represented /sɔ/ (though English "heard", which

---

1. Chomsky states explicitly (*Syntactic Structures*, p. 109): 'A linguistic level is a method of representing utterances. It has a finite *vocabulary* of symbols ... which can be placed in a linear sequence to form *strings* of symbols by an operation called *concatenation* and symbolized by +. Thus on the morphemic level in English we have the vocabulary elements *the, boy, S, past, come,* etc. and we can form the string, *the + boy + S + come + past* (which would be carried by the morphophonemic rules into the string of elements /ðɪbóyz#kéym/....' Here we have yet another example of the confusion of moneme and morpheme, *come* and 'past'.

at the input stage might be /hīr/+*past*, might be represented /hir≠d/. ...' Here it is quite unclear why the selection of /sɔ̄/ as the past tense of /sɔ̄/ is included in the phonological component. It might be regarded as a 'morphophonemic rule', but this is no more than saying that the past tense of *see* is *saw*. The information which enables us to convert the terminal string at this point is stored first in the monematicon under *saw*, where there is a cross-reference to the grammar under Past Tense (irregular forms). What is relevant to the phonological component is the *keneme* /sɔ̄/, that is the vocable which signals 'past tense of *see*'. But this is represented in Chomsky's own exposition as a string of phoneme symbols, and this notation is meaningless unless we have been given explicit information about what they stand for. This seems to imply the usual phonemic analysis. That this is implicit in the theory is shown by the phonological comment on /hīr#d/ to the effect that later rules will be applied 'which convert ī to e in many contexts and convert lax, non-compact vowels to [ɨ] before /r/ (+Consonant)'.

In plain terms, what is here contrasted as an example of the ordering of rules is first the formation of the regular and irregular past tenses, and secondly the deviant pronunciation of the apparently regular form *heard*. This is brought into connexion with similar oddities, and a 'general rule' is formulated to the effect that /hīrd/ is to be performed as [hɜ:d]. Presumably a special saving rule would have to be devised to exclude *feared, geared, jeered, leered, reared, sheared, queered, speared* and *veered*.

As another example of the 'systematic phonemic' level of generation he gives a representation of the phrase *telegraphic code*:

[NP [Adj [N Pre tele] [Stem græf]] ik] # [N kōd]

This representation in terms of segments and junctures is virtually identical with our monemic analysis of the phrase *transformational grammar* (see pp. 144f). For Noun Phrase is first analysed into Adjective+Noun, and then the formation of the adjective is sketched: first the derivation from the noun *telegraph* by the affix *-ic*, the noun being made up of the prefix *tele-* plus the stem *graph-*. To reach the output stage, where the representation will be in terms of phones and prosodies, rules will be required governing *inter alia* the placement and gradation of the stresses which are

partly determined by the grammatical structure. This final
stage is called the level of systematic phonetics. For the representation at the lowest level (which in our terminology turns a 'logos'
into an utterance) Chomsky prefers to use bundles of acoustic
features. This has already been discussed above (pp. 82ff). This
is held to be 'more economical' than a phonemic description.

The issue turns on the status of the 'formatives' which appear
at certain stages of the generation. What interpretation is to be
given to a 'stem' such as /græf/? The rewrite rule is incompre-
hensible without the prior existence of an inventory like our
monematicon. This will list /græf/ as a string of symbols the
meaning of which must be given in the prolegomena to the inventory. It is hard to see how this can be done except by contrast
and itemization of utterances leading to an inventory of minimal
meaningful elements. The notation represents, of course, merely
the vocable side of the 'stem', i.e. the 'keneme', and this appears
as a string of phoneme symbols having statable relations to the
phonic phenomena which are the primary data of the observer.
It is from among these data that the linguist selects the allophones
which are grouped together to form the phonemes. That the
theory of the phonological component makes provision for what
we have called 'performance rules' is clear from recent formulations. The phonological rules are 'rules which relate phonemes to
allophones'. Phonology is to be given the 'explicit conception . . .
as a generative device which associates phonological and phonetic
representations'. The fact remains that the notation used by
transformationists implies the existence of an alphabet of phoneme
symbols, and an explicit 'grammar' must explain them before it
uses them. Householder (1965) has examined the theses of the TG
phonological component and has come to the conclusion that
'something like traditional phonemes must continue to be part, at
least, of the terminal alphabet of the phonological grammar'. *Sub
judice lis est.*

TRANSFORMATIONAL GRAMMAR AND SPEAKER PSYCHOLOGY

A generative grammar has been defined as 'the set of rules and
principles that determine the normal use of language'. The task

of the linguist is 'to construct a theory of the grammar of the speaker-hearer', the 'person who knows the language', and it is the 'competent speaker' who is the prime object of study by the linguist.

This puts linguistics squarely within the field of psychology. The object of enquiry is by definition 'the person who knows the language'. This contrasts sharply with the attitude of those linguists whose stated concern it is to observe and describe an extensive corpus, potentially unlimited, of acts of speech. The confrontation between the two schools of thought may therefore start by asking what is involved in 'knowing the language', for this use of the term 'language' is evidently different from that preferred in this book. For us, 'to know the language' is tantamount to competent application ('performance' in our sense) of a given description, since 'language' is the term applied to the description of the speech data in terms of elements at different levels of analysis and their modes of combination. Speech, if considered as 'generated' by the application of rules (the Way Down), may be regarded in this sense as 'the use of language' by the speaker. Although the number of elements in the description is finite, the number of 'logoi' generated by the various rules of combination is in effect infinite. Hence an adequate description will not only cover all the utterances observed; it should also enable the person who faithfully applies the rules of the description both to form utterances appropriate to situational requirements (i.e. intelligible and acceptable to native speakers) and to give a correct interpretation to (i.e. to 'understand') utterances in the speech exchanges of the community under observation. Such a description is thus neutral as to speaker and hearer.

The position of Chomsky is not greatly different from this despite his insistence on the primary importance of the psychology of the speaker. For him a person who 'knows the language' is one who has 'internalized' a set of rules which constitute the grammar. Such a competent speaker is tentatively endowed by the TG theorist with a certain mental constitution. But this cannot be directly scrutinized by inspection or introspection. Hence this mental constitution is said to be characterized by the linguist's theory.

It will now be clear that common to the two schools of thought is a set of rules. For Chomsky these are the observables which give an inkling of an unobservable mental constitution. It is thus pertinent to ask how such 'rules' become observables? Evidently they are the product of the describer of speech. If we take up our stance as philosophical observers of the describer as he carries out his technical operations on speech material (in so doing we shall be 'metalinguists'), we shall describe the description he produces as the result of the reaction of the theorizing linguist to his chosen material. We shall infer that he sees his material in this theoretical guise because he has a certain mental constitution. His competence at theorizing is subject to the test of 'application', i.e. acceptability of his products ('sentences') in the given community. In brief, we may say that the linguist, confronted with his material, externalizes a 'grammar'[1] thanks to his mental constitution. Yet the theorist of speaker 'performance' defines 'competence' as the 'internalizing of grammar'. Apply this now to the learner *par excellence*, the native child who becomes 'competent' and gets to 'know the language' in the sense that it becomes able to form and understand new utterances in unfailing supply in response to situational requirements. It is now deemed to possess a certain mental constitution and to possess 'knowledge of the language'. This means, according to Chomsky, that it has 'internalized' a grammar analogous to that externalized by the theoretician, who does so by virtue of a certain mental constitution. The definition of 'knowledge of language' is thus completely circular, while 'internalization' is an empty concept.

Chomsky holds that the psychology of 'competence' is best conceived along the following lines. The linguistic scientist, *qua* observer of speakers, is faced with a kind of black box, the internal structure and workings of which are not available to direct scrutiny. The only observable data are the input and output of the device.

---

1. This is a wider sense of 'grammar' than propounded above, p. 96. The application of the term grammar to the whole description, including the lexicon, obscures an essential distinction. Grammar, in the traditional sense, is a set of rules. To generate utterances (the performance of logoi) we need to know the lexicon, and this is a collection of *ad hoc* directives not amenable to rule. This fact conflicts with transformationist use of the term grammar.

In setting up his theory of its internal structure the investigator will ascribe to it certain components and specified interactions to account for the relationship between input and output.

From the above it will be clear that what is common to both schools of thought is the study of the output of the device we call the speaker–hearer. These are the speech data, and we can concentrate on the differences in the rules and principles which, after their establishment, are hypothetically ascribed to the workings of the said 'black box'. To put it briefly, performance provides the evidence which prompts the framing of hypotheses about 'competence'.

EPILOGUE

Chomsky's own declaration that TG is essentially a return to old-time methods of grammatical description and that his innovations are largely notational has not unnaturally caused disquiet and dissent among the enormous band of disciples whom he has attracted and dominated during the last decade and a half. In fact, the notational innovations are merely the reflex of a logical purging of old-time grammatical practices. All schools of linguists would agree that the nature of speech and the inherited mental constitution of the speaker and observer (for the speaker during his apprenticeship is inevitably an observer) makes it inevitable that a description should be structured. There is no non-structural linguistics. This has meant that grammars have been a legitimate object of scrutiny and study by those mathematicians and logicians who are concerned with structures in general. Much of Chomsky's purely technical work is concerned with the logical form of grammars. The lack of training in modern logic and the relevant part of mathematics has inevitably made Chomsky's more technical expositions unintelligible and often pointless to practising linguists. Still, an introductory manual of transformational grammar has given the assurance that 'for the construction of transformational grammars nothing whatsoever in the way of a mathematical background is necessary'.[1] Yet all grammarians would subscribe to the requirement that a grammar should be a theory in the form

---

1. E. Bach, *An Introduction to Transformational Grammar*, 13.

of a set of statements 'which tells us in a formal and explicit way which strings of the basic elements of the language are permitted' and in so doing should make explicit the relations between the elements in a given terminal string, such an explicit statement of the relations being a description of the structure of the string. The final word may be left to one of the most outstanding of his English disciples: 'Chomsky's most original and probably most enduring contribution to linguistics is the mathematical rigour and precision with which he formalized the properties of alternative systems of grammatical description.'[1]

It must be remembered that Chomsky was reacting against a form of linguistics which was taught in the nineteen-forties. One of the leading figures of this school of thought, C. F. Hockett, has recently[2] recanted and emphasized 'that transformations are largely a corrective to certain temporary extremisms of the 1940s, a reintroduction, with improvements and under a new name, of certain useful features of the Bloomfieldian and Sapirian view of language that we had set aside'. This view of language, as we have seen, has a long ancestry, as Chomsky has emphasized.

---

1. J. Lyons, *Chomsky*, 42.
2. *The State of the Art*, pp. 31ff.

8

Semantics
The Use of Words

In previous chapters the essential function of utterances as a means of communication between members of a given society has not been the focus of attention. In phonology all that is necessary to know is that the vocables are different in meaning. In the grammar, too, we have abstracted from detailed consideration of meanings of individual words and concentrated on their site-availability. In this way we have devised a means of generating abstract formal structures ('sentences') which underly the manifold utterances which are our primary data. A user of such a grammatical description has learned how to set the functional sites in relation to one another and how to prepare potential occupants morphologically. But there comes a point when he requires to know how to signal HARE EAT LETTUCE as a present event requiring urgent action (small capitals are used for the extra-linguistic part of the speaker's world). He will not be satisfied with the advice to frame a 'sentence' with the structure $NP_1 + V + NP_2$. To alarm the German gardener he must choose the particular 'occupants' *Hase + fressen + Salat* and form them into the 'logos' *Ein Hase frisst den Salat*. Our next task, then, if we are to complete the description of the language is 'to try and understand the final selection of lexical items in particular patterns in a given instance of a sentence as used in a live situation'.[1] The signal value of such an utterance

---

1. A. McIntosh, *Language*, 37 (1961), 329. The author uses the term

is a product of the lexical meaning of the site-occupants and the 'grammatical meaning' of the particular structure of sites into which they are inserted.

SOME BASIC TERMS

The central problem of language is 'meaning', but despite the fact that scholars have found it possible to compile useful dictionaries of a multitude of languages, their work has remained on a rule-of-thumb basis. A recent textbook declares: 'No one has presented even the outlines of a satisfactory and comprehensive theory of semantics.' There is no generally accepted definition of the central term 'meaning'. The difficulties are such that in some schools of 'structural linguistics' semantics has been banished from the realm of science altogether.[1] If, however, we regard theory as talk about practice, the problems may at least be identified if we limit ourselves in the first instance to describing the operations[2] of

---

'sentence' for which, as explained above, we should prefer 'logos', the performance of which on a particular occasion is an 'utterance'.

1. Particularly in America linguists, under the influence of Leonard Bloomfield, were unwilling to accept 'mental' data, with the result that scientific attention was concentrated on the sounds emitted by the informant. Meaning was defined as 'the situation in which the speaker utters [the linguistic form] and the response which it calls forth in the hearer' (*Language*, 139). The utterance is a response by the speaker to the stimulus of the situation. Since situations are manifold and include the whole of the speaker's world, 'In order to give a scientifically accurate definition of meaning for every form of a language, we should have to have a scientifically accurate knowledge of everything in the speakers' world.' This obviously lies outside the competence of the linguist and this explains why semantics has remained the weak point in our science and is likely to remain so.

S. Ullman shares this despondency: '[The definition of meaning] is fundamental to the analysis of any symbol, linguistic or otherwise, but the philologist cannot hope to solve it by his own efforts' (*Archivum Linguisticum*, 8, 12).

2. Lyons subscribes to the operational approach to the problems of meaning: an adequate linguistic theory of semantics 'must employ concepts that are operationally definable in terms of empirical techniques. This requirement yields a criterion of the **operational adequacy** of the theory. It needs no justification, for it is widely accepted by linguists. We must reject any theory of semantics the terms of which neither refer to observables nor are reducible to observables' (*Structural Semantics*, 1).

those scholars who state that they are engaged in 'semantics'. First we may define the term itself.

At the outset the point was made that what the linguist examines is a mode of social behaviour—the use of vocal sounds in the service of social cooperation. The primary data are the utterances, the vocal configurations produced by the speaker, and the effects they are observed to have on the hearer in given social situations. Each utterance thus has by definition a 'use', and we learn the language by imitation of the native 'usage'. If the primary phenomenon, the utterance, is defined as significant[1] sound, that is something that stands for something other than itself (a *sēma*), then the relation between the vocal 'expression' and the social use to which it is put may be termed 'semantic'. Such a use may be viewed from three angles: (1) the speaker who produces the utterance with an intention, (2) the utterance itself and its observed effects, (3) the hearer who interprets the incoming signal. For (1) we may use a technical term which the Greeks themselves employed for the meaning of a word: this is their word for 'intention'—*dianoia*.[2] Such an 'intention' was transferred metaphorically to the word itself, that is to the relation (2): thus the Greeks wrote of what a word 'wishes' (*bouletai*). A distinct technical term, however, is required for this relation, i.e. of the 'expression' to its 'content'. On the lines of *phenomenon* one might simply transliterate the Greek passive participle 'what is signalled' as *semenomenon*. Alternatively, we might apply the common English expression 'sense'[3] in this restricted technical way. For (3) the term *interpretation* will do.

The tasks facing the descriptive semantician fall under two main headings: (1) the compilation of an inventory of semantic units and (2) its structuring. In the first place, once the signal values of the whole utterances have been established (let us call this their

---

1. Significance (or meaningfulness) is a primitive term in linguistics. What is given is the functioning speech community. If there is a consistent measure of response to an utterance, we can say that there is evidence of its acceptability in context and situation. The utterance will be said to be 'significant'.

2. The sense 'intention' which lies behind our word 'meaning' is still uppermost in expressions like ' *What did you mean by that?* '

3. See below for a proposal to relate 'sense' to 'meaning'.

'*purport*'), the attempt must be made to reduce the corpus to an inventory of semantic units, the sum total of those meaningful items which can be reassembled to make up 'useful' utterances in the manifold social situations in which the speaker may find himself. This is the 'first articulation'. In considering the problems of the description of the monemes and their reassembly to form 'logoi' (performed as 'utterances') it was found expedient to set up an intermediate theoretical unit, the 'word'. After the monematicon has been simplified by the construction of the grammar, the 'non-regular' residue will be reorganized to form an inventory of 'words', as thus defined. Each word will be provided with a grammatical index which assigns it to its appropriate syntactic site or sites. Every such entry will also contain appropriate morphological information so that the user will know what shape the word will assume in a given site: e.g. 'Lat. *puella* "girl"', 1st declension'. From the group of forms which such a variable 'word' may assume one may be arbitrarily chosen as a lemma in the inventory to represent the whole group. Better still, an abstract form called a 'stem' can be used, e.g. *puellā-*. Such an abstract word-form is often called a lexeme (see Chapter 5), and the inventory of lexemes, which is the second stage of the monematicon, is called the lexicon.

Once such a lexicon has been compiled, the question will arise whether any means can be devised of 'structuring' it, that is of seeing whether any relations can be detected among these inventorized semantic units which will enable us to group them together; the statement of the relations holding among the members of a group will be called its 'structure'. A structured group of lexical items will be called a *lexical system*.

THE LEXICON

From this outline it will be clear that the first task of the describer is the interpretation of utterances and their dismemberment. For this task the linguist will need to take into account the whole speech situation. Each speech event is embedded in a situation which will comprise the speaker, the hearer and some portion of their 'world'. The 'world' is not merely their geographical environment; it also

includes the society in which they live with all its material culture,
complex usages, beliefs, institutions and conventions, including
the 'language'. Even this will not always suffice for a correct interpretation of utterances. For the most part we shall have to take
account of what has been said earlier than the particular utterance
under scrutiny, and in some cases what is going to be said later
(e.g. *what I mean is this*). The term which it would be most
natural to use for the purely linguistic framework of a particular
utterance is *context*, literally 'what is woven together'.[1] Thus in
addition to the lexical and grammatical clues offered by the utterance the observer, who watches the reactions of hearer to speaker
as he interprets the incoming signals, will have to use clues offered
(1) by the context, (2) by the situation and (3) his knowledge of his
'world', that is the general 'cultural' conditioning to which the
speaker and hearer have been exposed as members of the society
to which they belong.

In establishing the semantic function of the several components
of a given utterance it is evident that situational analysis must go
hand in hand with linguistic dismemberment. In this task both
language-learner and language-describer use the principle of
minimality. In an utterance such as *Go and get the bread* a vast
number of words can be substituted for (or 'commuted with') the
final item, and the observer of the speech situations will learn to
pick out the features of the physical environment to associate with
the substituted words: *sugar, milk, hammer, chisel*, and so on. This
relation between a vocable and an object from the world of perception is called 'reference': the vocable is said to refer to a
referent. Obviously, no theory of semantics can dispense with
reference.

---

1. It is a pity that many linguists apply this useful term of our natural
language to the situation and even speak of 'the context of situation', with the
result that they have to coin *co-text* for the linguistic context; others include in
context what we have called 'world': 'It [context] must also be taken to include
the tacit acceptance by the speaker and hearer of all relevant conventions, beliefs,
and presuppositions "taken for granted" by the members of the speech-community to which the speaker and hearer belong' (J. Lyons, *Introduction*, 413). This is
considered as an argument against the possibility of constructing a complete
theory of the meaning of utterances.

The relationship between vocable and referent is, of course, an arbitrary one which becomes established in the mind of the speaker–hearer of a given community as part of the cultural conditioning to which he is subjected as he gradually grows into full membership of the community. Some semantic theorists have therefore insisted that psychologically a word comes into existence as the result of an association of a phonic image (an 'engram' corresponding with the form of the vocable and somehow imprinted on the brain) with a mental concept. Certainly the referent of (say) the vocable *tree* /trij/ is not any individual object of the observable world but the class of such objects, and classification is a mental activity. This 'conceptual' view of the nature of the linguistic sign is commonly represented by the so-called semiotic triangle (Fig. 26), which brings out by a dotted line the fact that

Thought or reference

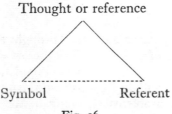

Symbol   Referent

Fig. 26.

there is no direct relation between the vocable and the referent. However, since both vocable and referent belong to the physical world, the facts would be more accurately represented if the link-up of both aspects of the linguistic sign were shown at the mental level, turning the triangle into a quadrilateral (Fig. 27).[1] An extreme conceptualist doctrine would dispense with the observable phonetic word (the vocable) and the 'thing' altogether. The linguist is held not to be concerned with the non-linguistic world

---

1. This would meet an objection made against the 'semiotic triangle', namely that the distinction between vocable and 'sense' 'implies a kind of psychophysical parallelism modelled on the metaphysics of body and soul and combining two heterogeneous elements, one physical and the other mental'. In reply to this the point has rightly been made that in linguistic theory the phonemic word is not an object of the physical world but an abstract construct.

as such. What is conveyed by the vocable (the 'name'), its reference or thought (no distinction being made between these two terms), is called its 'sense'. There is a reciprocal relationship between the name and the sense: the thought of a pencil evokes the name *pencil* in the speaker while the hearer perceives the name and thinks of the thing. It is to this reciprocal relationship that the term 'meaning' is applied.

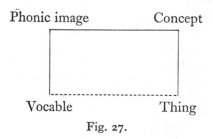

Fig. 27.

A number of objections have been brought against the 'dualist' (conceptual) theory of meaning. While the associationist hypothesis may well be of use to the student of 'linguistic competence', the descriptive linguist will do well to avoid the difficult psychological and philosophical problems attaching to the 'concept' and the 'phonic image' and devote himself in the first instance to studying the use of words in utterances produced in context and in situation. The combination of context and situation we shall call the 'setting' of a word.

There is no real distinction between such an 'operationalist' and the 'mentalist' approach. Certainly the meaning of an utterance (its 'purport') is gathered from its use in situation, and the assignment of vocables to objects of the physical world is on the face of it the simplest semantic relationship. But the observer must credit the speaker–hearer with much the same mental constitution as he claims for himself, first and foremost the ability to classify. As noted above, the 'reference' of a word like *table* is not an object of the physical world but the class of such objects. Thus even if we keep to 'reference' in the narrowest definition, we cannot avoid a 'mentalist' approach. But right from the start the speaker–hearer is introduced to less tangible aspects of his world. From his earliest years he encounters terms of approval and disapproval such as, *good, bad, naughty, nice, nasty,* for which it would be difficult to establish a 'referent'. The use of such words is learned to the accompaniment of immediately experienced features of the situation such as a frowning face, the scolding voice and the slap on the backside. We have our noses rubbed in the moral mess. Again, how can we interpret *I think, I believe, I hope, I feel,* except in mentalist terms? Yet these, too, we learn operationally as we attain to the 'concept of mind'.

In essence the task of the lexicologist is likewise essentially operationalist. 'Purports' are scanned for differences. Difference of 'purport' is the fundamental relation which permits analysis on the semantic, no less than on the phonological and morphological levels. Differences of purport could be registered simply by listing the utterances of the corpus according to grades of difference from total to minimal, the limiting case being sameness of purport. This would be an uneconomical mode of description, and in practice we attempt a description (as with phonemes and morphemes) in terms of minimal items and their interrelationships (their modes of combination). With the lexicon, too, we have recourse to the principle of minimality: purports are contrasted to locate their differences in single commutable items.[1] These are the units of semantic description, the words, or rather their abstract representations, the lexemes (see p. 121). The contribution made by such a unit to the overall purport of an utterance we propose to call the 'sense' of a word. It follows that a 'sense' thus defined can be determined only for a word used in a particular context (that is the rest of the utterance together with the wider speech context) in a particular situation against the background of the 'world'. This is why a lexicon entry quotes a word in typical sentences, often with an indication of the situation, e.g. the law courts, the stage, etc.

Once the lexicographer has completed his task of analysis along these lines, he will find that for many words he has to record a

---

1. The important point must be made again that the corpus assembled by the describer will include much material from 'mother–child' situations, when utterances tend to be minimal.

number of different 'senses'. This phenomenon is called 'multiple meaning' or polysemy. Polysemous words may have considerable semantic spread or range. For such a 'scatter' of senses connected with a single vocable we might employ the ambiguous term from ordinary language 'meaning'. If this suggestion were adopted, the 'meaning' of a word would be made up of a number of different 'senses'. The relation of 'meaning' to 'senses' would be then much like the relation of the phoneme to the environment-bound phones. As with the phoneme, which was described as the HCF of the allophones, the meaning of a word might be 'defined' by a formula which would express the semantic HCF[1] of the 'senses' which it comprises. If we remember that the 'senses' are elicited by the observation of the part played by a word in the purport of utterances, it follows that the 'meaning' thus devised will be a general formula giving directions for the use of the word, these directions requiring closer specifications according to context and situation. This is precisely what lexicographers do in practice. 'Meaning' on this view is the construct of the describing linguist. If we generate a 'logos' by applying the rules of the description (the Way Down), then the 'senses' appear as the realizations of the 'meaning', just as the allophones are the realizations of the phoneme.

Semantic definitions often present the lexicographer with intractable problems. To take an example from German, it is difficult to find a definition which would subsume both *Schloss* 'castle' and *Schloss* 'lock'. From the standpoint of purely synchronic descriptive linguistics it is irrelevant that both senses had a common origin and that the castle was so named because it 'locked' a means of communication, whether a road or river. For the German today *Schloss* has no such associations. The decision must be a practical one, for after all the description of a language in the last resort must satisfy a practical purpose even though such a description may come under the scrutiny of the philosopher of scientific method. If the linguist finds difficulty in devising a definition which will relate both 'castle' and 'lock', then he may

---

1. Highest common factor implies that we can 'factorize' the 'senses'. On this problem, see p. 183.

well decide that he has to do with two homonyms like *hare* and
hair. He will assign irreconcilable groups of senses to different
words, quite regardless of his knowledge of their one-time
etymological identity. In so doing he will also be rendering a
correct account of native intuition. Experiments with German
children have revealed complete unawareness of any connection
between the two words *Schloss*.

If native intuition is to be our guide, the decision will be reversed
in the case of the English *ear* (of corn). The unlearned speaker is
quite unaware that this word was once distinct in sound from *ear*,
the organ of hearing, as the German cognates, (*die*) *Ähre*, (*das*) *Ohr*
show. From the synchronic point of view the difference in origin
is irrelevant. The speaker, by a process similar to 'popular etymology' (see p. 250), regards the 'ear' of corn as a figurative use of
ear, on all fours with uses like *Little pitchers have long ears*. If English
were a language without history, then linguists would doubtless
draw much the same conclusion as the untutored speaker.

THE FORM OF SEMANTIC STATEMENTS

In practice scholars have found no insuperable difficulty in
puzzling out the 'senses' of words in context and situation, and
the dictionaries they have compiled ('in paradisiac innocence', to
quote a recent theorist[1]) have been found useful by language
learners. The form of the semantic statements made in dictionaries
and the modes of definition are, of course, a legitimate object of
scrutiny by the theorist of linguistic descriptions. His demands
will be all the more rigorous if a semantic theory is required not
merely to account for the facts of the corpus but also to provide
a basis for the 'use of language' by the speaker, for his 'competence'. One of the main problems is to find a 'universal semantic
alphabet' of semantic 'features' parallel to the universal phonetic
alphabet in terms of which we describe the sounds of language.
Only if this project is feasible can we hope, so it is argued, to
devise a satisfactory way of describing 'senses' and their interrelationships, that is to present an account of semantic structure.

---

1. U. Weinreich, 'Explorations in Semantic Theory', in *Current Trends in Linguistics*, 3, 395.

Recently proposals have been made[1] in the framework of transformational generative grammar for devising a means of semantic statement which would account for the ability of hearers to understand utterances. The theory envisages two parts: (1) a dictionary and (2) a set of 'projection rules'. The dictionary contains the statements of 'meanings' (our 'senses') for a given word. The projection rules are devised to account for the way in which a hearer copes with the problem of polysemy and reduces the ambiguity of certain words by use of the context. Several points must be made before we examine the proposals. KF deal with utterances in isolation from the situations of which they form an essential part. This is an artificial restriction on real-life speech. Further, the problem of reference is excluded; the authors are not concerned with what might be regarded as the nuclear semantic phenomenon—the ability of the speaker to utter (say) *hare eat lettuce* (with appropriate grammatical forming) when faced with the situational configuration HARE EAT LETTUCE. Thus at the outset a semantic theory which is not concerned with the speaker's knowledge of the world or with the relationship of the utterance to situation cannot be otherwise than defective.

What KF are interested in is a very restricted phenomenon, the capacity of the hearer to give the correct interpretation to incoming ambiguous signals. He is regarded as being in the possession of a dictionary which records the different senses of (say) the word *bachelor*. We have to account for his successful performance, that is his ability to choose the one meant from among the theoretically large number of possible 'readings' of a given string of polysemous words. An adequate theory will have to mark every semantic property or relation.

We start our exposition as before with a look at traditional methods in dictionary compilation. The *Shorter Oxford English Dictionary* lists the following senses for bachelor: (1) A young knight who followed the banner of another; a novice in arms. Hence b. Knight bachelor, a simple knight. . . . (2) A junior member, or 'yeoman' of a trade guild, or City Company. (3) A

---

1. The authors are J. J. Katz and J. A. Fodor (see also Katz and Postal, 1964). The abbreviation KF is used in this discussion.

man or woman who has taken the first degree at a university. (4) An unmarried man (of marriageable age). This order of entries is obviously dictated by the overall strategy of the OED, which was originally the *New English Dictionary of the Philological Society on Historical Principles*. Such a diachronic point of view is, we repeat, alien to the purposes of synchronic description. If we follow the intuition of the native speaker and watch the progress of language acquisition by children, then we should unhesitatingly put (4) as the main sense. Opinions may differ about the grading of the other senses. In the modern community (3) has a reference, but we tend to speak of a BA, BSc, BMus, and so on. As for (1), which is the earliest sense, it becomes known from reading history books, while the Knight Bachelor usually becomes familiar only as the resolution of KB, e.g. *The Principal got a KB in the Birthday Honours*. Thus while the historical statement about the development of the sense range would start with the junior rank in the institution of chivalry, see the academic use as a simple transfer of the term to the junior position of the Bachelors vis-à-vis the Masters, and regard the present main use as an example of generalization (see below, p. 311), the scatter of senses in present-day use could be represented as a constellation with an outsize sun as its focus (there is no place for the obsolete (2)):

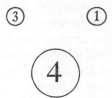

What is important to stress is that even in university circles the word would be taken in sense (4) unless it were collocated with *degree*, or of *Arts*, etc. We speak enviously and disparagingly of 'the bachelor Dons'.

The dictionary is an unstructured inventory of items. In its articles it shows the collocations of words, that is their syntagmatic relations, by displaying them in typical 'contexts'; but it does not assign a word to its site in a structure of semantic relations. *Roget's*

Thesaurus of English Words and Phrases is an attempt to see words in this light. The vocabulary is ordered into six classes: (I) Abstract relations, (II) Space, (III) Matter, (IV) Intellect, (V) Volition and (VI) Affections. (VI) includes a subdivision (III) Sympathetic, with a subdivision 1° Social, and it is here that we find the terms relating to 'marriage', 'celibacy' and 'divorce'. One might devise other such conceptual schemes with a primary division of the world into Animal, Vegetable and Mineral. Under Animal would come Human, with successive subdivisions into Society, Institutions and Family, where Marriage, etc., would find its logical place. A thesaurus is thus a kind of semantic map covering the whole field of senses, each sense being provided with a set of conceptual grid references which determine its unique place on the map.

KF's dictionary is conceived along these lines. Their diagram of the senses of *bachelor* is shown in Fig. 28 (note the addition of the technical sense 5. 'Adult seal without mate during the breeding season').

The format of a typical dictionary entry, as proposed in the new theory, comprises (1) a syntactical category, (2) a semantic description and (3) a statement of restrictions on occurrence. (1) is already provided for in our own model, in which the processed monematicon is provided with grammatical indexes which cross-refer to the grammar. What appears to be new is the stipulation that the description must consist of a sequence of 'semantic markers' followed, in some cases, by a 'distinguisher'. It is on the markers that the projection rules operate in order to reduce ambiguity. In the diagram the markers are placed within parentheses and the distinguishers in square brackets. What first strikes one as unsatisfactory in a mode of representation intended to account for the intuition of the speaker–hearer is the failure to distinguish 'usual' from 'occasional' meaning and the mixture of everyday and obsolete usage. No less important is the wide separation of 5 from 4 along separate paths of derivation when it is simply a way of saying 'an unmarried seal'.[1] A more serious

---

1. One could easily correct the statement *That seal is a bachelor* by saying: *No, I'm afraid he is a widower. His mate was killed yesterday.*

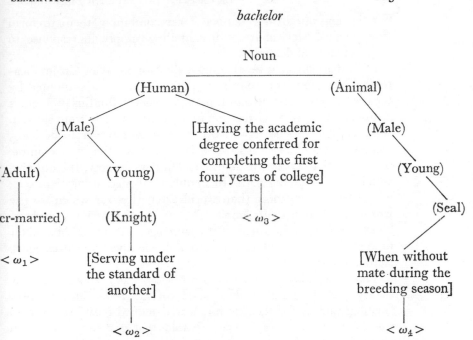

Fig. 28.

objection to the theory is that theoretically there is no clear dividing line between marker and distinguisher. The markers are the 'formal elements that a semantic component uses to express general semantic properties', whereas the distinguishers 'are the elements employed to represent what is idiosyncratic about the meaning of a lexical item'. General semantic properties are, of course, the work of the categorizing linguist. It is by this means that we take a global 'meaning' and analyse it exhaustively into conceptual 'elements', the configuration of which defines the said meaning. KF write that 'semantic markers and distinguishers are intended as symbolic devices which represent atomic concepts out of which the sense of a lexical item is synthesized'. Here we have an attempt to reach back to semantic 'atoms'. The analysis into such constituent concepts would thus appear to be part of our Way Up. If the theory is to account for competence, then we must suppose such 'atomic concepts' to be stored in the mind, which has the appropriate mechanism for recombining them to form 'idiosyncratic' lexical items in unfailing supply in response to novel situational demands.

KF's diagram may be examined first for its Way Up implications. Their first dichotomy into Animal/Human is prompted by the necessity to trace out a unit path for sense 5. But this problem is created by the previous decision to separate it widely from sense 4. As already suggested, another linguist might prefer to derive 5 from 4 in accordance with the self-evident fact that it is a simple personification. Our own 'markers' Human, Society, Institutions, which have diverging paths to Family, Chivalry, Education, etc., would be nothing more than world categories, for which we use words of the language as labels. The same is true of KF's markers. They are couched in words of the language, but it would be better to put them in small capitals to indicate their world-category status: ANIMAL, etc.

This brings us to what is least satisfactory about the new theory, namely the anomalous status of the *ad hoc* and complex 'distinguishers', for there is no clearly defined meaning given to the term 'idiosyncratic'. We are told that a distinguisher will occur only once in the dictionary for it marks the ultimate step in differentiation, what separates the meaning of a given lexical item from the ones closest in meaning. In fact the distinguishers given in Fig. 28 are, once again, all 'world specifications', and each of these could equally well be represented as a cluster or configuration of markers. The resort to distinguishers would appear to be simply a symptom of the theoreticians' reluctance to multiply markers. They want to keep markers down to a manageable number, otherwise the theory would have so many 'elements' as to become unworkable and unsuitable for a machine. Whatever their motive, the authors make no firm theoretical distinction between markers and distinguishers.

Perhaps the most serious criticism which can be brought against the authors is, however, that there seems to be no place for creativity. Transformational grammar constantly stresses this aspect of human speech and reproaches corpus-based descriptions with failure to account for it. One detail in the treatment of *bachelor* has already been singled out: the failure to give recognition

to the transferred use of *bachelor* as applied to a seal. Now the
creativity of the speaker does not reside in the generation of abstract syntactic structures, which in fact are comparatively few in
number. Originality in the creation of 'logoi' is given scope mainly
in the choice and combination of lexemes to fill the structural sites.
Not merely this, but the chosen lexeme may be given a sense
which lies outside the established sense-range recorded in the lexicon, which cannot be otherwise than corpus-based. It is this
process of sense-extension, largely by metaphorical invention,
that the semantic theorist concerned with creativity must envisage.
What confronts him in real-life speech is the human capacity for
seeing similarity often in widely separated experiences and the
power of image-making, in a word, imagination. KF's modest
attempt to account for 'disambiguation' is far from being an
adequate semantic theory and particularly so within the framework
of transformational generative grammar.

The projection rules operate on the structural description given
by the syntactic component.[1] They are applied from bottom to
top of the constituent structure tree and readings are assigned
to the groups of lexical items dominated by 'nodes'. Type 1
projection rules are of this kind: they amalgamate the readings
of the lower level constituents to form a new reading. This derived
reading is assigned to the node dominating the items amalgamated.
Amalgamation involves joining matching pairs of readings, that
is (in our terminology) selecting that combination from among the
possible 'senses' associated with the lexical items involved which
'makes sense'. Thus if NP dominates *a rubber ball* there is mutual
selection from among the numerous senses both of *rubber* and of
ball. If one of the markers of *rubber* is 'Material' and one of *ball*
'Physical object' the hearer rejects the sense 'a social assembly for
the purpose of dancing'. This commonsense procedure is formulated thus: 'A pair of readings is joined if one of them satisfies the
selection restrictions of the other' (KP, 21). What remains

---

1. Note that in our model of linguistic description the generation of abstract
syntactic structures has priority over lexemic 'cladding'. Lyons also assumes
'that the morphological and syntactic structure of the language of the text has
been previously described . . . and that no difficulty is experienced in identifying
the grammatical units which occur in the text' (*Structural Semantics*, 10).

unexplained (and this the linguist takes for granted) is the 'sense-making' capacity of the hearer. That a speaker 'talks sense' and the hearer 'makes sense' of utterances is implicit in the definition of the linguist's object of investigation. His task is to determine what sense is made by utterances, to seek for a means of describing 'purports' economically. This involves 'atomization' and, concomitantly, structural relations of such atoms.

COMPONENTIAL ANALYSIS: THE ATOMIZATION OF MEANING

KF's markers such as Animate, Human, Male, etc., are prompted in part by the desire to account for the preclusion of unacceptable combinations of words such as *pregnant boy*. In the last resort the complexities they face are due to loading the grammar with more than it can conveniently bear. It would seem more promising to account for semantic compatibility and incompatibility by componential analysis.

The Danish scholar L. Hjelmslev maintained that the two planes of expression and content were 'isomorphic'. By this he meant that content could be analysed into smaller and smaller components independently of the expression and that in the final analysis we should reach ultimate content components corresponding to the phonemes or phonetic features, the elements of expression. These he called 'content-figurae'. Hjelmslev believed that he was a pioneer in attempting such a reduction of content to ultimate components: '. . . such an analysis into content-figurae has never been made or even attempted in linguistics'. There is, however, a fundamental difficulty. If the analysis of 'content' is to be really independent of 'expression', how can we obtain an uncontained content? Hjelmslev in one of his few illustrations takes as entities of content 'ram', 'ewe', 'man', 'woman', 'boy', 'girl', 'stallion', 'mare', 'sheep', 'human being,' 'child', 'horse', 'he', 'she'. By a series of oppositions, he claimed, we can reduce this inventory to a smaller number of entities 'he', 'she', 'sheep', 'human being', 'child', 'horse', because 'ram' and 'ewe' can be accounted for as 'he sheep' and 'she sheep' and so on. By introducing a new opposition 'adult: non-adult' we can also account for 'child', 'calf', 'foal', and so on, and by a combination

of the two 'figurae', for 'boy', 'girl', 'heifer', 'filly', etc. But
if such analyses are carried out in real independence from expression, then the uncontained content we are analysing is the WORLD.
It is inadmissible to use linguistic expressions such as 'he' and
'she' unless they are taken merely as labels for observables we
classify as differences of sex. World analysis and classification
should not be identified with content-analysis. From a semantic
point of view we can say that the words *calf*, *foal* and *child* have
something in common; but this something relates to the entities
referred to by the vocables. The point will be brought out by the
fuller notation used above. What {*calf*~'calf'} and {*child*~
'child'} have in common is established by the relations which
CALF has to COW and BULL, and CHILD to MAN and WOMAN. True
content analysis would have to operate on 'calf' and 'child' and
not on CALF and CHILD. However, world features such as ANIMATE,
HUMAN, ADULT, FEMALE, are commonly taken as 'semantic components', and various terms have been proposed for them:
'sememe', 'plereme', 'content-figurae' and, as we have seen,
'semantic markers'. But the term 'semantic' applies only to the
relation between the vocable and its 'senses'. It is a function of
signals, and in linguistics we can speak only of the semantic
components of utterances (or of 'logoi' if we consider them as
products of 'generation'). The semantic components of 'man'
are not to be identified with the attributes of MAN; otherwise
we might be in difficulty over accounting for the sense of such
derivatives as *mannish*, *manly*, to say nothing of phrases like *a real
man*.

STRUCTURIZING THE LEXICON

The main problem facing the descriptive semantician, once he has
dissolved the utterances into their meaningful components and
established their senses, is to figure out the modes and means
whereby such elements are reassembled and how the global
purport of a 'logos' emerges from the joint contributions of its
components. Inevitably this involves stating the inter-relationships
between the senses, and this is tantamount to statements of semantic structures. There are three possible ways in which we can seek

to structurize the lexicon. In the first place it is evident that the senses comprised under a 'meaning' bear a relation to one another. Secondly, the purport of a sentence is structured by the very fact that it is a product of the contributions of its components. These relations form the subject of syntagmatic semantics. Finally, since the contributions of various components, and indeed the lexicon entries themselves, were ascertained by contrasting utterance with utterance and by 'commuting' components, we can set up paradigmatic systems consisting of elements which are interchangeable at specified semantic 'places'. The opposition of the members of such a paradigmatic system should help in componential analysis, which seeks to dissolve meaning into 'semantic features'.

PATTERNS OF POLYSEMY

The difficulty in semantics (and what distinguishes it from grammar) is the low level of generality attainable. Statements of meaning are in the first place *ad hoc*, and the lexicon was regarded as that residue of the monematicon which was not amenable to 'rule'. Certain general patterns can, however, be discerned in polysemy. The general mechanism of the extension of sense range was already sketched out by Dr. Johnson in the Preface to his *Dictionary*: 'As by the cultivation of various sciences a language is amplified, it will be more furnished with words deflected from their original sense: the geometrician will talk of a courtier's *zenith*, or the *eccentric* virtue of a wild hero, and the physician of *sanguine* expectations and *phlegmatic* delays. Copiousness of speech will give opportunities to capricious choice, by which some words will be preferred and other degraded. Vicissitudes of fashion will enforce the new or extend the significance of known terms. The tropes of poetry will make hourly encroachments and the metaphorical will become the current sense.'

These suggestions sketch out the possibility of detecting patterns of polysemy. Some degree of generality could be attained by analysing the semantic paths taken by words of similar meaning in different languages or by following the divergence of meaning of etymologically related words. The English word *mark* may serve as an example. Its semantic ramifications within English and the related languages may be represented diagrammatically:

MARK

I   Indication, point out, draw attention to, say.
    Characteristic.
    Target, aim, goal; winning post; throw; conjecture; opinion.

II Boundary mark
    (Space) limit, measure, territory;
    (Time) opportune moment, appointed time; season, year.
    (Metaphorical) decision, judgment.

III Outline
    shape, form, mode, manner.

A compilation of semantic scatters under keywords is a crying need in semantic studies, especially in etymology, for there it would set limits to the present subjectivity in judgments on semantic connectedness (see Chapter 13).

SYNTAGMATIC SEMANTICS: COLLOCATION, SELECTION

Above we spoke of the necessity to mark every semantic property or relation that plays a part in the hearer's ability to understand utterances. In the previous section, while we have focused on the senses of a single word, it was clear that 'senses' emerge from the study of words in their various settings. The practice of lexicographers does justice to this basic fact of speech since they display words in typical contexts. To put it another way, the lexical entry shows the 'collocations' of a given word. Such collocational statements are in a sense 'structural' since they state relations holding between lexical items. The theorist will envisage the possibility that the collocational facts registered in dictionary citations may fall into patterns and be amenable to description in general terms. It must be borne in mind that the 'sufficient degree of abstraction' attainable in description is a practical question determined by the linguist, just as he decides when to stop rule-making (the 'limit of grammaticality') and to make *ad hoc* statements.

The study of collocations and the mutual selections of lexical items has been called 'lexis'.[1] The relations of each word to every other word is a task of immense complexity which is feasible only with the help of large computers. There is an essential difference between grammatical structure and semantic structure. In the grammar we are concerned with the relations of comparatively few classes of items (site-occupancy) at different levels of complexity ranging from the whole sentence down to the monemes. In the lexicon the items themselves function as the terms of the structural relationships. In the grammar the relations are complex and highly abstract. In the lexicon the terms are an 'open-ended set', but the relations are extremely simple. Because of this the study of collocations is still in its infancy. One of the basic difficulties, once the focal item has been established, is to determine the stretch of context which provides the frame within which collocations are observed and stated. From the situational or notional point of view it is easy to see that for a stretch of discourse concerned with letter-writing we can predict that the speaker will require words like, *paper, pen, ink, envelope, stamp, post-office, pillar-box*, etc. The difficulties are much more formidable if we abstract from situation and simply programme the computer to detect the collocations of the given words in the text alone.

Some collocations are trivial in that they reflect 'world' co-occurrences: e.g. the selective restriction of the verb *bark* mainly to *dog, quack* to *duck, neigh* to *horse*, and so on. Other much discussed examples of collocational restrictions are implicit in the definitions of the words concerned and again in the world-relations which such definitions reflect. If *to eat* is to 'ingest solid food', it follows that it will collocate with *bread, cheese, meat*, etc. and not with *water, tea, beer*, etc. If a distinction is made in the theory between 'sentence' as an abstract structure of functional sites, and 'logos' as a particular assemblage of words occupying such sites, it will be simply incorrect to say that the 'logos' *The vegetarian drinks nuts* may be generated by the grammar. The grammarian does not need to excogitate elaborate built-in con-

---

1. See J. McH. Sinclair, 'Beginning the Study of Lexis', in *In Memory of J. R. Firth* (1966), 410–430.

straints to preclude such 'generates'. The restriction of the lexical items which can co-occur with *eat* is given in the definition of this verb. On the Way Up the linguist records the collocations of *eat* and correlates the collocated terms with observables which he classes as 'food' as opposed to 'drink'. Within the conceptual field of 'ingestion' we make an opposition of solid and liquid with a corresponding distinction of verbs. These distinctions enter into the definitions of the verbs *eat* and *drink* and are in effect a restriction on the range of collocability. The class of nouns which can occupy the direct object site after the verb *eat* comprises those which are 'hyponyms' (see p. 197) of the class 'solid foods'.[1] Such a statement is a fragment of lexical structure. On the Way Down we can say that *eat* automatically 'selects' the nouns for solid foodstuffs and excludes those of liquids. 'Logoi' generated in obedience to this rule will be 'acceptable'. But 'acceptability' is merely the reflection of 'usage', which was the starting point of the Way Up. One final point may be made apropos of this example. 'Collocation' alone will not suffice to state the restrictions of co-occurrence. In the case of the verb *eat* the site 'direct object' will have to be specified. If the verb is active, a different set of collocable items would have to be stated for the 'subject' site.

The fabrication of 'sentences' with unacceptable collocations such as the notorious *Colourless green ideas sleep furiously* conjures up a pseudo-problem created by the failure to draw the proper limits of grammatical statement. The number of 'logoi' generated by site-occupancies is infinite, but they are all assignable to a comparatively small number of 'sentences' (abstract 'site-structures') generated by the grammar. On the other hand if we were to encounter *Colourless green ideas sleep furiously* not as a grammarian's figment but in real-life speech (or writing), we should normally rule out deliberate mystification, accept the utterance as a genuine attempt to make a communication, and try

---

1. An exception to the rule would have to be stated for those speakers who 'eat' their soup. If we were concerned with 'competence', we should have to impute to the speaker–hearer some such abstract formulation of the collocable range of *eat* and *drink*, so that he would use one or the other when faced with some new foodstuff or beverage.

to 'make sense' of it. The position and form of the words, all of
which are familiar, will establish the structure of site occupation
(NP + VP). In devising the semantic 'cladding' of this structure
we should try to select from the manifold possibilities senses that
are compatible with one another. The noun *ideas* rules out the
literal sense of *green*, but we recall that this adjective has the transferred sense 'immature'. Similarly *colourless* could be taken as
'insipid', 'unoriginal', and the like. *Sleep* might well mean 'lie
dormant'. Finally, *furiously* could be taken 'proleptically' implying
that the awakening would be terrible. As for a 'situation', we
could imagine this form of words applying to student unrest.

Of greater theoretical and practical interest are the arbitrary
restrictions on collocations. From the available material (theoretically extendable at will) the collocations of a given word can be
stated. As with the 'senses', we can detect frequent and less
frequent, normal and unusual collocations, the limiting case being
an exclusive mutual determination, such as *spick and span*. Such
instances are most economically treated as single lexical entries:
spick and span.[1] Closely resembling these are the words which are
confined to a single collocation: *toil and moil, might and main,
without let or hindrance*.

PARADIGMATIC SEMANTICS: THE STRUCTURE OF THE VOCABULARY

A recent survey of work on the semantic structure of language[2]
begins with a section entitled 'The state of our ignorance', in the
course of which the observation is made that 'The scarcity of
relevant data is in itself a major obstacle to the elaboration of
workable hypotheses.' The major works on semantics concentrate
on the meanings of words in theoretical isolation and little attention
is paid to the 'combinatory semantics of connected discourse'.
In this section we are no longer concerned with the relations of
words in utterances ('in the chain') but with the systematic

---

1. In general it may be stated that the lexical item is not always coextensive
with the word. Notorious examples are the idiomatic English verbal compounds
like *put up with, lie up, do in*, etc.

2. U. Weinreich, 'On the Semantic Structure of Language', in *Universals of
Language* (ed. J. H. Greenberg), 1966, 142–216.

relations which come to light by comparing utterance with utterance and gathering words into paradigmatic sets, that is groups of words which can occupy the same 'place' in a given frame. A simple example of such a set with a structural relationship among its members are the terms for weight-classes in boxing: *bantam, feather, light, welter, middle, heavy*. The bodily weights of men form an unbroken continuum which is segmented at arbitrarily chosen points, as is the case also in the standard measurements of weights: *ton, hundredweight, stone, pound, ounce, dram, grain*.

Other structured sets arise from the description of social organizations. An oft-quoted example is the set of terms for military rank: *private, corporal, sergeant*, etc., whose 'structure' emerges from a statement of military 'pecking order'. Another key social organization much studied by semanticians is the family. While the biological constants 'father', 'mother', 'children (sons, daughters)' remain, a given social and legal system may require clear distinctions not found necessary elsewhere. Every reader of Homer knows the difficulty of grasping the meaning of terms like *einateres* 'wives of brothers or of husband's brothers'. Hungarian made do until comparatively recent times without words for 'brother' and 'sister' although it possessed words of more restricted significance for younger and elder brother and sister. English lacked a common term corresponding to German *Geschwister* until 1897, when the Old English word *sibling* 'relative' was pressed into use to designate children having one or both parents in common.

Less arbitrary, because the basic terms reflect the physiological mechanism of vision,[1] are the colour terms. The spectrum of colours in nature is a continuous band, and the way this is carved up in distinct segments may differ from language to language.

---

1. The light-sensitive surface of the eye is so arranged that light between wavelengths of about 760 mμ (red) and 380 mμ (violet) can be perceived. If the whole range is presented we experience it as colourless, grey or white, while complete absorption of it gives the impression of black. The phenomenon of colour vision depends probably on the presence of three distinct types of receptors which are maximally sensitive to different wavelengths, blue, green and red.

Statements about such cultural differences have become a commonplace of structural semantics. Russian has two adjectives corresponding to the English word *blue*: *sinij* means 'dark blue' and *goluboj* 'azure, sky-blue'. Latin distinguishes between white (*albus*) and shining white (*candidus*), with a parallel difference for black (*ater* and *niger*). Some languages lack terms distinguishing between green and blue or brown and grey, and so on. A child growing up in a given community is acculturated to the native system of colour references by learning to draw the limits between the continuous terms in the series which covers the spectral band. At first it may learn certain basic colours from a box of beads differing only in their colours: *green, blue, yellow, red*. At this stage the words are associated with brute 'item experiences'. We cannot yet say that the series is ordered in any way or that the child knows the 'position' of each term with respect to others. This knowledge will come from other experiences such as the sight of a rainbow or the operation of traffic lights. It is these which impose an order on the set of terms so that the relationship of colour becomes meaningful, and on this basis increasing fineness of distinction is achieved *pari passu* with the acquisition of new terms like *mauve, puce*.

The colour terms also have a logical relationship in that they are all subsumed in the concept 'colour'. In linguistic terms we can say that they are all 'hyponyms' (see below p. 197) of the word *colour*.

CONCEPTUAL FIELDS

The point has already been made that semantic structure is often the reflection of 'world' structures, and this is particularly the case of the social 'world'. The social order is itself in the final instance also a construct of the pattern-making tendencies of the human mind,[1] and it would be surprising if this did not show itself in the ways man talks about social institutions. Certain striking examples of this are of importance in diachronic semantics and will be more conveniently discussed in a later chapter (see pp. 365ff). But

---

1. I owe this phrase to W. J. Entwistle.

since the diachronic approach is in essence merely the comparison of descriptions, certain key ideas and methods may be illustrated here.

The study of conceptual fields is associated with the name of the German scholar J. Trier and in particular with one special study. Trier was first concerned with the social structure of the Middle Ages about the year 1200, when there was a sharp cleavage between the feudal nobility and the non-noble population. To fulfil its special obligations each class required its own form of 'know-how'. Knowledge of the arts of the gentleman (the courtier) was comprised in the term *kunst*, whereas the banausic[1] skills were designated collectively as *list*. Both kinds of know-how were special kinds of *wîsheit*, the overall term for wisdom of every kind. About a century later the relationship of the terms within the conceptual field of 'knowledge' showed a different picture. *List* has suffered the consequences of its banausic associations and had progressed towards its modern meaning 'cunning',[2] and a new term *wizzen*, the substantivized infinitive of the verb 'to know' appears as the new member of the trinity *wîsheit, kunst, wizzen*. But in the meantime society had changed, too, so that the cleavage between the courtly and the non-courtly spheres and their particular know-how was blurred. But *wîsheit* had ceased to be the superordinate term dominating the other two. It had become specialized to denote religious and mystical experience. *Kunst* is used with reference to the 'higher' forms of knowledge and adumbrates the modern sense of 'art'. *Wizzen*, while being used in the general sense 'knowledge', had also the connotations 'skill' and 'technical know-how'.

---

1. Adjective from the Greek term *banausos*, a word for the artisan class. The Greek disdain for the mechanical arts is reflected in Aristotle's dictum that in the best form of state the *banausos* will not possess citizenship. Aristotle also uses the abstract noun *banausia* in the sense 'vulgarity, bad taste', while Hippocrates gives the sense 'quackery, charlatanism'.

2. It is of interest that our own word *cunning*, a derivative of the verb *kunnan* 'know', as a noun kept its meaning 'learning, wisdom' until the fourteenth century, 'skilful deceit, craftiness' being first attested in the sixteenth century. The dates for the meanings of the adjective are 'learned', thirteenth century; 'able, skilful', fourteenth century; 'crafty, artful', sixteenth century.

A different approach to the subject of 'semantic fields' has been followed by G. Matoré. Like Trier and others he holds that the word should not be regarded in isolation but as an element entering into larger units which can be classified hierarchically. But this he achieves by starting with social structures. This is where he differs from Trier. He gives prior importance to WORLD phenomena and in particular to social phenomena. He has gone so far as to define lexicology as a sociological discipline which uses linguistic material in the form of words. Matoré examines different aspects of social life, such as law, religion, politics, arts and crafts, sport and so on, and he claims that in attempting to 'explain' a society we should start with a study of the vocabulary. As a basis for a diachronic view of the development of the vocabulary the history of French is carved up into 'generations' of some thirty-three years' duration. The history of the vocabulary emerges from a comparison of the descriptions of these successive 'states of the language'. Each of these states is organized into a hierarchy of conceptual fields or spheres, the structure of which is described with reference to *mots-témoins* and *mots-clés*, 'witness-words' and 'key-words'. *Mots-témoins* are new coinages which testify to the emergence of new ideas and ideals which stamp the thought and influence the actions of particular epochs. A modern example would be 'underdeveloped peoples' and 'underprivileged classes'. Certain of these *mots-témoins* are of particular importance in that they form the nucleus of a notional field so that the structure can be stated by reference to them. These are the *mots-clés* 'key-words'. Examples often singled out are the notion of the *honnête homme* in the seventeenth century and the *philosophe* as a social type in the eighteenth century. This was the Age of Reason with its rejection of authority and tradition to the end of securing *bonheur*. The influence of these leading ideas is worked out in science, art, economic life, etc., and the vocabulary relating to these new notions, ideals and practices is 'structured' accordingly.

The field approach to semantic problems gave rise to a number of appealing metaphors which presented the vocabulary as a number of fields which were like a jigsaw puzzle or mosaic in which the pieces fitted neatly into one another to make a complete picture. In fact this approach yields convincing results only in a few parts of the vocabulary, those chiefly concerned with intellectual and moral terms.

Recently an interesting attempt has been made to combine 'field' semantics with a transformational approach to grammar. The author, J. Lyons,[1] also chose to examine as the object of enquiry certain words of the intellectual vocabulary of ancient Greek. He first examines Greek nouns that denote members of occupational classes like carpenter, farmer, bronzesmith, geometer, physician, potter, and so on. Such persons with specialist specifications are grouped together in Greek under the class *dēmiourgoi*, which is roughly translated as 'craftsman'. To each such Npt (Noun personal technical) corresponds a verb denoting the practice of such a specialist: e.g. *iatros* 'medico', *iatreuein* 'practise medicine'. Finally, there are terms which name each particular form of 'know-how'. These are either derivatives from the Npt or from the corresponding verb: *iatrikē/iatreusis*. The class name which subsumes all these various forms of 'know-how' is *tekhnē*, a word which is roughly translated as 'craft', or 'skill' or 'art'.

demiourgós	tékhnē		Corresponding Verb
astronómos	astronomikḗ	astronomía	astronomeîn
geōmétrēs	geōmetrikḗ	geometría	geōmetreîn
iatrós	iatrikḗ	iátreusis	iatreúein
hippeús	hippikḗ	—	hippeúein
huphántēs	huphantikḗ	—	huphaínein

Fig. 29. The field of *tékhnē* (after J. Lyons).

Lyons tabulates (Fig. 29) these well-known facets and points out that there are two kinds of relationships: those represented in the columns and those represented in the rows. The relationship between the class term and the terms which it subsumes is one of 'hyponymy'. This is a logical relationship. Such a logical arrangement of this part of the lexicon gives us a lexical sub-system

---

1. *Structural Semantics*, 1963.

'dominated by' *tékhnē* and *dēmiourgós*. This gives us an insight into what is meant by lexical sub-system. Since it is set up on the logical principle of hyponymy and involves the notion of class inclusion, it follows that the sub-system cannot be set up without prior establishment of the senses of the words involved. The text itself draws attention to the logical relation in presenting expressions such as 'carpentry, navigation, farming and other *tekhnai*' or 'carpenters, bronzesmiths, musicians and other such *demiourgoi*'.

Lyons is concerned largely with the horizontal extension of the sets of terms: what in historical philology is called productive word-formation. What analytical operations lie behind the statements of relationship that are implied in the tabulation? How do we establish that *iatrikḗ* is the Nt corresponding to Npt *iatrós*? According to Lyons the statement of intralingual relations is a set of implications each of the following form: if the speaker of the language can significantly assert (or deny) a sentence X, then he can significantly assert (or deny) a sentence Y. The statement must also say something about the paired sentences in terms of sameness and difference of meaning.

The corpus may present considerable difficulties to this procedure, since the sentences do not occur in the simple and neat form which will reveal at first glance the logical relationships of implication, and sameness or difference of meaning, localized in the lexemes between which we wish to establish relationships. Lyons uses transformational techniques to secure this simplicity and transparency. He reduces the complex sentences given in the corpus to one or more kernel sentences. He first classifies the lexemes of column 1 as Npt, those of column 2 as Nt, and those of column 4 as Vt. Ntp are found to occur in kernel sentences of the form

$$Np/einai \text{ ('be') } /Npt$$

Such a sentence (*John be carpenter*) can be brought into relationship with sentences of a different type in respect to significance and equivalence of implication. Such relations of implication and equivalence constitute for Lyons the 'meaning' of the lexemes in question. Here we see at its clearest the logical foundation of his structural semantics. A further example will bring this out.

Np *ékhein* Nt
John have carpentry

Such 'have' sentences prompt the question 'where did he get it
from?' (i.e. the particular 'know-how'). A relation of consequence
holds between *ékhein* ('have') in such contexts and the verbs
meaning 'take' (*lambánein*) and 'acquire' (*ktâsthai*). In this way
another logical relationship is elicited. We now take a further step:
the verbs 'have', 'take', 'acquire' have a wide range of application.
If we restrict this extensive field of application to that of learning a
technē we get a set of terms with a similar set of relationships:
epístasthai 'know', *manthánein* 'learn', and *didáskein* 'teach'. The
logical relations between kernel sentences containing the verb
epístasthai are worked out, and Lyons reaches the conclusion that
the structural principles of the field of *tekhnē* 'know-how' are
transformational derivations from sentences containing *epístasthai*
'to know'. By this means we establish the existence within the
vocabulary of Plato of a lexical field structured by the relations that
hold between *tekhnē* 'know-how', *epístasthai* 'to know-how' and
demiourgós 'the knower-how'.[1]

The question now arises whether this field of 'know-how' is
part of a wider field. The answer is 'yes'. This emerges from the
study of the relationship of the verb *epístasthai* to two other verbs,
both of which we translate as 'to know'. One of these is *gignóskein*,
which is used in Greek chiefly with a personal noun as direct
object. Greek in fact makes a distinction roughly parallel to that
between French *savoir* and *connaître*. The more general term
which subsumes *epístasthai* and *gignóskein* is *eidénai*.

It remains to discuss what Lyons singles out as 'one of the principal theoretical points that is being made in this work'. This is
that 'the meaning of a given linguistic unit is defined by the set of
paradigmatic relations that the given unit contracts with other
units of the language (in the context or contexts in which it occurs)
without any attempt being made to set up 'contents' for these
units'. This seems to be contradicted by his own heuristic operations. Units are set in such relationships by being made the focus

---

1. This is my own formulation of his findings.

of a frame. Thus the restrictions of *gignôskein* to 'knowing a person' emerged from the observation that with this verb the 'object site' was mostly occupied by a Np. Such a generalized formulation as

$$\text{Np}/gign\hat{o}skein/\text{Np}$$

is called an 'environment class'. It is couched partly in functional-categorial terms (Noun) and partly in 'world' terms (Person). Lyons chooses to call this 'world' classification 'semantic'. At all events the 'sense' must be established in the usual analytical way before we can set the verb in relationship to *epístasthai* and *eidénai*. It is also difficult to see how we can establish relations of 'incompatibility' or 'sameness of meaning' without knowledge of the 'sense' of the units in question.

The logical approach also pervades the chapter on 'Structural Semantics' in Lyons's *Introduction to Theoretical Linguistics*. The chief difficulty which the reader will find is the peculiar use of the word 'sense'. For us a 'sense' of a given lexical item is the contribution it makes, in a given context and situation, to the global purport of the utterance. By the usual analytical procedures the linguist elicits from the observed utterances a number of different senses which he duly records against the given lexical item. We speak of a word having many senses and on this basis we establish sense-relations. Lyons rejects this practice and theory and insists on the priority of sense-relations. He writes: 'There would seem to be no more reason to postulate a set of "senses" associated with the lexical items in a system than there is to postulate a set of 'lengths' inherent in physical objects.' For him the question 'what is the sense of x?' ... is methodologically reducible to a set of questions each of which is relational: 'Does sense-relation R_1 hold between x and y?' He defines the 'sense' of a lexical item as 'the set of relations which hold between the item in question and other items in the same lexical system'. Here the key term is 'same lexical system'. It is difficult to see how the implied prior establishment of a system is feasible without the prior analytical operations carried out by practising lexicographers. How can a system *taste* with its hyponyms *bitter, sour, sweet* be set up unless we know the applications of these words in particular contexts?

The chief sense-relations studied by Lyons are incompatibility, hyponymy and antonymy.

INCOMPATIBILITY, ANTONYMY, HYPONYMY

It is maintained that incompatibility, along with hyponymy, is among 'the constitutive principles *par excellence* of the structure of the vocabulary' and that 'it is hard to imagine how a language in which incompatibility . . . played no part could function at all'.[1] This takes us back to the first step in analysis. Fundamental was the item experience (see pp. 34f), which is basic to every linguistic level. In semantics we are concerned first with the itemization of utterances and in particular with their purports. The apprehension of an item 'I' means the singling out of 'I' from its 'non-I' frame. This affirmation of an 'I' implies the existence of 'non-I' with which it is incompatible. We could not know that *black* is incompatible with *white* unless we had previously heard such utterances as *Bring me the black cotton, No, that is the white cotton* and learned that these different items are related to certain distinct features of observable objects. 'Incompatibility' is no less operative as an analytical and structural principle in phonology, morphology and syntax. In fact it is a constitutive principle of our 'world'. It would be difficult to imagine a 'world', not merely a language, in which incompatibility played no part.

Among the words incompatible with a given word, its antonyms (semantic opposites) occupy a specially important part in the structure of the vocabulary. This again mirrors a basic capacity of the mind, which in its perception and articulation of the world proceeds by comparison and distinction, the fundamental operations being affirmation and negation: 'This is "I", that other is "not-I".' So it is not surprising that all languages present numerous examples of antonymous pairs like *child/adult, male/female, front/back, up/down, straight/crooked*, and so on.

The problem has been posed whether such terms exist because it is a characteristic of the human mind to think in opposites or whether we think in opposites because of the pre-existence of a

---

1. *Structural Semantics*, 70, 78.

large number of such pairs in our native language. Another such problem is whether we perceive smells in an unstructured way, quite unlike the sensations of colour, because we have not inherited a systematized vocabulary of smell-terms with our native language. That human societies have not evolved such a set of terms for smells is doubtless connected with the physiological mechanisms which are quite unlike those for colour perception (see above, p. 193).

Antonymy must be established by reference to the 'sense' of the terms involved, and this means that the relationship emerges in context and situation. *White* is not everywhere the antonym of black. We can say that *Things look black* but not *Things look white*. *Near* is the antonym of *far*, and *narrow* that of *wide*. But there is no term *near and narrow* corresponding to *far and wide*. *Far-sighted* has as its antonym *short-sighted*. The latter in an optical sense has a synonym *near-sighted*, the antonym of which is *long-sighted*. Yet in many contexts *long* and *short* are antonymous. But in the context *short (measure)* the antonym is *full (measure)*. Thus, according to context, *short* has a number of different antonyms: *far*, *long*, *full*.

It has been noted that some antonymous pairs represent absolute poles (e.g. one is either *alive* or *dead*, *male* or *female*). Such polar terms are called complementaries. Other pairs of opposite meaning are gradable. Such are the adjectives susceptible of 'elative' use like the Latin comparatives of the type *pulchrior* 'rather pretty, quite pretty'. If the standard of comparison is made explicit (as in the ablative of comparison), then we talk of the 'comparative degree' of the adjective. Such adjectives are often used with tacit reference to an implicit scale. The problem arises only if we abstract from the context. A 'large house' can be a 'small castle'. A 'tall girl' may be of moderate height for a man. A 'high jump' for a flea may be negligible for a kangaroo. As Lyons puts it 'such words as *big* and *small*, or *good* and *bad* do not refer to independent "opposite" qualities, but are merely lexical devices for grading "more than" or "less than" with respect to some explicit norm'.

Closely related to such antonymous pairs are those which express the terms of a two-way relation. *Married* is the relation between husband and wife, a *child* has *parents*, a *giver* implies a *recipient*, a *buyer* implies a *seller*, a *borrower* a *lender*. The technical term 'converseness' has been proposed for this relationship.

Along with incompatibility Lyons includes hyponymy as the most fundamental of paradigmatic relations. This, too, is no less the reflection of a basic characteristic of the mind: the capacity to classify. If I wish to protect my fruit trees against damage by hares and roe-deer, I go to the shop and ask for something against *Wildbiss* (German, literally 'game-bite'). *Wild* is the superordinate term in German which has *Hase* ('hare') and *Reh* ('roe-deer') among its hyponyms. *Red, yellow, green*, etc., are the hyponyms of *colour*. Military ranks included *private, corporal, sergeant*, etc. *Love, hatred, fear, hope*, etc., are the hyponyms of *emotion*. The *professions*, which originally were confined to the callings of divinity, law and medicine, now include also the military and technical professions.

SYNONYMY

In our terminology synonymy is a 'sense relation' not a 'meaning-relation'. This implies that we establish synonymy when in a given utterance two or more items can be interchanged without any alteration in the purport of the utterance. In that case all these interchangeable items would make the same contribution and so would have 'the same sense': the *new porter will start (begin) work next week*. But *start* and *begin* are not synonymous in all their senses. *The horse started back, she started when I came into the room suddenly*. In neither of these can *begin* be substituted. So *begin* and *start* differ in their 'meanings' (as defined on p. 178) even though they share some 'senses'. To put it another way, synonymy is context-bound. *Commence* would also claim a place in this synonymous group but the stylistic overtones of the word set it apart. To quote *The Shorter Oxford Dictionary*: 'Formerly more formal than *begin*; now often an affected substitute.'

There are thus two limitations on synonymy. The usual requirement of interchangeability in all contexts is tantamount to defining the relationship in terms of 'meaning' rather than 'sense'. That there should be 'not the slightest change either in cognitive or emotive import' presupposes a clear distinction

between the message conveyed and the emotional impact made by
the utterance or some of its constituents. That words have pleasant
and unpleasant associations is undoubtedly true. Moreover, as
Ullmann has stated[1] 'the possibility of choosing between two or
more alternatives is fundamental to our modern conception of
style, and synonymy affords one of the most clear-cut examples of
such choice'. In this connexion one must not ignore the physical
characteristics of the vocable. Phonetic and prosodic characteristics
will influence the acceptability of a word in different genres and
metres. If all these considerations are taken as defining synonymy,
total interchangeability with cognitive, emotive and aesthetic
equivalence, then we can subscribe to the view that there are few
synonyms in any language. If the conditions are less strict, then
the linguist will extend the range of synonymy. Lyons finds it
preferable to restrict the phenomenon to 'cognitive synonymy'.
For diachronic study the emotional overtones of words play an
important part in the growth and decay of the vocabulary (see
Chapter 13), and if we take the view, argued below, that the
diachronic approach is essentially the comparison of descriptions,
then the emotive aspects of the vocabulary deserve recognition in
descriptive linguistics, and this is particularly important for the
fate of competing synonyms.

  Despite the undoubted interest of the manifold approaches to
the problem of structurizing the lexicon, we should not close our
eyes to the meagreness of the results to date. In a recent book on
the problems of translation G. Mounin[2] refers to the undoubted
fact that during the last thirty or forty years very little advance has
been made in semantics. Nothing has been achieved which is
comparable to the systematic constructions achieved in phonology
and grammar. No semantic elements on a par with the phoneme or
the morpheme have emerged and still less anything corresponding
to the distinctive features of phonology. So far are we from a
formal and functional structure of the lexicon that the idea of the
'isomorphism' of expression and content remains a programmatic
dream.

---

1. *Semantics* (1962), 151.
2. *Les problèmes théoriques de la traduction*, 1963.

Part 2

Historical and Comparative
(Diachronic) Linguistics

9

Sound Change

Chapter 3 was devoted to investigating the nature of the sounds of language and the conditions of their production by the human speaker. Such a study is an indispensable preliminary to the scientific description of the sounds of any language whatsoever. The linguist, however, is not content with the mere description of existing languages; he seeks to trace their history as well. It has already been remarked that all languages are subject to continuous change. It is with these changes that the linguist must concern himself. Like workers in other sciences, his first task is to establish the facts of the multiple and diverse changes of language, and then to try to discover the laws which underlie them.

In the five centuries between Alfred and Shakespeare the English language changed so much that to the uninitiated it seems incredible that Old English is the direct parent of the English we speak today, or that any language transmitted directly from parent to child should have changed its character so profoundly in the course of a few generations. The following passage of Old English is to all intents and purposes for the modern reader written in a foreign language:

Us is riht micel,	For us it is much right
That we rodera weard,	That we the Guardian of the skies,
Wereda wuldor-cining,	The glory-King of hosts,
Wordum herigen,	With our words praise,
Modum lufien,	In our minds love.

It will be instructive to trace one of these changes throughout its history in English. In the word *mód* the long vowel (marked with an accent) was at a later date written double to show that it was long: *mood*. In the course of time this sound [oː] came to be pronounced [uw] as it is in modern English, although the spelling remained unchanged. Now this change in pronunciation, which took place in the fifteenth century, was not an isolated phenomenon confined to one word. The contrast of other Old English words in the following table, which contain the same sound *ō*, with their modern English equivalents reveals the same change of pronunciation:

cól,	cool	móna,	moon
stól,	stool	nón,	noon
tól,	tool	bróm,	broom
tóþ,	tooth	dóm,	doom
gós,	goose	glóm,	gloom
sóna,	soon	bród,	brood

Here we arrive within grasp of a basic principle of historical linguistics—the regularity of phonetic change. It has been observed that Old English *ó* [oː] has in every instance[1] been replaced in modern English by the sound [uw]. A similar regularity is to be observed in other changes which have taken place in our language. Thus the Old English *ā* has become [oɑ] in modern English, as is shown by the words in the following list:

ác,	oak	sápe,	soap
fá,	foe	gát,	goat
hál,	whole	bát,	boat
hám,	home	tácen,	token
hálig,	holy	rád,	road
stán,	stone	hláf,	loaf
ráp,	rope	áþ,	oath

Nor are such phenomena confined to English alone. Regular phonetic changes have been observed in all languages for which we have adequate records. In French, the language evolved from

---

1. But see p. 209.

Latin, which became the language of Gaul after its conquest by the Romans, the vulgar Latin long *ē* changed regularly to a sound [wa], which is represented in French by the spelling *oi*: e.g. *sē > soi; mē > moi; tē > toi; rēgem > roi; lēgem > loi; trēs > trois; mēnsis > mois; crēdere > croire*. In modern High German the sound [t] was changed regularly (in certain circumstances) to the affricate [ts] represented in writing by *z*. This may be clearly seen by a juxtaposition of German words with related English words which have preserved the original sound:

tongue,	Zunge	town,	Zaun
tide,	Zeit	tile,	Ziegel
tin,	Zinn	tear,	Zähre[1]
token,	Zeichen	toll,	Zoll
timber,	Zimmer	to,	zu
twenty,	zwanzig	tug,	Zug
ten,	zehn	tinder,	Zünder
tell,	zählen	tap,	Zapfen
	twig,	Zweig	

Now all such changes, in so far as they are regular, can be formulated in the form of a 'law'. We say that in High German the initial voiceless dental plosive changed (in certain positions) to a voiceless dental affricate.[2] Such a formulation of a sound change is called a sound law. A sound law refers to the treatment of a sound only under certain given conditions, in particular environments, so that if the sound in question occurs in a word under conditions other than those stipulated by the law, then the law will not apply. Thus the above rules as to the change of Old English *ā* to [oɑ] will have to be modified to except cases where this sound is preceded by a consonant [w], when it changes to [uw]. The Old English words *hwā, twā, swāpen*, for instance, are represented in modern English by *who, two, swoop* (with [uw] instead of [oɑ]). Yet another development is exemplified in *ought* [ɔːt], which goes back to OE *āhte*, where the raising of [ɔː] to [oɑ] was inhibited by the following *h* (cf. *naught* from OE *nāht*). Similarly in French words where *ē*

---

1. Now poetical, the everyday word being *Träne*.
2. Similar changes affected the other voiceless plosives *p* and *k*.

was followed in the next syllable by an *i*, it changed to an [i] instead of [wa], e.g. *fēci > fis; prēsi > pris.*

Similarly with the High German consonant shift, the voiceless stops (*p, t, k*), medially between vowels and finally after a vowel, were not affricated but were changed to the corresponding voiceless fricatives. Examples are: *open/offen; sheep/Schaf; eat/essen; foot/ Fuss.* The examples, however, do not constitute exceptions to the law. The stipulations referring to their special conditions are part and parcel of the law, and a statement which omitted them would simply be incomplete and inaccurate; just as Boyle's Law concerning the relations of pressure and volume in gases would be incomplete without the stipulation as to constancy of temperature. Such a phonetic law admits of no exceptions; for after a considerable amount of controversy,[1] there seems no room for doubt that phonetic changes take place regularly. This principle may be formulated in the following way: when in one word of a language the sound *x* changes into *y*, it will be found that the sound *x* changes into *y* in every word in which it occurs *under the same conditions* in that language *as spoken at the time.* The italicized reservations are important and must now be discussed.

A sound change, for reasons that are as yet unclear, does not continue indefinitely but only operates for a limited time, and it affects only those words of the language which contain that particular sound *in the period during which the sound law is operating.* So when we assert the regularity of the Old English [ā] to [oɔ], it will be no valid objection to point to words like *father.* For at the time when the Old English [ā] started on its development to [oɔ], the word *father* did not contain this sound, but was pronounced *făder* (from OE *fæder*), so that it was not affected by the change under consideration. Actually the sound change exemplified in the development *făder > fāder* took place in the thirteenth century (*circa* 1250), while the first stage of the development [ā > oɔ], [ā > ɔ:], was completed about the year 1200. The temporal limitation of the sound law gives rise to a different type of apparent exception. In modern English words like *dame* (pronounced [deɪm]) a long *ā* has undergone a different change from that dis-

---

1. See below Chapter 12.

cussed above. This, however, does not invalidate the sound law in question. The change of OE $\bar{a}$ to [ɔː] was completed long before the fifteenth century and it ceased to operate. The word *dame* is of French origin, and it entered the language after that date, so it could not partake in the change. It was subsequently affected by the new change which began in the fifteenth century, when the long $\bar{a}$ was fronted to [ɛː] and eventually to [eɪ], as can be observed in words like *place, cage, trace*, which have the same origin.[1]

We must now proceed to the discussion of the second of the above italicized reservations. A sound law is limited not merely in time but in space as well. The people of different districts speak in different ways: that is to say, they have their own dialect. The dialect of Lancashire is different from that of Devonshire, and both differ from Lowland Scots. A sound law can only refer to a small linguistic group in which there exists for all practical purposes uniformity of speech. Thus each dialect will have its own peculiar set of sound laws. Words may be borrowed, however, by one group from another which has been affected by a different set of sound changes. In such a case the borrowed word will stand out because of its foreign aspect, apparently transgressing the laws of its host. Thus, although in English the word *whole*[2] from *hāl* (cf. German *heil*) is regular in its treatment of $\bar{a}$, *hale* does not conform to the rule that $\bar{a}$ becomes [oɒ]. This word, however, entered standard English in modern times from the northern dialects. These were unaffected by the change of $\bar{a}$ to [oɒ], which was confined to the southern half of England, but it partook of the change of $\bar{a} >$ [eɪ] which has just been discussed in the case of *dame*. Such dialect mixture[3] and inter-borrowing accounts for a great number of the doublets which seem to refute the sound law principle.

An obvious exception to the above law about the development of Old English $\bar{a}$ is offered by the pronunciation of *one* (OE *ān*, OS

---

1. *Fāder* was affected by this change, and it is from this form that the dialect *feyther* [feɪðə] has evolved. The received pronunciation owes its origin to the short-vowelled form contained in the analogical genitive *fădres*.

2. The spelling with initial *w* reflects a dialect pronunciation. *Whore* (OE *hōre*) is another such spelling.

3. For a fuller treatment of linguistic borrowing see Chapter 12.

ēn, ON *einn*, Goth. *ains*) as [wʌn]. According to the law we should expect [oɒn], as we actually have in *only, atone, alone*. The received pronunciation [wʌn] appears to be an intrusion from a western dialect. A similar development is to be seen in the pronunciation of *oak* and *oats* (OE *ātan*) as [wʌk] and [wʌts]. Dialect mixture also accounts for the discrepancy in the initial consonants of *fox* and *vixen*.

Sometimes the intruders come from further afield. Thus the following pairs of words, though derived ultimately from the same source, have come by different routes into the English language and have been subjected to different influences in their travels: *shirt, skirt; school, shoal; no, nay; ship, skiff*. Nearly all languages contain specimens of such dialect mixture. In German Low and High forms occur side by side: *Ecke* 'corner', *Egge* 'harrow'; *Waffe* 'weapon', *Wappen* 'coat-of-arms'; *Teich* 'pond', *Deich* 'dyke'; *sanft* 'gentle', *sachte* 'soft'. Latin contains two nouns from the verb *coquo* 'to cook'. One is *coquīna* 'kitchen', a native Latin word with the regular Latin sound treatment, while *popīna* 'cook shop', is a loan word from the Osco-Umbrian dialect group with the characteristic sound representation of that group, which replaces the q^w sound (labio-velar) by a labial, e.g. Oscan *pis* = Lat. *quis*. We see, then, that in discussing the history of any word it is essential to take into consideration the factors of time and space.

Up till now in our consideration of sound changes we have employed what is known as the historical method. The history of sounds in a given language has been elicited by comparing words from different texts at different periods from the earliest recorded state down to the present day. The task of the linguistic historian becomes more complicated in practice (though the method is fundamentally the same) when he has to deal with a group of related[1] languages, the parent form of which is not directly attested. Yet here, too, the sound law principle is no less clearly operative. If we suppose that a sound *x* existed in a parent language and that this sound changed regularly in three 'daughter' languages into *a, b* and *c* respectively (see Fig. 30), when the parent language is obliterated, the only fact to be observed will be that these three

---

1. The term 'relationship' was defined on p. 22.

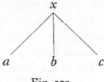

Fig. 30a.

languages L, L′, L″ contain a series of etymologically related words which are phonetically similar but not identical. There will be in fact a parallelism of sounds in this series of words. Thus if the parent language contained the words *pat, pot, pit,* and in one of its descendants the sound *P* is changed to *V*, in a second to *F* and in a third to *B*, after the extinction of the parent language, investigators will merely be able to observe the following correspondences in a series of words of related meaning:

L	L′	L″
Vat	*Fat*	*Bat*
Vot	*Fot*	*Bot*
Vit	*Fit*	*Bit*

Such a *parallelism* of arbitrary sound symbols could not be accidental any more than absolute *identity* would be (see Chapter 1). The fact of relationship thus being established, by comparing such sets of words we arrive at a formula which sums up the sound correspondences: $V = F = B$. It is obvious that this correspondence can be explained only by reference to a common source from which these related languages are derived. Thus we may postulate the sound *$*x$* of the parent language and say that this sound *$*x$* in every word in which it occurred under the same conditions changed in L into V, in L′ into F, and in L″ into B. This process can be repeated with every sound of the above words, and we should then arrive at a hypothetical reconstruction of the primitive words *$*xay$*, *$*xoy$* and *$*xiy$*. Nothing is known, however, with certainty of the actual nature of the sounds of this reconstructed parent language. In the case of far-going similarity of sound among widely diverse languages the probability would be that the sounds of the parent language approximated closely to the sounds of its descendants; but in a case like the above no assertion could be made about the character of the sound which became V, F and B respectively in the derived languages. It might have been any one of these sounds or something different again like *ph* or *bh*.

Some examples from actual languages may serve to elucidate this point. If we compare the above series of Old English *ā*-words with their modern German correspondents, e.g.

stone	Stein	loaf	Laib
oak	Eiche	oath	Eid
whole	heil	holy	heilig
home	Heim	token	Zeichen
	goat	Geiss	

we see that in all these cases an [oʊ] in modern English corresponds to the German diphthong [ai]. For the above-mentioned reasons we are compelled to explain this parallelism by reference to a common source. But from a study of German and English alone we could not say what this parent sound was. The comparison with other Germanic languages makes it likely that the sound was a diphthong [ai], since Old English stands alone among its sister languages in presenting a vowel [a:] in words with these phonemic correspondences.

GOTHIC	OLD NORSE	OLD SAXON	OLD ENGLISH
stains	steinn	stên	stān
	eik	êk	āc
hails	heill	hêl	hāl
haims	heimr	hêm	hām
gaits	geit	gêt	gāt
hlaifs	hleifr		hlāf
aiþs	eiðr	êth	āþ
taikns	teikn	têkan	tācen

In the Romance languages, again, we may observe a correspondence of the sounds [k], [tʃ], [ts], [s], [θ] in a series of related words:

SARDIN.	ITALIAN	ENGAD.	FRENCH	SPANISH
kentu	cento	cient	cent	ciento
kelu	cielo	cil	ciel	cielo
kerbu	cervo	cerf	cerf	cierbo
kera	cera	caira	cire	cera

In this case we are more fortunate since we have texts which attest the parent language—Latin. However, this does not provide a simple solution to the problem of the phonetic character of the parent sound, for it is only by complex deductions relating to the pronunciation of Latin that we know that the above words in all probability contained a /k/ sound: *centum, caelum, cervus, cera.*

The actual phonetic specification of the entities represented by the asterisked symbols is irrelevant to their essential character. What must be made clear is the logical nature of a 'reconstructed' sound attributed to the parent language. It is defined as that unknown phoneme which it is necessary to postulate in order to account for the observed phonemic parallelisms in words equated on the basis of sameness or similarity of meaning. In our fabricated example $*x$ simply sums up the correspondences $V = F = B$. It is merely a convenient symbolism for referring to observed phonemic parallelisms in a number of languages. These correspondences serve to define it. The symbol also serves another purpose. It functions as part of a kind of phonemic telephone exchange which enables us to put through calls from one language to another of the same family. If in etymology (see Chapter 13) we want to find possible relatives ('congeners') of a puzzling word, then we can connect up with the asterisked symbols and use the sound laws appropriate to the several members of the family to construct vocables of the corresponding pattern. If such vocables occur in the related languages, the texts are analysed to detect similarities of meaning.

In brief, the asterisked symbol is a theoretical construction which facilitates certain operations by the comparatist. Consequently it is not open to objections of a phonetic nature. Above the point was made that the phoneme is an abstraction devised to account for the observed sounds of speech. The asterisked symbol is at a stage further removed from reality. This postulated ancestral phoneme may be called a 'diaphoneme'. It does not claim to be a phonetic description of a sound uttered by Indo-Europeans.

The problem of the phonetic specification of the asterisked symbols and the operations which can be legitimately conducted with them arises in a still more controversial form when we project our entities back into epochs far removed from direct observation of speech and textual attestation of states of language. We may start with an example already used to establish the existence of a parent Indo-European language—the words for 'father': Latin *pater*, Greek *patér*, Sanskrit *pitár*, etc. (see p. 25). We start with the Germanic languages: OE (Old English) *fæder*, ON (Old Norse) *faðir*, OHG (Old High German) *fater*, Gothic *fadar*. All the words closely resemble one another and all have five phonemes in the same order. This implies that the successive mimetic processes (see p. 22) which have resulted in these parallel modes of social behaviour must be traceable back through successive communities to one ancestral community possessing a word of a pattern which, by regular but different processes of change, became the forms *fæder*, etc. in the historically attested languages. Let us symbolize this deduced form as *12345. By *1 is meant that diaphoneme which is postulated to account for the presence of the initial /f/ in related words. In the intervocalic position the correspondences are /d/, /t/ and /ð/. Here, too, an ancestral form must be postulated. But what was its phonetic nature? Was it one of these three alternatives or some other sound? The use of the numeral gets us out of the difficulty. Yet comparatists rightly prefer to symbolize the ancestral Common Germanic form as *fadēr*, using diaphonemic symbols instead of numerals because the numerals fail to indicate an important aspect of the observed facts. The phonemes of the compared languages are organized into a structure. They exhibit certain interrelationships, and these relationships must be reflected and easily recognizable in the symbols used to summarize the correspondences.

To pursue matters further, Germanic *fadēr* corresponds, as we saw, to Latin *pater*, etc. The validity of the equation is supported by a series of parallelisms in which an initial *p* in the related langu-

ages corresponds to Germanic f,[1] *piscis* = *fish*, *pecu* = Germ.
Vieh (English *fee* has undergone a change of meaning), etc. Since
the majority of the attested languages exhibit *p* we choose to
ascribe this phoneme to Indo-European.

The first vowel of *pater* brings us up against a difficult theoretical
problem. All languages show *a* except Sanskrit *pitár-*. The equation
is thus *a* = *i*. Now we cannot simply apply majority rule here and
postulate **a* and assume that this changed into *i* in Sanskrit. For
a series of word equations results in a number of different sets of
correspondences:

> *a* = *a* (Latin *ager* 'field', Greek *agrós*, Skt. *ajrás*)
> *i* = *i* (Greek *ímen* 'we go', Skt. *imás*)
> *a* = *i* (examples above).

To account for these three different equations scholars postulate
three different diaphonemes for Indo-European: **a*, **i* and **ə* (the
so-called shwa, a term taken from Hebrew grammar). It is apropos
of shwa that the structural approach to the diaphoneme becomes
important, for this sound cannot be isolated from its position in the
phonemic system of Indo-European.

It is often said that nineteenth-century linguists considered
sounds in isolation from their system. This is far from being the
truth, as may be seen from a consideration of certain systematic
features of the IE languages which go under the name of Ablaut
or vowel gradation. By Ablaut is meant the alternation of vowels to
serve morphological purposes such as is exemplified in the English
sing/sang/sung, *drive/drove/driven*. This phenomenon is found in
all Indo-European languages. It appears at its most transparent in
Greek. The Ablaut grades of the verb 'to leave' *leip-/loip-/lip-/*
offer a perfect parallel to our *drive/drove/driven*. The system is seen
at its simplest in roots which have a short vowel: *légō* 'I say',
lógos 'word' are examples of the *e*-grade and the *o*-grade (cf. Latin
tego 'I cover', *toga* 'a man's article of dress', a word cognate with
German *Dach* 'roof' and our word *thatch*). Besides these two
grades we have the zero grade in which the vowel disappears
altogether: *pet-* 'to fly', *pt-ésthai*, aorist infinitive, *pt-erón* 'feather'.

---

1. This is one item in a system of correspondences which are summed up in
'Grimm's Law' (see below).

To simplify the exposition we shall confine our remarks to the relationship between the *e*-grade and the zero grade.

The first point to be noticed is that whereas in a root of the pattern CVC (*pet-*) the zero grade is CC (*pt-*); in roots containing a diphthong (defined as vowel plus sonant), that is of the pattern CVSC, the zero grade has the form CSC. Such is the relation of *leip-* to *lip-*. Another example, containing this time a *u*-diphthong, is the Greek *peuth-* 'inquire, learn', with zero grade *puth-*. Similar relationships are observed in roots containing diphthongs in which the sonant second element is *m*, *n*, *r* and *l*. Syllabic sonants were postulated for Indo-European because of a puzzling series of correspondences which may be illustrated from the numerals 'seven', 'nine' and 'hundred':

Lat. sept*em*	Gk. hept*á*	Skt. sapt*á*	Goth. sib*un* < IE**septm̥*
nov*em*	enné(w)*a*	náv*a*	ni*un* < IE**newn̥*
ce*n*tum	hekat*ón*	śatám	hund < IE**kn̥tóm*

It was noticed that this equation was often to be observed in morphological positions where the zero grade was to be expected, that is parallel with examples like *lip-* and *puth-*. Thus in English, *drunk* represents the zero grade corresponding to the full grade *drink*. A disguised example is *numb*, which in fact is the past participle of the word *nim-* 'to take, seize' (cf. German *nehmen*). So it seemed reasonable to suppose that in Indo-European to an *e*-grade like *nem-* there corresponded a zero grade *nm-* and that in certain positions the *m* became syllabic (*m̥*) just like the *i* of *lip-*. This seemed not implausible phonetically because syllabic nasals are of frequent occurrence, for instance in examples like English *seven* [sɛvn̩]. This reason for approving is, of course, as irrelevant to the acceptance of the postulated diaphonemes as phonetic difficulty would be for their rejection. **m̥* is defined as that unknown IE phoneme which accounts for the equation *em* = *a* = *a* = *un*.

These sounds in the different languages show certain relationships with other members of the system, certain structural features, and these must be represented in an adequate symbolism. This demand is met by postulating the opposition **em/m̥*. Similarly we postulate **en/n̥*, *er/r̥*, *el/l̥* to account for alternations like OE *bindan/bunden*, *weorpan/wurden*, *helpan/hulpon*.

We may now take the next step, which similarly sites the shwa
*$ə$ in its structural position. Another type of the IE Ablaut
system is exemplified in Latin *stāre*/*stătus* (cf. Gk. *stā-*/*stătos*).
The corresponding form in Sanskrit shows an *ĭ*: *sthitás*. Here we
encounter the equation $a = ə = i$ which occurred in the words for
'father'. Consequently we can symbolize the IE Ablaut relations
as *$ā$/$ə$. On the basis of equations like *dō-num*/*dătus*, *fē-ci*/*făcio* we
can also postulate *$ō$/$ə$ and *$ē$/$ə$. Now this is untidy as a system, and
we propose to restate the symbolism so as to bring these skew Ablaut
relations into line with the others. There it was observed that we
could construct the *e*-grade simply by inserting the vowel *e in
the zero grade: *lip-*/*leip*, etc. This operation can be carried out on
the zero grades exhibiting shwa. If we follow the same patterns, we
should substitute *$eə$ for *$ē$, *$ā$ and *$ō$. However, we should
then have to state the law which derives these long vowels from
the original diphthongs, for it would be an offence against the
sound law principle if we postulated three different treatments of
only one original diphthong. We get round this difficulty by
writing *$eə_1 > ē$, *$eə_2 > ā$, and *$eə_3 > ō$. Analysis of the structural
relations thus forces us to postulate three sonants instead of one. At
the same time we are obliged to make certain inferences about their
phonetic effects, $ə_1$ lengthens a previous *e* but leaves its quality
unchanged; $ə_2$ lengthens a previous *e* and changes its quality to *a*;
$ə_3$ lengthens a previous *e* and changes its quality to *o*.

By these algebraic devices we can achieve a neat and simple
representation of the IE Ablaut relationships:

E	Zero
pet-	pt
leiq^w-[1]	liq^w-
bheudh-	bhudh-
nem-	nm-
gen-	gn-
derk-	drk-
pel-	pl-
dheə$_1$-	dhə$_1$-

---

1. *q^w represents the IE voiceless 'labio-velar' (see p. 61).

E   Zero

$ste\vartheta_2$- $st\vartheta_2$-

$de\vartheta_3$- $d\vartheta_3$-

There is a further bonus besides the achievement of a tidier symbolism to represent Ablaut relations. The German scholar K. Verner observed at the time when the sound law principle was being evolved that we must discover rules for apparent exceptions to the sound laws. Now the Sanskrit derivatives of the postulated zero grade *$st\vartheta_2tós$ is *sthitás*, which exhibits an unexplained aspiration of the *t* preceding *ϑ_2*. We can now account for this by ascribing another phonetic feature to *ϑ_2* besides its *a*-colouring: it aspirates the preceding *t*.

The most remarkable triumph of this structural analysis, which goes back to de Saussure (1879), came with the decipherment of Hittite in 1915. It was pointed out by the Polish scholar J. Kurylowicz that the postulated *ϑ* corresponded in many places to a Hittite phoneme which we transcribe as *ḫ*. Not only this, but where other IE languages like Latin and Greek have a root beginning with a vowel *a* or *o*, Hittite sometimes shows an *ḫ*. Examples are:

Lat. *ante* 'before'   Gk. *antí*   Hitt. *ḫanti*

os 'bone'   *os-téon*   *ḫastai*

The Hittite evidence lent support to the view previously expressed that the 'shwas' were in fact sounds produced in the larynx or pharynx (see p. 42). Hence the term 'laryngeal theory' applied to the analysis. Nowadays the symbols ϑ_1, ϑ_2 and ϑ_3 are commonly replaced by H_1, H_2, H_3.

The laryngeal theory made new word equations possible, and a new doctrine relating to the form of the typical IE root was put forward.[1] No IE root begins with a vowel but they are all of the form CVC. Where the attested forms appear to contradict this principle, this is due to disappearance of an initial *H*. Thus, instead of postulating a root *ed- to account for the equation English *eat*, Latin *edo*, Greek *ed*-, Sanskrit *admi*, Hittite *edmi*, we now write *H_1ed-. Similarly for *ag- 'drive, lead' (Lat. *ago*, Gk.

---

1. E. Benveniste, *Origines de la formation des noms*, Chapter IX.

ágō, Skt. *ájāmi*, etc.) and **od-* 'smell' (Lat. *odor*, Gk. *odmḗ*, etc.) we substitute $*H_2$ *eg-* and $*H_3$ *ed-* respectively. To these notations we append the sound laws $*H_1e->e-$, $*H_2e->a-$, $*H_3e->o-$.

While every Indo-European root is triliteral of the type CVC, to this root suffixes may be attached forming a 'base'. An example is **der-* 'wood, tree', which may be extended by the suffix *-w*. The base *der + w-* exhibits Ablaut gradation such that if the root is full, the suffix is zero (form I): **der + w*. If the root is zero, the suffix may be full (form II): **dr + ew*. Finally, both parts of the base may be zero (form III): **dr + w-*. From form I **der + w-* come Welsh *derwen* 'oak', Lithuanian *dervà* 'pinewood'; from form II **dr + ew-* are descended Gothic *triu*, English *tree*, which go back to Gmc. **trew-a-*. Finally to form III **dr + w-* are ascribed Skt. *dru-* 'wood', Albanian *dru* 'wood, tree', and Gk. *drŭs* 'oak'. From the sense 'oak', by a natural transference, the derivatives of this base came to be used in the meaning of 'firm, strong, healthy'. Of this we have an example in OE *trum* (cf. Skt. *druma-* 'tree'). In a similar sense, 'steadfast, trustworthy', we have the congeners of English *true*: OE *trēowe*, OS *triuwi*, Germ. *treu*, Gothic *triggws*, all from Gmc. **trew-wa-* and ultimately from IE **drew-wo-*, an adjectival derivative from form I.

A similar pattern of base forms is discernible in the words for 'knee':

I	II	III
*gen + w-	**gn + ew-*	**gn + w-*

From I come Lat. *genu*, Hitt. *genu*; from II Goth. *kniu*, OE *cnēo*, Engl. *knee*, from Gmc. **knew-a-*, going back to IE **gnew-o*. III appears in Gk. *gnú-petos* 'falling on the knee', *gnúx* 'kneeling', and elsewhere.

The Ablaut relations are obscured if either the root or the suffix contained a laryngeal. Thus the root **gen-* 'beget', with Ablaut grades *gen/gon/gn*, may be extended by the suffix-H_1. This base assumes the three forms

I	II	III
gen + H_1-	*gn + eH_1-*	*gn + H_1-*

From I come forms of the shape *gene-* (Gk. *genetḗr*); from II those with *gnē-* (Gk. *gnésios* 'genuine, legitimate'); and from III those with *gn-* (Gk. *neo-gn-ós* 'newly born').

The theory enables us to account neatly for the relationship between the English verbs *eke* (originally meaning 'increase') and *wax* (e.g. the moon 'waxing and waning'). The verbs are traceable to a root $*H_2ew-$, which can be extended by means of the suffix *-eg*. The theory of the base envisages the forms:

I	II	III
H_2ew+g-	H_2w+eg-	H_2w+g-

Form I will appear as $*aug$ since $H_2e > a$. This we have in Latin *augeo*, *augur*, etc., and in the Germanic words corresponding to Gothic *aukan*. The Germanic root *auk-* appears in OE in the past participle *ēacen* 'increased, strong, pregnant', and in the substantive *ēaca* 'increase'. The present-day verb *eke* in the phrase 'eke out' goes back to this OE form.

As for form II, Greek, besides the form *aux-*, has forms of the shape *awex-*. These are of the greatest interest since they derive from a form of the base extended by means of the morpheme *-s-*, which we also see in the Latin word *auxilium*. The theoretical base form is thus $*H_2w+eg+s-$. In the Greek prothetic vowel *a-* we have a reflection of the initial preconsonantal laryngeal. The Germanic forms which include English *wax* (OE *weaxan*) are traced to CGermc. $*waxs-$, IE $*H_2wogs-$, with *o*-grade of form II.

The explanation of the prothetic vowel in certain Greek forms like *awex-* is yet another bonus of the laryngeal theory. An obvious example is *onoma*, which corresponds to Latin *nōmen* and our own word *name*.

INTERNAL RECONSTRUCTION

The laryngeal theory may be taken as an illustration of what is known as internal reconstruction. In this method we use the pattern of facts observed in synchronic analysis of a language state to draw deductions about the genesis of the pattern. Thus in Latin the compound verbs corresponding to *cado* 'fall' show an *i* instead of an *a*: *in-cido*. The same pattern of facts is discernible elsewhere: e.g. *facio/inter-ficio*. These facts enable us to set up a rule about the treatment of medial short *a* at some time in the history of Latin. Another observation enables us to be more precise. The past participle *factus* of the simple verb appears in the compound as *interfectus*. This pattern of facts is repeated elsewhere, e.g. *aptus/ineptus*, *castus/incestus*. The two types of vowel change are linked to the type of syllable in which the vowels occur. In an open syllable such as *fa-*, the *a* changes to *i*, whereas the change of *a* to *e* took place in closed syllables, e.g. *fac-tus > (con)-fec-tus*.

In Greek internal reconstruction enables us to deduce an important sound law known as Grassmann's Law. The word for 'hair' shows a peculiar alternation of aspirated and unaspirated plosive consonants in its declension: nom. *thrix*, gen. *trikhós*. This alternation is observed elsewhere, as emerges clearly from the following tabulation:

thrík-s 'hair' (n.s.)	*trikh-ós* (g.s.)
thrép-sō 'I shall rear'	*tréph-ō* 'I rear'
hék-sō 'I shall have'	*ékh-ō* 'I have'

What is common in this pattern of facts is that the alternating consonant has the unaspirated form if the next syllable begins with an aspirated stop. The rule deduced (Grassmann's Law) is that we have to do with an instance of dissimilation (see pp. 63ff). If a syllable begins and ends with aspirated plosives or if successive syllables begin with such sounds, then the first consonant loses its aspiration. The rule is seen at its clearest in those places where reduplication of the root takes place, as in the formation of the perfect tense. Thus in the perfect stem of the verb *pheug-* 'flee' (cf. Lat. *fugio* with zero grade), we should expect **phe-pheug-*.[1] Instead we find *pe-pheug-*, with dissimilatory loss of the first aspiration.

The verb *ekh-* 'have' gives us a clue about the chronological stage at which Grassmann's Law operated. We have the following grades of Ablaut:

E	O	Zero
ékh- (*ō*)	*ókh-*(*os*)	*skh-* (aorist infinitive *skh-eîn*)

---

1. Actually the *o*-grade would be normal, but this is a complication irrelevant to the point at issue here.

As shown above, from the zero grade we can construct the original full grade *sekh-. Now an initial antevocalic s- in Greek becomes aspirated, as can easily be seen from the numerals 'six' and 'seven': héx and heptá from IE *s(w)eks and *septm̥. Thus *sekh- would first become *hekh-, which by Grassmann's Law yields the form actually found in Greek, ékhō 'I have'. The change of initial antevocalic s- to h- is one of the constitutive features of Greek. In fact, if criteria were being sought to determine the stage at which we speak of 'Greek' as opposed to 'Indo-European', then the aspiration of s- would rank high as a boundary mark. But Grassmann's Law could not operate in the verb *sekh- until this change had taken place. It follows then that Grassmann's Law must be cited chronologically within the history of Greek proper, even though a similar change took place in Sanskrit. This conclusion is supported by another example. Among the words relating to 'burial', the verb tháptō contrasts with the noun táphos 'tomb'. Again we observe the alternation of an aspirated and unaspirated consonant, the latter being positioned before an aspirated plosive at the onset of the following syllable. It appears that we must posit *tháptō and *tháphos. What remains to be explained is the form of the verbal stem. Briefly, this is assigned to a present tense stem in Indo-European formed by means of the morpheme -j-: *thaph-j-. In Greek the cluster -ph-j- became pt, with loss of the aspiration. Now, if Grassmann's Law had operated before this particular sound change took place, then *thaph- would have become taph-, and the 'yodization' (for this term see p. 65) would have produced the form *táptō 'I bury'. Since we have in fact thaptō, we must site Grassmann's Law after the process of 'yodization'. These examples will serve as an illustration not only of internal reconstruction but also of the way in which, in certain cases, the relative chronology of the sound laws can be determined.

CHANGES IN PHONEMIC STRUCTURE

So far we have considered isolated examples of sound changes. The question now arises how such changes affect the phonemic structure of the languages concerned, for as was explained in Chapter 4, the phonemes of a language serve to keep the vocables apart. A. Meillet expressed this basic principle in the phrase that 'langue' is a system 'où tout se tient' (where all parts support one another). That this is not so can be shown by numerous examples of phonemic convergence, that is where originally distinct phonemes merge. This produces puzzling distortions in the patterns of phonemic parallelisms from which we formulate the sound laws. We may revert to the example of parallelism exemplified in the English *oak*, German *Eiche*. Examples like *drive* [draɪv], German *treiben* [traibən] cut across this pattern. Other examples of this second patterning are *swine/Schwein*, *shine/scheinen*. The two different patterns of phonetic parallelism are due to the actions of different series of sound change which may be represented in the following tabulation, which leaves out a number of intermediate stages:

IE *ei	IE *oi
Gmc. ī	Gmc. *ai
Germ. [ai]	Germ. [ai]

The first stage of the change of [i:] towards the diphthong [ai] in present-day English took place in the period between Chaucer and Shakespeare. It forms part of the number of vowel changes which are collectively called 'The Great Vowel Shift' and provide a stock illustration of a change in phonemic structure. The changes are schematically represented in the following tabulations, which are an over-simplification of the complicated historical processes.

The first table shows the relation of the OE long vowels to those of ME, in the form of a vowel triangle (see p. 72) representing degrees of tongue raising towards front and back.

ī > ī	ȳ > ī	ū > ū
ē > ē		ō > ō
ǣ > ɛ̄		
	ā > ɔ̄	

The points to be observed are (1) the loss of the opposition between [ī] and [ȳ] and the empty slot created by the raising and backing of [ā]. This lowest position in the structure was filled *inter alia* by lengthening of OE *a* in certain cases (e.g. *nama > nāme*) and by the influx of Norman-French words like *dame* and *rage*. The 'Great Shift' thus produced the following system, the stages being Middle English (Chaucer), Early New English (Shakespeare) and Late New English.

$$(4)\ \bar{\imath} > \partial i > a\iota \qquad\qquad (7)\ \bar{u} > \partial u > a\omega$$
$$(3)\ \bar{e} > \bar{\imath} > ij \qquad\qquad (6)\ \bar{o} > \bar{u} > uw$$
$$(2)\ \bar{\varepsilon} > \bar{e} > ij \qquad (5)\ \bar{\jmath} > \bar{o} > o\omega$$
$$(1)\ \bar{a} > \bar{\varepsilon} > e\iota$$

Examples are:

(1) *name* (OE *nama*, CGmc. **namōn*), (2) *clean* (OE *clæne*, WGmc. **klainiz*), (3) *green* (OE *grēne*, CGmc. *grōnjaz*), (4) *time* (OE *tīma*), (5) *oak* (OE *āc*, CGmc. **aiks*), (6) *food* (OE *fōda* from **fōðon*), (7) *now* (OE *nŭ*). The overall tendency of the Great Vowel Shift was a step by step raising of the long vowels, each member of the system keeping its distance, the highest vowels becoming diphthongized.

GRIMM'S LAW

Another famous example of an overall change in a phonemic structure is summed up in Grimm's Law.[1] It relates to the changes in the Indo-European consonants which took place in Common Germanic. By observation of phonemic parallelisms among the related languages scholars have built the following picture of the Indo-European consonantal phonemes:

	Voiced Aspirated	Voiced	Voiceless
Labials	bh	b	p
Dentals	dh	d	t
Dorsals	gh	g	k
Labio-Velars	$g^w h$	g^w	q^w

---

1. The 'sound shift' (not called a 'law' by Grimm) was first formulated by Jakob Grimm in the second edition of his *Deutsche Grammatik* (1822), but the sound correspondences were first observed and exemplified by the Danish scholar Rasmus Rask in 1818.

In addition to this rich variety of plosive consonants,[1] the only fricative attributed to Indo-European is the sibilant *s. Grimm's Law is most simply formulated by saying that the members of the system as represented in the above table took a step to the right, those in the last column becoming the corresponding voiceless fricatives. Thus $bh > b$, $b > p$, $p > f$, $dh > d$, $d > t$, $t > \theta$; $gh > g$, $g > k$, $k > \chi$; $g^w h > g^w$, $g^w > q^w$, $q^w > \chi^w$. This is, however, an over-simplification,[2] and discussion of these changes and of the modification of the 'law' by 'Verner's Law' will be found in Appendix B. It may also be pointed out that Grassmann's Law relating to the dissimilation of the aspirates (see above) also accounts for certain apparent exceptions to Grimm's Law.

THE NATURE OF 'SOUND LAWS'

The use of the term sound law to denote such changes as have been discussed above is liable to lead to misconceptions as to the nature of these formulae. It must be emphasized that a sound law is not a law in the sense in which it is used in the physical sciences. Sound laws do not enable us to *predict* linguistic events as a law of chemistry predicts material change; nor are sound laws of universal application. Thus the sound [ā] in English changed at one time into [oɔ] and at another time into the diphthong [eɪ]. Neither of these changes could have been predicted, and the 'law' that refers to them is not a statement of causality; it is merely a record of what has occurred. In other words it is a formulation of accomplished change, formulation of which is possible because the change has occurred regularly. This is a basic tenet of historical linguistics—that where a sound change takes place, it is accomplished in all cases where the sound in question occurs.[3] This principle was enunciated in its most uncompromising form by Leskien, who declared that 'the sound laws act with blind necessity'. It acted as a salutary influence in stiffening philological methods at a time when sporadic changes were admitted freely

---

1. The voiceless aspirates, which are disputed, have been omitted.

2. The sounds developing from IE aspirates ascribed to Protogermanic were probably voiced fricatives: *v, *d, *g which later developed into b, d, g.

3. I.e. under the conditions stipulated by the law.

and etymology was delivered into the hands of the dilettante. It could not be upheld, however, in this downright form, and nowadays the 'inviolable' sound laws have become toned down to formulations of accomplished change.

THE CAUSES OF SOUND CHANGE

The causes of sound change are obscure.[1] Although many suggestions have been put forward, none is entirely satisfactory. In the first place the term 'sound change' is itself misleading. A sound once uttered is gone and lost forever. What we actually mean by sound change is that the members of a given speech community in the course of time come to pronounce a word [kuwl] instead of [kɔːl]. This means that they substitute a sound [uw] for a sound [ɔː], so that it would be more correct to speak of 'sound substitution' or 'replacement' than 'sound change'. Hence what is called a sound change is not a process in the external world independent of human action, but a change of habits by a group of speakers. The common formulation that 'languages change' also tends to obscure this essential fact. It is the reason for this change of habits that we now have to examine.

In seeking an explanation of sound replacement we must be clear what it is we are trying to explain. To this end precision must be given to the analysis and classification of sound changes. What the linguist in effect does is to contrast certain components of utterances (the phonemes) at different historical stages. But in thus tracing the history of the phonemes it is necessary to bear in mind the abstract nature of the phoneme. What corresponds to it in the utterance is a group of allophones (see p. 69), and it is these which must be the object of scrutiny by the historical linguist who seeks to describe the changing habits of utterance. Since the allophones are described in terms of features, either articulatory

---

1. For combinative changes due to purely phonetic reasons like economy of effort, influence of neighbouring sounds, etc., see Chapter 3. The changes discussed here are those spontaneous changes for which no reason can be detected from their immediate phonetic environment.

or acoustic, it follows that statements of change will also have featural specifications. An example of this is the statement that the IE voiced plosives became voiceless in Germanic. The articulatory features were grouped according to 'place' and 'manner' (see pp. 74ff), and we may classify sound changes accordingly. The rule just enunciated describes a change in the manner of articulation of the IE plosives. In this class comes also the change of the IE voiced aspirated plosives to voiceless fricatives (two features of 'manner'). 'Place' is involved in the change of the OE velar fricative to the labio-dental fricative in modern English: e.g. *ruh > rough*, where the spelling attests the survival of the old sound in Middle English.

The allophones of a given phoneme may all go their separate ways and be drawn into the orbit of other phonemes, so that the original phoneme is lost altogether. Such was the fate of the IE labio-velar consonants q^w, g^w, gh^w, in Greek. On the evidence of the Linear B texts (see p. 260) these phonemes survived until the end of the Mycenaean Bronze Age (roughly twelfth century B.C.). But when we next encounter Greek in the alphabetic script beginning in the eighth century B.C., we find that they are represented (in Attic) by dentals before front vowels, by labials before back vowels and consonants, and by dorsals in the neighbourhood

Fig. 30b.

of a *u*-sound.[1] Unquestionably, these later representatives, which belong to different phonemes of Classical Greek, originated in different positional allophones of the Mycenaean labio-velars, which subsequently were eliminated from the phoneme inventory of Greek.

Such phonemic split does not always result in the loss of the phonemes concerned. A case in point is the development of the allophones of the Latin dorsal plosives (see p. 74) in French and

---

1. This last change had taken place by Mycenaean times.

other Romance languages. One of the allophones retained its original character (*collum* > [ku]), although the others changed to *s* (*centum* > [sã]) or ʃ(*campus* > [ʃã]). An extreme case of phonemic splitting is offered by the treatment of West Germanic *a* in Old English.[1] In different conditions it appears variously as /æ/ (*dæʒ, daʒas* n. pl. 'day'), /ɔ/ (*noma* 'name'), /ea/ (*heard*, Germ. *hart*, NE *hard*), /ō/ (*ʒōs*, from **gans* with loss of *n* and compensatory lengthening of the vowel, which also changed its quality, NE *goose*; *tooth* is another example of this change, from W Gmc **tanþ-*); /e/ (*bed(d)*, cf. Goth. *badi* from Gmc **baðjam*).

The last example illustrates the phenomenon known as Umlaut, which should be carefully distinguished from Ablaut (see above). Umlaut is the name given to a common form of assimilation in which a vowel was fronted under the influence of an /i/ or /j/ in the following syllable. The modern English irregular plurals like *geese, mice*, etc., are due to the umlauting of the root vowel under the influence of the plural ending **-iz* (e.g. **mūsiz* > OE *mȳs*). Another such example is the modern word *guest*, which has a more complicated history. It goes back to an Old Norse *gestr*, which superseded the pure OE form, both going back to CGmc **ʒastiz*, which corresponds to IE **ghostis*, cf. Latin *hostis*. An example showing the influence of a following /j/ is seen in the causative form of the verb *fall*, **falljan* > *fell*.

Sometimes sound developments lead to the emergence of a new phoneme. A stock example is the English velar nasal /ŋ/. Originally this was an allophone of the /n/ phoneme before velar stops; but when the final /g/ was lost in words like *rung* (OE *hrung*), the phonemic contrast with *run* was carried by the final /ŋ/. This accounts for the limited distribution of this phoneme in modern English. Above a device was suggested for eliminating it from the inventory of English phonemes (see p. 72). Similar is the case of a comparatively recent phoneme, the voiced fricative /ʒ/, which came into being as the result of the palatalization of /z/ and the importation of French words containing this sound. This, too, is of limited distribution, and it is open to the describer to eliminate it from the inventory by regarding it as a cluster.

---

1. See M. Lehnert, *Altenglisches Elementarbuch*, p. 51.

Allophonic changes which are due to the influence of neighbouring sounds are collectively known as conditioned sound changes, or
combinative changes. Opposed to these are the unconditioned
changes in which all instances of the phoneme show a uniform
change. A good example of such a change is the reduction of the
IE short vowels $e/o/a/$ to a in Indo-Iranian (see Appendix B, p.
383).

Once the various sound changes have been classified and given
modern phonemic descriptions, the question of the causation may
be approached. It may be said at the outset that nothing very
plausible has been put forward and that suggestions tend to be
speculative. Why should the Greeks of the Iron Age have abandoned the pronunciation of the labio-velars with which their
Bronze Age forerunners experienced apparently little difficulty?
In trying to find an answer to such particular questions and to the
universal fact of sound drift in language some scholars stress the
difficulty that the child finds in learning its native language. Its
imitation of its parents and the persons of its environment is
imperfect, and in the course of generations the accumulation of
such slight imperceptible changes results in the profound modifications which the historical study of language brings to light. It has
been suggested that it is in times of war and turbulence, when
parents cannot devote much time to their children's education,
that languages undergo the most rapid changes. It might be further
pointed out that speech is in its essence the reproduction of a
pattern of sounds. With this we may contrast the process of copying a picture. In doing this we can constantly refer to the original.
In reproducing sounds, however, which once produced are gone
for ever, we have to rely entirely on the auditory memory, so that
speech actually involves a copying of copies. Memory being
imperfect, this leads to a continuous process of slight modifications which has been aptly called 'linguistic drift'. It has not been
shown conclusively, however, that the pronunciation of an individual varies after his speech habits have been formed in childhood,
exception being made, of course, for those individuals who change
their place of domicile, or who for reasons of snobbery or policy
deliberately attempt to acquire the speech habit of a different
social class. Moreover, such arguments, even if admitted, would

explain the general fact of 'drift' and not the particular direction and results of the changes. Why did the Romans preserve *quid* (*$q^w id$) and the Greeks change it to *ti*?

More attractive is the thesis that mixture of peoples is a prime cause of sound change. Throughout history there is evidence of migration, wars and conquest resulting in a mixture of differently speaking populations. The Romans conquered Gaul, and Latin superseded Celtic as the language of that country. We may be sure, it is argued, that the conquered Celts, even if they adopted the Latin language, preserved the speech habits of their native tongue; that they in fact spoke Latin with a Celtic accent. It has been suggested that the fronting of the [u] sound to [y] in French is due to Celtic influence. Plausibility is lent to this theory by the fact that the same change occurs in Celtic languages like Welsh, and in those Germanic dialects which were subject to Celtic influence.[1] A similar explanation has been cogently urged in the case of those profound changes of the Indo-European consonants that took place in Germanic (see Appendix B for details). These changes have been attributed to a peculiarity of the pre-Indo-European peoples on which the Germanic-speaking tribes impinged and imposed themselves. Similar changes occur in Celtic, where *p* becomes *h*, in Armenian, in Latin dialects, and in Spanish. Scholars have assumed the influence of a pre-Indo-European substratum to explain all these widely scattered phenomena. It is, however, highly improbable that a uniform language or languages of similar phonetic characteristics should have extended over so wide an area, and it ignores the fact that other Indo-European speakers settled in the intervening areas without being affected by these changes.[2] Most probably, the similar changes in these languages must be explained each by its own

---

1. It should be noted, however, that the change of *u* to *y* does not occur in all Celtic languages, and that it probably does not go back as far as Gaulish.

2. It is possible that Grimm's Law operated in a smaller area than appears, since after the first two of the above changes the Germans expanded south and west. Moreover, if mixture of peoples is a potent cause of speech change, it is strange that Finnish (where Finns, Swedes and Russians have constantly mixed) is so conservative, while Norwegian, comparatively isolated, changed even more rapidly than English.

special circumstances. After all, the change of voiced consonants to voiceless occurred a second time (in the High German dialects) without any admixture of foreign peoples. Still more cogently, the change of the labio-velars in Greek occurred long after the establishment of the Greeks in the Balkan peninsula, whether the date of the invasion is fixed at 1900 B.C., 1600 B.C. or 1300 B.C.

Another theory put forward distinguishes between the origin of a sound change and its spread. Its sponsors point out that no two individual members of a speech community speak exactly alike. The very difference in the physical structure of the vocal organs gives each person his distinctive voice and his own peculiar pronunciation. But apart from this consideration there are other causes of individual difference which are psychological rather than physical. These are the favourite words and expressions which characterize individual speakers. Further, within a speech community we find differences which are based on distinctions of class and occupation. Thus various craftsmen and handiworkers have vocabularies which are unintelligible to the layman.[1] A bargee speaks differently from a student, and a professor differently from a charwoman. Thus we see that the appearance of unity in a language even at one particular period is illusory. A speech community is comprised of members each of whom possesses his own peculiar dialect.[2] Owing to class distinctions or personal ability, certain members of the community become objects of respect and admiration, and their habits of clothing and speech, etc., are imitated by their admirers. In this way mannerisms and even defects of speech on the part of a leading personality may become a norm and by imitation may affect the speech of a whole community. A later chapter will show that speech changes do actually spread out gradually from a centre like waves.

More recently scholars have approached the problem of sound change from the structural point of view. The most thoroughgoing attempt has been made by the French scholar A. Martinet.[3] He

---

1. See below Chapters 12 and 14.
2. The speech of a single individual is called an 'idiolect'. On this see Chapter 12.
3. *Économie des changements phonétiques*, 1955.

lays stress on certain fundamental factors of the speech act. A speaker seeks to express himself and communicates with his hearers by means of utterances. His primary concern is therefore to make himself clearly understood. On the level of sound this urge will tend to secure phonemic systems of maximal clarity. Complementary to this is another human characteristic, namely the tendency to secure results with as little expenditure of effort as possible (the principle of 'economy of effort'). In the case of speech this means the tendency towards 'least effort' in the employment of the vocal organs. These tendencies work themselves out in various ways. Thus in a vocalic system with three degrees of opening the intermediate vowel /e/ will tend to station itself at the acoustic middle point between low /a/ and high /i/. In this way maximum 'equilibrium' of the system is achieved. As for economy of effort (and memory), the functional load in different phonemes will have implications for their history. A phoneme which contributes little to the generation of utterances will tend to be eliminated. Such is the fate threatening the phoneme /œ̃/ in French which is yielding up its small territory to /ɛ̃/. Further, if the system is such that all its members provide mutual support, a change in the performance of one may well affect its neighbours, which must make compensatory changes in order to preserve their distinctiveness. Yet despite the sophistication of the techniques employed and the often illuminating observations of details, we find that little or nothing has been contributed to such simple questions as why the Mycenaean labio-velars split in Attic-Ionic into *p* and *t* but evolved to *p* in the Aeolic dialects. Why did *bh* remain unchanged in Sanskrit, change to *b* in Germanic and to *f/b* in Latin? There are further fundamental objections. If throughout human history there has been this effort to achieve integration and equilibrium in the system and to achieve clarity by least effort, why it is that stability and changelessness have not been achieved long since?

On the contrary, what we observe is the eternal instability of language, which is the basic empirical principle of historical linguistics. As for the clarity and least effort, did the Greeks of the Classical period ask questions more or less distinctly by using *ti* rather than *qʷi*? And if the Mycenaeans made less effort by eliminating the final consonant of IE *$q^w id$, was it because they were more efficient speakers than the Romans who a thousand or more years later still said *quid*, leaving it to their descendants in France and Italy to catch up with Greek achievement with their *que* and *che*? It is fair to add that Martinet himself insists on the limitations of his approach and the partial nature of his proposed explanations. He writes: 'At every moment the honest diachronist will have to confess his ignorance, his incapability of finding an explanation of this or that feature, positive or negative, of the events he is studying.' Martinet's work, in fact, is concerned chiefly not with establishing the causes of upsets in a theoretically perfect phonological system but with 'what happens within such systems once disequilibrium has been brought about'.

The above suggested reasons for sound change, it must be insisted, are all mere hypotheses. It is probable that there is no single cause of sound change, and all the factors we have mentioned may have played their part at one time or another. It must be pointed out, however, that our ignorance of the causes of sound change does not invalidate the sound laws. They are, as we have seen, merely formulations of observed fact, of sets of 'correspondences' or 'phonemic parallelisms'. In the same way zoology, from its morphological studies, has established a structure of evolutionary stages which is completely convincing. Yet the reasons given for changes such as the development of the horse's hoof are no more than hypotheses, the acceptance or rejection of which does not affect the main tenets or conclusions of the science. In so far the failure to discover the actual causes of sound change is irrelevant to the validity of the sound laws themselves; nor does it prevent their application to linguistic facts or their employment in processes of linguistic deduction.

10

Interaction of Form and Function

So far our attention has been concentrated on the external side of language. The physical nature of the sound symbol has been examined in all its aspects and an attempt has been made to discover the laws of change. This was the attitude that characterized the early history of our science. Until the middle of the last century linguistics had been dominated by concepts derived from the natural and the biological sciences. Language had been conceived as an organism, as a plant that grows and develops according to its own laws. This is, however, fundamentally false; for it cannot be too often insisted that languages are nothing more than noises which human beings make to serve particular ends. They cannot exist in separation from the speaker, and all the changes and modifications that are observed in languages must be conceived and explained as changes on the part of the speaker. So although linguists of that early period strove to establish laws as rigid as those of the natural sciences, they were thwarted by the existence of numerous apparent exceptions. But about 1875 a new group of linguists in Germany, known as the Young Grammarians,[1] began to criticize this concept of language. They pointed out that language is not merely sound but sense as well, and that our approach should be more akin to that of the psychologist than that of the natural scientist. In actual speech sounds do not occur in

---

1. Among the leading lights were A. Leskien, K. Brugmann and H. Osthoff.

isolation but in rhythmical groups; as words correlated or associated with certain mental contents which we call their meaning. Furthermore, these linguistic symbols are not present in the speaker's mind as a mere aggregate of unrelated facts. By a tendency inherent in the human mind they tend to gather in groups, the members of which, for obscure reasons, are linked together by a bond of association. The members of such an associational linguistic group tend to become similar in form, and any force which tends to disintegrate the groups and destroy the uniformity is resisted by the combined strength of all the constituents. This may be illustrated by the history of the declension of a noun or the conjugation of a verb; for such series of forms are among the closest-knit linguistic groups.

In early Latin, for instance, the word for 'tree' has the following declension: *arbōs*, *arbŏsem*, *arbŏses*, *arbŏsei*, etc. The unity of the concept finds its counterpart in the unity of the word stem. At a later period, however, an intervocalic -*s*- was changed into -*r*- so that the declension of the word now appeared as *arbōs*, *arbŏrem*, *arbŏris*, etc., the stem in the nominative being different from the other cases. The unity of the group is destroyed, but it tends to be restored: in classical Latin the nominative stem *arbor* is identical with that of the other cases. But here the -*r* is not, as in the other cases, the regular phonetic product of an intervocalic -*s*-. The causation is in this case different. Here a psychological force has come into play; for it was on the grounds of its functional connexion with *arborem*, etc., that the form *arbōs* was changed into *arbor*. The meaning of the word plays a decisive part. Form is affected by function. This tendency towards uniformity in a group of closely associated word forms, like a noun declension or the conjugation of a verb, is called 'levelling'. Some common examples from English will illustrate this point. The adjective *préferable* is often accented on the second syllable owing to its association with the verb *prefér* from which it is derived. Similarly *maintain* in popular usage makes a noun *maintainance* (for the 'irregular' *maintenance*), while the noun *nation* makes an adjective *national* with the first syllable pronounced as in the noun: [neɪʃənəl]. Levelling is a powerful creative and preservative force in all languages. In certain dialects of German, for instance, it has been responsible for the disappearance of the Umlaut forms of the verbs, forms like *er lauft, er tragt* replacing the standard *er läuft, er trägt*.

Thus far the examples have been straightforward and the theory simple. It cannot be denied that the various forms of a verbal conjugation are closely associated with one another. The same forces, however, are active outside this narrow range. For words that are related in meaning are also exposed to associational interference and tend to become similar in form. A case in point is the word *howitzer*. In the seventeenth century this replaced the form *howitz*, which was a borrowing from German *Haubitz*, a word which in its turn had come into German from the Czech *houfnice* 'stone sling, catapult' during the Hussite wars. The added suffix may owe its origin to the association of the word with *mortar*. French, too, borrowed the German word in the form *obus*, to which the suffix *-ier* was later added—*obusier*. Another instructive example of semantic interference is provided by the abstract nouns of spatial extent in English. It will be seen that the words *length, depth, breadth, width* form a closely knit functional group with a well-defined morphological characteristic: the ending *-th*. One word, however, that belongs functionally to this group stands apart: *height*. It is not surprising to find that this word in uneducated speech assumes a form which brings it into alignment with the group with which it is functionally connected: *heighth*.[1] Similarly the reflexive pronouns *myself, yourself, herself* are for the modern speaker compounded of the possessive adjective and the word *self*. Only *himself* and *themselves* are different. In some forms of speech unity is achieved, and they appear as *hisself* and *theirselves*. Again, from the adjective *low* we make the verb *lower*. Unfortunately the adjective *high* has no equivalent verb formation and the purist has to be content with the verb *raise*. The English schoolboy, however, sees no harm in 'highering' the saddle of his bicycle on the model of *low, lower*. It is unfortunate that this otherwise excellent addition to the language collides with *hire*.

---

1. This restores the original form of the suffix: OE *hēhþu*, Goth. *hauhiþa*. The standard form is of northern origin and is due to the dissimilation of *hþ* to *-ht*. Milton uses *highth*.

In vulgar Latin, too, the word *gravis* 'heavy' was changed to *grevis* on the model of its opposite, *levis*. It should be noted in passing that opposites form close associational groups. This explains the presence of the internal *-n-* in the French word *rendre* from the Latin *reddere*. It is due to the influence of its antonym *prendre* (Lat. *prendere* from *prehendere*). The words of relationship in English provide a further instance of the rapprochement of semantically related words. *Father*, *mother* and *brother* form a group whose functional (semantic) unity is mirrored in their phonetic similarity. But this was not so at an earlier period of the language; OE *fæder*, *mōdor*, *brōþor*, Chaucer *fader*, *moder*, *brother*; cf. German *Vater*, *Mutter*, *Bruder*. These are derived from Indo-European forms **pətér-*, **mātér-*, **bhráter-* respectively. The different development of the medial **-t-* in Germanic to *ð* and *þ* is due to the position of the accent in the parent language, which is mirrored faithfully in the corresponding Sanskrit words *pitár-*, *mātár-*, *bhrátar-*. By Verner's Law (see Appendix B) these became in Germanic **fader*, **mōðer*, **brōþer*, a state of affairs which is reflected in the above Germanic forms. Modern standard English, however, has levelled these related words and given them a similar form. But it is interesting to note that the regular forms *fader*, *mudder*, *brother* are still spoken in certain dialects of the North-West, for example in Cumberland.

Words that occur together also tend to increase their resemblance. Thus the word *woof* in everyday English occurs solely in the phrase the *warp and woof*, few people having any very precise idea of what it means. *Warp* is the name for the threads extended lengthwise in the loom, and it is connected with the German word *werfen* 'throw'. The *woof* is the name for the threads crossing the *warp* at right angles. It goes back to the OE *ōwef*, which is derived from *wefan* 'weave'. In Middle English *oof* became *woof* because of its close association with *warp*.

Numerals, too, exert often a mutual influence. In Latin the form *septuāginta* was made on the model of an extinct **octuaginta*, just as Vulgar Greek presents *hebdoēkonta* for *hebdomēkonta* 'seventy' and *odomēkonta*, on the other hand, for *ogdoēkonta* 'eighty'. Similarly in the Viennese dialect of German one hears not *elf*, *zwoelf*, but *oelf*, *zwoelf* 'eleven, twelve'. For Latin a study of the

Indo-European parallels would lead us to expect the series *septem, *noven, decem*. *Noven*, however, was subjected to group influence and appears as *novem*. In Greek the word for 'eight' *oktṓ* has dialect forms *hoktṓ* and *optṓ*, these showing in different ways the influence of the word for 'seven' *heptá*. This influence shows itself also in the occasional aspiration of *hennéa* 'nine' for regular *ennea*. In Old Church Slavonic the word for nine *devętĭ* has an initial *d* for *n* because of the influence of *desętĭ* 'ten'. Further, in English the regular phonetic products of *two-pence, three-pence* would be [tʌpəns] and [θɹɪpəns]. The latter form is, however, frequently modified to [θɹʌpəns].

Handicraft offers another example of the formal assimilation of words of similar meaning. The earlier form was *handcraft*, in which an *-i-* was inserted on the model of *handiwork*. The latter goes back to OE *handġeweorc*, a compound of *hand* and *ġeweorc*, a collective formation based on *weorc* 'work'. The prefix *ġe-* developed to *y* and *i*. The word was later (sixteenth century) analysed as *handy + work*, and from this a new adjective *handy* 'manual' was extracted.

Experiments have shown that words are associated not merely on grounds of meaning but also because of mere similarity of sound, so that an accidental phonetic resemblance will often induce words to follow parallel lines of development. The jocular past participle *thunk* of to *think* on the lines of the verb *sink, sunk* is an instance of a process that is richly creative in language. In the strong conjugation of English *wear* (*wore, worn*) we have a case in point. In OE *werian* had *werede* and *wered* as preterite and past participle respectively. The modern forms owe their origin to the influence of *tear*, etc.

From the dialects a considerable number of such analogical formations are quoted: *oblige/obloge, reap/rope, arrive/arrove, squeeze/squoze, fetch/fotch, sweat/swot*, etc. A complex example of such remodelling on the pattern of another verb is the verb *speak*. The OE form was *sprecan* (cf. German *sprechen*), which was superseded by *specan*. The preterite was *spæc* (which gave rise to the archaic *spake*) and the past participle *gespecen*. This cannot be the ancestor of our form *spoken*. This modern form is due to the fact that *specan* came under the influence of *brecan* 'break', past participle *brocen*. The analogical form *spoken* is attested as early as the thirteenth century.

This is paralleled in German by the verb *scheinen*, a strong verb like the English *shine*. It often forms a weak past tense *scheinte* on the model of verbs like *weinen*, with which it rhymes. In the same way a German child might still make a past tense *frug*[1] from *fragen* on the analogy of *tragen, trug: fragen, frug*. But the influence of *sagen, sagte*, which is closely related in sense, has proved stronger. We are also informed by the eminent Danish scholar, O. Jespersen, that his little son defended a similar formation *nak* (from *nikker*) instead of *nikkede*, thus: *stikker: stak, nikker: nak*.

Most scholars admit the existence and significance of these associational groups in linguistic development. They point, however, to a further decisive factor in producing change. An analogy is in its essence the replacement of an accepted form by a new form. We are concerned here with a productive and creative activity on the part of the speaker, whereas normally speaking involves the reproduction of inherited speech forms.[2] The immediate cause of such a new formation lies in the momentary or permanent embarrassment of the speaker. A child who says *throwed* may never have heard the accepted form; alternatively it may be merely a failure of memory on his part. But what concerns the linguist is how he goes to work in the creation of his new form. We must try to ascertain what forces are at work in its production. This, and this alone, constitutes a satisfactory explanation of analogy. We must, in other words, try to discover the nature of the groupings which are effective in analogical formations.

What are the associations which are likely to be effective in influencing the choice and form of linguistic symbols by a speaker? In the first place, the most powerful force will be extended by the thoughts uppermost in the speaker's mind. These are what he has just said and is going to say, in our terminology, the context. Scholars have called attention to the importance of the context in the genesis of new analogical creations. In vulgar Latin *senātus*

---

1. *Fragen* was a weak verb in OHG. The preterite *frug* is heard in dialect use.

2. That is, of course, as far as morphology is concerned.

often forms a genitive *senātī* (for *senātūs*). It has with great plausibility been suggested that this form owes its existence to the
continual employment of the word in the phrase *senātus populusque
Rōmānus* the correct genitive of which is *senātūs populīque Rōmānī*.
Similarly *illui*, the late Latin dative of *ille* (whence French *lui*),
originated in its constant use as the antecedent of the interrogative
cui.

In English the nursery phrase *teeny weeny* provides an example
of the reciprocal approximation of two words in a frequent phrase.
We should expect *tiny wee*; but *wee*[1] adopted the ending of its
companion and *tiny* has changed its vowel. Such rhyming groups
are a frequent phenomenon: *helter-skelter*, *pell-mell*, *hugger-mugger*.
The last is traced to ME *hoder* 'huddle, wrap up' and ME *mokere*
'hoard'. Constant association and similarity of meaning has led to
formal assimilation in the pair (1) *morning* and (2) *evening*. (1) goes
back to OE *morgen*, which developed to *morn*; (2) derives from
ǣfnung, a noun from the verb *ǣfnian* 'grow towards night'. The
extension of *morn* to *morning* on the pattern of *evening* is dated to
the thirteenth century.

We have so far been able to distinguish three main types of
analogical action: contextual influence, association by meaning,
and association by sound. There are, however, cases which cannot
be explained in any of these ways. When a child makes a plural
sheeps, it does so on the model of words like *cows*, *dogs*, *pigs*. The
process can be represented by a proportion, e.g.

$$\text{dog:dogs::cow:cows::sheep:}x$$
$$x = \text{sheeps}$$

This formulation was first made by the German philologist
Hermann Paul, and it is called after him 'Paul's Proportion
Formula'. It has for long remained the classical explanation of
analogical formations. It may be applied indeed to many of the
above cases which we have explained without its aid, e.g.

$$\text{low:lower::high:}x \therefore x = \text{higher}$$

---

1. *Wee* was originally a substantive going back to the Anglian form *wēg*
'weight'. It was chiefly used in the phrase *a little wee* 'a small quantity'. By
misinterpretation it came to be used as an adjective.

It has, however, been attacked in recent years. Much of this criticism might have been avoided if the earlier writers had been more careful in their choice of examples. Thus Paul in his treatment of the vulgar Latin genitive *senātī* explained it by the proportion

$$animus: animi:: senātus: x$$

But in this proportion the whole crux of the matter lies in the ':: '. It assumes quite unjustifiably an intimate connexion in the mind of the speaker between the two arms of the proportion. A critic might well ask why the word *animus* should occur to a speaker who is going to talk of *senātus*. But it is obvious that Paul did not mean his formula to be taken literally. He regarded *animus* merely as a specimen of the second declension.[1] In other words, he implied that *senātī* is one instance of the action of the second declension on the fourth.

It seems, however, certain that the naive, grammatically untrained, speaker is unconscious of declensional types, and that these are mere grammatical abstractions. This will be realized if we contrast the natural acquisition of a language by a native speaker. We learn Latin and Greek grammatically. That is, the facts of the language are presented to us in an orderly, systematic way. We see the declensions ordered and set out in neat rows; the accusative follows the nominative, the genitive the accusative, and so on. We note that the genitive ends variously in *-ae, -ārum, -ī, -ōrum*, etc. The native speaker, on the other hand, picks his language up in the course of his everyday life. Innumerable phrases are learnt by heart as they occur, with no order or system. The Roman child's first experience of the word for 'war' may have been in the genitive plural and quite a long time may have elapsed before the word *bellum* was heard. Nor would such a speaker be conscious of the functional equivalence of *mensae, reginārum, dominī, bellōrum, nāvium, jūdicis, senum, senātūs* as one author suggests.[2] It will now be evident that the grammatical grouping 'second declension' is a linguist's construct and that it cannot be endowed as an

---

1. So Hermann, *Lautgesetz and Analogie*, 1931.
2. The very term 'genitive', of course, denotes a complex set of syntactical relationships; there is no unity either of form or of function.

entity with a psychological force capable of modifying words of a different type.

Yet another part of the old theory has become dubious on closer inspection. It was supposed that the nouns of the second declension overpowered and ousted those of the fourth because they were superior in numbers. But it has been pointed out that in some cases the reverse process has taken place, and that nouns like *fāgus* 'beech', are occasionally inflected like those of the fourth declension. Moreover, how could we explain the extraordinary tenacity of the strong verbs in English and German in the face of the immensely superior numbers of the so-called weak verbs? The truth is that military and democratic metaphors have little relevance to linguistic processes. The tenacity of a form depends not so much on the numbers of its 'supporters' as on the frequency with which it is used. The use of the word *senātus* fifty times has greater preservative force than the existence of fifty rare words of the second declension. It is impressed more indelibly on the speaker's memory. We must therefore replace the old 'lexico-graphical frequency' by a new concept—'density of usage'.

C. F. Hockett[1] points out that the verbs which preserve their 'irregularity' have a much higher frequency in modern English texts than those which have gone over to the regular 'weak' conjugation. An example is *help*, which originally had the preterite *halp*, a form which survived until the fifteenth century. It was then 'levelled' to *holp* under the influence of the past participle *holpen*. The analogical form *helped* appeared as early as the thir-teenth century. This was a northern form which found its way into Standard English.

In spite of these criticisms the proportion formula is still indispensable to philological theory, for many analogies can be only explained with its help. Thus in ancient Greek the second person of the verb is distinguished from the third person by the addition of an -*s*.

E.g. *légei*   'he says'   *êlthe*   'he came'
       légei-s 'you say'   *êlthe-s*   'you came'

The corresponding forms of the imperative, however, are second person *elthé*, third person *elthétō*. In the Cyprian dialect a remarkable form of the second person singular of the aorist imperative is attested: *elthétō-s* 'come' instead of the normal *elthé*. This can only be explained by the proportion formula:

e.g.   êlthe:êlthe-s :: elthétō:x

A formula alone is, however, merely an empty schema, and it offers no real explanation unless we can interpret it in terms of speaker mentality; for, as we saw above, a 'linguistic change' is always a change on the part of the speaker. What process does the above formula represent? How does the speaker come to attach a definite 'you'-meaning to the addition of the sound -*s* to the third person singular? The point to be determined is whether the speaker does, consciously or unconsciously, analyse words into parts as the grammarian does and endow each part with meaning. For instance, in the group of words *give, giver, gift*, does the speaker abstract the constant element *giv-*, which is for him charged with the meaning of the whole sphere of giving? When *giver* is compared with words like *buyer, doer, killer*, etc., does he become aware of an element -*er* with the value 'agent'? This would explain why the speaker can construct from the verb *sell* the agent noun *seller*, even if he was previously unaware that this word exists. An examination of several phenomena in English will show quite clearly that the native speaker is in many cases aware of the existence and value of the word-fragments (monemes) into which grammatical analysis dissolves words. A child feels that *sheep* and *feet* are not plurals, and it pluralizes them by the addition of an -*s*: *sheeps, feets*. But this feeling is not confined to children. Words like *Chinese, Maltese*, etc., are also felt as plurals owing to the final -*s*, and from these vulgar singular nouns *Chinee, Maltee* have been created. Similarly *peas* was originally a singular (as it is in *pease-pudding*), while *cherry* has also been singularized from an Anglo-Norman form *cherise* corresponding to the French *cérise*. On the other hand the word *riches* (from *richesse*) and *alms*[1] now

---

1. This goes back to the Greek *eleēmosynē* 'compassionateness' which, appearing in OE as *ælmysse*, developed to ME *almes* and later to *alms*.

take plural verbs, although they were really singular. Another example of the same kind is *eaves*. This comes from a Germanic derivative of **oƀ-* 'over', which is reflected in Gothic *ubizwa* and OE *efes*.

An example of a double plural on the lines of the child's '*feets*' is provided by the word *breeches*. This comes from an OE word found only in the plural *brēċ*. Because it lacked the distinctive plural ending, in modern English this has become *breeches*. The word *book*, on the other hand, (OE *bōc, bēċ*), the regular plural of which would be **beech* in modern English, has made a new plural *books*, just as *cows*, *foes*, *eyes* have banished *kine*, *foen*, *eyen* from the standard language. The weak past tenses in English provide another instance which shows how in the speaker's consciousness speech elements become charged with a specific meaning. Children constantly coin forms like *lighted*, *seed*, *brokened*, showing that they feel that a final *-d* is the mark of the past passive participle. Such formations are attested from the dialects both for the past tense and the past participle. Recorded are *begunned*, *doved* (from *dive*), *droved*, *drunked*, etc., and [dʌnd] for *done*, [friznt] for *frozen* and, more grotesque, [skwoznd] for *squeezed*.

This then is the real significance of Paul's proportion formula. It symbolizes the process (conscious or unconscious) of analysis by which the speaker becomes aware of the existence and the value of certain speech elements. A full statement of the proportion would contain all the words from which the speaker extracts a significant element. For the sake of brevity only one representative of the type which forms the model is taken for the left arm of the proportion. Thus in the above proportion

$$\text{êlthe:êlthe-s}::\text{elthétō:}x$$

the example in the left arm is merely a representative of all those verbs which distinguish the second person singular from the third by the addition of a final *-s*.

Forms like *breeches* and *brokened* are examples of what is known as 'hypercharacterization'. In the second example the child felt that *broken* was insufficiently characterized as a past participle. Such 'repair' of forms deemed to be not clearly characterized is a constant feature of language. An example which will illustrate a number of points made in this chapter is offered by the degrees of comparison of the adjective *near*. This was in origin actually the comparative of the adjective which appears in present-day English in the guise *nigh* and goes back to OE *nēah*. German *nah*, *näher*, *nächst* show the degrees of comparison, the OE forms being *nēarra* (ME *ner*, *nar*) and *nīexsta*. All the forms thus survive in *nigh*, *near*, *next*. *Near* was, however, felt to be insufficiently characterized as a comparative, and in the sixteenth century the hypercharacterized *nearer* appears. From this, by what is known as 'back-formation', the positive *near* was extracted, and a regular superlative *nearest* has been substituted for *next*, which still survives in a more restricted semantic application. Similar has been the history of *far*, which was by origin a comparative form but was taken as a positive and so gave rise to the comparative *farrer*. This in its turn came under the influence of the semantically similar word *further*; hence the modern form *farther*. Parallel with these examples is the genesis of the regular series *late*, *later*, *latest*. The regular comparative (OE *lætra*) is now represented by *latter*, and the superlative (OE *latost*) by *last*. The regular modern forms appeared in the sixteenth century. Another 'hypercharacterized' comparative form is *lesser*, as in *lesser evil*. The French *plusieurs* likewise goes back to hypercharacterized Latin *plūsiōrēs*, in which the regular comparative suffix *-ior-* was added to the comparative form *plūs*.

The doctrine of analogy in the classic formulation by Paul has remained virtually untouched by the revolution in linguistic thinking, and the exposition in Bloomfield's *Language* is still Young Grammarian in spirit. In 1949 an attempt was made by the eminent Polish Indo-Europeanist, J. Kurylowicz, to formulate some general rules relating to analogical processes. These were of an abstract and *a priori* character. His first rule may serve as an example. 'A bipartite morpheme tends to assimilate an isofunctional morpheme which comprises only one of the two elements, i.e. the compound morpheme replaces the simple morpheme.' By way of illustration the plural of strong masculine nouns in German may be analysed. In OHG the plural of an *a*-stem like *tag* 'day' was *tag-a*; on the other hand, an *i*-stem like *gast* 'guest' formed its plural *gest-i*. In the latter we may distinguish the plural morpheme proper -*i* from the purely phonetic phenomenon, the umlauting of the root vowel *a* to *e*. But this contrast changed its character once the final vowels -*a* and -*i* had both changed to -*e*. At this stage both classes exhibited the same plural ending -*e*, but they are distinguished by the extra phenomenon of Umlaut. This means that in the case of *Gäste* we have to do with a compound plural morpheme. What we observe in the history of the language, according to Kurylowicz, is an extension of Umlaut plurals at the cost of others. Hence his general rule. However, this is merely a tendency, for there are still plenty of plurals in German of the type *Tage*.

Kurylowicz's rules were tested by scrutiny of a considerable amount of modern material by another Polish scholar, W. Mańczak, and his conclusion was that 'one must recognize that the majority of the facts mentioned above fall outside the formulas of M. Kurylowicz'. W. P. Lehmann in his summary of the debate has commented:[1] '. . . if the rules cannot be established in contemporary languages, their application to earlier periods may be artistic rather than scientific.'

How difficult it is to set up rules for analogical processes may be seen from a consideration of the development of the verb 'to be' in Greek, Latin and English. In Indo-European the root **es-* appeared in its full form in the singular and in its zero grade *s-* in the plural. The reconstructed conjugation of the present tense is as follows.

	Sing.	Pl.
1	**es-mi*	**s-mes*, **s-mos*
2	**es-(s)i*	**s-te*
3	**es-ti*	**s-enti*

In Greek the full form of the root is carried over into the plural: hence forms like *este* 'ye are'. In the first person **es-mes* yields the dialect form *eimes*, with regular development of the cluster -*sm*-; but in Attic *esmen* the -*s*- has been restored analogically from the second person. In the third person **es-enti*, with analogical introduction of the full grade, would proceed regularly to *e-henti*,

---

1. *Historical Linguistics*, 189.

further to *ehensi* and finally to *eisi*, as in certain dialects like Attic. Another dialect form *enti* evidently goes back to **s-enti*, from which we should expect **henti*; but this form has lost its aspiration on the analogy of the singular *esti*.

In Latin the zero grade of the root is still evident in *sumus* 'we are' and *sunt* 'they are'. Under the influence of the latter (and perhaps also the subjunctive *sim*) the first person singular has been refashioned to *sum*. On the other hand the second person singular *es(s)* has exerted an influence on the corresponding plural form *estis*, which now shows the full grade of the root.

The history of the corresponding English forms is far more complex. In the first place the conjugation of the 'copulative' verb is made up from four distinct roots:[1] *es-*, Gmc. *ar-* (**or-*), **bheu*, and *wes-*. The forms *am* and *is* are the only survivors in modern English of the root *es-*; but in OE the forms *sind, sindon* are also found, and they survived into early Middle English. The corresponding form in German is *sind*. Further, a subjunctive corresponding to the Latin *siem, sim*, etc., occurs in OE *sīe*, plural *sīen*, German *sei*. With the second person singular OE *eart* and the plural forms *aron, earon* we have representatives of the second root. Interesting is that these are in origin perfect forms, and it may well be that the root is *ar-* 'arrive'. The third root originally meant 'grow, become'. It is represented in the OE second person singular *bist*, which also had a future sense. It survives in modern dialect use and finds its exact equivalent in German *Du bist*. A plural form is *bēoþ*.

Thus OE had no fewer than three forms of the plural: *sind(on)*, *aron* and *bēoþ*. The second has become the standard form, but the last still survives in modern dialect use, where we find a completely regularized conjugation: *I be, you be*. In other dialects *m* for *am* is used also in the plural: *we'm, they'm*, etc. Another form of levelling has taken place in spoken Swedish where an invariable *är* (pronounced [ɛ]) has replaced the complex irregularities of the inherited Germanic conjugation.

---

1. This patchwork kind of paradigm is known as 'suppletion': an example is the Greek verb 'to see', which makes its present tense from *hor-*, its future and perfect from *op-* and its aorist from the root *weid-*.

Analogies are not the only product of the interaction between form and function in language. We have seen that no speaker is completely familiar with every detail of his native language, and by a process natural to the human mind a strange word or expression is often identified or associated with something familiar. This process is exemplified in the amusing malapropisms committed by half-educated persons who attempt to use words that they do not fully understand. H. G. Wells' Mr. Polly is an illuminating, if extravagant, example. The author was once informed by a servant, when he called on an invalid friend, that the doctors were holding a 'consummation' in the drawing room. 'Just consecrate on this' and 'ornamatic machine' are further examples from the same source.

The British sailors of the last century converted the classifical names of the warships *Bellerophon* and *Iphigenia* into the *Billy Ruffian* and the *Niffy Jane*. At a stipendiary's court a witness once volunteered the information that his street was a *coal sack* (meaning *cul-de-sac*). Such formations are by no means confined to the uneducated. As we have said, they are merely instances of a widespread tendency on the part of human beings to identify the unknown with the known. Many such 'popular etymologies' have become part of the accepted language. One of the German national dishes is fermented cabbage called *Sauerkraut*. This word was adopted by the French from the neighbouring Alemannic dialects in which the word appears as *surkrut*. It has been modified, however, to *choucroute*, the first part of the word, *sur-* (*sauer*) being identified with the French word for cabbage, *chou*. A strange 'naturalization' of a foreign word is the Middle High German word for a 'cross-bow', *Armbrust*, literally 'arm-breast'. This goes back to later Latin *arcuballista* 'bow-catapult'. This developed to *arbalista*, which appears in Old French as *arbaleste*. A form similar to the German is the Old Norse *armbrist*.

In English the phrase *leg cutlet* suggests the idea of a small piece of meat cut off the leg. Actually this word has nothing to do with cutting. It is of the same origin as the French *côtelette*, which is a derivative of the Latin *costa* 'side or rib' and means 'a little rib'. A further example from the realm of food is the vulgar *sparrow-grass* instead of *asparagus*. An Austrian peasant once informed the author that a certain vegetable had a '*brennetanten Geschmack*' confusing the foreign loan-word *penetrant* with the native *brennend* ('burning'). The word *liquorice* has an interesting history. It is derived from a Greek word *glukurriza* meaning 'sweet root'. The word was adopted by the Romans, who associated the first part of the word with their native words *liquidus*, *liqueo*, etc., and transformed it into *liquiritia*. Similarly the word *oreichalkos* 'mountain copper' appears in Latin as *aurichalcum*, the first part *orei-* (*oros* 'mountain') being identified with the Latin word *aurum* 'gold'. A final example from English to illustrate this point. The expression *by-law* to the modern speaker is associated with words like *by-road* and suggests laws connected with minor local affairs not of national significance. Thus we speak of *railway by-laws, by-laws of the Thames Conservancy Board*, etc. The word, however, originally meant 'town law', *by* being the Scandinavian word for town which is to be seen in many place names like *Whitby*, *Rugby*, etc.[1]

These examples lead to the consideration of another type of confusion that influences linguistic form. In most languages there exist numerous synonymous words and phrases which provide alternative forms of expression for the same thought. Very often when we wish to say something, both synonyms arise together to consciousness and compete, as it were, for utterance. This results frequently in mixed 'portmanteau' forms that are called 'contaminations' or 'blends'. A schoolmaster once spoiled a moving peroration by a reference to *symblems* of liberty (mixture of *symbol* and *emblem*). The author was once accused of looking '*dejectent*' (*dejected* × *despondent*), and further of trying to '*evoid*' the issue. A student once wrote in an essay on Roman history that 'a fleet was sent to *harage* (*harass* × *ravage*) the coast of Carthage'. Similarly the slang word *mingy* seems to have arisen from the union of *stingy* and *mean*. *Diminish* is a blend of *diminue* (French

---

1. A few more examples: the author in his youth was always excited by the prospect of a 'bomb-fire' on Guy Fawkes Day. This word *bonfire* was, of course, at one time a 'bone-fire' in which dead bodies were burnt. Before a classical education brought enlightenment he thought that roads were covered with 'ash-falt'. *Asphalt* is actually a Greek word meaning roughly 'non-skid'.

diminuer) and the archaic *minish*, which is derived from old French *menusier* (Vulgar Latin **minutiare*). Recent additions to the list are *brunch*, a meal combining *breakfast* and *lunch*, and *smog*, a blend of *smoke* and *fog*.

Such phenomena are not confined to words alone. Contamination plays a large part in the syntax, too, of every language. Uneducated speakers are particularly liable to the confusion of constructions, expressions like *in the beginning part of the week* (*at the beginning* × *in the first part*) and *he changed from one reverse to the other* being extremely common. But they are not entirely absent from the standard language either. The following example is an extremely subtle case which would scarcely be noticed without closer inspection: *The bell had scarcely rung than he appeared in the hall* (blend of *no sooner . . . than* × *scarcely . . . when*). The constructions of words of similar meaning are often confused, this being perhaps the most frequent type of contamination. Thus the common vulgarism *different to* is most probably due to the influence of synonymous expressions like *opposed to*.[1]

To sum up the main conclusions of this chapter, a few examples may be quoted in which all the forces discussed above have played their part. The processes of analogy and contamination are well exemplified in the declensions of the Latin words *iter* and *iecur*. From a comparison of the related languages we know that the latter word was once declined *iecur*, **iecinis*. In early Latin, however, we find the genitive singular *iecoris* on the analogy of words like *fulgur*, *fulgoris*, just as *femur* in Plautus has a genitive *feminis*, but in classical Latin *femoris*. The classical Latin genitive *iecinoris* must be due to the contamination of these two forms *iecoris* × *iecinis*. Similarly *itineris*, the genitive of *iter*, is compounded of the old form *itinis* and a later analogical form *iteris*. In this noun, however, at a later date levelling restored the unity of the declension by producing the new nominative *itiner*, a 'back formation'.

We must now turn our attention to certain phenomena of a rather different kind which must also be explained by reference to

---

1. This is a perfectly natural, and indeed universal, phenomenon. The normal usage *averse to* is increasingly giving way to the pedantic *averse from*.

function. The purpose of the speaker is to convey a message; that is to say his speech must be intelligible. Now human beings like to perform their task with as little effort as possible, and language is no exception to this rule. Consequently a speaker will normally tend to say the minimum that is required to make himself understood, and those parts of words that are not essential to the meaning will tend to be left unsaid. This process the speaker, in his natural indolence, will carry as far as he is permitted, until in fact he is pulled up with a 'I beg your pardon' from the hearer. We may say that intelligibility forms the limit of linguistic attrition.

The way in which parts of speech that have no function tend to become atrophied and to drop out is well illustrated by the history of the Indo-European case endings. Indo-European had a system of at least eight cases, and the simple case endings were alone sufficient to express grammatical and concrete relations. Thus the Latin *domum* meant 'to the house', *domī* 'at the house', and so on. But linguistic symbols are exposed to constant weakening, and speakers continually strive after clarity and forcefulness. Consequently, in order to define more precisely the meaning of the cases, adverbial particles were inserted (*in*, *ex*, *ab*, etc.). They were at first not bound closely with the cases; but in the course of time the constant use of certain particles with certain cases produced in speech consciousness a feeling that such a relation was necessary. The particles are now felt to 'govern' a certain case. The once independent adverbs become 'prepositions'. This is the linguistic state at which classical Greek and Latin had arrived. Gradually, however, the meaning became centred in the once superfluous preposition and the case endings, deprived of their function, tend to be eliminated. Once this is accomplished a language has progressed from a 'synthetic' to an 'analytic' state; that is, it has evolved from the linguistic state in which syntactical relations are expressed by word inflection to one in which they are expressed by independent wordlets. The whole development may be seen in the following example: Plautus uses *temperī*, the old locative for 'in time'. In Cicero we find *tempore*, where the ablative has usurped the function of the locative.[1] In Livy's time

---

1. Such fusion of case forms and functions is called 'syncretism'.

the case force has been weakened and he employs *in tempore*. Modern French carries the process to its logical conclusion and dispenses with the case ending, the whole meaning being expressed by a preposition: *à temps*.

11

Writing

Our consideration of language and its problems in the previous chapters has been based upon the fact that languages are systems of significant sounds. We must now approach our subject from a new angle. It is a remarkable fact that in a civilized community linguistic behaviour, both active and passive, that is to say linguistic expression and understanding, are largely carried on without the use of vocal sounds at all. In this book, in which the author is behaving linguistically in order to influence the mind of his readers, there is no contact from mouth to ear such as we have assumed in our previous disquisitions. Instead of this the writer has caused marks to be made on paper; the reader sees these marks, and from these visual impressions he interprets the author's meaning. Yet we call this *linguistic* behaviour; and the book, or rather its contents, constitutes *linguistic* matter, although the tongue (*lingua*) has not been called upon to articulate a single sound.

Our ability to perform such acts of communication and interpretation again rests upon training in early childhood. After the laborious process of learning the auditory symbols that constitute our language, we were next compelled to acquire a new system of symbols. By an intricate pedagogic apparatus of picture-books, pencils, and paper, chalks, slates, and blackboards, our minds were impressed with the fact that certain intricate shapes refer to particular sounds. In other words, we were compelled to submit our linguistic knowledge to a process of phonemic analysis, to realise that all our speech may be reduced to a series of easily distinguishable sounds, and that these sounds may be represented by visual symbols. This system of writing and the different mode of linguistic behaviour which it makes possible open up a series of new problems. To approach them we must first consider how this remarkable alignment of writing and sound, of visual and auditory impressions came into being. We must trace the history of the alphabet.

Fig. 31.

The earliest and most primitive stage of graphic symbolization consists of picture writing. A more or less complicated event is depicted as a totality without reference to any linguistic analysis or description of that event. Figure 31, which reproduces part of a famous Egyptian document,[1] will illustrate what is meant. The flattened oval at the base of the complex represents a land, and this land is further identified by papyrus growing on it—it is the papyrus land, the Nile delta. The head attached to it represents the inhabitants of this land. The falcon is the symbol for the king, and the fact that he is leading the head by a string indicates that he conquered the land and took its inhabitants prisoners. It must be

---

1. The so-called 'Narmer Palette'.

emphasized that in this type of graphic representation there is little or no connexion with the *linguistic* expression of the idea or event. There is no articulation of the picture to correspond to the words into which the sentence may be analysed. Nevertheless the very fact that the event must be symbolized stimulates the mind to analysis. For symbolization implies schematization; that is, the choice of the most significant factors and moments in the event complex. Such an analysis constitutes the next stage in the development of writing. The picture, instead of being conceived as a totality referring as such to a complex event, now denotes a single idea or object. Figure 32 gives a selection of such 'ideographic'

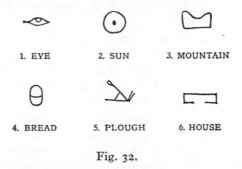

1. EYE   2. SUN   3. MOUNTAIN

4. BREAD   5. PLOUGH   6. HOUSE

Fig. 32.

hieroglyphs, as they are called. Here again stress must be laid upon the fact that at this stage the graphic symbol refers directly to the idea. It has as yet no connexion with the linguistic sound symbol. Writing and speech are, in fact, still two independent symbolic systems that serve to represent ideas. This fact may be schematized as in Fig. 33. The most significant step in the history of writing

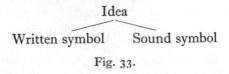

Fig. 33.

was taken when the third side of the triangle was completed, and the graphic symbol was taken to represent not an idea but the sounds of the corresponding word. Writing then became not an idiographic but a *phonetic* system. Suppose in an ideographic system we have two symbols, denoting 'man' and denoting 'age'; in the new system these symbols will merely represent the groups of sounds *man* and *age*, so that by their juxtaposition we could represent the word *manage*. Such 'rebus' devices are common in the history of script. A further advance in technique was made when the pictures were taken to represent not the whole phonetic word, but merely the first syllable of the word. In this way the so-called syllabaries, such as we find in Crete, Cyprus and Japan, most probably evolved. The alphabetic stage was finally reached when the symbol was used to denote the first sound of the word of which it is a sketch. This is known as the 'acrophonic' principle.

Two main stages can thus be detected in the evolution of script. In the first stage meaning is conveyed by pictorial means without the intermediacy of language. This has been called 'semasiography'. This is followed by the stage of 'phonography', when the symbols render the sounds of speech. At first the signs refer to the whole words or rather their vocables: the signs are said to be 'logograms'. Successive adaptations turn the logograms into 'syllabograms', and finally the characters are made to refer to single phonemes. This stage was reached by about the fifteenth century B.C. in the West Semitic alphabet. This script, however, simply renders the consonantal skeleton of the words and leaves the vowels without notation.

It should be realized that the actual history of scripts does not correspond to this smooth theoretical progression. Human beings are conservative in their writing habits, and it rarely happens that a perfectly rational solution is found to the problem of the graphic representation of speech. At each stage of progress much useless junk remains. By way of illustration a sample of the only script invented for an Indo-European language may be analysed. This is the so-called Hittite Hieroglyph script, which was used in the Hittite empire as a monumental script for texts written in Luvian, one of the Anatolian group (see Appendix A) of languages. The script remained in use after the fall of the Hittite empire, and in fact the great majority of the texts which have come to light belong

Fig. 34. A Hieroglyph Hittite inscription from Carchemish. The language
is closely related to Luvian.

to the later period. Such a late text is the one from Carchemish on
the Euphrates (see Fig. 34). The text runs from right to left in the
first line, and then from left to right and so on. This style of writing
is called 'boustrophedon' (Greek for 'as the ox turns'). The signs
face the beginning of the line, and they are read in short columns
starting at the top of the first column in the line after the standing
figure pointing to himself, which signifies 'I' (Luvian *Amu*). The
first sentence can be transliterated:

AMU -*wa-mi-a* ᴹ *A- a+ra-a+ra-a* -*s* JUDGE-*na-s* GOD+
BIRD-*ta-na-sa-mi-a-s ta+si-sa-pa-ru-wa-ti-a-s* MAN-*ti-
a-s*.

The words in capitals represent ideograms and they are followed by phonetic complements written syllabically. Before the second word there is an oblique stroke which is used to introduce a proper name;[1] the third word is a title which is sometimes written out in full *tarawanas*. In the fourth word the double ideogram is possibly to be read phonetically, giving the word *istanasmias* 'of My Sun', this being the equivalent of 'his Majesty'. The last word means 'vassal'. The whole sentence thus reads: 'I am A'araras, Judge, vassal of His Majesty T.' Two further points may be noted. There is a word division sign |c, and some words, e.g. names of towns and countries, are followed by classifying signs, the so-called determinatives, e.g. $Ka + r\text{-}ga\text{-}mi\text{-}sa\text{-}\bar{\imath}\text{-}s$ ^{CITY}.

Compared to this cumbrous system the script used by the Greeks of the Mycenaean epoch, Linear B, is simplicity itself. Linear B is the third stage of the Cretan script; this began with pictographs or ideograms, which were subsequently simplified into schematic linear forms. This linear script had two phases: the earlier form, Linear A, was in widespread use in Crete, and the language is unknown. Linear B was used chiefly on the Greek mainland, and it was in all probability introduced into Crete when the Mycenaeans took possession of the island. Clay tablets inscribed in this script have been found in abundance at Knossos in north central Crete, but so far the only specimens found in other parts of the island have been painted inscriptions on vases.

On the Linear B tablets (see Fig. 35) the continuous text is written purely with syllabograms. The so-called ideograms are in fact accountancy symbols which are followed by numerals. One line will suffice to illustrate the comparative simplicity of the script as against Hittite hieroglyph.

> jo-do-so-si ko-re-te-re ... ka-ko na-wi-jo pa-ta-jo-i-qe
>   e-ke-si-qe ai-ka-sa-ma
> *hōs dōsonsi koretēres ... khalkon nāwion paltaioihiq^we*
>   *enkhessiq^we aiksmans*
> 'How the k. (officials) are to give temple bronze as tips for arrows and spears'.

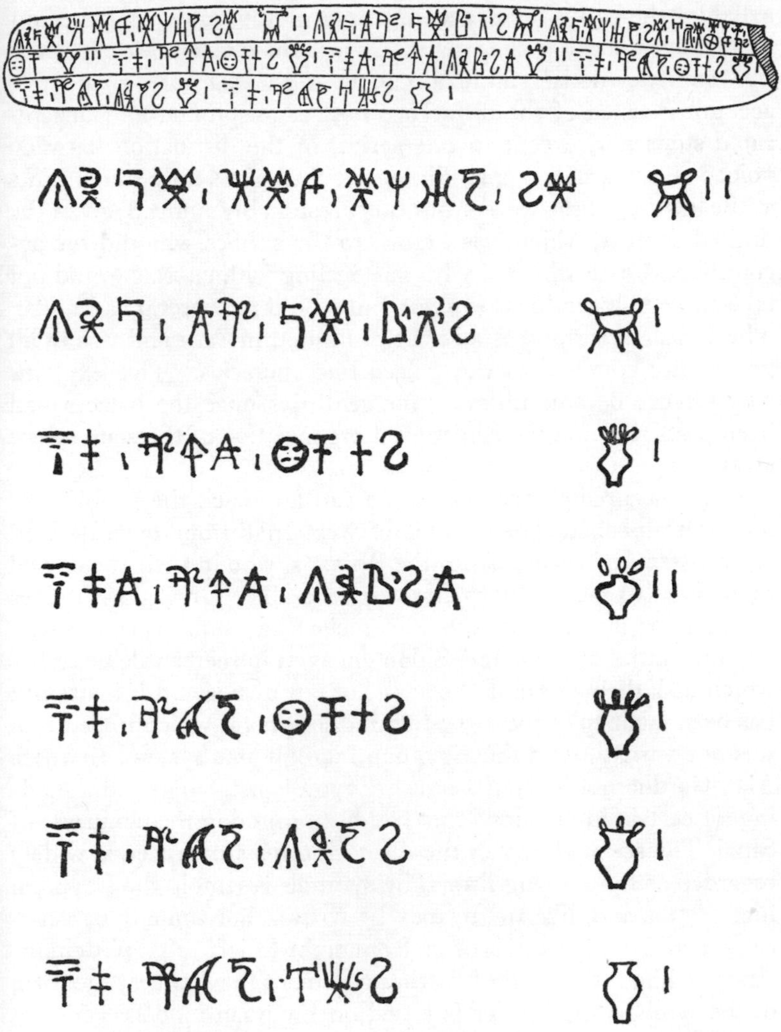

Fig. 35. The Tripod tablet from Pylos discovered after the communication of the decipherment. In the last three entries the sole change in the ideogram entry is the number of handles. This correlates with the sole change in the text, the last word indicating the number of handles. The word for 'four' begins with the 'currant-bun' sign.

The script is a pure syllabary. In analysing the Greek words into syllables the script takes account only of the vowel and the immediately preceding consonant. Consonant clusters are rendered by 'empty vowels': an example is *-ka-sa-ma* for *-ksma-*. No account is taken of the difference between aspirated and unaspirated stops nor, except in one series, of the distinction between voiced and voiceless stops. The script thus gives only rough hints at the identity of the words, but this presumably sufficed, given the limited context, which was known to the scribes who did the accounting. A man who knew he was dealing with BRONZE would not take *ka-ko* to mean 'evil' (*kakós*), but would interpret it as *khalkós*. The Linear B script was a script of limited literacy and was in all probability confined to the palace bureaucracies.[1] This explains why Greece became illiterate for centuries once the palaces had been destroyed and the centralized organization of the state swept away.

After the preliminary survey we can approach the problem of our own alphabet. The nations of western Europe have derived their systems of writing from the Romans, who in their turn owed their alphabet ultimately to Greek sources. The Greeks themselves traced their alphabet to the Phoenicians, a Semitic people who from the cities of Tyre and Sidon engaged in mercantile activities which took them as far as the coasts of our own island. An attempt has been made to connect the Semitic scripts (of which Phoenician was one variety) with the Egyptian hieroglyphic system. In 1916, Alan Gardiner, a leading English Egyptologist, suggested a reading for certain inscriptions that had been found in the peninsula of Sinai. The script in which these inscriptions are written is widely regarded as the missing link. The symbols resemble the Egyptian hieroglyphs and, like them, may be written horizontally or vertically, and from left to right or from right to left. Fig. 36 demonstrates without the need of further comment the fact that the form of the symbols themselves is based on Egyptian models, and that they have a close resemblance to the oldest Semitic scripts. The only difficulty is that they have a different phonetic value. Light was thrown on this problem when it was realized that the *names* of

1. The use on clay vessels is only an apparent exception.

the Semitic symbols designate the *objects* which the Sinai symbols depict. That is to say, the Sinai symbols refer to the *Semitic names* of the objects which the Egyptian hieroglyphs represented. This could suggest that a Semitic-speaking people adopted the Egyptian script, but made the signs refer to the corresponding words of their own language. By the acrophonic principle the symbols were made to represent the first sounds of these Semitic words and so the alphabet was evolved. The accompanying table (Fig. 36)

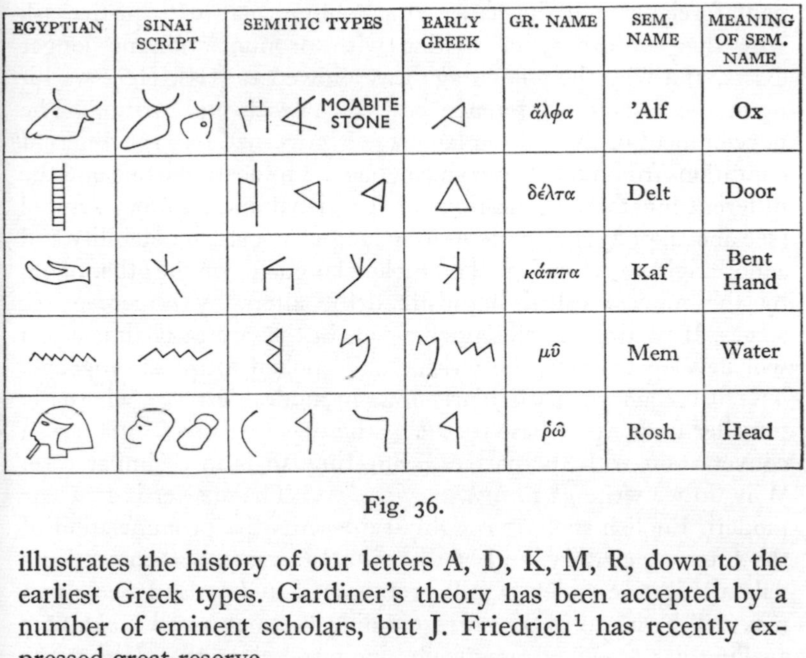

EGYPTIAN	SINAI SCRIPT	SEMITIC TYPES	EARLY GREEK	GR. NAME	SEM. NAME	MEANING OF SEM. NAME
		MOABITE STONE		ἄλφα	'Alf	Ox
				δέλτα	Delt	Door
				κάππα	Kaf	Bent Hand
				μῦ	Mem	Water
				ῥῶ	Rosh	Head

Fig. 36.

illustrates the history of our letters A, D, K, M, R, down to the earliest Greek types. Gardiner's theory has been accepted by a number of eminent scholars, but J. Friedrich[1] has recently expressed great reserve.

In the alphabet we seem to have reached a solution of the problem of written representation of speech that is at once simple and adequate. This is made clear if we compare the alphabetic system with the syllabaries which were their immediate predecessors in the line of evolution. If a language has five vowel sounds, then it must have a separate symbol to render the combination of each

1. *Geschichte der Schrift*, pp. 60–61.

consonant with each vowel. Thus there must be a separate symbol for the sound combinations *pa, pe, pi, po, pu*; so that a language with sixteen consonants would require a syllabary with eighty signs to represent all combinations with its five vowels. The alphabetic system, on the other hand, with its one-sound-one-symbol principle, finds 16 + 5 symbols adequate to perform the same task. With this invention perfection seems to have been reached; and, it may be added, the invention of an alphabet (by gradual stages) took place only once in human history. Yet in England the indignant foreigner and the harassed schoolboy may with justice ask why this conformity of writing with pronunciation no longer exists, and why the golden age was allowed to pass. Here we hit upon the essential difference between speech and writing. The development of the written language is governed by very different conditions from that of spoken language. The act of writing and the different mnemonic conditions of the visual and auditory symbol (see above, p. 231) give the written language a greater stability and a more rigid conservatism. The spoken language, on the other hand, by the process called linguistic drift, alters by imperceptible stages. If writing remains unchanged, in the course of time a gap will develop between the written and spoken forms of language. The discrepancy is particularly crass in modern Greece, where the traveller finds the debased Attic of the newspapers of little use in conversation with the natives.[1] But English is in a similar case. Why do we write *gh* in *light, right, sight*? The answer is that our modern English spelling roughly represents the pronunciation of the fifteenth century, and at that time *gh* was meant to render a palatal fricative which is still pronounced in Lowland Scots and may still be heard in the corresponding German word *Licht*. Our spelling has remained practically unaltered since that date, while pronunciation has undergone such profound changes that the link between speech and writing has almost been severed. Irish is in an even worse plight. Where *saoghal = sil, oidhche = i*, we may indeed say that one writes Oxford and pronounces Cambridge. The

---

1. The 'pure language' (*kathareuousa*) used in writing goes back to the 'common language' (*koinē*) of post-classical times. The popular speech (*dēmotikē*) is the natural descendant of the Greek spoken throughout the ages.

difficulties of such spellings are so great for certain types of people that there has been at regular intervals a great clamour for spelling reform. But there are several considerations which should deter from precipitate action. A problem of a similar kind exists in China, where the authorities have often been urged to abandon their own cumbersome method of writing and to adopt the western European alphabetic script. The reflections of an eminent Sinologist on this question are relevant to our own problem. I paraphrase and supplement them in the following paragraph.[1]

In China, as in early Egypt, the script was nothing more than a system of stylized and simplified pictures. That is to say, the visual symbols referred directly to the idea *via* the spoken word. This means that the literature of millennia is at once opened to the student who learns the 4000-odd visual symbols which we are told is sufficient for everyday use. He is not burdened with the task of learning Middle Chinese and Old Chinese. No dialect complications arise such as trouble the student of Classical Greek who, to appreciate Homer, Sappho, Herodotus and Demosthenes, must learn as many varieties of speech. Moreover, though the different parts of China have spoken dialects that are mutually unintelligible, an edict written in the ancient characters is immediately comprehensible to the literate in every province. Yet we are told that if a Cantonese were to read it aloud, the sounds would convey absolutely nothing to a speaker of the Pekinese dialect. Thus the Chinese script is the sole instrument of universal communication in China, and as such it is the backbone of Chinese culture. If the traditional script is abandoned and replaced by an alphabetic script, the schoolboy (and the European) would be saved infinite pains. But against this the Chinese would lose the heritage of a literature that has endured and grown for millennia. Moreover, a phonetic document written in the Pekin dialect would be unintelligible elsewhere. The unity of China, as of all administrative areas, depends entirely on the existence of a common means of communication (see next chapter). This work has hitherto been performed through the medium of the universally intelligible script. If this is abandoned, where is the *koine* that would take its place? Karlgren has

---

1. B. Karlgren, *Sound and Symbol in Chinese*, Oxford, 1923.

well said: 'If China does not abandon its peculiar script in favour of our alphabetic writing, this is not due to any stupid or obdurate conservatism . . . the day the Chinese discard it they will surrender the very foundation of their culture.'[1]

The same warning holds good for our problem. The student of language is aware that in the first place any reformed system of spelling might well be out of date in fifty years. Secondly, in what orthography are we to print the masterpieces of English literature? To ascribe modern pronunciation to Shakespeare would be falsification. Yet if we preserved the old spelling for such works and applied the modern orthography only to modern texts, teaching it in the primary schools, then English literature would become a closed book to all who had not the time and patience to learn the old orthography. To those who have learned to write *lait* the old *light* will be as foreign as the German *Licht*. The traditional orthography, like Chinese script, is a unifying bond which holds together the whole of English literature since the fifteenth century. Any adequate attempt at modernization would lock the doors of English literature to all except the erudite.

Apart from this difficulty of learning, this misrelation between speech and writing has important linguistic consequences. As children we were impressed with the fact that the alphabet is a phonetic system. We learned to associate certain shapes with certain sounds. This naive attitude to writing persists with most uneducated people. They write as they speak, and very often speak as they read. These are the two aspects of the interaction of speech and writing which we must now consider.

The sounds of dead languages are known to us only from their script, and it is from variations in spelling that we have to deduce the development of sounds. In this we are aided by the tendency of uneducated people to write phonetically. In vulgar Greek texts we find the signs $\varepsilon\iota$, η, ι used indiscriminately. From this we must deduce the fact that the sounds once represented by these symbols were no longer distinguished; for symbols will not be interchanged

---

1. For a recent survey and assessment of the various projects for the reform and eventual alphabetization of the Chinese script see R. A. D. Forrest, *The Chinese Language*, 2nd ed. (1965), pp. 260–263.

unless they have the same value. This conclusion is borne out by reference to modern Greek, where we find that all these symbols are pronounced [i]. Similarly in Latin we observe that an *n* before an *s* or *f* is often left out, e.g. CESOR or COSUL (for *censor* and *consul*). On the other hand, it is often put where it is not required, such as *thensaurus, formonsus*. From this we can deduce the fact that *n* was no longer pronounced in such circumstances. It was in fact a 'silent letter'. In this way such alternative spellings as *whight, fite* will inform the future philologist of the phonetic value of *gh* in such combinations.

In numerous instances we find the spelling has influenced the pronunciation of even educated speakers. The word *author*, for instance, is derived from French *auteur* and ultimately from the Latin *auctor*, so that there is no justification for the [θ] pronunciation of the medial consonant. This has a complex origin. In Latin many Greek words which contained an aspirated consonant were transcribed either with or without the aspirate. Thus *māchanā* was transcribed as *macina* or *machina*, *theātron* as *teatro* or *theatro*, both forms having the same pronunciation. In later times the reason for this uncertainty of spelling was no longer understood, and it was thought permissible to write an aspiration after any voiceless plosive. So we find pure Latin words like *praeco*, *centurio* written *praechones, centhuriones*. This indiscriminate use of the aspirate persisted with scribes throughout manuscript tradition, so that the French word *auteur* was written in English as *author*.[1] It is the influence of this spelling that has produced the modern pronunciation. The English word *fault* has a similar history. In many English words like *calm, talk* (and in certain dialects even words like *milk*) the *l* was no longer pronounced. Then, like other silent letters, it was inserted where it had no justification (see above). Thus the frequent Scots name *Chalmers* is no more than a differentiated form of *Chambers*, although uninformed Southerners pronounce the *l*. The pronunciation of many French words in our language has been mutilated because of accidents of orthography. *Fault* is derived from French *faute*. In Middle English it is written

---

1. The Latinized spellings *auctour* and *auctor* were common in the fifteenth and sixteenth centuries, while the intrusive -*h*- appears in the sixteenth century.

both *faute* and *faulte*.[1] Pope evidently pronounced the word still in its proper way for he makes it rhyme with *thought* and *wrought*. But modern educated pronunciation has been misguided by the parasitic *l*. The word *realm* from Old French *reaume*, written even in Middle English as *reaume*, has suffered the same fate.

---

1. The form *fault* was due to pedantry; for these spellings were never meant to represent pronunciation, but merely to indicate the Latin origin of the word *fallita*. A particularly crass example of this is the word *doubt*, where a *b* was inserted to indicate its connexion with *dubitare*, although even Old French exhibits a form *dote*, *dute*. For a list of modern spelling pronunciations see the collection in I. C. Ward, *The Phonetics of English*.

12

Dialects

The discussion of the relations of speech to writing opens up a new series of linguistic problems. The sound laws, we saw, are statements about the development of particular sounds in particular languages. Thus we say that the Indo-European word *pətēr develops into the English word *father*. But what is the English word *father*? Although as printed on this page it is something that is understood by every English-speaking person, yet the actual spoken rendering of this visual symbol differs greatly from person to person. The unity of the written word is only an apparent unity, for each separate locality in England has a different pronunciation. Thus from a phonetic point of view there is no single English word *father*, but only a series of resemblant vocables. Differentiation may be carried further than the pronunciation of 'each separate locality'. In the last resort, each individual has his own way of speaking, his favourite words and turns of phrases, in a word his own 'idiolect'. It is evident that this description of the speech habits of a community cannot be undertaken without some intuitive identification of the different idiolects. This brings us back to the basic 'item experience' which is taken as 'given' by the linguist. On this basis D. Jones devised the concept of the 'diaphone' to encompass the individual variants of what we have called a stoecheum. He wrote:[1] 'It is convenient to have a name for a family of sounds consisting of the sound used by one speaker in a particular set of words (said in isolation) together with

---

1. *The Phoneme*, p. 195.

corresponding though different sounds used by other speakers of the same language. Such a family may be termed a "diaphone".' What Jones was doing was to 'identify' a word, say *get*, and record the different ways of pronouncing the vowel. The variants were plotted on the vowel quadrilateral to give the diaphonic area of the English vowel in question. The point has already been stressed that such a 'vowel' is an abstraction set up for the purposes of description, and the same is true of the 'language' as a whole. It is in this sense that 'language' is a rigid system. The 'language' produced by the describer inevitably reflects his basic assumption about the validity of the 'item experience'. Each such description assumes 'an ideal speaker-listener, in a perfectly homogeneous speech-community' (Chomsky). Such an approach must result in a simplification and misrepresentation even of the speech of a single individual whose 'idiolect' comprises different styles according to the particular situation, and these change throughout his speaking life. The concept of a 'rigid' language also raises difficulties in diachronic work. C. F. Hockett has recently written:[1] 'We ignored the whole problem of the implications for language design of the fact of linguistic change, and vice versa.'

These considerations suggest a new approach to linguistic problems which will take more account of the varieties of speech in a given community, i.e. the dialects of a given language.[2]

The systematic study of regional dialects began in earnest in the last quarter of the nineteenth century. The dispute about the inviolability of the sound laws prompted investigators to test their theories on the living dialects of the countryside, where speech may be studied in its natural setting, free from the distortions and over-simplifications inseparable from written representation. The seeds of this movement were first sown in Germany, but it was in France that they first bore fruit. Here Jules Gilliéron, with the aid of his colleague Edmond Edmont, undertook the investigation of the *patois* of the Gallo-Romance territory. A questionnaire of about two thousand words and sentences embodying important

---

1. *State of the Art*, p. 31.
2. On the relation of the terms 'dialect' and 'language', see p. 274.

points of phonology, lexicography and syntax was drawn up, and Edmont travelled about France and recorded the local equivalents in some 650 centres distributed over the whole country. Each item of the questionnaire was allotted a separate map, and on this map all the dialect equivalents were plotted in the places where they occurred, so that it was possible to see at a glance the distribution of each separate phenomenon over the Gallo-Romance territory.

The material collected by a single phonetically trained field worker is certainly more reliable than that provided by any number of amateurs. However, in the nature of things the network of places covered by a man working single-handed is bound to fall far short of the optimum. In the Survey of the Scottish dialects[1] it was estimated that a field worker in five years could collect information from only two hundred dialect speakers; but to obtain an adequate picture, data from more like two thousand localities would be required. For this reason the indirect method of obtaining information was also used when it was a question of eliciting responses for which the precise phonetic description was irrelevant, for instance whether the dialect uses *branks* or *buffets* for 'mumps'. To this end a copy of the questionnaire was sent to almost every rural school in Scotland and to a selection of city schools. The schoolmaster was asked to hand it to a suitable local person, i.e. 'one who was middle-aged or over, a native of the district, and not one addicted to confusing what he had heard in local use with words he had read only in books'. This mass of information tends to be self-confirmatory, while it inevitably throws up problems which can be subsequently cleared up by field workers. In this way the coverage of a region is denser and the skill of the trained workers more efficiently deployed. The indirect method was also used by Georg Wenker for the survey of the German dialects. With government support he sent round a list of some forty sentences embodying linguistic points considered important, with the request that they should be translated by the schoolmasters into the local dialect. In this way he obtained some 40,000 different dialect specimens. It is con-

---

1. See A. McIntosh, *Introduction to a Survey of Scottish Dialects*, 1952.

sidered that 'the value of a great mass of material acquired by means of a carefully organized postal questionnaire is such as to far outweigh the disadvantage that is is not written phonetically'.[1]

The questionnaire will cover points of pronunciation (e.g. whether the word for 'stone' is pronounced *stane* or *steen*); points of morphology (e.g. whether the preterite of 'climb' is *klam* or *klom* or *klumb* or *climbed*); and, most especially, the choice of a whole series of different words for one and the same thing (e.g. *weaver*, *ettercap*, *netterie* for 'spider'). The plotting of this mass of information on maps throws up its distribution in a vivid way. By superimposition of maps the distribution of different phenomena may be compared. This opens up new possibilities of solving old linguistic problems which proved intractable to traditional philological methods.

In the first place we must consider the verdict of dialect geography upon the sound law question. At first sight the dialect maps seem to deal a crushing blow to the neogrammarian dogma, for no two words seem to have exactly the same sound treatment. Figure 37 illustrates such a case. It shows the treatment in French of Latin words in which an initial *k*-sound is followed by the vowel *a*. In standard French it usually becomes [ʃ] (e.g. *caldum* > *chaud* [ʃo]), but the *k* is preserved in certain dialects in the north and south. On the dialect map a line is drawn enclosing all places which have the same sound treatment. Such a line is called an 'isogloss'. Figure 37 is a composite map made by superimposing the maps of the words *chandelle* (*candēla*), *chanter* (*cantāre*), *champ* (*campus*), *chambre* (*camera*). It will be seen that in the centre of France the *k* under these conditions regularly becomes *ch*, but that in the north and south, where it is preserved, the lines of the different words do not exactly coincide. That is to say that in some dialects on the border of the *k*-territory and the [ʃ]-territory the treatment varies from word to word, so that in these dialects there can be no talk of rigid sound laws. The experience derived from such dialect studies led Gilliéron and his followers to deny the truth of the sound-law dogma, and to condemn it as an artificial and sterile approach to linguistic problems. Before

---

1. A. McIntosh, *Survey*, p. 78.

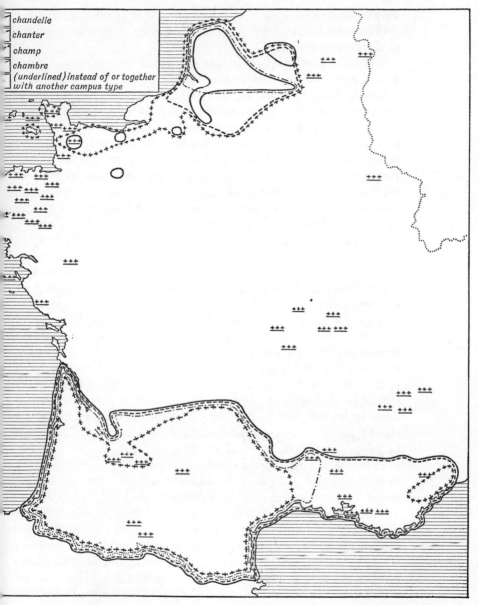

Fig. 37. (After Jaberg, *Sprachgeographie*, Aarau, 1908.)

discussing this question it will be convenient to mention another problem that has troubled dialect investigators. This is the problem of dialect boundaries.

The definition and delimitation of dialects have puzzled a number of linguists. An additional question is how far differentiation must go before difference of 'dialect' becomes difference of 'language'. In seeking ways to determine the latter problem some scholars have proposed the criterion of mutual intelligibility; but this immediately runs into difficulties. Romance scholars have pointed out that if we proceed from Southern Italy northwards to the French frontier and then through Gallo-Romance territory to the Channel coast, we traverse dialects which merge gradually, so that those on either side of the Franco-Italian frontier have greater mutual intelligibility than, say, the dialects of Turin and Taranto. Yet Torinese is classified as an Italian dialect. So it is contrary to ordinary usage to say that forms of which are mutually unintelligible constitute different languages. On the other hand if mutual intelligibility is the criterion for classification as 'dialects', we run into the opposite difficulty with Danish, Swedish and Norwegian, for speakers of these languages find little difficulty in communication. Another suggestion is a non-linguistic one: a form of speech used in an independent national state is a 'language' and not a 'dialect'. This would mean that we should have to speak of the American language, the Australian language, and so on. It should be obvious that linguistic science cannot permit its definitions to be determined by non-linguistic criteria. It would be absurd to leave it to politicians to decide whether Scots is a language or a dialect.

In fact we are once again faced with a pseudo-problem inherent in our terminology. There is no either/or relation between the two terms language and dialect. The term 'dialect' implies a superordinate term. When we say: 'he speaks a dialect', we imply 'a dialect of X'. In other words we mean 'a variety of X'. No zoologist would give a moment's serious attention to the question 'Is this a dachshund or a dog?' The opposition dialect/language involves the logical nature of these linguistic terms. The descriptions D, D_1, D_2, etc., of certain locally restricted forms of speech are said to be dialects of language L, when L is set up as a higher

order entity which subsumes their resemblances. L is of a higher
order of abstraction than the descriptive systems which are
compared in order to set L up. Thus Danish, Swedish and Norwegian from this point of view can be said to be dialects of
'Scandinavian'. The English language we set up on the basis of
our dialect survey can in its turn be said to be a dialect of West
Germanic.

The superordinate linguistic entity set up to account for the
resemblances of a given number of 'dialects' has already been
discussed under the comparative method (see Chapter 1). The
description and comparison of the resemblant forms of speech
within a national territory is no different in theory. From this
point of view the 'language' is a 'diasystem'. The dialect/language
crux arises from a non-technical use of linguistic terminology.
One of the modes of speech used in a given national territory may
become endowed with particular prestige and gradually come to be
accepted as the 'standard form' and be regarded as the English
language *par excellence*. From the technical point of view this mode
of speaking is also a dialect. It is the standard dialect of the
English people.

We may now return to the question of dialect boundaries. The
Romance dialects spoken in Italy and France appear, as we have
said, as a continuum of speech forms shading into one another.
Thus it would appear just as impossible to fix a dialect boundary
as it is to mark a definite place in the spectrum where yellow stops
and orange begins. The dialect maps again seem to bear out this
contention, for the various isoglosses seldom coincide to form a
clear-cut boundary marking off dialects one from the other. But
they seem rather to go each its own separate way.[1]

Such data as these, furnished by dialect geographical researches,
have led scholars to give a negative answer to the question: 'Are

---

1. This result of linguistic geography was predicted by Hugo Schuchardt
in 1870, twenty-six years before Gilliéron's Atlas began to appear: 'If we now
draw up a map on which we enter the lines encompassing (*Umfassungslinien*=
isoglosses) all possible phonetic and morphological phenomena whereby Latin
has changed to Romance, on this criss-cross of lines we shall see some denser or
darker places where several meet, i.e. we shall establish transitional zones'
(Schuchardt-Brevier, p. 187).

there dialect boundaries?' This question, however, is obscure and even absurd in its very formulation. It contains two, or rather three, questions in one. The first should be 'Are there differences between dialects?'; to this the answer is obviously in the affirmative. The second is 'May two dialects have many or most peculiarities in common, so that they may be classified as a group?' This is of course possible, but not necessary. Conditions vary in fact from country to country, as we shall see later when we compare Germany with France. But the presence or absence of this condition does not help or hinder the division of dialects. The definition of a dialect is the sum of its characteristics. Any one single difference will serve to mark it off from its neighbours. The fact that it has certain characteristics in common with the neighbours in the south and others again in common with those on the north side does not obscure the fact that it is different from both. It is therefore obvious that we can always distinguish between dialects. But this brings us to the third implication of the question we are discussing. To plot the geographical distribution of speech forms on a map is another question altogether. In fact the question 'Are there dialect boundaries?' is absurd, and it will be seen in all its absurdity if it is put in the right way. When we ask 'What is a dialect boundary?', we mean 'Can we draw a line on a map which will represent a distinction and a demarcation between two or more forms of speech?' But forms of speech are not physical objects like towns, rivers, mountains, which have fixed position in a physical world. Those who posed the question forgot the truism that words and sentences are merely human actions, and that they cannot exist apart from human beings who produce them. There is no such physical entity as a dialect, but only dialect speakers.[1] The question should then be put in this form: 'Are there boundaries for dialect speakers?' Now it is seen in all its absurdity, divested of its pseudo-scientific aspect. If I, as a speaker of a south-western dialect, move to Manchester, that involves a shift of a dialect boundary. Such extensive geographical displacements on a large scale, are, of course, rare, the bulk of

---

1. That is of course from the geographical point of view. On language as a super-individual entity, see above.

the population being stable within comparatively narrow limits. Nevertheless, even under primitive transport conditions, movements of population are constantly taking place. A farmer goes to market, converses and does business with his acquaintances from different districts. He may take his bride from a distant village. She brings her dialect with her, and although she tends to become assimilated to the dialect of her new home, she has some influence on her neighbours and her children, so that slight changes may be produced in isolated individuals of that community. It is in this way that the so-called dialect boundaries continually shift and fluctuate. It is the natural result of social intercourse and communication and the geographical instability of human beings. Consequently, by the very nature of the thing, there can be no *clear-cut* line between varieties of dialect speech.

We may now return to the discussion of the sound laws. Figure 37 shows clearly that there are territories enclosed and separated by bundles of lines within which sound treatment is regular. It is only in the buffer regions between such territories that confusion is recorded. Such facts, however, do not invalidate the dogma of sound law inviolability propounded by the neo-grammarians; for they, too, had envisaged the possibility of dialect intermixture and borrowing providing apparent exceptions to the sound law.[1] All that dialect geography has done is to show that such borrowing takes place far more frequently and intensively than we had supposed. It will suffice to quote the words of an eminent dialect geographer on this very question: 'Nous ne croyons pas que le géographie linguistique doive sérieusement saper le solide édifice élevé par la rigoreuse méthode des néo-grammariens.'[2]

We may now turn from the problem of defining the differences and distinctions between dialects to that of accounting for similarities. From a dialect map we see that each separate linguistic phenomenon extends over a definite area bounded by an isogloss. The boundaries of different phenomena often coincide, and such

---

1. See above on *popina*, etc.
2. 'We do not believe that linguistic geography must seriously undermine the solid structure erected by the rigorous method of the neo-grammarians.'

bundles of lines mark out territories within which the dialects have various characteristics in common. This is the cartographical representation of what we understand by a group of dialects. This is not to say that all members of such a group have every important characteristic in common or that it excludes the possibility of their sharing peculiarities with a dialect outside their group. Nevertheless, within such a bundle of isoglosses there is a palpable degree of uniformity, and it is our task to explain how and why such a uniformity comes about.

The existence of such a dialect area raises two complementary questions: (1) 'What are the circumstances and conditions that produce uniformity of speech within a given area?' and (2) 'What is the nature of the obstacles which check the expansion of a certain form of speech and limit its area?' We shall first attempt to find an answer to the question as to what produces a greater or lesser degree of uniformity within a given geographical area. In the first chapter we discussed the tendency of language to constant change. The individual, dependent on his memory for the reproduction of sound symbols and concerned only to produce the required effects on the hearer with the minimum of effort, is particularly exposed to the phenomenon characterized as linguistic drift. But to this disintegrating tendency of the individual which, left unchecked, would lead to anarchy and mutual unintelligibility, there is opposed the integrating force of the community. Accordingly we should expect to find that within any community the uniformity of speech varies directly with the intensity of intercourse; for constant communication tends to iron out individual idiosyncrasies. Wherever there exists a centre of social activity of any kind at which people come together regularly, whether it be for marketing, for festivities, religious or secular, or merely for the business of political administration, there we have a uniformizing force that will be manifested in all the cultural phenomena of that region, and most particularly in its speech. Isolated communities, on the other hand, will exhibit eccentricities of language, just as a recluse, deprived of the criticism and examples of his fellows, develops eccentricities of behaviour and deportment. We shall now see what light dialect geography throws on this relation between social communications and speech differentiation.

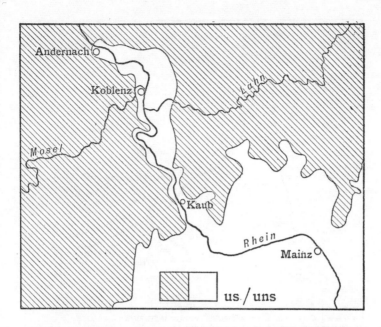

Fig. 38. (From Bach, A., *Deutsche Mundartforschung*, Heidelberg, 1934.)

In the first place we shall consider how far ease of communication facilitates the spread of speech forms. The geographical method of dialect investigation in various countries has gone to show that speech forms spread furthest and quickest along lines of communication like river valleys, important roads, etc. Figure 38 illustrates the distribution of the representatives of the standard German word *uns*, which in Low German, as in English, drops the *n*. The map shows clearly how the *uns*-form has spread from the south and is penetrating the *us*-territory along the natural road formed by the Rhine valley. Figure 39 shows how in the south of France an important series of isoglosses follows the old trade road that joins the Mediterranean to the Atlantic Ocean, while even the side road depicted on the map is accompanied by diverging isoglosses. This example shows clearly how linguistic changes follow a line of communication and spread out laterally from that line. Speech, like disease, spreads quickest where contact

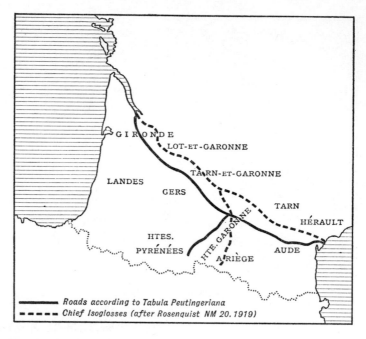

Fig. 39. (From Gamillscheg, E., *Sprachgeographie*, Leipzig, 1928.)

is closest and intercourse most intense. To sum up our argument, I quote a striking passage from Ellis's *Early English Pronunciation*, which reveals to what extent the radiation of speech forms depends on communications. With reference to the dialect of the Old Colne Valley (6 N.N.E. Burnley), his informant writes that as a boy he had 'special opportunity of hearing handloom weavers who lived in the small farm cottages on the hillside in what was known in old times as Pendle and Trawden Forests. During the twenty years he had been away from the district the dialect had completely changed and become a bastard Yorkshire, from *the mechanics who were engaged in fitting the mill machinery and from the "hands" who cross and recross the Pennine chain.*'

We can now examine the counter proposition—how isolation secures immunity from such speech infection. Isolation does not necessarily mean geographical remoteness, although that, as will be shown later, is often an important factor. The barriers that check the expansion of certain forms of speech, are, in fact, obstacles to social communication; and such obstacles, as post-war politics amply illustrates, are often entirely artificial and man-made. Let us consider in order the possible reasons for the position of modern dialect boundaries. Of various theories that have been put forward the most generally accepted until recent times was that the modern distribution is based on old tribal distinctions. In Germany, for instance, dialects had long been classed according to the old tribal divisions into Franconian, Alemannic, Saxon, etc., the underlying assumption being that the differences of speech existing at the time of the migrations have been perpetuated down to the present day, and that the boundaries between them have remained more or less fixed. But it has been pointed out in the first place that the 'tribes' were not homo-geneous either in race or in language. The Angles and Saxons, for instance, who conquered Britain were accompanied by Jutes, Frisians, Suevians, etc. Moreover, present-day linguistic unity cannot be taken to prove that this unity has existed at all times. Silesia, for instance, was settled by colonists drawn from Upper, Middle and Lower Germany. Yet until the recent expulsion from Poland, the dialect of this territory was fairly uniform over its whole area, although it contains a mixture of elements from all the above regions. It must be said, then, that the old tribal distinctions are of little or no significance for the delimitation of modern dialects.[1]

Geographical barriers as such have surprisingly little effect on linguistic conditions. Rivers, as was shown above (Fig. 38), act more often as means of communication than as obstacles, so that they do not always coincide with a dialect boundary. Where there

---

1. This refers, of course, to the German dialects. In English, though the old distinctions have been greatly modified, the main groups of English dialects do still correspond roughly to the old kingdoms, and the old kingdoms were more or less tribal in origin. It is important for the history of the dialects that *administrative boundaries* in England have always corresponded to a great extent with the boundaries of the old kingdoms, so that it is probable that this factor has been really decisive in the delimitation of the dialects. But we must reserve judgment in this question until we have the English dialect atlas completed.

is such a coincidence, it is mostly due to the circumstances that the river forms a political boundary, and it is the latter which must be held responsible for the division of dialect.[1] The same may be said of all geographical features. In so far as they determine ease or difficulty of communication and provide natural limits for political and administrative areas, they are indirectly responsible for dialect distribution and delimitation. Where, however, such areas transcend the natural geographical limits, it is the former which are of major importance for the history of the dialect. Thus we are told that the Mont Blanc massif does not coincide with any linguistic boundary, whereas the Pyrenees do.

We have so far discussed the ways taken by wandering speech forms and the obstacles to their progress. We have not yet considered why certain new forms of speech are preferred by speakers of a particular dialect. Leaving aside for the moment the adoption of new words to designate new cultural objects like *potato*, *coffee*, etc.,[2] it appears to be mainly a question of linguistic prestige. We in England are particularly sensitive to dialect differences as indicative of social class. So much so that Bernard Shaw has remarked that it is impossible for any Englishman to open his mouth without making some of his fellow countrymen either hate or despise him. The dialect of the educated Londoner, which attained standing and prestige as the language of the Court in the seventeenth century, has now been adopted by most educated Englishmen with only slight individual distinctions. This state of

---

1. In this connexion Dauzat (p. 160) makes the following comment: 'A river if it is crossed by bridges and easily navigable, need form no hindrance to communication, and consequently it does not form a linguistic boundary. If, however, it is broad and bridges are rare, it isolates the two banks. Thus the lower Loire in France forms a clear-cut dialect boundary. Similarly the Allier, which until 1830 was not bridged anywhere in the department of Puy-de-Dôme, separates two widely diverging linguistic territories. It has been pointed out (A. H. Smith, *TPS*, 1936) that the river Whorfe still appears as the dividing line between the Northern and Midland development of OE *ā* (W. Germ. *ai*): north of the Whorfe OE *bān* 'bone', *stān* 'stone' appear as [biən], [stiən], but south of the river as [buən], [stuən]. Smith concludes that 'it would seem that the demarcation between [buən] and [biən] goes back to the time of the Anglian settlement'.
2. See Chapter 14.

affairs is nevertheless merely an extreme example of a universal tendency. It is in fact only one manifestation of the human urge to emulate and imitate those whom we consider our betters. The habits, manners and fashions of the upper classes are followed with blind and unquestioning obedience by the *petite bourgeoisie*, and Savile Row penetrates by degrees to Petticoat Lane. In speech, history has repeated itself in every country where a centre of culture and administration has been set up. In ancient Greece, where every city state was a law and a power unto itself, each such region spoke its own peculiar dialect. Later the city-state was superseded and the Greek world was unified under Alexander and his successors. A new common language was evolved for the purpose of administration, a language which, being pruned of certain local peculiarities of Attic, could serve as a means of communication throughout those territories. This was the *koinē*, the language of the chancelleries that replaced and swept out of existence the ancient local dialects. It was from this language that, after the break-up of the Greek world and the interruption of communications, the modern Greek dialects (with one exception) were evolved. In Italy the process was repeated. In the early history of the peninsula Latin was merely the dialect of Latium and, more particularly, of the city of Rome. In other cities and parts of Italy different languages were spoken: Oscan and Umbrian (both related to Latin), Etruscan, Greek, etc. As Rome became mistress of Italy and the centre of administration, she imposed her language on her Italian subjects and eventually a great part of her empire, so that throughout Spain, Gaul, Raetia and Dacia, a fairly uniform type of vulgar Latin was spoken. After the failure of the central administration consequent on the barbarian raids, the Latin spoken in each of these separate provinces developed independently into modern Romance languages—Portuguese, Spanish, French, Rhaeto-Romance, Rumanian, etc.[1]

The dialect maps illustrate the same process in the linguistic microcosm. They show plainly how words are radiated from centres of culture and administration and how the standard literary languages gradually replace the *patois* of the countryside.

1. See W. D. Elcock, *The Romance Languages*.

Thus Low German is distinguished from High German by the absence of diphthongization, a peculiarity which it shares with Lowland Scots as opposed to standard English. The accompanying sketch (Fig. 40) of the distribution *hus/haus* forms shows how Berlin and its immediate surroundings, though actually in Low German territory, form an area in which the diphthongized pronunciation of the standard language is predominant. England

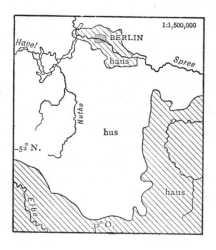

Fig. 40. (After Mertes, *Geograph. Zts.* 28, 392.)

has as yet no complete dialect atlas, but the following quotation from the introduction to Wright's *Dialect Dictionary* gives an indication of the same phenomenon in our own country. Speaking of the collection of material in dialects spoken within twenty-five miles of London: he says: 'In these regions the dialects are hopelessly mixed, and are now practically worthless for philological purposes'.[1]

---

1. This argument is often advanced by those who decry the value of an English dialect atlas. The truth is that dialects never were pure. Moreover, the distribution of scattered dialect remnants is often as informative as maps of richer texture (see below on *trabs*).

A cultural centre infects not only its own immediate environment but also any area or locality with which it has communications. Now there is often more intense communication between large towns than between those towns and their immediate countryside. Consequently speech-forms leap, as it were, from town to town over the intervening country. Thus in France the dialect maps show that the dialect of Paris infects first towns like Bordeaux, Lyons, Marseilles, and from these centres in their turn the forms of the standard language are relayed to the surrounding districts.

Perhaps the most interesting of the phenomena brought to light by the study of dialect geography are those that develop on the frontiers where two or more dialects come into collision. In such a buffer territory the inhabitants are usually able to understand two forms of speech even if they practise only one; the result it that they often possess two dialect equivalents for what they wish to express. By the psychological process discussed in a previous chapter this gives rise to contaminations, phenomena that occur with a far greater frequency than the study of the written texts alone would lead one to suspect. The two accompanying maps (Figs. 41 and 42) show the distribution of the words for *she* and *without* in North England. In the Northwest Midlands the word for 'she' appears as [u:], unstressed [u]. This goes back to ME *hō* OE *hēo*. The form *she* [ʃi:] appears in two separate regions, (1) the South East Midlands with the unstressed form [ʃɪ] and (2) the North with the unstressed form [ʃə]. In the buffer area between the area of [u:] and that of [ʃi:] a form [ʃu:] is recorded. Apropos of this form (Windhill district of the West Riding) Wright wrote: 'For the present the form ʃu: still remains a riddle.' His reason was that the ME *shō* from OE *sēo* would not become [ʃu:] but [ʃiu] in the modern dialect. Its geographical position suggests that the most attractive explanation is that the form is due to contamination of [u:] and [ʃi] in the modern dialect. The explanation may be more complicated than appears from this simplified account.[1] In ME and OE the pronouns *hē* 'he' and *hēo* 'she' converged to *he*. To overcome the ambiguity the demonstrative form *sēo* was

1. See E. Dieth, *Essays and Studies*, 1946, p. 99.

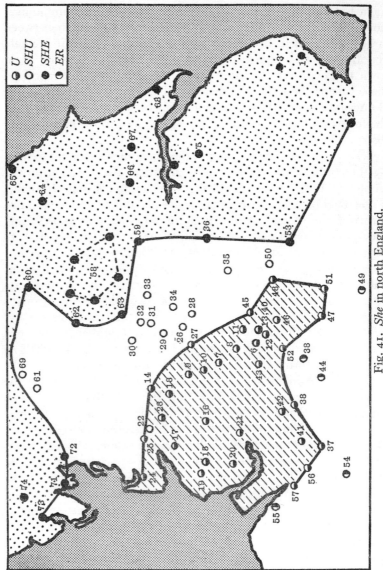

Fig. 41. *She* in north England.

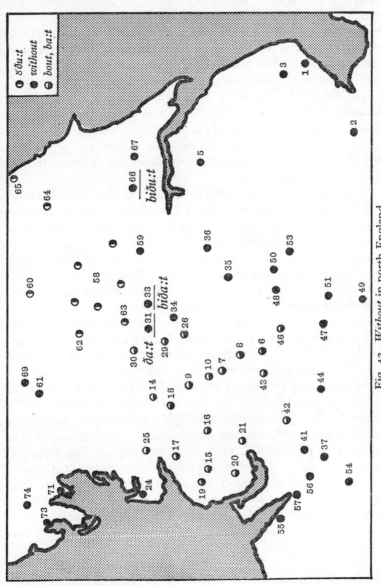

Fig. 42. *Without* in north England.

pressed into service, which by different developments had become [ʃeː] and [ʃoː]. Sporadic survivals of ME *shō* have been detected in the Northern *she* area, and it has been suggested that the descendants of *shō* are to be regarded as 'genuine' forms in Northumbrian, *she* being a secondary intrusion. Dieth, therefore, while accepting the Windhill *shu* as a contamination, would regard it as a blend of [ʃiu] and [uː]. The picture of the distribution elicited by the *Survey of English Dialects* does not materially alter that based on Ellis's collection. [ʃuː] forms are recorded in Yorkshire at points 18 (Spofforth), 22 (Wibsey), 23 (Leeds), 26 (Thornhill), 27 (Carleton), 29 (Golcar), 21 (Skelmanthorpe) and 32 (Ecclesfield).

Anyone who is familiar with the song 'On Ilkley Moor' knows that in Yorkshire they say [baːt] for *without*. The dialect map reveals a form *bithut* where the dialect and the standard form collide.[1] The distribution of the forms is seen in Fig. 42.

There seems to be no doubt that dialect speakers are acutely conscious of the peculiarities of their neighbours' dialect. Ellis records the fact that Fylde (12 N.W.N. of Preston) people have concocted a sentence 'ai m baun daun th taun to bai a raund paund a butə' to mock the South Lancashire people who come to Blackpool and who are accused of saying 'aːm guin daːn t taːn t bai ə raːnd paːnd a buːtə', substituting the vowel [aː] for their own diphthong [au]. But sometimes such an automatic substitution of a sound does not produce the desired result. Much music-hall humour is based on the fact that the Lancashire dialect is distinguished from standard English by the treatment of the sound *u* in words like *much*, *but*, etc. (pronounced [mɒtʃ] as opposed to southern English [mʌtʃ], etc.). Consequently, in their efforts to speak standard English the natives of the country substitute an [ʌ] wherever the [u]-sound occurs in their own dialect. This results in enormities like [bʌtʃə] for [bɒtʃə]. Such hyperdialectal forms are known as 'false regressions'. They are common in all countries where attempts are made to speak another dialect than

---

1. In the *Survey of English Dialects* the blend [biðuːt] is recorded only in Rillington and even there it is characterized as 'old' alongside more recent [wiðuːt].

one's own. One of the most striking features of the Berlin dialect is that in many words it substitutes *j* for *g*. The famous sentence *ik habe eene jut jebratene Jans jejessen* 'I have eaten a well-roasted Goose' is meant to ridicule this feature of the dialect. The Berliner who in his attempt to speak standard High German substitutes a *g* for *j* often overshoots the mark and produces flowers like *ein guter Gunge* (instead of *Junge*). In Germany, further, the Low German dialects are distinguished from the High German by the so-called sound shift, which affected the plosive consonants. Thus *tal* 'number' became *Zahl* in High German, and *tam* 'tame' became *zahm*. Dialect speakers, conscious of this correspondence *t/z* often make errors when attempting to speak High German. *Zeller* for *Teller* 'plate' is a well-known example. Standard English contains some forms which have a similar origin. In vulgar pronunciation an *n* was often omitted before a plosive consonant, producing forms like *Brummagem* for *Birmingham*. In the effort to avoid vulgarity an *n* was often inserted where it was not required. Such was the origin of forms like *messenger*, *passenger*, *scavenger*, etc., the correct forms of which can be seen in the corresponding French words *messager*, *passager* and Anglo-Norman *scawager*.

Standard English contains a number of such 'hyperurbanisms'. It is a characteristic of certain dialects to pronounce an intervocalic dental plosive as an *-r-*. Thus, *what's the matter?* is heard as [wɔzəmarə]. Mistaken reaction against a vulgarism of pronunciation seems to be responsible for the form *paddock* in English. Actually this word is derived from OE *pearroc* (cf. German *Pferch*), which appears in ME as *parrock*, a pronunciation which still persists in dialect use. Apparently the country gentlemen who heard this word in the mouths of their servants took it for a vulgarism and 'corrected' it to *paddock*. On the other hand, we consent to eat *porridge* for breakfast although this is an instance of the same phonetic vulgarism, the correct form being *pottage*. In the form for the receptacle *porringer* we have an example of the intrusive *-n-*. A more complex example is the word *pediment* 'triangular gable-like part crowning a façade', first attested in the seventeenth century. This form is a refashioning of the earlier form *periment*, which is thought to be a corruption by workmen or rustics of the word *pyramid*.

From the foregoing paragraphs it will be obvious that what is essential in the methodology of dialect geography is the interpretation of speech forms in space. The social intercourse that determines linguistic contact is fundamentally a question of contiguity and movement in space, so that speech, like all cultural phenomena, is limited and determined by geographical factors. Very often the mere geographical position of a word gives an answer to problems that cannot be solved by traditional philological methods. Thus Gilliéron in a series of studies has been able to show clearly the factors which lead to the disappearance of words. Some districts of France still use derivatives of the Latin word *gallus* for the cock. In neighbouring regions this word is unknown and has been replaced by such obvious makeshifts as *vicaire*, *faisan*, etc. Now we know that in these regions the Latin words *gallus* (cock) and *cattus* (cat) would both have become *gat* in accordance with the sound laws operative in those dialects. This intolerable homonymity made it necessary for a substitute to be found for one of them. The factor of homonymity in word mortality is, of course, not a discovery of dialect geography (see Chapter 13). What was new about Gilliéron's approach was the direct proof that this method affords. The striking fact is that the area *gallus* 'cock' is limited by the isogloss that marks out the limit of the region when final *ll* becomes *t*, that is where *gallus* becomes *gat*. Within this region there would be homonymity between *cattus* and *gallus*, and consequently *gallus* is unknown. As Dauzat puts it, '*the cat killed the cock*'. It has been mentioned above that Latin *mulgēre*, 'to milk' has been displaced by a descendant of *trahere*. *Mulgēre*, however, is preserved in southern France. Its disappearance in the northern dialects was occasioned by the fact that in these districts regular phonetic development would have rendered it homonymous with *moudre* (from *molere* 'to grind'). A final example to illustrate this principle. Of the Latin word *trabs* 'beam' only a few scattered remnants remain in the French dialects. These have the phonetic form *trau*. If the map representing the distribution is superimposed on the map *trou* 'hole' the causality of this distribution springs to eye. For the localities with *trau* meaning 'beam' lie with one exception round about the region where *trau* means 'hole'.[1] The one point where both are in use lies on the border of these two territories, and it is thus merely an exception which goes to prove the rule. Elsewhere the two forms are mutually exclusive.

The map *trabs* opens up other fascinating problems of dialect geography—those of word stratigraphy. Given a distribution of various words of identical meaning, the question arises how such a distribution originated. Figure 43 shows the distribution of *trabs* survivals in France as revealed by the map *poutre* 'beam'. Its territory is fairly compact, comprising eastern France towards French Switzerland, almost the whole of Savoy, and a horizontal strip that traverses France towards the mouth of the Garonne. There is one isolated point in the extreme south. Now these points show clearly that the distribution of this ancient word was far more widespread than it is today. They are the islands that indicate a submerged continent; or, in another metaphor, the surface outcrops that reveal a hidden stratum. It is from this comparison with geology that the term 'word stratigraphy' is taken. A proof that the conclusions as to the extent of this hidden stratum are correct is furnished by reference to the maps *chevron* 'rafter', *fenil* 'hayloft', *seuil* 'threshold, door-sill', which reveal derivatives of *trabs* for these objects in many intervening districts, and thus justify the conclusion that the basic word *trabs*, from which these derivatives were made, also existed in these parts. If we add these places to the distribution of *trabs*, it completes the picture that we had formed from the *poutre* map. The patch on the extreme south is freed from its isolation and the Rhone valley is again seen as the path along which the invader has spread. The points in the extreme north, west and southwest seem to indicate that this ancient word once extended over the whole of France and was only later submerged by other alternatives. This conclusion is borne out by the historical evidence afforded by a study of the texts.

One more example to illustrate the value of word stratigraphy in

---

1. To put it differently, *trau* 'beam' only occurs in those localities which have another word for 'hole', e.g. *creux* or *pertuis*. For further examples see Jaberg, *op. cit.*, p. 86, to whose article I am indebted for the above.

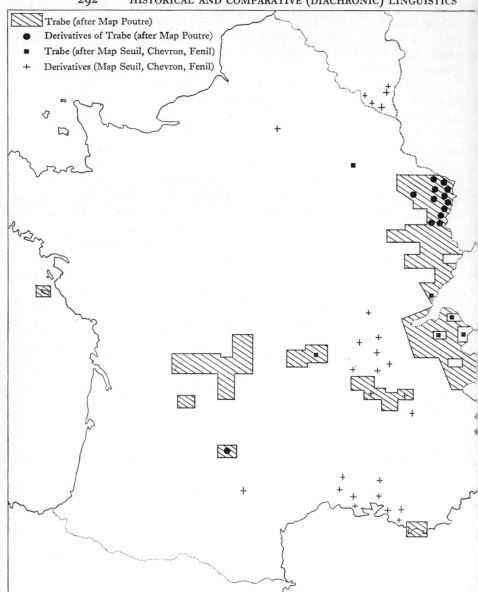

Fig. 43. The distribution of *trabs* on the basis of the maps: *poutre, chevron, fenil, seuil* (after Jaberg, *Arch. f. d. Stud. d. neuer. Spr.* 119).

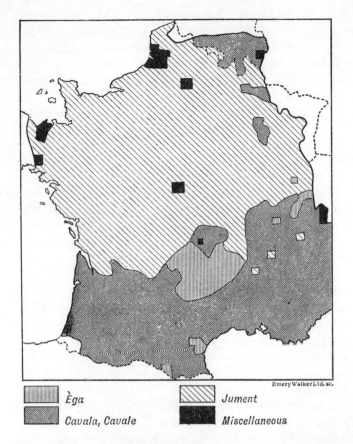

Fig. 44. (After Dauzat, *La géographie linguistique*, Paris, 1922.)

illuminating the history of a language. The French dialects have a variety of words to designate the 'mare'. The standard word *jument* extends over practically the whole of northern and central France and is beginning to descend the Rhone valley (Fig. 44). In the extreme south the most common term is *cavala*, a word that has invaded France from northern Italy. But most interesting is the form *ega*, derived directly from the Latin word *equa*. Its distribution is informative. It survives only in a small region of the central uplands and in a few isolated points in the south and in the Alps; that is, in more or less inaccessible places cut off from communication with the outside world.[1] It is precisely in such a situation that we should expect a dialect to be most immune from the influence of the standard language (see above). We should rightly conclude that this is the most ancient stratum. The distribution of *cavala* is also instructive. Apart from its principal demesne in the south, it occupies fairly extensive islands in eastern and northern France, so that we may conclude that its territory once extended unbroken between these limits, and that it has been disintegrated by the pressure of the standard form radiating from Paris.

In conclusion one might say that if speech is conventional social activity resting on imitation, on the contact of man with man, then the distribution of likenesses and differences of speech, when projected on to a map, will be a mirror of human relationships, of their gathering together and drawing apart.

APPLICATIONS OF LINGUISTIC GEOGRAPHY: THE NEO-LINGUISTS

Dialect Maps like *Jument* and *Poutre* reveal that remote and isolated areas tend to be immune from the influence of the standard language. All this is the result of the truism that people do not imitate those with whom they have little or no contact. It is such maps that have led linguistic geographers to declare that marginal areas tend to become archaic. But this is true only within limits, that is to say that isolated communities are less exposed to the influence of *innovations* proceeding from the standard language. The fact is that linguists, no less than archaeologists, tend to be antiquarians at heart. Jacob Grimm showed his romantic enthusiasm for the works of the folk when he wrote in the preface to the German Grammar: 'Six hundred years ago every rustic knew, that is to say practised daily, perfections and niceties in the German language of which the best grammarians nowadays do not dream.' In this spirit scholars naturally tended to concentrate on the old phenomena preserved in dialect and so came to exaggerate the archaism of the country dialects. Henry Sweet wrote: 'Superficial observers have discovered the Gothic of Ulfilas in

---

1. In much the same regions the archaic word *trabs* is preserved.

various German dialects, none of them being on the average more archaic than the ordinary literary German. These sensational results are generally obtained by picking out those forms which are more archaic than the corresponding ones of the standard language, forms which occur in every dialect, and ignoring the equally numerous and striking cases in which the advantage is decidedly on the side of the literary language.' Despite these warnings the supposed archaisms of marginal areas have been elevated into universal linguistic principles by the Neo-linguistic School. Before proceeding to an examination of their theses the point must be made again that the impingement of the standard language on a dialect speaker is a phenomenon of bilingualism or 'bidialectalism'. When the patois fails him either as an effective means of communication or for social reasons, the standard language offers its services. It is ubiquitous, he understands it and can accept what it offers, even if only in a modified way. With this reminder of the field of linguistic forces at play we can turn to the doctrines of the neolinguists.

The neolinguist theses were elaborated by the Italian scholar M. Bartoli in his *Introduzione alla neolinguistica* (1925). His approach to linguistic problems is also known as 'areal linguistics'. It is in effect the application of the principles and findings of dialect geography to the relations holding between different languages. Among the Romance languages the following facts of distribution may be observed:

	Iberia	Gallia	Italia	Dacia[1]
'mare'	equa	caballa	caballa	equa
'head'	caput	testa	caput	caput
'sheep'	ovis	ovis	pecora	ovis

Generalizing from such carefully selected examples Bartoli held that the lateral, flanking, or marginal areas contrast with the central areas, and so he set up two principles:

(1) Of two linguistic stages the earlier stage is usually preserved in the more isolated of the two areas.

---

1. Dacia was the Roman province corresponding roughly to present-day Rumania.

(2) The stage attested in lateral (marginal) areas is usually the earlier stage, provided the central area is not the more isolated.

The word 'usually' must be stressed because Bartoli was well aware of such contrary patterns as

	Iberia	Gallia	Italia	Dacia
'bird'	passer	avis	avis	passer

It is to be noted that Bartoli and the neolinguists reject the polygenesis of linguistic phenomena. They tend rather to postulate a single centre of innovation with subsequent spread from a centre of 'radiation'. By use of the various principles, of which two have been singled out for mention, Bartoli traced certain innovations in Romance to various centres of origin. From this base he proceeded to attack the neogrammarian doctrines and methods. For instance, he argued that there is no need to postulate shwa (*ə) to account for the correspondence of Skt. *pitar-*: Lat. *pater* (see above p. 217). The vowel *a* is observed over a greater area and 'the greater of two areas ("area maggiore") usually preserves the earlier stage of the development, provided the lesser area ("area minore") is not more isolated and does not consist of marginal areas'. It follows from this principle that *a* represents an earlier stage than *i*. Bartoli adds what he considers a stronger reason: Sanskrit and other southern Indo-European languages have many innovations not found in northern languages of the family, which were 'more isolated'.

It is this concept of 'isolation' which is focal. It must be examined more closely, together with the purely geographical concept of 'marginal area', in its bearing on the dynamic principle 'the spread of innovation', for these lie at the heart of Bartoli's doctrines. What is fundamental in linguistic geography is that a given area of speech, say France, is the field of linguistic forces which operate because speech is essentially a mimetic process. These forces can operate only (a) where there is mutual intelligibility and (b) where geographical contiguity ensures the necessary contact of speaker with speaker. The patois gives way to the standard language because (a) the speakers of the patois are brought into linguistic contact with speakers of the standard language and

(b) the standard language enjoys social prestige or provides a ready-made substitute if the patois resources for some reason or other become defective as a means of communication. An isolated patois will go its own way, and the result will be that it will in some respects be more archaic, and in others more innovating, than the standard language. Both its archaisms and its innovations will tend to persist if the pressure of the standard language is reduced because of difficulties of communication. The traffic of inter-dialect exchange is less intense than in more accessible areas. But the essential fact underlying all these acts of imitation is the fact of bilingualism. If the speech of others is unintelligible, there will be no imitation and no influence. I may live in close proximity to Welshmen, but as far as I am concerned as a speaker of English they can mutate their consonants, incorporate their pronouns and all the rest without the slightest difference to my speech. Without extensive bilingualism two mutually unintelligible modes of speech cannot have any profound effect on each other.

Despite these self-evident truths the neolinguistic doctrines have been applied to the relationships between the Indo-European languages, and the technical literature abounds with references to 'marginal features' and even 'colonial areas'. It may be asked what sense there is in dubbing Sanskrit as the language of either a central or marginal area. Towards the end of the third millennium B.C. we may suppose that Indo-Iranian, Anatolian, Greek and all the rest existed in widely separated geographical regions and had become mutually unintelligible languages. At this stage of linguistic history where was the prestigious standard language? Where was the centre of radiation without which the terms 'central' and 'marginal' are meaningless? What careers were open to well-spoken talents? Where was the prevailing bilingualism, the contact of man with man, which alone makes possible the unbroken chain of mimetic processes that underlie the spread of linguistic forms from centres of radiation?

A few examples will make clear the difficulties. *Aqua* is said to be older than Greek *hudōr*, because the latter is found in 'central', that is innovating, areas. Congeners of *aqua* are found in Germanic (Goth. *ahva*, OE *ēa*, still preserved in *is-land*) and in Celtic (only in place names!). The relatives of *hudōr* are more widespread, in fact the majority of Indo-European languages present the word. Significant is the occurrence in Germanic (e.g. Engl. *water*) alongside of the *aqua* representatives, and in Umbrian *utur*, which is not only closely related to Latin but also in close geographical proximity. Moreover, the word shows a highly archaic form of declension with a stem alternation *r/n*: this is exemplified in the Gothic genitive *watins*, with which we may compare the *r/n* alternation in Hittite *wadar*, loc. sing. *wedeni*. There can be little doubt that *water* belongs to the oldest stratum of Indo-European words and that its geographical position on the 'Indo-European map' is irrelevant. According to neolinguistic theory Latin would have to be more 'marginal' than Umbrian. It remains to add that Celtic on the extreme western periphery has substituted a new word: Ir. *dobur*, Welsh *dwfr*, Bret. *dour*, a word which is also considered to enter into Germanic place-names, i.e. *Verno-dubrum* 'alder-water'.

The point need not be laboured further. The fundamental concepts of areal linguistics, centre of innovation, marginality and the like, largely derived from the study of the behaviour of dialects in centrally organized states in which a given set of social forces governs the patterning of the linguistic data, have no validity when applied to a totally different set of linguistic data, i.e. the relationships of mutually unintelligible languages scattered over immense geographical areas. The methods and principles of linguistic geography apply strictly only to synchronic material collected from closely cohering dialects. To permit the application of such principles to the Indo-European dialects we should have first to reduce the available material, attested at widely different dates and under different circumstances, to a synchronic basis. We should, for instance, first have to reconstruct (say) the Celtic of 2000 B.C., and set it in the geographical position it occupied at that date, and similarly with all the major IE groups. How difficult and disputed such reconstructions would be, to say nothing of their geographical determination, needs no emphasis. In particular, concordances and discordances of vocabulary among the IE languages must be treated with the greatest caution. Languages easily replace their ancient inherited stock of words because of linguistic and historical accidents. So it is permissible to doubt whether, for instance, the preservation of the word for 'king' *rēg- which is attested for Celtic, Italic and Indo-Iranian, is due simply to the geographical position of these 'marginal' languages. Greek does not present the word; but the crucial question is when it was replaced. We know that at the end of the Mycenaean world ca. 1200 B.C., the Greeks used the word *wanax* for 'king', whereas in classical times (and in Homer) this has been replaced by *basileus*, a word which seems originally to have denoted a local functionary of quite subordinate status. Thus if *wanax* replaced *rēg- in the second millennium after the Greeks entered the Balkan peninsula, this innovation has nothing to do with the 'central' position of Greek among the IE languages. It is a fact on all fours with the replacement of the word for 'water' in 'marginal' Celtic and the replacement of the ancient word for 'horse' *ekwos by a derivative *hrossan 'the leaper, runner' in West Germanic (the ancient word surviving in OE *eoh*).

Examples could be multiplied but this could do no more than reinforce the warning given long ago in an influential exposition of linguistic geography.[1] 'When applied to the past, and particularly to the ancient languages, the geographical method requires very careful handling indeed, as its cogency and effectiveness are reduced in proportion to the remoteness, lack of precise localization, and dissimilarity of the material treated.'

---

1. I. Iordan–J. Orr, *An Introduction to Romance Linguistics*, revised by R. Posner, 1970 (p. 271).

13

Etymology and Change of Meaning

Etymology is the quintessence of the comparative method, yet there are few discussions of this subject, or even mentions of it, in modern handbooks of linguistics. One scholar has even gone so far as to call the typical etymological dictionary 'an old curiosity shop'. Yet it remains true that laymen and young students feel the fascination of word history, and many of the greatest scholars have devoted much of their lives to etymological work. The subject is of immense complexity in practice, but at least some basic principles deserve discussion in an introductory manual.

The comparative method rests on the intuitive judgment that the resemblances of S(ound)-M(eaning) items of different languages cannot be due to chance, this being a consequence of the arbitrary connexion between the vocable and its meaning (see Chapter 1). The sound laws are deduced in the first place by observation of regularities of correspondence between the vocables of words and monemes that are equated on the basis of their meaning. To detect the relatives of a given word or moneme in this way is to write its etymology. It follows that an acceptable etymology must account both for the S and M sides of the item in question. It was the discovery of the sound law principle that delivered etymology from dilettantism and from the reproach that etymology is a science in which the consonants counts for very little and the vowels for nothing at all.

The tempting equation of English *have* with Latin *habēre*, of identical meaning, is a case in point. But this must be rejected because it does not fit into the patterns of sound correspondences between Germanic and Italic. For instance, Latin *h-* derives from IE **gh-*, while Germanic *h-* goes back to **k-*. The modern English form goes back to OE *habban*, which in its turn descended from CGmc. **χabēn*, and scholars are inclined to link this up with the IE root **kap-*, which is reflected in Latin *capio* 'take'.

Words change, however, not only in their sounds but also in their meaning; but as yet linguistics has little or nothing to offer in the way of regularities in semantic change comparable to the sound law principle. The problems of etymological research may then be reviewed first from the easier side, that is the establishment of the phonemic correspondences between words which are identical in meaning.

The intuitive identification of English *hand* and *finger* with German *Hand* and *Finger* would meet with little resistance. With *tongue* and *Zunge* we encounter the correspondence $t = z$ which was discussed above (p. 209), and the etymological equation is supported by examples which account for this difference between the two words as the result of a sound law. This leads on to the equation *tooth: Zahn*. The words are identical in meaning and the initial consonants fall under the sound law just mentioned. But the etymologist must account for all the differences between the words and bring them under similar formulas of regularity. To do this we must look for other relatives. Here a fundamental principle of etymological research must be enunciated. It has been formulated as 'Look for Latin etymologies on the Tiber, not on the Ganges.' This means that etymology must begin at home, in the bosom of the family. For an English etymology we must first scan the resources of English, followed by those of West Germanic and Common Germanic before venturing further afield. Among the Germanic representatives of *tooth* we find Old Saxon *tand*, while Old High German offers both *zan* and *zand*. Gothic *tunpus*, too, shows that the word stem ended with an *n* plus a dental consonant. But there the vowel of the stem is aberrant. Scholars, therefore, posit a Common Germanic form with stem alternation: **tanpuz/tunpus*. There is a sound law to the effect that in Old English the *n* was dropped before the dental fricative, as the result of which the vowel was lengthened and changed to ō. This vowel, by the changes already reviewed (p. 208) eventually developed into [uw]; hence the modern form [tuwþ]. A similar loss of *n* before [þ] is seen in *mouth*, which corresponds to the German *Mund*, while the Gothic form is *munþs*. In this word the vowel *u* was also lengthened in Old English and was later subject to the diphthongization already commented on p. 284. Hence the modern form [maoþ].

The as yet unexplained alternation of the vowel *a* and *u*, in the postulated Common Germanic forms *tanþ-/tunþ-*, still leaves us open to reproach. For guidance we must consult more distantly related members of the family. Here we resort to the diaphonemic 'telephone exchange' of Indo-European. First using the lines provided by Grimm's Law, from *t—þ we link up with IE *d—t. From here we can put calls through to Latin *dent-*, OIr. *dēt*, Welsh *dant*, Lithuanian *dantìs* Greek *odont-*, etc. Here, too, we find an alternation of vowels (to say nothing of the puzzling prothetic vowel of Greek). The clue to the problem is provided by Sanskrit, which has a declension *dan*, accus. *dántam*, gen. *datás*. This reveals that the stem exhibited an Ablaut alternation in the declension (see p. 217), so that we have to posit IE *dont-/dnt-. The sonant nasal which appears in the zero grade (see p. 218) developed regularly to *un* in Germanic: hence Gothic *tunþus*. In other Germanic languages levelling of the stem also took place (see p. 237), but most of them generalized the *dont- forms, which became quite regularly *tanþ-*, since short *o* was changed to *a* in Germanic. In Latin the zero-grade form was generalized and *dnt- proceeded quite regularly to *dent-*.[1]

It now remains to account for the prothetic vowel of Greek *odont-*. In the first place note must be taken of the fact that in one dialect (Aeolic) a form *edont-* is attested, and it looks as though *odont-* is simply due to assimilation of *e* to the *o* of the stem. The prothetic vowel can be accounted for first by Benveniste's theory of the root (see pp. 220ff), which posits that all IE roots have the form CVC, the apparent exceptions of the type VC being due to the loss of a laryngeal consonant. Following this, we should deduce

---

1. In ODEE *dent-* is mistakenly referred to a form *dent-* with full *e*-grade.

that the prothetic vowel in *edont-* is the reflex of a laryngeal consonant in the anteconsonantal position such as would come about in the zero grade: $*H_1d\text{-}ont\text{-}$. If we now subject this complex stem to morphological analysis, it appears as a derivative from the zero grade of a root by means of the suffix *-ont-*. The full grade corresponding to H_1d- would be $*H_1ed$-. It is this which lies behind the verbal root *ed-* 'eat'. Consequently, scholars refer both the English *eat* and *tooth* (together with their congeners in other languages) to one and the same root. The root is simply the common core of this whole family of words; and to site any of the words in its family is to etymologize it. In fact, the proper object of etymological enquiry is not the isolated word but the word family; and the family cannot be established without family ties, and this means the study of word formation.

The example just worked brings out the fact that morphological structure and meaning are essential ingredients of an etymology no less than sound correspondences. With *tooth* and *eat* the meaning has been held constant, but this rarely happens in etymological research. Words change their meaning in strange and unpredictable ways as well as their shape. A case in point is our word *sad*. The semantic equivalent of this in German is *traurig*; but by applying the rules of sound correspondence we can pick out a German word *satt* 'replete, satiated'. Despite the semantic gap, scholars agree in equating this German word with our *sad*, and this poses a semantic problem which must be discussed systematically. First a search for other relatives must be made, and this offers little difficulty if the meaning 'satiated' is accepted as basic. In Germanic we have ON *saðr*, Goth. *saþs*; in Ir. *sathech*, in Latin *satis*. Greek sound developments make the root difficult to recognize, since antevocalic *s-* and intervocalic *-s-* were both changed to the aspirate, which was dropped intervocalically. Once this rule is applied the Homeric adjective *a(h)atos* 'insatiable' (from $*\eta\text{-}s\theta tos$) and the adverb *ha-dēn* 'filled to repletion' (from $*s\theta\text{-}d\bar{e}n$) are seen to belong to the family. But Greek also offers words which show the root in a different form with a final *-s* but without the initial aspirate, e.g. *asē* 'surfeit, loathing'. This poses a double problem.

New light was thrown on this and on the whole family of words when Anatolian texts (Palaic and Hieroglyph Hittite, see Appendix A, p. 384) presented a root *ḫas-*, meaning 'fill with drink', 'abundance'. It was this which suggested a revised morphological analysis and revealed connexions with unrecognized members of the family.

Again we establish family ties by morphological analysis. Using Benveniste's theory of the root and the laryngeal hypothesis we can posit the following variants of the extended root, the base being $*H_2es + H_2$ (see p. 221).

I	II	III
$H_2es + H_2$	$H_2s + eH_2$	$H_2s + H_2$

Form II, according to the rules, would yield *sā-*, and this unexpectedly brings the Latin adjective *sānus* under scrutiny, because the morphological analysis from $*H_2s\text{-}eH_2\text{-}nos$ is parallel with that of *plānus* from $*pl\text{-}eH_2\text{-}nos$ (the root being **pel-* which is extended by the element $-H_2$). The standard works on Latin etymology leave the word *sānus* isolated: 'No similar word is found elsewhere.'[1] Basically the word means 'in good health', and it is also applied to mental health. This word provides a good example of the problem which more often than not faces the etymologist. He must rely on his judgment in bridging the semantic gap. Here the gap is between 'replete' and 'healthy'. It so happens that the earliest example of the Greek use of the verb *as-* (Linear B text of the Bronze Age) is concerned with the fattening of young pigs. This context fits in well with the Bronze Age attestation of the verb *ḫas-* 'fill with drink' in the Anatolian group. It is thus permissible to suppose that the word belongs in Indo-European to the technical language of animal husbandry. The original technical meaning of *sānus* may therefore have been 'well-fed', 'in good condition'. It is interesting to note that *sānus* continued to be used in the vocabulary of animal husbandry, for in Late Latin the derived verb *sānāre* meant 'to castrate'.

We now return to the semantic problem offered by the wayward member of the family, the English *sad*. The first step is to plot the semantic scatter or range of the word. ODEE divides the scatter into two sections:

---

1. Ernout-Meillet. *sub. voc.*

A. †sated, weary OE; †steadfast, firm; †grave, serious; sorrowful XIV; deplorably disappointing or bad XVII.
B. †solid, dense XIII (cf. *sad-iron*, solid flat-iron); dark-coloured (cf. G. *sattblau*, etc.,) XVI; (of bread, etc.) that has not 'risen' XVII.

Evidently 'solidity' has developed from the notion 'stuffed full'.

This article shows the strange ramifications of meaning that a word can pursue and makes clear how much is left to the ingenuity of the etymologist in the absence of extensive documentation such as lies behind the above dictionary article. In the absence of such evidence an etymologist might be tempted to underpin the connexion of *sad* with *satt* by simple reference to the parallel colloquial use of 'fed up'. It also brings out how a small piece of new evidence, such as the Anatolian *ḫas-* can transform a problem. A final point may be added which concerns the nature of etymology itself. In a sense a successful etymological find constitutes a verification of the theories which lead to that find. It was by applying the theories relating to the laryngeals and the guises assumed by Indo-European roots and bases that *sānus* was seen as a possible member of the *satis* family. The strength of the verification lies in the semantic approximation. The fact remains that on the 'meaning' side of word equations much has to be left to individual judgment, so much so that in the last resort much of etymology is a matter of opinion—not a very satisfactory state of affairs for what aspires to be a rigorous science. It follows that intensive research into semantic change, the systematic analysis and presentation of semantic ranges and ramifications, are a *sine qua non* for the etymologist.

For an example we may revert to the problem presented by the Latin *habēre*, the connexion of which with the Germanic family represented by our *have* was rejected for diaphonemic reasons. In searching for a more acceptable solution for the verb, the first step is to analyse it morphologically. It is parallel to verbal forms like *valēre* 'to be well' and *patēre* 'to be open', these words being referable to the root **wel-* and **pet-*[1] respectively. Verbs of this

---

1. **pet* meant 'spread, stretch'. It is represented in our word *fathom*, the measure of the outspread arms.

morphological shape in Latin express a state. On this analogy we should set up a root *heb-, and by using the diaphonemic telephone exchange we should link up with an IE root *ghebh. If we now put a call through to Germanic, our correspondents would turn out to be Gothic *giban* and OHG *geban*, OE *giefan*, *gefan*, from which the modern form *give* is descended. All these are referred to a CGmc *ȝeƀan*, on which ODEE remarks 'with no certain IE cogns.' The problem is the semantic gap between 'give' and 'have, possess'. However, *habēre*, as already pointed out, is a verb expressing a state. A similar gap yawns between *iacio* 'throw' and *iacēre* 'lie'. Ernout-Meillet comment on the latter 'to be in a state of someone or something that has been thrown'. The semantic gap between the Germanic and the Latin words may therefore not be unbridgeable. The problem must be tackled by tracing out the semantic ramifications of words denoting 'giving' and 'taking', which are surprisingly equivocal. For instance, the Greek root *nem-* 'distribute' appears in Germanic for the meaning 'take': e.g. German *nehmen*. From this root we have the OE adjective *nǣmel* 'quick at seizing', which has yielded the modern word *nimble*.

CHANGE OF MEANING

It will now be amply clear that it is no less true of meaning than of sounds that language is in a constant state of flux. The facts of change are established by comparing descriptions, in the case of semantic change by comparison of lexicons that register the use of words at different dates. This means that comparison is based on the vocable, the 'sameness of which' is secured by sound correspondence. It is here that we see the essential circularity of method. The sound laws are established by comparing the vocables of words whose meaning is 'the same', and changes of meaning are established by comparing words whose vocables are 'the same'. Above (p. 177) it emerged that the 'meaning' of a word is in effect a more or less wide range of 'senses'. It follows that 'change of meaning' will consist in modifications of the sense-range. Since the senses emerge from the use of words in context and situation (see p. 177), in searching for the causes of semantic change we must look to the speaker and his reaction to his world in the effort to make a communication. The 'intention' of the speaker provides the driving force; the 'world', which includes the hearer, provides the conditioning circumstances.

Semantic change comes to the notice of the learner as soon as he starts to study texts of an earlier period. A glance at any text of Chaucer and Shakespeare makes this clear. For although the spelling hides to a large extent the changes of pronunciation which have taken place in our language since those authors wrote, even so, understanding is possible only with the help of a glossary, because many of their words no longer exist or have survived only with considerable modification of meaning. A few examples, taken at random, will serve as illustrations.

> This *sely* widwe and *eek* hir doghtres two
> Herden thise hennes crye and maken *wo*
> And out at dores *sterten* they *anoon*, etc.
>
> (Chaucer, *The Nun's Priest Tale*)

Sely is the modern word *silly* which goes back to OE *sǣlig* 'happy, blessed' which through 'innocent', 'simple' has developed to 'simple-minded', 'foolish'; *eek* 'also' is related to German *auch* 'also'; *stir* has the meaning of 'move briskly, energetically'; *anoon* goes back to OE *on ān* 'into one' and *on āne* 'in one', which had the meaning 'into or in one body, state' and 'at once', hence later 'soon, shortly'.

> O, *train* me not, sweet mermaid, with thy note,
> To drown me in thy sister's flood of tears.
>
> (Shakespeare, *Comedy of Errors* III. ii. 45)

Here *train* means 'to entice, allure', while the corresponding noun meant 'treachery, guile, deceit'. Another example might be quoted from a more recent author. Dr Johnson, in a criticism of Milton's *Lycidas*, remarked that the poem was 'easy, vulgar and therefore disgusting'. A modern reader might object to the severity of this judgment did he not know that 'easy' meant 'facile' or 'commonplace', *vulgar*[1] merely 'popular' and *disgusting* no more than 'in bad taste'.

From these few examples it will be clear that we establish the facts of semantic change by comparing lexicons that record the vocabulary in use at different dates. This means that comparisons are based on the vocable and that the differences are detected in the meaning attached to one and the same vocable at different dates. As for the causes of semantic change, they lie in the effort of the speaker to convey his messages effectively in an ever-changing world. A large part of changes of meaning can be summed up in the phrase 'old words in a new world'. As regards the nature and classification of the changes, this will be discussed in detail below. By way of preliminary some basic points must be recalled. In any act of symbolic reference we must distinguish the 'world reference' of a vocable from the attitude of the speaker and hearer towards it. *My bicycle* and *that old crock* may have the same 'referent', but the two expressions convey a different attitude towards it. So a broad division of semantic changes would be into those which involve a change of the vocable-referent relation and those which involve a different aspect of, or attitude towards, one and the same referent.

A speaker faced with the task of calling the hearer's attention to a given referent may, of course, coin an entirely new word (e.g. *campylognathus*).[2] Such an addition to the vocabulary of his language does not involve any semantic change, and it consequently lies outside the scope of this chapter. On the other hand, the speaker may apply a word to this referent which had previously denoted another referent; that is to say, he uses the word in a different sense. Now such changes of the word-referent relation cannot be made haphazard. If I say 'donkey' when I mean 'tortoise', the hearer will simply fail to understand me. Here again we see that the development of the linguistic instrument is guided

---

1. Cf. Shakespeare's 'tis a vulgar proof that verie oft we pitty enemies', where 'vulgar proof' means 'common experience'.

2. An often quoted example of such a coinage is the term *gas*, which was invented by van Helmont on the basis of the Greek *chaos*: 'I have called that spirit *gas* as not far from the *chaos* of the ancients'.

and limited by the function which it has to fulfil. The speaker, in his effort to communicate new facts, new thoughts and new experiences, may use his language actively and creatively. But all his inventions and adaptations have to pass the test of intelligibility and to find the approval of the hearer. Only those expressions which can fulfil these functions can hope to gain general acceptance and to become part of the language. Semantic changes then, like other linguistic phenomena, can only be fully understood by reference to the living traffic of speech exchange. These are the general principles which we must keep in mind in the following paragraphs.

All sound patterns of speech have the power of evoking certain responses in the hearer, and this is one aspect of the meaning of those sound patterns. But can we say what is *the* meaning of the word *glass*? We may look in the *glass* when combing our hair; we may drink a *glass* at the public-house; we may tap the *glass* to see if it is wise to take a raincoat. In each case the word *glass* has a different sense. Similarly the word *engagement* means basically 'the putting of a person under a pledge (*en gage*)',[1] but it acquires a variety of meanings in different contexts, as may be seen from the following examples: 'Their *engagement* will be announced'; 'sorry I have another *engagement*'; 'his *engagement* will be terminated at the end of the quarter'. The verb *engage* could also mean 'attach, charm', hence the sense *engaging*. A glance at the *Oxford Dictionary* shows that such a 'multiple meaning' (see above, p. 178) is a feature of many words of our language. As was shown above, the fact is that words are not strictly limited to a fixed and definite significance as mathematical symbols are. Ordinary speech may be regarded as a series of rough hints which the hearer must interpret in order to arrive at the meaning which the speaker wishes to convey. Thus the word *glass* is a clue of fairly wide significance which is narrowed down by the context in which it occurs. The context is important not only because of the part it plays in determining the intended meaning of a word in a given

---

1. Both *gage* and *wage* go back (by different routes) to Gmc *waðjan*, which also lies behind our word *wed*. The corresponding Latin word *vad-* meant 'surety'.

situation; it is also one of the most potent factors in the semantic changes which words of every language may undergo.

In the first place continual usage in a fixed context may result in restricting the meaning of a word of fairly wide significance merely to one aspect of that meaning. Before proceeding further it will be necessary to discuss what is meant by 'aspect'. Most objects, qualities and events in the world of the speaker are complex; that is to say, they consist of a totality of distinguishable parts of which some may be relevant to the speaker's purpose and others not. Consequently the attention tends to be focused on these (momentarily) essential parts to the neglect of the others. G. Stern quotes the example of *horn*. In the phrase *a horn spoon* it is the material aspect of the horn that predominates. On the other hand, when a musician speaks of a *horn* with reference to a brass instrument, it is the function that has crowded out the other characteristics of a horn. The development of the meaning of the word from the animal's horn (used as a musical instrument) to that of a metal musical instrument has only been possible by this selective attention to function; for the extension of the word *horn* to an instrument made of a different material rests on similarity of function (see below on metaphor).

Now the aspect regarded as essential differs with the predominant interests of the speaker. Thus a *glass* will mean something different to a sailor, a publican or an actress. The word *play* suggests different ideas to a musician, a gambler, a footballer or an actor. That is to say, the *usual* meaning will be different in each case, the meaning which springs to mind when the word is heard in isolation. In different contexts, of course, all speakers of the language will be able to divine the intended meaning; but the distinction between the *usual* meaning and the *occasional* meaning of a word, differing as it does from speaker to speaker according to his predominant interests, is of fundamental importance. It is in these professional environments that words become restricted to a special significance.

If a farmer remarks that his *birds* are *laying well*, we guess without further elucidation that his fowl are laying a satisfactory number of eggs. This type of change is extremely frequent. The word *fowl* itself in the above sentence once meant any kind of bird, as for instance in the Biblical phrase 'the fowl of the air'. The corresponding word in German, *Vogel*, still retains its original meaning.[1] Similarly in modern Greek the word *ornis* (originally 'bird') means 'chicken'. On the other hand, in French the Latin *avica* (a derivative of *avis* 'bird') has become *oie* 'goose'. In this way many Latin words of originally wide significance have become restricted in French to technical operations on the farm. Thus *pondre*, from Lat. *ponere* 'to lay, to put' now means only 'to lay eggs'; *traire* from *trahere* 'to draw', means 'to milk cows', while *couver* 'to brood' is derived from *cubāre* 'to lie', just as in English we say 'the hens are sitting'. Such restrictions of meaning are to be understood from the peculiar relations that exist between individuals engaged in the same trade or occupation. Stern remarks (p. 305): 'The basis for the comprehension of a single word is not that word alone but also a mass of context: concomitant circumstances, situation, knowledge of the topic, of the speaker's habits, opinions, etc.' In the special languages of the trades and professions there is a greater intimacy between speaker and hearer. They have common objects and habits of thought; the referents are more narrowly circumscribed and more intimately known than when speakers of different professions converse. Consequently the linguistic hints required to communicate the speaker's intention need not be so definite. That is why a farmer can speak vaguely of his 'birds' 'laying'. Each of these words is adequate in the restricted context and situation to convey unambiguous meaning. In this way words of wide sense-range become restricted in their application.

Words and phrases, however, find their way from the special languages into the general language—that is, the one in common everyday use by all members of the community. We do not need to be a sailor to know what 'half seas over' means, and most people are familiar with the meaning of 'a *hot-bed* of vice' long before attaining the gardening age.[2] But perhaps the most striking example

---

1. The word is traceable to CGmc* *foglaz*, *fuglaz, which may be a dissimilation of *fluglaz*, this being a derivative of the verb **fleuʒ-**fluʒ, 'to fly'.

2. Of a class of students questioned by me only one knew what a *hot-bed* was, although they all understood the meaning of the phrase.

of the influence of a profession on the language of the community
is provided by the vocabulary of the early Christian Church, which
sets its special stamp on a long series of words originally of wide
significance: *redemptio, salvatio, conventus, saeculum* provide
sufficient illustration.[1] An interesting example of such specialization of meaning is to be seen in the English word *spice*. This
actually comes from the Latin *species* 'form, appearance, kind'.
The Roman lawyers, under the influence of Greek philosophical
ideas of form and matter (*eidos* and *hulē*, translated into Latin as
species and *materia*), argued that wine is the *speciēs* derived from
the *materia* grapes. From this it developed into the idea of 'produce', 'wares', 'merchandise', and it has been plausibly suggested
that this change of meaning developed in the language of the
customs officials. It is from this meaning of the word that the
French and German names for the grocer's shop—*épicerie*,
Spezereiwarenhandlung—developed. From this it became further
limited in English to the modern meaning of *spice*, while in the
Yorkshire dialect it frequently denotes 'sweets'.

As a counterpart to restriction of meaning we may cite some
words which have undergone an extension of meaning. This again
can be understood from the relation between the technical and
general languages. The craftsman needs a variety of terms to
denote (to him) essential differences of detail. The carpenter has
many words for the different kinds of saw, but the layman is
content with one word for the whole category. Arabic, again, has
numerous words for camel, and such a multiplicity of terms to
distinguish minute differences of concrete detail is believed to
be a characteristic of many 'undeveloped' peoples, who are more
concerned with the concrete details of practical life than the discussion of categories.[2] With the growth of civilization, however, work

---

1. See my *Latin Language*, Chapter VII.
2. It is often argued that this proves a certain intellectual backwardness on
the part of such peoples. It may, however, equally well be put forward as
evidence to the contrary. The author, for instance, until comparatively recent
times, did not know the difference between pine, fir, spruce and larch. He classed
such trees under the vague category of 'Christmas trees'. Does this prove an
intellectual superiority over those nature lovers familiar with such fine distinctions? Actually differentiation and distinction arise from practical needs rather

is divided and men are grouped as professionals and laymen. To the laymen technical details are irrelevant or indeed unknown. Thus Dauzat has pointed out that in some regions of France the name of the ram is confined to the language of shepherds and stock-raisers; a shoemaker did not know the word and confused the ram with the ewe.[1] In this way the name for one member of a class of things may come to be used for the whole class. In French the word *panier* is derived from *pānārium* originally meaning 'a bread basket' (*pānis* 'bread').[2] *Butcher* comes from the French *boucher*, who originally sold goat's meat (*bouc*).[3] *Trouver* 'to find' comes perhaps from the Latin *tropāre*, which originally had the technical meaning 'to make variations on a religious melody'. From this it acquired its modern meaning through the intermediary idea of 'improvisation', 'invention'. A more interesting proposal, which has appealed to many scholars, was elaborated by the Austrian scholar Hugo Schuchardt. He traced the origin of the word to the language of fishermen. There is evidence from Sardinia that it was the practice to disturb (*turbāre*) the water in order to catch fish. Hence the verb developed the sense 'take or find fish', hence 'to find' in general. In reaching this explanation Schuchardt had made a special study of fishing methods (see Iordan–Orr–Posner, 1970, 54).

The farm, again, has supplied the general language with a large number of words originally referring to its own technical operations. The Roman farmer who ground out a certain amount of flour from a given quantity of corn called this his *ēmolumentum*, from *molo* 'to grind'. Afterwards it came to be used of any sort of profit or wage. Similarly the word *salary* is derived from *salārium*

---

than intellectual backwardness. A camel dealer can conduct his business far more efficiently with his numerous specialized terms than with our one. What may be called the focal vocabulary is likely to be more finely differentiated.

1. In Dundee, Ellis records the fact that 'fowls are called (henz) of both sexes'.

2. In English *pannier* normally means a large basket carried by a beast of burden.

3. Such an extension of meaning is conditioned, of course, by the development of civilization. On the relationship between language and culture, see Chapter 14.

originally a money allowance made to Roman soldiers to buy salt. A man who was 'rich in lands' was *locu-plēs* (*locus* being the equivalent of Greek *klēros* 'a plot of land'). Later the word was used to denote any rich man whatever the substance of his wealth might be. Similarly *pecūnia*, money, is a collective noun originally denoting cattle or flocks (*pecus*). This development is paralleled in English, where *fee* is cognate with the German *Vieh* which still denotes 'animal, beast'.[1] This contrasts with the development of *cattle* which comes via the French *capitale*,[2] which in Late Latin signified property in general. We have a variant of the same word which preserves the old meaning in the phrase '*goods and chattels*'. The same change of meaning is found in Greek, where *ktēnos* 'cattle' is from the same root as *ktāomai*, to possess. Again, the farmer's wife who gave her slaves a weighed quantity of wool to spin and weave called this their *pensum* (from *pendo* 'to weigh'). It was from this that the general meaning 'task' developed.

But perhaps the most fruitful source of extensions of meanings is the metaphorical employment of words, as when we speak of the 'foot' of a mountain, the 'head' of a firm. Frequent use in this may result in words losing their original narrow signification, so that its etymological origin is forgotten. Ships may be 'manned' by women. Our steamships 'sail' at definite times. The word 'equip' has a similar origin. It came ultimately from the ON *skipa* 'man a vessel', but also 'fit up, arrange'. A mediaeval Latin form *eschipare* is known, but the wider meaning 'equipment' is already present in the Anglo-Norman *eskipeson*. The French *équiper* in this sense is not attested before the sixteenth century. Similarly, the Greeks had a word *boukoleîsthai* which means literally 'to look after cows'. But it was later possible to say *híppous boukoleîsthai*, literally 'to cowherd horses', just as in English we talk of 'shepherding' even persons into an enclosure. Another example of the same tendency is the French *joncher*, which meant originally 'to strew the roads with rushes' (*jonc*). But

---

1. Doubt is cast on the etymology by E. Benveniste, who argues that *peku* originally denoted 'personal possession'. This often took the form of livestock, and it is in this way that the application of the term became *restricted* to 'livestock' and further specialized to smaller animals, and finally to 'sheep'.

2. On the origin of *capitale*, see Chapter 14.

nowadays the verb has the general meaning 'to strew', so that we can say *joncher de fleurs, d'herbe*, etc. In Old French, again, the word *habiller* meant 'to prepare, to fit out'.[1] Its meaning varied according to the profession, whether butcher, gardener or tailor. But it was frequently used of preparing and equipping a knight for battle. It is from this usage that the modern meaning 'to dress' developed. It will now be profitable to examine the phenomenon of metaphor in greater detail.

It has already been remarked that language is a series of hints from which the hearer has to piece together the sense intended. The hints, however, may vary in plainness. It is wearisome to hear a spade always called a spade, and often the hearer is more stimulated by allusiveness of expression which requires a greater effort of imagination or thought on his part. To achieve this, linguistic symbolism turns to its service what is perhaps the most remarkable quality of the human mind—its capacity for analogy: that is the ability to perceive similarity of quality or relationship in dissimilar objects or situations. This constitutes the mental basis of what is known as metaphor. If I call a man 'a whale of a cricketer', of all the characteristics possessed by a whale, the context enables the speaker to focus his attention on the one which is relevant to the particular situation. In so far as the understanding of the metaphor is a process of selective attention similar to that discussed above. The creation of the metaphor by the speaker, however, presents rather a different problem. If I wish to express a quality 'dirty', that quality has in the past been allied to notions as different as 'pig' and 'chimney sweep'. Consequently the thought of 'dirty' will evoke the thought of these different wholes of which it has formed a part. The peculiar effect of a metaphor is due to the tension which exists between the literal and the figurative meaning. When a metaphorical expression is understood, the hearer interprets the linguistic hint correctly; that is to say, his attention is drawn to the referent referred to by the speaker. At the same time he remains aware to some extent of the literal meaning of the expression, so that the two spheres of the actual

---

1. *Habiller* is from *habilis*, literally 'holdable', hence 'handy, manageable, fit', etc.

(occasional) referent and the literal (usual) referent are fused together. The actual referent becomes charged with the colour and emotional qualities of the literal referent. If the metaphor is original, a new set of relations is established in the perceived world and the mind of the hearer is stimulated and enriched.

Many of these perceptions of similarity on which metaphors are based actually take place automatically by the process known to the psychologist as synaesthesia.[1] Thus in many people different musical tones and timbres evoke distinct sensations of colours: an oboe evoking perhaps blue, a cello red and a flute green. S. Ullmann quotes in this connexion the lines by Rimbaud:

> A noir, E blanc, I rouge, U vert, O bleu, voyelles
> Je dirai quelque jour vos naissances latentes.

These associations are utilized in linguistic symbolism, particularly in designating mental states. It is well known that colours have a great psychological effect. *Black* can imply 'malignant', 'baneful', 'sinister', 'iniquitous', 'dismal', 'gloomy'. A man can be 'black-listed'. Trades unions declare products to be 'black'. They also remember a certain disastrous day as 'Black Friday'. The Romans, too, called days of ill-omen *dies atri*. Black magic, however, while suggesting horror and mystery, owes its origin to a misunderstanding of the Greek word *nekromanteia* 'oracle of the dead'. In mediaeval Latin, by a natural popular etymology, the first element *nekro-* 'corpse' was confused with the Latin word *niger* 'black' and the word assumed the form *nigromantia*. Our modern poetasters have not been slow to seize the chance that melancholic *blue* rhymes with *two* and *you*. This word is recorded in the sense of 'low-spirited' as early as the sixteenth century. We also speak of being in a *blue funk*. By contrast we may tend to view the world through *rosy spectacles*.

Such associations are called synaesthetic if they are brought about by automatic processes in the nervous system. On this narrow basis word-artists have raised such literary extravagances as

---

1. See S. Ullmann, *Principles*, pp. 266–289. He defines synaesthesia as 'a special kind of name-transfer through association between the senses'.

Soft music like perfume, and sweet light
Golden with audible odours exquisite[1]

More often, however, the mechanism of the metaphor is that of
simple association of ideas. Thus the various aspects of an activity
or an object form a complex of ideas which is so closely knit that
any member of the group is capable of evoking in the mind of the
hearer the other members of that group. The activity of writing,
for instance, requires such physical objects as pens, paper, ink,
rubbers, desks. It is this association of these objects with the
particular activity that gives them the power of calling up in a
suitable context the whole activity and profession of writing. This
is the *pen-is-mightier-than-the-sword* type of metaphor familiar
to us from our school exercises. By the same mental process the
stage may symbolize the acting profession, the knife surgery, while
the hammer and sickle on the Russian flag suggests the union of
industry and agriculture. In such cases the association is suggested
by actual juxtaposition and connexion in the perceived world, the
mind being more or less passive. But the human mind is also
capable of discerning similarities in widely different objects and
situations. Thus a speaker, wishing to convey a particular quality
vividly to the hearer, may mention an object which possesses that
characteristic to a striking degree. A person which is worthy and
good but uninteresting may be called a 'dumpling' or 'suet pud-
ding'. In the same way, animals may serve as symbols of
physical and moral qualities. A snake suggests slyness and
cunning, a monkey mischief, a fox craftiness, a lion courage, a
tiger ferocity, power and speed.

Even more complicated are the metaphors which involve an
analysis of situations that bring out essential similarities, such as
in expressions like *to foul one's own nest, not to let the grass grow
under one's feet.* The comparisons that spring to the mind are
often those taken from the profession, trade or occupation in which
we are habitually engaged. In this way languages are enriched by
metaphors taken from technical vocabularies. The operations of
agriculture and farming are here again mirrored in a host of

---

1. Quoted by Ullmann, p. 275.

expressive metaphors. *To plough the sand, plough a lonely furrow, do the spade work, sow one's wild oats, to weed out, reap a rich harvest, thrash*[1] *a subject out, separate the grain from the chaff* do not exhaust the list. Many English words contain hidden Roman metaphors taken from the same source. To *propagate* means literally 'to set out layers or slips'. *Delirium* is connected with the Latin word *dēlīrāre* 'to get out of the furrow when ploughing (*dē līrā*)'. *Precocious* originally meant 'flowering or fruiting too early' and this is close to the Latin *praecox*, which was used of fruit ripening too early. The word is a compound of *prae* and the root *coqu-* 'cook', a verb which was also used of the process of ripening. Sailors, as we should expect, have presented us with a large number of metaphors, e.g. '*to sail close to the wind*'. Life may be *smooth sailing*, and we can *rest on our oars*. If difficulties come our way and we fail to *weather the storm*, we may be *on our beam ends* or even *on the rocks*.

It will be noticed that these expressions are mostly so trite that the metaphor is hardly noticed. A metaphor becomes so usual in a language that for the new generation growing up and learning the language it is the normal, everyday term. It loses its colour and picturesqueness and all of the peculiar evocative power that it had for the older generation; so much so, that the later generation may be completely unaware of the original meaning.[2]

In this way metaphors taken from obsolete sports and occupations survive. Hunting with hawks was a favourite sport in

---

1. The standard word is *thresh*, cf. German *dreschen*. The by-form *thrash* (cf. OE *pærscan*) has taken on the meaning 'chastise by beating'.
2. This is what Stern seems to mean by 'adequation', although, curiously enough, he classes the process as a type of sense change. In discussing the change of (animal's) horn to musical instrument, he remarks that the meaning undergoes adequation to what is now considered by speakers as the main characteristic of the referent. But surely this whole process does not take place in the mind of one speaker. The process of change is a long development, which cannot be understood without bringing in the transference of linguistic knowledge from one generation to another. This so-called adequation seems to be no more than the different linguistic conditioning which those later learners will get when the new usage has become frequent in the language. Thus if a child hears the word *horn* mainly in connexion with musical instruments, then it will learn the referent of the vocable just as it does those of *flute, spoon*, etc.

mediaeval times and though it has long ceased to be practised, its memory is perpetuated by fossilized metaphors. To *reclaim* is literally to 'call back' (*reclāmāre*) the hawk after the flight. To reclaim the hawk the falconer made use of a pipe called a *lure*, an old French word for 'bait' specialized in this sense.[1] This is the source from which our 'lure' metaphors are derived.[2] To *pounce upon* is another metaphor that recalls old mediaeval sport, *pounces* being the name for the foreclaws of the hawk. Sport, generally, as we should expect, has made a considerable contribution to English vocabulary. How many people realize that *to turn the tables* is a metaphor taken from the game of backgammon or that *jeopardy* is *jeu parti*, a chess problem? From the tournament we have to *take a tilt at*[3] or to *break a lance*. To *throw down the gauntlet* is another phrase recalling mediaeval custom. But to *run the gauntlet* has nothing at all to do with this. Actually *gauntlet* in this phrase has been transformed by popular etymology from *gat-lopp*, a Swedish word meaning 'lane-run'.[4] In the Thirty Years War the Swedes used to subject their prisoners to this peculiar ordeal. They were made to run stripped to the waist between two rows of soldiers, forming a 'lane', who struck at them with knotted cords or sticks. Archery, again, has bequeathed us many expressions, e.g. to *have two strings to one's bow*, to *have a quiver full*, to *shoot one's bolt*, *draw a long bow*, etc.

Metaphors recall not only obsolete sports but obsolete occupations as well. The expression *a garbled version* is interesting in this connexion. The word *garble* reached England by a round-about and complicated journey. It derives originally from an Indo-European root **krei*, which appears as *cerno* in Latin and *krīnō* in

---

1. This word is of Germanic origin, *loðr*; the modern German word *Luder* now means 'a whore'.

2. The sense of 'a tempting thing' goes back to Chaucer.

3. The 'tilt' was technically the barrier separating the combatants and was secondarily applied to the exercise itself.

4. This is also the original sense of the English word *gate*, as contained in street names like *Highgate*, etc. This word is derived from Old Norse *gata*, and it is related to the German *Gasse*. It must not be confused with the other word *gate*, which is derived from the Old English *geat*, the Old Norse equivalent of which, *gat*, means 'opening'.

Greek.[1] In both these languages the verb is used most frequently in a metaphorical sense, 'distinguish, perceive, judge, accuse'. Latin has a derived noun *crībrum*, 'a sieve', which retains the original significance of the root. In its diminutive form *crībellum* it was borrowed into Arabic in the forms *ghirbāl* 'sieve', whence *gharbala* 'sift'. In this guise it became a term of Mediterranean commerce (Italian *garbellare*, French *garbeller*), and this was brought by the Moorish occupation into Spanish, where a noun *garbillar* was formed to denote a person who sifted spices. It came to England with the spice trade. In the sixteenth century the word *garbler* still denoted a sort of food inspector who went round sifting spices to make sure that they had not been adulterated. The verb eventually developed the metaphorical meaning 'to pick out, to make a selection' (of facts) to convey a false impression, which is its modern meaning.

Sometimes metaphors, particularly those which have become proverbial, preserve fossilized words and phrases, the meaning of which is no longer correctly understood. Thus in the phrase *buy a pig in a poke*, the word *poke* means 'a bag' just as in the corresponding German metaphor *eine Katze im Sack kaufen*. It is a by-form of *pouch*, only the diminutive form *pocket* being preserved in standard English.[2] In such cases the general sense of the phrase is understood, but the meaning of its separate elements is forgotten. Thus to the modern German the phrase *in Hülle und Fülle* conveys nothing more than 'in plenty, in abundance'. That is to say the last word determines the whole meaning. The phrase originally meant 'clothing' (*Hülle*)[3] and 'food' (*Fülle*). Similarly *kurz und bündig*[4] originally meant 'short and strong'; but the idea of brevity, conciseness, is the only one expressed by the

---

1. Cf. Welsh *go-grynu* 'sift' from **upo-krĭ-n-ō*; Latin *ex-crē-mentum*, literally 'what is sifted out', belongs to the same family.

2. *Poke* goes back to Anglo-Norman *poque, poke*, which correspond to Old French *poche*, from which we have *pouch*.

3. *Hülle* derives from a root **kel* 'cover, hide', which gives rise to *cell*, *clandestine*, *occult*, etc., all of Latin origin and connected with the verb *cēlare* 'conceal'.

4. *Bündig* is connected with the verb *binden* 'bind'. It meant 'binding', 'strong and firm'.

modern phrase. Such misunderstandings may lead to curious transformations of meaning. *To tell one's beads*, for instance, meant literally 'to count one's prayers', *tell* being connected with the German *zählen* 'to count', a meaning preserved in the noun *teller*, used of a person who counts votes. *Bead* is derived from Old English *gebed* 'prayer'. The word acquired its modern sense from the Roman Catholic form of a prayer, the rosary, in which fifteen decades of Aves are repeated, each decade being preceded by a Pater Noster and followed by a Gloria. For keeping count of this, a string holding one hundred and sixty-five beads was used.

Such cases are of great theoretical importance. It seems fairly clear that the meaning of phrases and sentences is not built up by the hearer from the meaning of their separate elements (words and inflections), but that he grasps their meaning as total impressions. In a given context one single hint may suffice to enable the hearer to jump to an understanding. J. Piaget has observed that such 'syncretistic understanding' is common among children. They jump to a conclusion and then interpret the details of the utterance in the light of this conclusion as a function of the general schema. This is precisely what has happened in the case of telling one's beads. It is, of course, true that the person is keeping count of his prayers by counting the beads. Consequently the hearer makes a correct reference to the event described. But he interprets the details in a different way from that intended by the speaker. What is important is that the speaker cannot correct this misapprehension in the hearer *because he does not know of it*; for it is only from the behaviour of the hearer that the speaker can know whether he has been successful in conveying his meaning or not. Since in this case the behaviour evoked in the hearer is precisely what the speaker intended, the hearer exhibiting awareness of the indicated situation, there is nothing to show that, though the answer is right, the 'arithmetic' is wrong.

Many instances of semantic change due to such false interpretations are quoted in the handbooks. The word *premises* is a case in point. Legal documents relating to the conveying and renting of property often begin with a detailed description of the property in question and thereafter in the body of the document refer to it as 'the premises', i.e. 'the aforesaid' (*praemissa*). It is easy to see how the word later was understood, or rather misunderstood, in its modern sense. Stern (p. 368) quotes the example of *knot*. The speed of the vessel was once measured by paying out a line furnished with knots at every fifty feet, the number of knots running out in half a minute being equal to the number of nautical miles that a ship would sail in an hour. The speed was therefore defined as so many 'knots'. Landlubbers hearing the phrase understand it as a measure of linear distance and commit the solecism of saying 'ten knots per hour'. Another fossil like *kurz und bündig* is the word *let* in *without let or hindrance*. This word comes from the Anglo-Saxon *lettan*[1] 'to hinder' which was dropped owing to the fact that it became homonymous with *lætan* 'to allow' of precisely the opposite meaning, for such an ambiguity is intolerable in any language (see below).

So far we have been concerned with the mere intellectual context of words. But words, besides being tokens for conveying meaning, have characteristics of their own. The English words *horse, steed, nag, gee-gee* all refer to the same animal; but the emotional colouring is different in each case. *Horse* is the everyday word, the word with the least emotional content. *Steed*,[2] on the other hand, belongs to the language of poetry. It is exalted, dignified and majestic, while *gee-gee* is a playful, nursery word. Most civilized languages have such sets of so-called synonyms at their disposal. German, for instance, has *Pferd*,[3] *Ross*, and *Gaul*. English distinguishes *face* and *countenance*; German coresponds with *Gesicht* and *Antlitz*. The different tone and status of words makes the choice of words a delicate problem to ensure that their emotional contents are not discordant with one another or with the situation in which they are used.

---

1. This goes back to *latjan* 'delay', a derivative of *lata* 'slow', which gave rise to *late*.

2. OE *stēda* 'stallion'; cf. *stud* from *stōðō, which is a derivative from the root IE, *stā- 'stand', from which we get *steading* and (via Latin) *stable*. German *Stute* 'mare' also belongs to the same family.

3. This word has a strange history. Latin borrowed from Gaulish the word for a post-horse, *verēdus*, and this was compounded with the Greek proposition *para* 'alongside', *paraverēdus* 'extra-horse'. This appears in OHG as *pferifrīd*, *pferīd*. The old French form *palefrei* is the source of our *palfrey*.

Insensitivity to such shades of meaning is one of the striking marks of the uneducated or half-educated. 'Charladies' *commence* scrubbing, have had *sufficient* to eat, ask when the lady of the house will be *at liberty*. No local authority would think of building *tenements* for workers, for this word has associations with 'teeming slum'. Unemployment commissions used to concern themselves in the bad old days with *standards of adequate nourishment*, whereas the working man simply wanted enough to eat. Stern puritans once condemned *gambling on horses* when more frivolous mortals saw no harm in *a flutter on the gee-gees* (but this is no longer a 'contemporary' expression). Death in all societies is a subject which called for a delicate choice of words. We say 'he passed away', the Germans use the expression *entschlafen* 'fall asleep', while the Roman said *supremum diem obiit* 'met his last day'. From this phrase the word *obire* alone developed this meaning, and it is from this that we have the word *obituary*.

This reluctance to use the direct term for an unpleasant object or situation gives rise to what is called 'euphemism'. Primitive languages provide striking illustrations of such bans placed upon words of a certain type. The word for the primitive man is endowed with an awful power. The name is inseparable from the thing; and whoever knows the name has power over the thing which it denotes. We hear that in some savage tribes the women are forbidden to use any word which resembles the name of their husbands for fear some harm might be caused by this. But such taboo is by no means confined to primitive languages. There are numerous things which we should prefer not to mention, but if they must be mentioned, we pretend to talk about something else. Physical processes are peculiarly subject to taboo in our society. In English it is rapidly becoming impossible to find an acceptable designation for the place of defecation. We have called it variously the *privy*, the *closet* (little room), the *lavatory* (the washing-place) and we are now being driven from the *cloak-room* into the *toilet*.[1] But our

---

1. This is a diminutive of the word for 'cloth' *toile*. First attested in the sense of a cloth cover for the dressing table, it came to mean the table itself. Its application to a lady's dress dates from the nineteenth century. ODEE does not mention the modern euphemism.

neighbours are just as perplexed. The Germans get out of the difficulty by using French words: *Pissoir*, *Toilette*, *Klosett*, etc. The French also have a variety of expressions: *les lieux*, *quelque part*, *le water*, etc. Then, again, in speaking of the physical characteristics of our friends we try to find the kindest words possible. We say *stout* in preference to *fat*, although this word originally meant 'strong', just as the French use *fort* and the German *stark* in the same sense. We prefer to call an unattractive girl *plain* or *homely*. *Buxom* has gone through a wide range of sense which shows how euphemisms wear out. The word is derived from OE *būgan* 'bend', so that its original meaning was, like German *biegsam*, 'pliant'. At various periods we meet with the senses 'flexible', 'compliant', 'blithe' (which originally meant 'mild' and 'merciful'), 'comely', and finally 'plump'. Certain articles of clothing again are preferably not mentioned in polite society. The old word *smock* was replaced by *shift* and this, again, by *chemise*, but this too deteriorated, more particularly after a vulgar singular *shimmy* was made from it. Nowadays we speak generally of a *slip*. It is strange to what length prudery can go. The Victorian use of *limbs* for legs is a case in point, and Austrians prefer to speak of *Füsse* 'feet' rather than *Beine* 'legs'. In America it is thought indelicate to refer to the *breast* of a chicken and the euphemism *white meat* is used instead. On the other hand, the American lady who rather shocks us by informing us that she has been *sick*[1] all day is merely using the word in the old sense of 'unwell', which we find paralleled in the German expression *siech und krank* and in nouns like *Bleichsucht* 'anaemia'. In German *siech* has also been replaced by a euphemism, *krank*, which originally meant 'thin, weak'.

The urge towards euphemism is manifested in a peculiar way in the so-called veiled languages. Here, again, for reason of modesty, secrecy or humour, the downright expression is avoided and only hinted at by using a form of words that resembles that expression. The following are among the best known examples: *to go down Sheet Lane into Bedfordshire*; *he that fetches his wife from Shrewsbury* ('marries a shrew') *must carry her to Staffordshire*

---

1. The sense of 'vomiting' developed in the seventeenth century.

('use the stick') *or else live in Cumberland*[1] ('in sorrow'). In French we find similar expressions such as *aller à Versailles* ('*se verser*'), *aller à Rouen* ('*se ruiner*').

A euphemism is usually only temporarily effective, for it is the thing or the idea which is distasteful or unpleasant. So, very soon the euphemism itself acquires the taint which banished its predecessor.[2] This is what causes a deterioration in the meaning of words. The word for a girl and woman in French provides a remarkable illustration of this process. The word *garce* has long been impossible, but nowadays even *fille* is occasionally avoided in some circles. In German, too, the history of the *Dirne* is parallel. In the southern districts it is still used in its old significance of 'girl', particularly in the diminutive form *Dirndl*, which has also become the name of a dress. In the standard language it has the meaning of 'prostitute'. The corresponding words in English for woman and girl show a similar degradation. *Wench*, which is attested in the sense of 'young woman, girl' in the thirteenth century, is still used in some dialects as the normal word. Its original meaning must have been 'unsteady, inconstant' for it is derived from a verb **wank-* 'waver' (cf. German *wanken*). However, by the fourteenth century *wench* was applied not only to a maidservant but also a wanton woman. Even *housewife* has come down in the world in the old pronunciation *hussy, huzzy*. In the sixteenth century is still had the original meaning, but by the following century it had already acquired the connotation 'bold and shameless' and 'a light woman'.

The modern romantic idyllification of the farmer and rustic life has no counterpart as yet in the history of language. In fact languages have consistently used the words of country dwellers as terms of reproach. The Romans drew an invidious distinction between *urbānus* and *rusticus*. The city dweller was polished and

---

1. This expression alludes to the obsolete word *cumber* 'harass', 'burden, load'.

2. The process of deterioration is precisely the same as the wearing out of metaphors. It is a type of what Stern calls 'adequation'. Since the euphemism is learned by the child as the normal everyday term, the word or phrase refers, in its language system, directly to its unpleasant referent and no metaphor clothes its nakedness.

courteous and the countryman clumsy and boorish. Greek parallels this with the opposition of *asteîos* and *ágroikos*. The word *boor* itself originally meant 'farmer',[1] the corresponding German word *Bauer* still retaining this meaning. In French the same taint attaches to the words *rustre, paysan*. Similarly the word *vilain* is derived from *villānus* and meant a person who was attached to the manor house (*villa*), a serf or *villein*. The names of the servant class in general tend to degenerate. *Knave* is related to the German *Knabe*. It had gone successively through the stages 'boy', 'servant',[2] 'scoundrel'.[3] Similarly *maid*, a shortened form of *maiden* (cf. German *Mädchen*) had already acquired the sense 'female servant' by the fourteenth century. German *Magd* has undergone the same development.

The history of the Latin *gallīna* provides an interesting example of deterioration. It originally meant 'hen', while *pulla*, once applied to any young animal, was specialized in the meaning 'chicken'. In selling livestock age is an important factor in price, whether the beasts are intended for consumption or reproduction. Consequently the farmer will give the most advantageous description of his wares. Every 'fowl' becomes a *pulla*. This had a remarkable effect on the meaning of *gallīna*, which is preserved in various French dialects in the meaning of 'an old hen which no longer lays' and then, by extension, it is applied to any old sterile female. In one other dialect it has again been specialized in the sense of a 'sterile sow'.

It has already been remarked that words are not merely colourless counters for the exchange of ideas. Language is used not only to impart information, but to influence behaviour, to impart commands, to arouse wonder, indignation and horror. The speaker is instinctively a rhetorician, and to effect his purpose of arousing emotion he chooses words and phrases that are most highly tinged and charged with emotional content. Contrast the bare efficiency of the expression 'we shall be killed' with the picturesque

---

1. Still in the fifteenth century; the meaning 'rustic, clownish fellow' appears in the following century.
2. OE *cnafa* meant both 'boy' and 'male servant'.
3. Already in the thirteenth century.

horror of 'we shall be murdered in our beds'. It is particularly in politics, where the arousing of mass emotion is more effective than any appeal to reason, that such devices are most frequently used. It was once found convenient to call socialists 'Bolsheviks', a name then associated in the mind of the public with high explosives, systematic rape and mass murder. Their opponents retaliated with 'Tory', a word then redolent of port wine, child labour and gunboats. But in all forms of speech, particularly the vulgar variety, we may observe such striving after effects. Surprise finds expressions in hyperbolic ('overshooting the mark') phrases like *thunderstruck, you could have knocked me down with a feather*. Slang is one manifestation of this search for vividness and picturesqueness of expression. A face has been called variously *mug, dial, phiz*, etc.,; the head a *crust, a coconut, a turnip*. Many of these words find their way from the street into the drawing-room, become part of the accepted language, and even oust their respective rivals. The French word *tête* is derived from Latin *testa* a word meaning 'pot', which was current slang for 'head' among the Roman populace. *Caput* (*chef*) survives only in a metaphorical sense. In exactly the same way the German *Kopf*, originally meaning 'bowl', has replaced in everyday language the older *Haupt*, which is now confined to poetry and the elevated language. This type reminds us of the use of *mug* in English slang, while perhaps *gob* 'mouth', heard frequently in Lancashire, is possibly connected with the diminutive form *goblet*.[1]

In many cases the use of slang has a result precisely the opposite of the deterioration discussed above. Thus the word *gore*, for instance, now a polite and elevated synonym for 'blood', once signified 'dung, filth', while *plucky*, applied in modern usage to the more trivial manifestations of courage, is derived from *pluck* meaning 'innards'.[2] The social elevation of such words may be explained from that peculiar manifestation of snobbishness that

---

1. ODEE links *gob* 'lump' with OF *gobe, goube* 'mouthful, lump' and tentatively connects the word with Gaelic *gob* 'beak', Irish *gob* 'bill, mouth'. In that case *gob* will be a transfer of a word denoting part of an animal to that of a human being; cf. *snout, paw*, etc.

2. Those parts which are 'plucked out'.

flourishes among the *enfants terribles* of the young sets, who regard a self-conscious vulgarity as a mask of enlightenment and emancipation and spice their conversation with the profanities and expletives of the gutter. Since they are often adopted by their elders anxious to escape from the stigma of age and 'stuffiness', the vulgarities of the streets are honoured by reception into our best society. It is curious to note that *guts* has gone exactly the same way as *plucky*. Other ameliorations are a result of the peculiar use of pejoratives as endearments. Children are called *scamps*,[1] *rascals*,[2] *wicked little devils* and the like in tones of rapturous approval. Similarly *naughty*, originally 'good for naught', 'depraved', has acquired a playful ring, while the development of *pretty* (OE *prættig* 'crafty, wily') to its modern meaning may be paralleled by the modern American phrase *a cunning child*. Another Americanism *he is just crazy*[3] *about her* throws light on another English word, *fond*, which is the past participle of *fonnen* 'to be foolish'.

The social elevation of such words is merely one aspect of the weakening to which all such violent expressions are exposed. Just as over-spiced foods soon jade the palate and are found insipid, so words lose their force and colour. The rapidity of such weakening may be aptly illustrated from film advertising. We now refuse to be interested or influenced by such strident superlatives as *stupendous*, *thrilling*, *enthralling*. In this way many words of our language have become but shadows of their former selves. Thus *annoy* is derived ultimately from the vulgar Latin *inodiāre*, which was created from the phrase *in odio esse* 'to be hateful'. At one time it could mean 'molest, injure'. In French the word has become even weaker in meaning, for *ennuyer* signifies merely 'vex'. *Gêner* has travelled the same road. Derived from the Old French *gehener* 'to torture', it means now no more than 'embarrass'. Adverbs of degree are especially exposed to linguistic corrosion of this kind. In English adverbs like *frightfully*, *awfully* (*I am frightfully sorry, I am awfully glad*) mean scarcely more than *very*. The German, too, says

---

1. Originally a highway robber.
2. Originally 'inferior deer of a herd', 'belonging to the rabble'.
3. *Crazy* is derived from the noun *craze* 'crack', 'flow', and in its application to an unsound mind it is paralleled by *cracked* and *crack-pot*.

furchtbar komisch, entsetzlich gross ('frightfully funny', 'horribly big'), and the French are capable of *rudement, furieusement, terriblement, fichtrement,* etc. Such expressions in time lose much of their original meaning and become expressions of degree. Thus *very good* once meant 'in truth good', while German *sehr traurig* meant 'sorely sad'.[1]

The speaker, we have said, is intent on effect and uses all the means at his disposal to attain his end. But linguistic phenomena mirror another human characteristic which has been described as economy of effort. The speaker will be content under normal circumstances to use the minimum of energy which is necessary for conveying the message. We have already remarked that the absolute limit of linguistic attrition is intelligibility. Frequent phrases like *Good morning, Guten Tag* are reduced to *morning, Tag,* or to a mere mumble, a mere vocal gesture, just as the English schoolboy in politer days, contented himself with a tug on his cap instead of taking it off. Such syncopations often result in strange changes in the meaning of words.[2] A *private* is short for a *private soldier*; a *rifle* is a *rifle gun*, that is with a special groove inside the barrel; *street* is derived from Latin *strata via*, just as the French *chaussée* stands for *via calceata*. A *terrier* has nothing to do with 'tearing' or 'terror'; it is simply a *(chien) terrier*, i.e. a dog which was used for hunting burrowing animals, like the German *Dachshund (terrier* from the Latin *terrārius*). In French we have further *fromage* from *(caseum) formaticum, sanglier* 'boar' from *(porcus) singularis; hiver* 'winter' from *(tempus) hibernum* (cf. Sp. *estio* 'summer'=*tempus æstivum*). Such shortenings are particularly common when an object is called by the place of its origin. So we speak of a *Panama* (hat), *Chianti, Burgundy, Champagne* (wines), *Cashmere* (cloth), *Gruyère* (cheese). A large number of our words

1. The OE adverb *sāre,* 'with great grief, etc.', is now used in dialect in much the same way as German *sehr.*

2. In all types of linguistic change it is essential to distinguish the motive forces from the conditioning circumstances. In the above instance the motive force is the speaker's urge towards economy of effort; the conditioning circumstances are the context and the situation in which the shortening is attempted, together with the resources of the personal language systems of the speaker and hearer.

denoting cultural objects and produce originated in this way. A *cherry* (Fr. *cérise*) is the fruit from Kerasos, which was first brought to Rome by Lucullus. The *peach* (Fr. *pêche*, German *Pfirsich*) is the Persian apple (Lat. *malum persicum*), while *currants* owe their name to Corinth and *damsons* to Damascus. *Copper* is the metal mined in Cyprus, *florins* were first struck in Florence, while *dollar* is shortened from *Joachimstaler*, Joachimstal being the place in Bohemia where there were once famous silver mines. The names of many cloths and fabrics indicate the place where they were once manufactured. Damascus has given us *damask*, Mosul on the Euphrates *muslin*, and Kamerijk (Cambrai) *cambric*. *Gamash* goes back to the Arabic *ghadāmasī* 'from Ghadāmas' a town in Tripoli where an esteemed kind of leather was made. *Galosh*, on the other hand, is from OF *galoche*, which is descended from *gallicula*, 'a Gaulish (sandal)'. *Sherry* (older form *sherris*) is a Spanish wine from Jerez. The type of pottery known as *faience* (Fr. *faïence*) actually originated in the Italian town of Faenza (Roman Faventia).

In the same way names of persons have become part of our language and are used as appellatives. *Sandwiches* are said to have been first made by the Earl of Sandwich, who hit upon this way of eating meat and bread so as to avoid leaving the gambling-table. We use other proper names when we *macadamize* our roads, wear *wellingtons* and test the *voltage* of our batteries, while Admiral Vernon, nicknamed Grogram,[1] Grog for short, gave his name to the diluted rum which in 1740 was ordered to be issued to the sailors instead of neat rum.

In conclusion we must deal briefly with the question of the disappearance of words. We reserve until Chapter 14 the discussion of those words whose disappearance is due to cultural development. The word *toga*, the name of the garment worn by Roman men, passed out of use with the change in fashion. In the same way obsolete beliefs, cults and ideas lose their names. They no longer form any part of the speaker's mental world, so that the means of their expression lapse into desuetude and are forgotten.

---

1. So called because the clothes he affected were made of *grogram* (i.e. *gros grain*), a coarse cloth.

To this category belong old English words like *ealh* 'temple', *blōt* 'victim' and *ād* 'the funeral pyre'.

In dealing with the problem of word mortality, as with other linguistic problems, we must constantly bear in mind that the main function of language is to convey meaning to the hearer. For this to be carried out efficiently the message must be clear; that is to say, the symbols used must be unambiguous. If the speaker uses an unclear symbol, his failure to communicate his meaning prompts him to seek a substitute word or phrase, so that the ambiguous word, being avoided, drops out of use. In our discussion of the word *let* we remarked that *lettan* 'to hinder' ceased to be used because of the danger of confusion with its homonym *let* from *lætan* 'to allow, to permit'. We now discuss further examples which will make clear the effects of homonymity on the vocabulary of a language.

In French dialects lying roughly south of a line drawn from Bordeaux to the Vosges 'to saw' was at one time expressed by derivatives of the Latin word *serrāre*. The word survives today only in four scattered areas. The question arises, what were the causes that brought about the disappearance of *serrāre* over large areas of its original domain. Gilliéron showed that the mortal defect of this word was its resemblance to another common word of this territory—the derivatives of *serāre* 'to close'. There were in fact two homonymous words *ser(r)āre* 'to saw' and *serāre* 'to close'. In but few places have the patois tolerated the confusion. Elsewhere they have either retained *ser(r)āre* 'saw' rejecting *serāre*, or preserved the latter at the cost of the former. That is to say the two words are in the southern patois almost everywhere mutually exclusive. Where *ser(r)āre* ('saw') has disappeared, the gap has been filled with words of the type *sectāre*, *secāre*, *resecāre*, etc. We see the same forces at work in the disappearance of *ouvrer* 'to work', the destructive homonym being in this case *ouvrir* 'to open'. Again, the phonetic development of the Latin *aestimare* > *esmer* > *émer* brought it into collision with *aimer* from *amāre*. This struggle in the standard language was ended by the intervention of the savants, who reconstituted *estimer* directly from the Latin word. Gilliéron, however, argues that the close struggle between the two verbs *aimer* and *émer* has left permanent marks on the morphology and syntax of the verb 'to love', both the strong forms of the plural *aimons*, etc., and constructions like *j'aime mieux danser* (but *j'aime à danser*) being proper to the verb *émer* < *aestimāre*.

Another example of the phenomenon is found in the words for 'blackbird'. In the Gallo-Roman territory *merula* 'blackbird' has been preserved; but in the Wallon territory, through the development *merula* > *la mierle* > *la mielle* and the loss of the distinction between masculine and feminine forms of the definite article (*le, la, le*), *le mielle* from *mérula* became indistinguishable from *le miel* 'honey' (Latin *mel*). As a consequence of this intolerable homonymity both these words were replaced by unambiguous substitutes, e.g. *lam* (i.e. *larme*) for 'honey' and *mauvis* for 'blackbird'. In those regions, however, where the difference of the article provides a distinguishing mark the two words have remained in use.

Scholars have suggested homonymity as a cause for the disappearance of many words in English. *Grētan* 'to cry' has been killed by *grētan* 'to greet'; *hrūm* 'soot' collided with *rūm* 'room'. Further, *ādl* 'disease' is said to have dropped out owing to its resemblance to *addle* 'filth'.[1] *Disease*, however, is a euphemism so that the disappearance of *ādl* may be due also in part to the reasons discussed above.

The reluctance to use a word because of its resemblance to another is not always due to the danger of confusion or ambiguity. Often accidental phonetic resemblance will awaken undesirable associations. Lecturers and schoolmasters all know the hushed hilarity prompted by *a bloody battle*. For similar reasons we speak nowadays rather of a *donkey* than of an *ass*, while in French the word *connil* (*cuniculus*) through entanglement, by jest or otherwise, with the French word from the Latin *cunnus* (*membrum muliebre*) has been replaced by *lapin*.

The presence of numerous homonyms in English raises an objection that calls for a modification of the above-stated principle. *Hare* and *hair* are pronounced alike, yet neither word shows any signs of becoming moribund. The reason is that in no conceivable situation could any ambiguity arise. The person who goes to

---

1. *Addled* is now used only of a rotten egg. In OE *adela* meant 'stinking urine or other liquid filth'.

market to buy a *hare* can use the word without risk of his requirements being misunderstood. Nor will a barber, on receiving a
request for a hair cut, expect anything like a rabbit to be produced
from the hat. The principle then must read: homonymity causes
linguistic disturbances only when it exists between words that
in given contexts and situations would cause misunderstandings.
This means that the words must belong to the same grammatical
category; thus there is no ambiguity between German *arm*
(adjective) and *Arm* (noun). Still more narrowly, *the words must
belong to the same sphere of ideas*. A typical instance of this was the
struggle between the French words for cat and cock (see p. 290).
Only in such limited circumstances will homonyms cease to be
efficient instruments of communication and expression; only in
such cases does phonetic resemblance become a disposing cause
of word mortality.

It is not only ambiguity which prompts the discarding of a
word. Often phonetic attrition proceeds so far as to reduce words
to mere fragments, which the speaker throws aside like worn-out
tools. Gilliéron has illustrated the results of such verbal decrepi-
tude by the history of the word *apem* 'bee' in the Gallo-Roman
territory. Its reduction by phonetic changes to the single sound [ɛ]
rendered it unsatisfactory as a means of communication. Speakers
cast about for a word of a fuller form and this they found in the
southern form, now standard French, *abeille*. Similar reasons may
be adduced for the disappearance of the uncompounded Latin
verb 'eat', *edo, ēs, ēst*, etc., and its replacement by various substitutes, such as the compound *comedo* or by the more forcible
word *manducāre* 'to chew', which is represented by the French
manger. In English such phonetic mutilation has been put forward
to explain why *āē(w)* has been supplanted by *law, custom, ēa* by
water, and *īg* by *island*. In all cases we can say that the criterion of
death or survival of linguistic elements is their efficiency as instruments of communication.

The preceding pages will have given an idea of the complexity
of semantic changes and their manifold causation. Much ingenuity
has gone into classification of semantic changes, but different
schemes proposed have contributed little or nothing to the understanding of the phenomena. We can understand how it is that a

farmer with his special interest and restricted situation can content himself with the vague verb 'put' apropos of the hens laying eggs. It does not help our understanding of the phenomenon to classify *pondre* as an instance of specialization or narrowing. It is noteworthy that S. Ullmann who in his *Principles of Semantics* has painstakingly reviewed the many schemes of classification proposed, writes in his concise work *Semantics* (p. 197): 'To survey all the overlapping schemes of classification, based on a variety of different criteria, would be a Herculean as well as a thankless task.' As for the causes of semantic change, we subscribe to the view that 'change of meaning can be brought about by an infinite multiplicity of causes' and further, that 'no matter how fine a mesh of distinctions one may devise, there will always be some cases which will slip through'. Most succinctly we might say that words come to be used in new senses because old words have to be used by new speakers in a new world.

THE STRUCTURAL PRINCIPLE IN ETYMOLOGY

The standard etymological dictionaries are the fruit of immense labours by scholars of the last century and a half. Texts have been subjected to minute exegesis and the sense-ranges of words have been registered in lexicons. By lexical comparison words have been shown either to change their sense-range or to disappear altogether. In this way a vast, if unsystematized, knowledge of semantic change has been acquired. Word-formational studies have organized words into families, clustering round a common element which is called the root. Finally, the sound laws have been applied to gather these national families of words into international comities. The traditional methods illustrated discursively above may be briefly reviewed by means of one more example.

The English word *cruel* goes back in the first instance to OF *cruel* and this in its turn is the descendant of Latin *crūdēlis*. The Latin word links up with the adjective *crūdus*, the basic meaning of which was 'bleeding' (e.g. of wounds), and thence it came to mean 'bloodthirsty, cruel'. Since it was applied to meat in the sense 'raw, uncooked', *crūdus* came to mean 'unprocessed' and even 'undigested'. Finally, in the sense of 'unripe' it passed to the notion of 'green' and 'vigorous' as in the phrase *crūda deō viridisque senectus* 'the god's old age is vigorous and green'. *Crūdus* in the basic sense 'bleeding' links up with *cruor*, which had the special sense of 'gore, i.e. shed and clotted blood' as opposed to *sanguis*, which signified 'blood in circulation'. From *cruor* an adjective *cruentus* was made (on the morphology see below) and this could also mean 'cruel, terrible'.

A root-form **crū-* accounts for words in other languages within much the same semantic sphere. In Celtic we have Irl. *cru* and Welsh *creu* 'shed blood' while Avestan (see Appendix A) presents *xrū-* 'raw meat'. Greek has the forms *kré(w)a* and *kré(w)as* 'flesh', the latter being paralleled by Sanskrit *kravís*, with an adjective *krūrá-* 'raw, bloody' made on an *r-* stem.

To account for this scatter of words an ancestral root **krew-* is postulated. If we now turn to Germanic, applying Grimm's Law, a number of words come to light derivable from a Common Germanic **χrawas*: OHG *(h)rao*, German *roh*, ON *hrár*, OE *hrēaw*, English *raw*. A number of words from other languages have found their way by different routes into English besides the genuine Germanic descendant *raw*. *Crude* is taken from the Latin *crūdus*, while *cruel*, as has already been said, is owed immediately to OF *cruel*. Less easily recognizable is *creosote*, the word for an antiseptic and wood preservative which was concocted in 1835 from the Greek *kreo-* 'flesh' and the root *sō-* 'save' (cf. *sōtēr* 'saviour').

That all these words are related is evident from the close similarity of sound and meaning, for they cover a narrow semantic range. However, an etymology will not be considered satisfactory until the derivation of the different stems is accounted for. These are intricate morphological problems, the full elucidation of which would go beyond the bounds of an introductory manual. In all probability we have to do with an ancient declensional pattern which is found in many of the words denoting parts of the body. A case in point has been discussed above (p. 252), i.e. the Latin word for 'thigh', which shows an alternation of *r* and *n* in the declension—nom. sg. *femur*, gen. sg. *feminis*. It is this we see also in *cruor/cruentus*. In the first place, then, we should postulate the Indo-European forms **krew-r/krew-n*. It is from an *r*-form that the Sanskrit *krūrá-* is derived.

Such are the methods and results of etymological research. Over the years large numbers of etymological dictionaries have appeared in the field of Indo-European linguistics, and much the same sets of facts have been presented from different angles: Sanskrit, Russian, Icelandic, Greek, Latin, etc., to say nothing of a new version of the standard work on Indo-European itself.[1] Perusal of these works leaves, together with the sense of admiration and gradituide for the work of these devoted scholars, some feeling of discouragement. The preface to the fourth edition of Ernout and Meillet's etymological dictionary of Latin states that Meillet's contribution on the etymological side (Ernout was concerned with tracing the history of words in Latin itself) has been left untouched on the grounds that very few of the etymologies proposed since his death would have been accepted by him because of their dubious and arbitrary nature. If this conservatism is justified, then one must conclude that, in default of new material, etymological work in the field of Indo-European has virtually reached the end of the road with present methods.

New vistas of research have been opened up by the application of the structural approach. A word-based etymological dictionary is in so far artificial as it treats words in isolation. But to wrest a word out of its context is to destroy, or to ignore, important aspects of the observed phenomenon. Speech is learned and used in the form of repetitive and habitual combinations of words. Everywhere we observe how one word provokes and elicits the presence of another. Such are word affinities, the collocations, which an adequate lexicon should record. Let us suppose we have two competing etymological possibilities. We must surely give the preference to the one which not only accounts for the members of the collocation separately but also for the collocation itself. A case in point is offered by the Latin words *mūnus* and *fungor*, for the verb has in early Latin a pronounced preference for the company of *mūnus* in the phrase *mūnere fungor*, an additional point being the ablative of the noun. There is general agreement among scholars about the etymology of *mūnus*, the older form of which was **moinos*. The word must first be subjected to a morpho-

---

1. J. Pokorny, *Indogermanisches etymologisches Wörterbuch*, 1951–1969.

logical analysis. It is a neuter *s*-stem from the *o*-grade of a root *mei* 'change, exchange'. This is an important fact, for there are numbers of such formations in Latin, and they cluster in the semantic sphere of 'social payments'. Examples are *pignus* 'pledge', *fēnus* 'interest on money lent' and perhaps[1] *fūnus* 'rites due to the dead'. The general sense of *mūnus* must, therefore, have been 'exchange gift', and the Latin use of the word can best be understood against a wide sociological background of the 'gift-exchange'. Such a gift once proferred and accepted creates a bond between the participants, a mutual 'obligation'.[2] Among the Romans this relationship was conceived of as a 'burden' which must be 'discharged' (i.e. 'unloaded'), and this explains why the terms *levis* 'light' and *gravis* 'heavy' constantly occur in passages relating to this subject. Another image was the 'bond' which must be 'untied'; this is the literal meaning of *solvere*, although we translate it as 'pay' (a debt). It is from this usage that we get the terms *solvent* and *solvency*. From the point of view of the giver of the *mūnus* what was conferred was a *beneficium*, and this automatically created its counterpart with the receiver—an *officium*, that is the obligation to requite the *beneficium*. Hence the *officium* was a 'duty' (a thing owed), and in the language of public administration it came to mean the tasks which a public official had to discharge.

Both giver and receiver were joined together by a *mūnus* in the relationship called *grātia*, and the recipient was *mūnis ac grātus*. A number of derivatives relating to social groups was made by the suffix *-icus* (e.g. *cīvicus*, *hosticus*, *classicus*), and there is evidence for the existence of a similar formation *mūnicus* from *muni-*. It is from this that a verb *commūnicāre* was derived. From another derivative *com-mūnis*, literally 'sharing a *muni*', the sense 'common' 'what is shared by all' developed. Finally we have the technical term *mūni-caps* > *municeps*, literally 'the taker of a *muni*', who was thereby bound to the giver. It is from this that we have the collective *municipium* 'a town subject to Rome'.

These gift-exchange arrangements also governed the Romans'

---

1. From a root *dheu-*.
2. *Obligāre* is a compound of *ligāre* 'to bind', cf. Engl. *ligament*, *ligature*.

dealings with their gods, who were treated on the principle *do ut des*, 'I give that you may give'. The offering bound the recipient god in the relationship of *grātia*, and it is this pagan notion that lies behind our use of the term 'the grace of God'.

There is less agreement about the word *fungor*; the most widely favoured solution credits the original root **bheug-* with the meaning 'enjoy', but this does not explain the extremely limited sense-range of the Latin verb. *Mūnus* was originally the most frequent collocation of *fungor*, but this word was soon joined by *officium* which, as we saw, was a near synonym of *mūnus*. Other nouns combined with the verb *fungor* were *perīculum* 'danger' and *vīta* 'life'. From *vīta functus* (and *dēfunctus*) we get the expression 'defunct'. It will be evident that an etymology of *fungor* based on the sense 'enjoy' will not fit the observed usage. What is required is the notion of 'release' and 'separation from'. It so happens that the root **bheug-* in Iranian has this very meaning: 'untie, deliver, save'. If we insert this sense, the whole Latin phrase *mūnere fungor* finds a satisfactory explanation. In the first place it illuminates the case of the noun (the ablative of separation) and the middle voice of the verb ('I untie myself'). Finally, the phrase fits into the sociological and terminological framework of the gift-exchange apparatus. The notion of untying also lies behind *solvere* (see above).

A number of important theoretical points can be made in the light of this example. In the first place the philological interpretation of the texts must establish the sense-range. This must be underpinned by a study of the whole family of words in the given language. The members of the family, as we have emphasized above, are detected by morphological analysis. Next, the collocations must be noted. Finally, the place of the word in the structure of terms relating to the same semantic sphere or conceptual field must be fixed.

Only after completion of this work within the given language should we start the search for the missing relatives in other languages.

Another example may be worked which uses the 'semantic maps' discussed above (pp. 188f). It concerns an important term of the moral vocabulary of Greek. The English word *token* 'sign, symbol' may serve as a starting point. This links up with the German *Zeichen* 'sign' and with words in many languages traceable to a root **deik-* 'mark, show'. Important is the use of derivatives of the word in the juridical sphere in the sense 'accuse' (Goth. *ga-teihan*, OHG *zīhan*, German *zeihen*).

In Sanskrit the derivatives keep close to the sense 'show, point', as in the verb *diśáti*, while the root noun *diś-* has the senses 'direction, region of the sky, manner'. In Latin, too, there are a number of derivatives of the root **deik-* with a sense 'show' 'point out', e.g. the compound *index*, which from meaning 'that which points' was specialized in the meaning 'forefinger'. However, the verb *dīco* and a large family of derivatives show the root specialized in the sense 'make known by speaking, say'.

In Greek we have an interesting semantic scatter. Most of the representatives of the root keep close to the notion of 'showing' (e.g. the verb *deiknumi* 'I show'), but it is significant that the root aorist *dikeîn* means 'to throw'. Most important is the noun *dikē* which in the main belongs to the juridical sphere. But though 'justice' is its most frequent meaning, there are indications that this is a specialized usage. In Homer the word can mean 'characteristic, usual mode of behaviour', and that this is ancient is shown by the fossilized accusative in phrases like *kunòs díkēn* 'after the manner of a dog'. *Dikē*, besides the sense 'justice', can also mean 'judicial process', 'judgment' and 'punishment'. Relying on this many scholars adhere to the view that *dikē* derives its juridical senses from the notion 'judgment pronounced'. This runs foul of an important etymological principle: the sense 'to say' is not found in Greek but in Latin. Moreover, the sense 'to throw' (*dikeîn*) must also be accounted for. It is here that the semantic map for 'mark' helps us. For there (see p. 189) we find that such words often develop the sense 'throw' as well as the juridical senses. That in fact the basic notion underlying *dikē* 'justice' was the 'boundary mark' is suggested by the structure of terms connected with this notion of justice. We have the opposition *ékdikos* 'unjust'; *éndikos* 'just' (literally 'outside' versus 'inside' *dikē*). Moreover, the offence is called *hyperbasiā* 'stepping over', 'transgression'. Further, notions of 'straight' and 'crooked' constantly appear in the contents of 'judgment'.[1]

Finally, many words of the Greek moral and juridical vocabulary revolve around the idea of 'distribution'. We find an integrated structure of moral terms reflecting a belief in the orderliness of the world which was the result of an elemental act of apportionment, whereby each component of the universe, gods, men and even natural objects, had its allotted portion, the boundaries of which might not be 'transgressed' without grave results. Over the whole system of 'apportionment' broods a spirit of 'Distribution'. This is *nemesis*, the abstract noun from the root *nem-* 'to distribute'. It is from this same root that the Greeks derived their word *nómos* 'law'. In such a complex semantic structure of terms within a given conceptual sphere or 'field' each member supports the other with a welcome increase in the probability of the solution. 'Probability' is a word which must be stressed. Despite all refinements of method and close attention to documentation the scholar must more often than not resign himself to a *non liquet*. Even for such common words as *girl, boy, lad, lass* the ODEE concludes that 'certainty is not attainable on the evidence'. Yet etymology retains its fascination, and etymological research, even though it fails in its ultimate goal, often yields valuable results. As Y. Malkiel has written:[2] '. . . creative etymology presupposes, on the part of its practitioner, a desire to transcend the domains of the obvious and the highly probable and to operate in the hazardous realm of the increasingly conjectural . . .'.

---

1. One vivid phrase about a judgment being drawn straight 'by line and set-square' brings out the underlying notion.

2. *Essays on Linguistic Themes*, p. 177.

Language and Culture

At a time when linguists for one reason or another felt it important to stress the 'autonomy' of linguistics a distinction was drawn between the linguistic and non-linguistic aspects of the speech situation with the implication that only the former constituted the proper object of the linguist's attention. However, without some understanding of the situational factors speech must remain unintelligible and hence undescribable. It follows that the linguist cannot escape being concerned with the whole speech situation, and all aspects of the situation are 'linguistic' in so far as they are relevant to the understanding of utterances. In plotting the sense-range of words we register the contextual (i.e. collocational) distributions (this is their purely linguistic distribution) and their cultural distributions, that is the situations in which they are found to occur. In tracing the ramifications of meaning the linguist, whether as a dictionary maker or etymologist, will find himself compelled to take into account the whole range of human concerns. Failure to do so reduces linguistics to aridity and sterility. Precisely because speech is embedded in the speaker's world, it is often possible to deduce from language information about historical contacts, social structure, religious beliefs and practices, folklore, techniques, and so on.

The most obvious examples are those from the world of material things. Above it was shown how the obsolence of a cultural object like the Roman *toga* results in the disappearance from the language of the word designating that object. As a corollary to this we have now to consider those cases where, as a result of cultural development, a word denotes entirely different things in the course of history. The word *pen*, for instance, originally meant 'feather' (Lat. *penna*), and it was strictly only applicable to the primitive quill-pen. The word was retained, however, throughout the development of the pen, so that the ancient word for 'feather' now denotes an instrument with a metal nib. Conversely, the analysis of the modern word and its relation to the word for 'feather' may teach us something about the early form of the pen. In this way the history of language and of culture ('words and things')[1] go hand in hand and provide mutual support and illumination. The present chapter is devoted to the examination of such relations between culture and language.

It is a remarkable fact that many of the Indo-European words for 'wall' have the basic meaning of 'wicker-work', 'wattle'. Thus the German word *Wand* is connected with the verb *winden* ('to wind, to intertwine'), while the selfsame verb is actually used in Old English of building a wall, e.g. *windan manigne smicerne wah* 'to weave many a fine wall'. The Slavonic languages also have words that suggest a similar mode of construction. Thus the old Slavonic *plotŭ* 'a fence' and modern Russian *plotnik* 'a carpenter' both contain a root that exists in our *plait*.[2] Ancient authors have repeatedly described this technique of building. Ovid's ... *et paries lento vimine textus erat*, 'and the wall was woven from the supple withe', recalls the above-quoted Old English passage. Excavations on prehistoric sites have also revealed its antiquity; for many fragments of burned clay have been found which bear distinct impressions of wicker-work. This is the type of construction known as wattle and daub. The wicker-

---

1. The school of philologists who have pursued this method of investigation have used this phrase as their slogan. Pioneers in this field were R. Meringer and H. Schuchardt. I am chiefly indebted in this chapter to articles by the former.

2. *Plait* goes back to OF *pleit* < **plicitum*, a substantivized use of the participle of the Latin verb *plicare*, from which we also get *ply*. The IE root was **plek-*, the genuine Germanic descendants of which include German *flechten* (OE *fleohtan*) and *flax*.

work forms the basis on which mud was smeared; or, alternatively, mud was smeared between two such wicker-work frames.[1]

There is another type of primitive building technique that is described by Vitruvius, the Roman writer on architecture, in the following words: 'Others used to construct walls by drying lumps of clay fastening them together with timber.' This mode of construction is recalled by the names for wall in many languages. The Greek word for wall is *teîkhos*, a root found in Italic and in our English word *dyke*. This goes back to a root IE *dheigh*- 'knead, mould, work in clay'. Our own word *dough* (German *Teig*) still stays close to the original meaning. *Dike* in the sense of 'embankment', which comes close to the Greek meaning, was probably a borrowing from the Dutch. In English dialects *dike* corresponds to *ditch*. In Latin the original meaning of the root is easily recognized in *figulus* 'potter', while *fictor* means 'pastry-cook' and 'sculptor' (cf. *figūra*). The verb *fingo* developed a wide range of senses including 'fashion', 'represent', 'imagine', 'invent', 'feign'. From the derived noun we get our word *fiction*.

In Old Persian the compound *pairi-daēza* also contains a derivative from this root with reference to a wall. It meant a park with a wall round it. This word passed *via* Greek and Latin into English in the form *paradise*. Thus we see that from this single Indo-European word 'to mould, work in clay', besides the word *dike* that recalls the old technique of wall-making, English possesses such different derivatives as *ditch*, *dough*, *feign*, *fiction*, *figment*, *figure*, *effigy* and *paradise*.

The Latin word *domus* (whence German *Dom* 'cathedral') and Russian *dom* 'house' are formed from a root *dem*- 'build', which originally referred to wooden construction. It is to this root that we trace the word *timber*, which in OE first meant 'a building' and later 'wood for building'. The corresponding German word

---

1. Meringer quotes Tacitus. *Germania*, xvi, *ne caementorum quidem apud illos aut tegularum usus*, to show that the primitive Germans did not build walls of bricks or stones and mortar. The fact that the German word *Mauer* 'stone wall', *Kalk* 'mortar', and *Ziegel* 'brick' are all Latin loan-words (*mūrus*, *calx* and *tegula* respectively) is a striking confirmation of this. It is interesting to note that French *bâtiment*, *bâtir* are Germanic loan-words derived from *bastjan* 'to plait'.

Zimmer means 'a room'. *Zimmermann*, however, is a 'carpenter', and the related Gothic verb *timrjan* 'to build' approaches closely to meaning of the Greek verb quoted above.

Another mysterious word that recalls an obsolete technique is the English word *window*, which means literally 'wind-eye'. The word 'eye' in many languages forms part of compound words denoting a window. Thus Gothic *auga-dauro* means 'eye-door'. Old English has *eagþyrel* 'eye-hole' and *eagduru* 'eye-door', but these were superseded by the ON *vindauga*. In Sanskrit we find

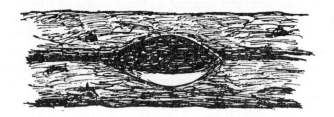

Fig. 45.

gavakṣa-('ox eye'), while Russian has *okno*, derived from a root connected with the Latin *oculus* (literally 'little eye'). In explanation of these forms it has been pointed out that the oldest houses were built either of wicker-work or of logs. In neither of these types is a large window of a square shape possible. In the case of wicker-work a square cut would easily cause splitting, while in log-houses the opening must be made between two logs, so that neither is excessively weakened. The accompanying illustration (Fig. 45) of a window in a log-house shows clearly the resemblance to an eye which gave rise to the names enumerated above.

By study of the 'things' Meringer attempted to clear up the connexion between the multifarious meanings of the German word group *Lade, Laden, laden, einladen*. The meaning of the word *laden* 'to load' is sufficiently illuminated by its near phonetic equation with the Old English *hlada* 'to load' and Slavic *klada* 'to lay, to put'. The noun *Lade* in the sense of 'drawer' seems also to approximate fairly closely to the old Norse *hlaða* 'a barn', both being assignable to the sense 'a depository', which is close to the meaning of the verb. The word *Laden* in the sense of 'shop' and 'window shutter' (*Fensterladen*) cannot be explained, however, without a study of the history of the objects to which these words refer. *Lade* meant a 'plank' (cf. Engl. *lath*),[1] which before the introduction of glass was the usual type of window shutter. Apart from that, it was used in the language of hawkers for the board on two trestles on which wares were exposed in the market place. This is the most primitive kind of shop. It was from these beginnings that the modern senses of the word developed. A study of cultural history also clears up the meaning of the words *einladen* 'to invite' and *Vorladung* 'summons'.

Fig. 46.

Meringer quotes an instructive example of the vagueness to which traditional etymologizing without a study of the cultural history is exposed. He quotes the relevant article by Kluge[2] as follows: 'For the meaning of the Germanic root *lap* compare Gothic *lapons* 'consolation, redemption', the adverbial *lapaleiko* 'very gladly' and modern High German *Luder*. An idea 'treat kindly', 'request' must be taken as point of departure; a root **lat* with this meaning has not yet been found among the other Indo-European languages.' Meringer in his attempt to explain this word has drawn attention to the widespread custom of requesting attendance at juridical proceedings by sending round a board. In certain parts of Bohemia such a 'Gebotbrett' is still sent from

---

1. This connexion is doubted in ODEE, which moots a connexion with Welsh *llath* (OIr. *st'at* < OCeltic **slathā*).

2. *Etymologisches Wörterbuch der deutschen Sprache.*

house to house. It consists of a wooden board provided with a handle (see Fig. 46), the proclamation being stuck or pinned on to it. *Laden* is therefore a verb derived from the noun *lap* meaning literally 'to board a person', this being a usage similar to denominatives like our 'blackball' or the Greek 'to ostracize'. Thus it was from this usage of *einladen, vorladen* to denote the sending of a board round to request attendance at Court that the modern general meaning of 'to invite, summon' developed.

Pagan is another word of which the etymology given on such speculative lines has proved unsatisfactory. *Pāgus*, of course, means a country district, and we are told that the word *pāgānus*, a country dweller, developed its modern meaning because it was in the country districts that the old religions persisted long after the towns had become christianized. A more attractive suggestion is based on the fact that the word *pāgānus* was used contemptuously by the Roman soldiers to denote 'civilians'. The early militant Christians made use of this army slang and contrasted themselves as soldiers of Christ with the *pāgānī* 'civilians' not yet enrolled in His army.

Of the material objects of civilization dress is perhaps the most subject to changes of fashion. In this field, too, the history of culture throws light on many a mysterious etymology. The English word *stocking*, for instance, is a derivative[1] of *stock*, which means literally 'a stump', something shortened or mutilated (cf. *trunks*). How have these garments come to possess such a curious name? The answer must be sought in the history of costume, and for the history of English costume we must turn to France. The oldest Romance word for trousers is derived from the Latin *brācae*. This is a Gaulish word borrowed from a Germanic source, the original meaning being 'buttock' (cf. *culotte*). It was in the first century of our era that a certain Caesina scandalized Rome by appearing in public clad in the long Gaelic trousers. The fashion soon caught on, however, and became general. Fashions changed in Rome and the trousers became knee breeches, a fashion that was adopted in their turn by the inhabitants of Gaul. The legs were clad in cloth gaiters, still to be seen in some parts of

---

1. ODEE comments 'of obscure formation'.

France. These gaiters sometimes had feet and were called *calceas* (Fr. *chausses*), a word that appeared in the Merovingian age and signified stockings throughout the whole of the Middle Ages. During the course of time, with the change of fashion, the stockings got longer and longer and the trousers shorter and shorter until, about the turn of the fourteenth century, the stockings grew up round the body and became a single garment—the tights. The *bracae* were submerged and became underpants. One century later the *chausses* were again divided into (*haut de*) *chausses*, shortened to *chausses*, 'trousers' and *bas* (*de chausses*) 'stockings' respectively. The corresponding English terms were *upper-stocks* and *nether-stocks*, referring to the upper and lower parts of the truncated garment. The word *stock* was reserved for the lower half of the split garment, and in the derived form *stocking* it has persisted down to the present day. Curiously enough, the word *trouser*, like *bracae*, is also derived from Celtic sources. It is a plural formation of an obsolete *trouse*, which comes from the Irish *triubhas* 'trews', a garment of close-fitting breeches which sometimes had stockings attached. Morphologically *trouse* was remodelled to *trousers* after *drawers*.

It has been pointed out that garments often pass from the possession of one sex to the other. The word *skirt*, a doublet of *shirt*[1] (see above), is a case in point. The French *jupe* has rather a more complicated history. The contrast of Italian *giubba* with Spanish *aljuba*, containing the Semitic definite article, suggests a Moorish or an Arabic source.[2] The word actually denoted a cotton garment worn by the Arabs, which the Crusaders gladly donned instead of their metal armour beneath the hot sun of the Holy Land. It thus found its way to Europe. But although in France the *jupe* has been appropriated by the female sex, it once referred to a male garment, as it still does in the German *Joppe*, a jacket. The English word *jumper* seems to come from the same source. Originally a heavy jersey worn by sailors it has been annexed by our sisters, the modern male having to be content with a 'pullover'.

---

1. ODEE comments: '. . . the corr. LG *schört* means "women's gown" locally'.

2. *Jubbah* (also *jibbah*) is the 'outer garment of Moslems and Parsees' (ODEE).

The *chemise* has a similar history, which begins in the soldiers' camp and ends in the boudoir. The earliest undergarment that we know of among the Romans was the *tūnica interior*. This was made of wool; but it was replaced later by a linen garment, the (*tūnica*) *līnea*. About the fourth century a new word appears— *camīsia*. According to Jerome (*Ep.* 64, 11), this was a foreign term (perhaps Gaulish or Germanic) for the close-fitting undergarment worn by soldiers: *Solent mīlitantes habēre līneas, quas camīsias vocant, sic aptas membrīs et adstrictās corporibus*, 'the soldiers usually wear linen shirts which they call *camīsiae*, closely fitting the limbs, tied close to the body'. This word was spread by the Roman army over the whole of Romania.[1] It is found even in non-Latin speaking territories under Roman influence, like Albania, Greece and, in the Arab word *kamis*. The old word *līnea* is now found only in three isolated parts of the Romance territory and, remarkably enough, in all three places it denotes a woman's undergarment.

We have seen above that cultural contacts result in an exchange of linguistic goods. Conversely the analysis of linguistic loans and borrowings throws light on the contact of cultures and on the relations of peoples, just as the archaeologists makes inferences from the distribution of pottery, ornaments and weapons, Thus, the Germanic words in French are largely concerned with war and weapons, law and politics. That the cultivation of the grapevine was brought to Germany by the Romans is clear from the fact that so many technical words connected with wine production are Latin loan-words: e.g. *Wein* (*vīnum*), *Most* 'new wine, must' (*mustum*), *Kelter* 'wine-press' (*calcātūra* 'stamping with the feet'). The fact that the Latin word for 'street' (*strāta via*) is so widespread in Europe would indicate, even without further historical or archaeological corroboration, that the Romans were great builders of roads. The Arabic elements in Spanish refer to agriculture and irrigation, astronomy and mathematics, chemistry and medicine, while practically the whole of Europe has banking and bookkeeping terms from Florence and Lombardy.[2]

---

1. The OE borrowing is *cemes*, cf. ME *kemes*.

2. The word *Lombard* itself was used in the seventeenth century in the sense 'bank, pawnshop'.

In the same way the composite culture of the English people is richly illuminated by the study of its loan-words. We have borrowed cultural words from widespread languages. *Potato* comes from the West Indies,[1] *algebra*[2] from the Arabs, *cheroot* from the Dravidian languages of southern India,[3] etc. From the Dutch we have many nautical terms such as *boom*,[4] *skipper* ('shipper'), *yacht* (*jaghtschip* 'chase vessel'). In art, too, we are considerably indebted to the Dutch schools as we see from the technical words for the craft. *Easel* is derived from the Dutch word *ezel*, connected with the German *Esel*, 'a donkey' (cf. *clothes-horse*). Other words from the same source are *etch*,[5] *sketch*[6] and *landscape*.

The greatest influence, however, was exerted on English by the Norman invasion, after which English became for three centuries almost exclusively a despised *patois*, spoken chiefly by serfs and underlings.[7] The social and cultural superiority of the Normans created a cleft in our language for which there are few parallels. The most often quoted example of this is the differentiation of the names for meats from the animals which provide them. The French-speaking nobles dignified the cow in its culinary aspect with the name *beef*, and the pig was transformed into *pork*, the sheep into *mutton*. It is remarkable how many table dainties have Norman-French names whereas the commonplace everyday foods retained their Anglo-Saxon names. Thus *bread* is Germanic, but

---

1. *Batata* is used in Haiti for the sweet potato.

2. First attested in the sense 'bone-setting'. The Arabs called this department of mathematics 'the science of redintegration (*aljebr*) and equation'.

3. Tamil *shuruṭṭu* 'roll of tobacco'.

4. 'tree or pole', related to German *Baum*, Engl. *beam*.

5. *Etsen*, cf. Germ. *ätzen* 'feed, bait; corrode (with acid)', all from Gmc. *atjan 'cause to eat'.

6. Ultimately from Italian *schizzo*, which goes back to Latin *schedius*, itself a borrowing from Greek *skhedios* 'on the spur of the moment, off-hand'.

7. Important factors in the emergence of Norman-French as a prestige language were: (1) the virtual extinction of the Anglo-Saxon nobility; (2) the filling of important positions in Church and State by Normans or other French-speaking foreigners; (3) their employment of French-speaking armed supporters; and (4) the influx of large numbers of merchants and craftsmen from France. French remained the normal language of intercourse among the upper classes for two hundred years after the Conquest (see A. C. Baugh, *History of the English Language*, pp. 131ff.).

biscuit[1] and *wafer*[2] have replaced *foca*. *Milk* goes back to OE *milc* but the Normans gave their name to the *cream*[3] (OE *fliete*). Of fish, too, *plaice*[4] appears instead of *facg*, *perch*[5] for *bærs*, and *salmon* for *leax*. The replacement of Old English words took place in fact over the whole range of what is called the higher culture. Thus Old English expressions for titles and ranks such as *æðeling*, *þegn* were replaced by *nobleman* and *baron*. In the realm of dress French custom soon replaced the English variety, and most of the old words died out. The general word *dress* appears instead of a multitude of native terms, e.g. *gierla*, *hæteru*, *hrægel*, *reaf*, *sceorp; cloak* instead of *basing*, *bratt*, *hacele*, etc. Expressions for war, law and administration are, as we should expect, also derived from Norman-French. Thus the Old English word *here* (German *Heer*) has been replaced by *army*. The word *war*, too, is of Norman-French origin, although the French in their turn had borrowed the word from Germanic sources. In the realm of government most of the Anglo-Saxon words were ousted. The Old English series *weald*, *geweald*, *wealdness*, were replaced by *power*, *dominion*, *government*, *control*. Even the noun *wealdend* succumbed to a French intruder, *prince*, while the Old English assembly the *witenagemot* gave way to *council*. But perhaps the most remarkable sign of Norman supremacy in England is the disappearance of English words for servant such as *þeow*, *þenestre*, etc., and their replacement by *minister*, *servant*.

Very often the very form of a word clearly indicates the country of its origin. Such words are Arabic terms that contain the definite article *al* (e.g. *alchemy*,[6] etc.). In the Romance languages there are a

---

1. OF *bescoit*, *bescuit* < *bis-coctus* 'twice-baked'.

2. From Middle Low German *wāfel*, which was borrowed into Norman French in the form of *waufre*, contrasting with OF *gaufre*.

3. OF *cresme*, which is regarded as a contamination of late Latin *crāma* (perhaps a Gaulish word) with *chrisma*, a loan-word from Greek *khrisma* 'anointing', 'unction'.

4. OF *plaïs*, which is traced to Late Latin *platessa*, a derivative from Greek *platús* 'broad, flat'.

5. OF *perche* < Lat. *perca* < Grk *pérkē*. The basic meaning was perhaps 'spotted'.

6. Arabic *alkīmīā*, in fact, contains the Greek loan-word *khēm(e)íā* 'art of alloying metals'.

number of Arabic words which appear in two forms (cf. above, on *aljuba*). Such a case is illustrated in the following table, which represents the distribution of the Romance derivatives of the Arabic word *makhāzin* (the plural of *makhzan* 'store-house') from which our *magazine* comes:

French: magasin	Portuguese: armazém
Italian: maggazino	Spanish: almacén
Catalan: magatzem	Catalan: almazèm

It is obvious from the form of the words, characterized by the presence or absence of the definite article, that the two groups of languages have derived their words from different sources. In the Iberian peninsula, of course, the word was introduced by the Moorish invasion and occupation. It appears, however, in the more easterly group at a much later date (thirteenth century), its borrowing being a consequence of the trade relations which existed between the eastern Mediterranean and the great commercial cities of the Christian countries. Actually *magazzenum* is first found in documents from Marseilles[1] to denote the depôts which the merchants of the city maintained in North Africa. The word for 'sugar' has a similar origin and it throws considerable light on historical relationships. The distribution is:

Portuguese: assucar	Italian: zucchero
Spanish: azúcar	French: sucre
Catalan: sucre	

We know that the Arabs attempted to establish sugar plantations (1) in Andalusia, and (2) in Sicily, these efforts being continued under the Normans and the Hohenstaufen rulers. The word spread, then, from two separate centres, as indicated by the distribution of the linguistic forms. The close political relationship of Catalonia and Sicily is faithfully reflected in the linguistic facts.

The progress of the conversion of pagan Europe may be traced in the distribution of words connected with religion. It is a curious fact that the words for 'church' in the Romance languages

---

1. For this and other details in this chapter I am indebted to W. v. Wartburg's article in *Neue Jahrbücher f. Paedagogik*, 1931, pp. 223ff.

are either derivatives from Greek *ekklēsiā* or *basilica* (e.g. Fr. *église*, Rum. *biserica*), whereas the corresponding Germanic terms go back to the Greek *kuriakón* (cf. Engl. *church*, Germ. *Kirche*). Similar distribution may be observed in the word for 'coffin'. The standard French word is *cercueil*, derived from the Greek *sarcophagus*; but of the whole Romance area only northern France has this word, the cognate languages having derivatives from Latin words, e.g. *vascellum, locellus, arca, capsa*. Holland and Germany agree with northern France in having *sarc* and *Sarg* respectively. In yet another word of the Church language we may observe a similar relationship. Instead of *Saturni dies* (English *Saturday*) French has *samedi*, corresponding to German *Samstag*, both of which go back to a Graeco-Oriental *sambaton*. Equivalents of this word are found in the Rhaeto-Romance dialects and the German dialects of the Danube basin and the Rhine as far as the boundary of the Church provinces of Trier and Cologne.[1] The geographical distribution of another day-name is also interesting in this connexion. Frings points out that when the Germans took over the names of the days from the Romans (fourth century A.D.), the classical names had been modified in the regions lying around the upper Rhine and south of the Danube under Graeco-Oriental influences:[2] the later Latin *media hebdoma* ('mid-week') still survives in certain dialects of France and in Rhaeto-Romance. The German translation of this loan-word appears in OHG as *mitta wecha*, German *Mittwoch*. This word, like *cyriakon, sarcophagus*, etc., conquered southern Germany and travelled northwards until it was held up at the northern boundary of the Church province of Trier and Mainz. North of this we find the *Wodansdag* domain of the North Sea region, to which England with its *Wednesday* belongs. According to Frings, these words show clearly the path along which Christianity came to the Germans; from Greece via the Goths.

This conclusion seems to be belied by the word *Priester*, which

---

1. T. Frings, *Germania Romana*, p. 27.

2. The Danube was an important strategic line for the Romans, and the continual passage of troops from one garrison to another was particularly favourable to the spread of cultural and linguistic elements.

goes back to a Greco-Latin *presbyter*, a word that signified in the whole Romania a Catholic priest. Its phonetic form shows clearly that it reached Germany by a different route, passing through Romance territory; for the Old High German form *prēstar* must be equated with the Old French *prestre*, which exhibits the effects of certain typical Old Romance sound changes. But other facts show that this is not the oldest German word for 'priest'. In the first place, this borrowing must have taken place after the High German sound shift, which transformed an initial *p* into *pf*. We see an example of this in the word *Pfund* from the Latin *pondus* (cf. English *pound*). If *prestre* had been borrowed before this time, we should have expected **Pfriester*. Hence this borrowing must be assigned at the earliest to the seventh or eighth century. Actually, precedence must be given to another Germanic word for 'priest' which exhibits the above-mentioned change from *p* to *pf*. This is *Pfaffe*, a word now only used in a contemptuous sense, much like the English *parson*. Its derivation direct from the Greek *papas* again marks out the road by which Christianity reached the Germans.[1]

It would be, of course, incorrect to say that this was the only source of Christian influence. Apart from the fact that there must have been isolated Christians among the Roman army of occupation on the Rhine, recent research has clearly shown that three distinct lines of Christian missionary activity converged on the region of the middle Rhine around Trier and Cologne. The first came from the periphery of the Romania Christiana—the Frankish mission; the second was the Anglo-Saxon mission at the mouth of the Rhine; and the third is evident in the forces radiating from southern Germany, which in its turn had been influenced by Gothic Christianity, drawing its inspiration from Greek sources. For the last, which was the most important, we have given evidence above; but both the first two have left their traces on the language. The standard word *Sonnabend* 'Saturday' is a case in point. For this word occupies a buffer region between the *saturni dies* territory of the North Sea and the *Samstag* dominion of the south.

---

1. See J. Jud, *Zeitschr. f. Roman. Philol.*, 38, 3; Frings, *op. cit.*, p. 29. It is only in Gothic and Slavonic that *papa* (Gk. *papâs*) denotes the *clericus minor*.

Sonnabend seems to have been introduced by Anglo-Saxon missionaries. It is the OE *sunnanæfen* ('Sunday eve'), a translation from the Church Latin *vigilia*.

The influence of the Christianity of France is illustrated in the above word *Priester*. *Easter* may be another word owed to the Frankish mission. This goes back to OE *ēastre*, which mostly occurs in the plural *ēastron* (cf. OHG *ōstarūn*, German *Ostern*). Bede derived the word from the goddess *Ēostre*, whose festival supposedly took place at the vernal equinox. The existence of such a goddess, is, however, extremely dubious, and in any case the Germanic *Austrōn is cognate with the Latin *aurōra* and other IE words meaning 'dawn'. The attractive suggestion has been made[1] that the West Germanic term originated in a translation of the term *alba(e)*, which meant not only the period after Easter, but also 'dawn' (French *aube*).

It is, however, necessary to add that these are late loanwords and that the relations of Germany and Gaul fall into two periods. During the first of these, the time of the Roman occupation, the Romans and romanized Celts were the linguistic givers. This was the time when cultural loan-words like OHG *muniʒʒa* (Lat. *monēta*), *Zoll* (cf. Engl. *toll*), from Greek *telōneîon*, via Gallo-Romance *toloneum*, *Pacht* ('lease', Latin *pactum*), *Kammer* 'chamber' (Lat. *camera*), *Keller* 'cellar' (Lat. *cellārium*), *Mauer* 'wall' (Lat. *mūrus*), found their way into German. At this time Christian influence from this source is betrayed by the word *Bischof* 'bishop', which is derived from the Greek *epískopos* via an Old Romance form *biscopus*. But despite their strong cultural influence, it is a remarkable fact that the Romans supplied the Germanic peoples with few words for weapons; on the contrary, in this sphere they were the borrowers. This is probably due to the fact that under the Empire military recruits were largely drawn from Germanic tribes. This historical fact goes to explain why the Germanic elements in vulgar Latin consist almost entirely of words drawn from the vocabulary of Germanic mercenaries. This was an omen for the time to come. For in the fourth century a

---

1. J. Knobloch, 'Der Ursprung von nhd. Ostern, engl. Easter', *Die Sprache* (1959), pp. 27–45.

Germanic people, the Franks, crossed the Rhine and began their penetration of Belgium and northern Gaul. By the year 486 they were in possession of a territory extending as far as the Loire. Christianity was overwhelmed for the time being, but it was re-introduced by missionaries from the south. It was through this Gallo-Frankish culture that the later Christian loan-words passed to their Germanic cousins on and beyond the Rhine (see above).

PLACE-NAMES

It is not only the large number of Germanic loan-words that reveal to us the Frankish invasion of Gaul. The names of their settlements indicate even today the areas in which they chiefly settled. In the department of Pas-de-Calais, for instance, we find a number of places the names of which contain Germanic personal names with a Gallo-Romance suffix *-iacum* tacked on, e.g. *Wisques* (*Witiacum*), *Wardrecques* (*Waldhariacum*). The investigation of place-names, indeed, is one of the most fascinating pursuits of the linguist, for they often provide important evidence which supplements and corroborates the work of the historian and the archaeologist.

Much light is thrown by place-names on the history of another Germanic tribe which carved out a kingdom from the moribund body of the Roman Empire—the Goths. In 257 A. D. the emperor Aurelian ceded the province of Dacia to the Goths. For many years they acted as allies to their Roman hosts and undertook the defence of the Danube frontier. Towards the end of the fourth century, however, the invasion of the Huns sent the West Goths off to seek a new abode. After wars and wanderings lasting nearly a quarter of a century, they founded a kingdom in south France. Here again the density of the place-names containing Gothic words and endings (e.g. *Les Goths, Le Goudeux, Goize = Gotia*) betrays the presence of those forgotten Germanic settlements.[1] In Spain, too, the name of the Goths lives in place-names like *Godos, Godojos, Godones*, etc.

---

1. For further details see Gamillscheg, *Romania Germanica*, 1934.

In England, again, history has received valuable help from linguistic research. It was about the year 450 when Vortigern called in the Teutons for help against the Picts and Scots. However, they soon turned against their hosts and ravaged the country northwards and southwards. It has been a moot point whether the Celts were exterminated by their Anglo-Saxon conquerors or whether they amalgamated with them, so that the present population of England is largely a mixture of the two races. The linguistic evidence supports the second alternative. For although Celtic loan-words are few in English, the large number of Celtic personal names recorded in Old English indicate that there was a prolonged and intimate contact between the two races. The distribution of place-names containing Celtic elements is also instructive. Names, for instance, like *Pendle Hill, Penhill, Penkridge, Pentrich*, containing the Welsh *pen* 'head'[1] are chiefly found in the counties of Dorsetshire, Wiltshire, Worcestershire, Staffordshire, Derbyshire and Lancashire, a distribution which indicates that at least in the western parts of England there were considerable remnants of a Celtic-speaking population. Thus, to mention only one remarkable instance, there is one cluster of Celtic place-names in the north-eastern corner of Dorsetshire, among the woodlands of Cranborne Chase, bounded on one side by the old entrenchment called Grim's Ditch. The whole area is dotted with remains of British villages. This is the conclusion reached by R. E. Zachrisson in a study entitled *Romans, Celts and Saxons in Ancient Britain*. He sums up the evidence of language, history and archaeology as follows: 'After the battle of Mount Badon the Teutonic invaders ruled over the eastern half of England, whereas the western half remained in British possession, exactly as in King Alfred's time, when a number of Scandinavian kingdoms were founded in the east of England, the so-called Dane-law. The British survivors in the Saxon half of England were very soon amalgamated with the conquerors. This accounts for the scarcity of Celtic elements in the place nomenclature in England. . . . The process of absorption

---

1. Place-names are often distorted by popular etymology, e.g. the *Sixpenny* Hundred in Dorsetshire really means the 'Saxons' Height', like *Pensax* in Worcestershire.

and amalgamation went on as the Anglo-Saxon conquest proceeded westwards, only that in these areas the number of British survivors must have been much larger than in the east. . . . The Britons were not exterminated but absorbed by their Saxon conquerors. Their civilization vanished but their race remained.'

New precision has been given to these findings by K. Jackson.[1] On a map recording the Brittonic river names in England (Fig. 47) three areas can be distinguished. In Area I, east of a line from the Yorkshire wolds to Salisbury Plain and the New Forest, 'Brittonic names are rare, and are confined almost exclusively to large and medium-sized rivers, such as the Trent, the Thames, the Thame, and the Darent'. What is of interest is that 'this area corresponds fairly closely with the extent of the primary English settlement down to about the first half of the sixth century; and in the South, roughly to what may have been the line along which the Saxons were halted for fifty years about 500 by the battle of Mount Badon'.

West of this is Area II, an intermediate strip, in which Brittonic river names are commoner and include more names of small rivers. 'Area II appears to agree pretty well with the movement of expansion of the Anglo-Saxon occupation which took place in the second half of the sixth century in the South and the first half of the seventh in the North. The hilly district between Tyne and Tees was probably one of the last parts of this Area to be settled by the Northumbrians.'

Area III lies west of Area II (see Fig. 47). It includes Cumberland, Westmorland, and part of Lancashire; south of this a strip lying along the Welsh border to the Bristol Channel; and southwest England with the exception of Cornwall (the boundary being marked by the River Tamar). This area is thick with Brittonic names, among which are the names of quite small streams. 'The sections involved agree remarkably well with the third and final stage of the Anglo-Saxon conquest.'

In Area IV, consisting of Wales and Monmouthshire, with the corner of Herefordshire southwest of the Wye, and Cornwall, the place-names are overwhelmingly Celtic as would be expected,

---

1. *Language and History in Early Britain*, pp. 219ff.

Fig. 47. (From Jackson, K., *Language and History in Early Britain*, Edinburgh University Press.)

'since these lands all remained Brittonic in speech till at least the Norman Conquest . . .'.

The Scandinavian settlements in England are also illuminated by a study of place-names.[1] Even one word like *Ingleby* ('village (or "farm") of the English') can reveal the intensive settlement of Yorkshire by Scandinavian invaders. For, as Mawer points out,[2] this is 'a name which would have no significance except in areas where the population was preponderantly Scandinavian with occasional survival of groups of the earliest inhabitants'. Then, again, linguistic evidence throws light on the part played by the Danes and Norsemen respectively in the Viking settlements in Yorkshire. The distribution of the place-names containing Danish elements like *thorpe* on the one hand, and the Norse *gill* on the other, reveals the Danish occupation densest around York, while the *gills* occur chiefly in the west and north of the county. Moreover, it now seems clear that 'the Norse settlers came in from the west, swarming over from Lancashire, Cumberland and Westmorland rather than from the east'. This is borne out by the fact that the Norse elements are densest on the north-west coast and become sparser as we move inland. Yet another interesting piece of historical evidence lies embedded in these Norse names: many of them contain Irish elements, e.g. the word *erg* 'shieling', a Norse loan-word from Irish which appears in names like *Airyholme* and *Eryholme*. *Irton* and *Irby*, again are compounds made from the words *Iri* and *Irar*, which were nicknames given to the Norsemen who had spent some time in Ireland. These Irish elements are a reminder of the fact that before the penetration and settlement of north-western England the Vikings made raids and settlements in Ireland, in the course of which they picked up Irish words. The word *cross* is one of the most interesting of them. It was brought over by the Viking invaders and figures in numerous place-names of Scandinavian England, e.g. *Ewcross* and *Osgoldcross* in the West Riding of Yorkshire.[3]

---

1. For the Scandinavian settlement of England see the map 10 in A. H. Smith, *English Place-Name Elements*, I.

2. *Acta philol. Scandinav.*, 1932, 1ff.

3. For the distribution of Irish-Norwegian place-names see the map II in A. H. Smith, *op. cit.*,

Place-names are also valuable in dialect study; they have been described as frozen dialect material. On this aspect of place-name study Smith has written:[1] '. . . a considerable regular phonological variation occurs with many elements, which is important in English dialectal studies, as for example with *cald*,[2] *hamm*, *scelf*,[3] *wella*,[4] *wilig*,[5] etc. Many of these dialectal varieties are very old, and when it is possible ultimately to plot the place-name examples in which they are found, they will provide a most valuable supplement to the material which already exists for determining the original boundaries of the Anglo-Saxon tribes and their dialects, especially in those areas where written texts are few or non-existent.' Further, since, 'most place-names . . . at least until the sixteenth century, adhere much more closely to local patterns of speech', it will be possible to detect the spread of dialect modes of speech beyond their original boundaries. A case in point is 'the spread of Midland forms like *cold* or *well* (**cald, wella**) into the South (where *chold* and *will* or *wull* would have been correct) . . .'.

LANGUAGE AND PREHISTORY

If our Proto-Indo-European is merely an abstract construction, a dialanguage useful only for certain operations of comparison, must it for all that 'remain hypothetical, a collection of formulae without reference in any known reality'?[6] Certainly, these formulae have some connexion with a social reality even though we may have only hazy notions about their 'realization' on the lips of men of bygone times. This follows from the nature of the relationship itself. For, it will be recalled, when we say that two languages are related, we mean that certain patterns of resemblance

1. *Op. cit.*, xxviii.
2. '*cold*': *cald* OE (Angl), *ceald* (Kent, West Saxon), *kaldr* (ON), *cald, cold* (ME).
3. 'a rock, a ledge, shelving terrain, a turret or pinnacle': *scelf* (Anglian, Kent), *sci(e)lf, scylf, scylp* (West Saxon), *scylfe* (Anglian, West Saxon).
4. 'a well, a spring, a stream': *wella, well(e)* (Anglian, Kent), *wiella, wielle, will(a), wyll(a), wylle* (West Saxon), *wælla, wælle* (Mercian).
5. 'Willow': '. . . from the material so far available . . . *welig* was the WSax. form and *wilig* the Anglian'.
6. E. Pulgram, *The Tongues of Italy*, p. 143.

can be explained only on the supposition that the resemblant
social habits are connected by an unbroken chain of mimetic
processes which link up at some unknown time and place in
prehistory. Whatever 'diasystem' we construct to account for
the resemblance of *beech* and *Buche*, implicit in this construction[1]
is the statement that in some community we call Proto-Germanic
an ancestral word of this diaphonemic shape was used to designate
this particular tree. This last point is important since it is by
reconstructed *meanings* that we can hope to penetrate into the
ancestral prehistorical world and provide the formulae with referents in reality. Since the basic equation of the compared words in
this case is based on phonemic parallels and identity of meaning,
the onus of proof is on the sceptic who would prefer to posit an
unknown ancestral meaning in common Germanic, which by
successive developments converged to the observed identity in
the Germanic languages. If it is thus reasonable to credit the
Proto-Germanic people with a knowledge of the beech-tree, then
this gives us an insight into an aspect of their physical world.
Consequently, in seeking for the 'homeland' of this prehistoric
people whose speech is reflected in the Common Germanic
dialanguage, it would be reasonable to rule out those parts of the
world where the beech tree is unknown.

Scholars have attempted to carry this line of argument back a
stage further in the effort to find guide-lines bearing on the homeland of the Proto-Indo-European people. In this the 'beech
argument' has largely figured, and the conclusion has been
drawn that this tree was likewise known to the Urvolk, so that they
must have lived within the beech area[2] and this rules out the
possibility of an Asian homeland. It is here that we run up against
the central difficulty in this style of argument: the problem of
semantic reconstruction. Certainly there are tree names in other
languages which stand in systematic phonemic correspondence
with *beech* and *Buche*: Latin *fāgus* 'beech', Greek *phágos*, *phēgos*
'a kind of oak'. It is the Greek meaning that introduces an

---

1. CGmc. *bōkjōn* is posited.
2. The beech boundary runs from Königsberg (Kaliningrad) on the Baltic
to Odessa. It does not grow east of that line.

element of uncertainty into the reconstruction of the original meaning, for tree names do change their referents.[1] For a long time the discussion turned on the relationship of certain other words: these words were Russian *boz* 'elder' and Kurdish *būz* 'a species of elm'. This last word is now generally excluded, but the fundamental uncertainty remains. Latin has many more words in common with Germanic,[2] and this has been taken as evidence for a long period of habitation in a common cultural area. Thus we cannot rule out the possibility that both language groups applied an Indo-European tree name of unknown reference to a common tree of their new environment.

Similar difficulties were encountered in attempting to find an answer to the question whether the Indo-Europeans were acquainted with the 'sea'. We must start with the Latin word *mare*, which has a number of congeners: Ir. *muir*, Welsh *mor* (cf. the Gaulish name *Aremorici* for the people who lived in what we now call the Armorican peninsula, which means 'those who live close to the sea'), Goth. *marei*, OSlav. *morje* (cf. *Pommerania*, which is derived from the ethnic name *Po-morjane* 'those who live on the sea'). But our own word *mere* now means 'a lake', cf. Dutch *meer* 'sea', 'pool'. Hence it is far from certain that the word originally referred to what we now understand by the 'sea', a point which is underlined by the fact that *marsh* is a derivative from the same word (WGmc. **mar-isk-*). A further point is that the word is absent from Greek, Armenian and Indo-Iranian. Thus we are reduced to a very small sum of knowledge indeed: a number of western Indo-European peoples possessed a word referring to a sheet of water, it being uncertain whether this was the open sea or an enclosed body of water.

No less indecisive was the so-called 'salmon' argument, by which is was hoped to locate the Urheimat on the shores of the Baltic. Old English possessed a word *leax*, related to Old Norse *lax* and Old High German *lahs* (Germ. *Lachs*), all meaning 'salmon'. Congeners are also found in Baltic and Slavic. Since this fish was believed to occur within the whole area that could be

---

1. For instance, Latin *quercus* 'oak' corresponds to OHG *forha* 'pine'.
2. See my *Latin Language*, pp. 17ff.

plausibly assigned to the Indo-Europeans, only in the rivers flowing into the Baltic, this was put forward as a cogent geographical indicator. Unfortunately the word occurs also in the most easterly of the attested Indo-European languages, in Tocharian, where *laks*, however, has the general meaning 'fish'. Since the special meaning 'salmon' occurs only in those languages with access to the salmon-rivers, it can be plausibly argued that the folk living in these regions applied an inherited word of general meaning to a particularly common or important species. We see an exact parallel to this procedure in a word used by the Ossetes, an Iranian-speaking people of the Caucasus. This is *læsæg*, which is certainly a relative of the *laks*-words, but is used with reference to a species of trout.

Not all reconstructed words present such semantic difficulties. Established with reasonable certainty is a complex vocabulary relating to animal husbandry (bovines, sheep and pigs), and there is a widespread word for the horse, (*ekwos*). But as soon as we attempt to penetrate beyond these bare facts and assess (say) the significance of this or that animal to the Indo-Europeans, difficulties and uncertainties arise. A case in point is the Indo-European word to which OE *féo* 'cattle' is assigned: *peku*. The OHG word is *fihu*, to which corresponds Skt. *paśu-*, Avest. *pasu-*, Lat. *pecū*. The semantic range of this widespread word is limited, and there is little doubt that it referred to large and small cattle. At this stage the siting of the word in its morphological family becomes pertinent. It is claimed that the morphological connexions show that the original meaning of *peku-* must have been 'wool sheep'. The reason for this is that from the root *pek-* are also derived words meaning 'fleece' (e.g. Greek *pékos*, *pókos*) and 'to comb' (Greek *pékō*). Other semantic ramifications of the same root have been taken as indicative that the main wealth of the Indo-Europeans consisted in cattle and that payments were made in this form. In the Gothic Bible, for instance, *faíhu* is used to translate the Greek word *argurion* 'money', and in this connexion the Latin word *pecūnia*, a derivative from *pecū-*, meaning 'money', is also usually quoted.

The form of the argument is simple: the word *peku* meant originally 'wool sheep', and certain uses of the word or its derivatives suggest that it also meant 'wealth' in general. However, in an acute study[1] E. Benveniste has shown the trap into which comparatists may fall. His conclusion is that *peku- originally meant 'moveable personal property' and that it was only by specialization in certain languages that it came to denote cattle, and the sheep in particular. Benveniste's study underlines the importance of strict methodology in such hazardous explorations. All important is the establishment of the earliest meanings in the texts available to us. In Vedic *paśu* is a collective term covering all domestic animals, and it may even include men, as is explicitly stated in a passage enumerating the five *paśu*. Benveniste interprets this new insight as a reflection of the pastoral society in which moveable wealth consisted of both animals and men. This is confirmed by the Iranian evidence, where we find the formula *pasu-vîra*, the second word meaning 'slave' or at least 'servant'. There are other cogent indications that *pasu* and *vîra* together constituted a man's personal chattels.

Of great importance is that this *phrase* is echoed in another part of the Indo-European world, in Italic, where in Umbrian prayers are said for the well-being of *uiro pequo*, where *uiro*, though etymologically related to Latin *vir*, in fact refers to persons of the third social order. A corresponding Latin prayer brings this out more clearly, for the formula *pastores pecuaque salva servassis* 'May you keep safe shepherds and flocks' corresponds to the Umbrian *uiro pequo ... salua seritu*. Another important point is that in Latin *pecūnia* never refers to the possession of cattle or sheep. Much the same is true of another derivative *pecūlium*, for this signified the personal possession of one whose right to possess was not recognized by law, e.g. what was given by a master to his slave or a father to his son. The semantic nucleus again is 'personal property', and this is no less apparent in the derivative *pecūlor* 'appropriate', whence *pecūlātus* 'embezzlement of public money'.

In Germanic the semantic range of *peku* is also instructive. It is only in Old High German that the word is used with reference to animals. In Gothic *faihu* invariably meant 'money', and the same is true when it enters into compounds, e.g. *faihufriks* 'avaricious'.

---

1. *Le vocabulaire des institutions indo-européennes*, I, 47 61.

It has nothing to do with the vocabulary of animal husbandry. The same is true of Old Norse, where the compound *félag* 'common property' gave rise to the derivative *félagi* 'comrade, companion', which passed into Old English and is the source of our word *fellow*.

Important lessons must be drawn from this study. The reconstructed meaning must rest firmly on close analysis of the earliest available texts, and these indicate a semantic development in some cultures from 'moveable possessions' to 'cattle' (large or small). It is significant that Greek, which lacks the word *peku*, offers a word *próbasis* (more frequently *próbaton*), which derives from the verb *probaínō* 'step forward'. The meaning 'sheep' must surely be due to an ellipse, and it so happens that we have an expression in Old Norse *gangandi fé* 'walking property' for 'cattle', which not only illuminates the Greek word but also shows incidentally that *fé* could not mean 'cattle'. In the semantic evolution of **peku* we have an example of the specialization of a word of general meaning, which is paralleled by the development of the Latin word *capitale* to our word *cattle*. The entry in the ODEE in fact may serve to sum up Benveniste's own sketch of the history of **peku*: 'The origin. gen. sense "wealth, property" became narrowed to "moveable property", esp. as typified by live-stock . . .'.

The final result of this study is to destroy the connexion between **peku* and **pek(t)*- 'comb'. It underlines the dangers of drawing conclusions about prehistoric peoples from etymological connexions which may be nothing more than homonyms.

If such difficulties are encountered in the semantic reconstruction of such down-to-earth terms as 'cattle', the enterprise becomes still more hazardous when we venture on to such fields as social structure, customs and religious beliefs. Yet terms reflecting the social order certainly exist. A case in point is the Latin word *cīvis* 'citizen'.[1] The corresponding Sanskrit word is *śeva-* 'friendly', but it is the Germanic word *heiwa-* which gives us a clue to the sociological background. In Gothic *heiwa-frauja*

---

1. See E. Benveniste, *Le vocabulaire des institutions indo-européennes*, II, 335ff.

means 'lord of the family' (translating Greek *oikodespotēs*). The same social setting is apparent in other Germanic words such as OHG *hīwo* 'husband', ON *hyske* 'family', etc. Benveniste concludes that **keiwo-* (**kiwo-*) in primitive Germanic referred to the family as constituted by the parents united by the bond of marriage, together with their offspring.

The root **kei-* may be traced in Old English, too, for *hīd*, earlier *hīgid* 'family', is traceable to **keiwitā-*. What is of particular interest is that the word was used as 'a measure of land reckoned as that sufficient to support a free family with dependants'. This intimate linkage of social units and landed property is found at other levels of the social structure (see below). Thus it is evident that Latin has turned to a wider institutional use a word meaning originally a member of the close family group which was set in opposition to the 'stranger', the *hostis*.

In all probability the Indo-European word for the family group was that represented by the Latin *domus*, 'the lord of the *domus*' being designated *dominus*. Elsewhere we find a compound to express the same, as in Greek **de(m)spota-*, Vedic *dam-pati-*, Avestan *dəng paitiš* (where *dəng* comes from **dams*). Above the level of the family as a 'house-community' came the clan; the Iranian terminology, which is clearly archaic, suggests that this social unit was designated by a term drawn from the root **gen-* 'beget'; this is *zantu*, literally 'the collectivity of those who are of the same birth'. Other words drawn from the same root are the Greek *génos*, 'race, kin, stock', Latin *gens* 'clan, stock' and the Germanic words represented by English *kind* 'birth, descent, race, kin, etc.' and the German *Kind* 'child'.

It was from such an opposition of those belonging to a given 'stock' against those who do not that the notion of 'free' as against 'unfree' arose. This is seen in derivatives from the root **leudh-*, which originally meant 'grow', as can be seen from the coincidence of Sanskrit *rudh-*, Avestan *rud-* and Gothic *liudan*. Corresponding nominal forms take the meaning of 'ethnic stock, people'. Further, in Greek *Eleuthia* is known as the goddess of vegetation,[1] but the

---

1. Cf. Latin *Līber* (equated with Bacchus) and the Venetic goddess *Louzera*. For this whole group of words see Benveniste, *op. cit.*, II, 321ff.

adjective *eleutheros*, evidently meaning originally 'one of the stock', came to mean 'free'. The same is true of the Latin *līber*, which also goes back to **leudheros*. A further specialization *līberī* 'children' must once have arisen from the notion of 'members of the genuine stock' as opposed to *servī* 'slaves'.

Recent research on the Latin term *plēbēs* has also proved important for the prehistory of institutions. This word, designating the lower order of citizens who had a long struggle for their rights against the noble patricians, is evidently derived from the root **plē* 'fill'. The same is true of the corresponding Greek term *plēthos*, which has been traced to a neuter noun **plētos*.[1] Of particular interest is the fact that a dialect form corresponding to the adjective *plētus* is glossed as 'slave' or '*dēmos*'. The Italian scholar M. Scovazzi has pointed out that in Frankish and Alemannic a corresponding Germanic word *fledus* is used with reference to the third order of society, coming below the *adelingi* 'nobles' and *frilingi* 'free men'. The Salic law, however, preserves another form, *litus*, for the same class of free men, and this recalls the word *leti* (*laeti*) which was used by the historian Ammianus Marcellinus with reference to the German colonists of low status serving in the army of Julian. The loss of the initial *p* in this word indicates a Celtic origin, and Scovazzi rightly concluded that here we have indirect evidence of a Celtic word corresponding to Germanic *flēdus*, Latin *plēbēs* and Greek *plēthos*. What is of especial importance is the siting of this technical term in a structure of semantic oppositions. It is this which enables us to take a tentative step towards the reconstruction of a social class distinction within the prehistoric society to which we must assign the term **plētus* in this technical sense: a distinction between the broad masses of free men (distinct from slaves) and the nobles. That this terminological coincidence is not due to chance and independent semantic development but an integral feature of this prehistoric society is suggested by an examination of other technical words from the same sphere.

We may begin with the Greek word *dēmos* (the Attic form of the

---

1. See O. Szemerényi, *Innsbrucker Beiträge z. Kulturwissenschaft*, Sonderheft, 15, 1962, 185.

original *dāmos*). This is one of those words which mean both a social group and the land with which it is associated (cf. *hide* above). The etymology of *dāmos* is secure: it comes from the root *dai- 'divide, apportion'. Thus *dāmos* meant literally 'share-land'. This is a finding of great interest since we find precisely such designations for the land of the non-noble order in a number of Indo-European languages: Welsh *rhandir*, OE *gedalland* and Hittite *takšannas*. The point is worth stressing that here we have terms, located at a particular place in a structured social vocabulary, which have the same semantic 'inner form'. It is fortunate that the Bronze Age texts, written in the Linear B script, dealing with land tenure show us a double structure in which the oppositions between social classes are paralleled by tenurial terms. Contrasting with the *dāmos* with its holdings of 'share-land' is the *telestas*, who in all probability held his land from the *wanax* 'king'. This term is a derivative from the noun *telos*, which is formed from the root *tel*- 'lift'. Thus the name literally means 'the man of the burden'. Strikingly in Hittite we find a parallel expression with the same 'inner form': in the case of the 'man of the (feudal) service', who derived his tenure from the palace, loyalty and disloyalty to his obligation is conceived as lifting and casting off the burden. If we turn to the Germanic world and scan this place in the structure, once again a term of the same meaning is encountered: the *baro*, a word which long ago was interpreted as meaning 'man of the burden (of service)'. Given such a pattern of semantic oppositions within the social vocabulary of a group of related languages, the difficulty which faces the linguist is to decide whether these resemblances are due to chance and independent invention or to the continuation of notions and institutions characterizing the ancestral society which is implied by the fact of linguistic relationship. His judgment will be swayed by an accumulation of such resemblances. That mode of landholding and social class were interrelated concepts is suggested by the study of another term.

Above reference was made to the *adalingi* 'nobles'. This is a derivative from the noun *adal*, which in Old High German means 'family, nobility'. Study of the family of words containing this element showed, however, that the word originally meant 'hereditary property',[1] as in OE *fæder-æpelo* 'ancestral property'. Once again we encounter a tenurial term which is also used for the social class distinguished by this type of holding. If we now seek for a parallel among the Indo-European languages, we are led to suggestive evidence bearing on the social structure of the Indo-European people.

The French scholar Vendryes long ago[2] pointed out that terms from the spheres of religion and law survived to a remarkable degree at the extremities of the Indo-European world, in Indo-Iranian and Celtic. The conclusion he drew, and which has been repeatedly reaffirmed since, is that these are 'societies of the same archaic structure . . . in which institutions and the relevant vocabulary have persisted which were lost elsewhere.'[3] Among the Indo-Iranians we find a division of society into three classes: priests, warrior-nobles and the common people. The last two in ancient India were designated by *kṣatrám* and *viś* (and by the derivatives *ksatríya-, vaiśya-*). *Viś* means roughly 'clan', that is the unit formed by several families; but it also denotes their place of habitation 'village' as in the Latin correspondent *vīcus*. What is germane to the search for a parallel of *Adel* 'property' is that *kṣatrám*, the opposed designation for the noble class, is a derivative from a verb which elsewhere means 'acquire, possess' (e.g. Greek *ktắomai*).

This leads to further exploration. The word *ārya-*, which the Indo-Iranians applied to themselves,[4] has long been the object of research and the subject of dispute. A close study by H. W. Bailey has shown, however, that the basic meaning of the root *ar-* is 'possess'. This is close to the meaning of the Greek verb *arnumi* 'acquire'. The possibility cannot, therefore, be excluded that *ārya-* parallels *Adel* and *kṣatrám*. It is a derivative from a noun *ari* meaning 'possession'. The conclusion is that *ārya-* once desig-

---

1. See S. Feist, *Vergleichendes Wörterbuch der gothischen Sprache*, p. 233: *ōpala-* 'free hereditary property', in Ablaut with *apala-* 'legal claim to a hereditament, legitimate relationship'.
2. *Mém. de la Soc. de Linguistique*, 20, 1918, 265ff.
3. Benveniste, *Vocab.*, II, 10.
4. The term was for long applied to the Indo-Europeans themselves and endowed with racial overtones.

nated the noble class: but when it came to be used as an ethnic term, its place was taken by *kṣatrám/kṣatriya*, a term meaning much the same thing.

The speculative character of this type of research will now be amply clear. The method has been to take the social structure attested so clearly in Indo-Iranian and the Celtic world as reflecting that of the ancestral Indo-Europeans and to focus etymological scrutiny on given places of the structure of social designations. In such structural sites we find either widespread words or word families, e.g. the important word family centring round the root **kei* or etymologically different words which nevertheless exhibit striking parallels of 'inner semantic forms', such as 'shareland', 'man of the burden', or 'man of the hereditament'. 'Speculative', is, let it be said, not meant to be a term of opprobrium. A 'speculator' is one who goes and looks, one who reconnoitres. The news he brings back must, of course, be subjected to close scrutiny. The etymologies just referred to are 'speaking words' whose literal meanings must be 'made sense of' by setting them in a hypothetical 'world'. One final example will make this clearer.

The subject of 'speculation' will be the word *fee*. On this the ODEE comments: 'estate in land (orig. in feudal tenure); payment for services or privileges'. It is referred to 'Rom. **feudum*, medL. *feodum, feudum* (IX) . . ., which has been derived from Frankish **fehu-ōd-* "cattle-property", i.e. OHG *fehu* (Germ. *Vieh*) = OE *fēo*, etc., . . ., and *ōd*, as in ALLODIUM, but the sense is not appropriate'. From this it emerges that the supposed Frankish *fehu-ōd* contrasts with *allōd-* 'absolute possession' and refers to a type of tenure which involves obligations to the granter. The difficulty lies in the literal meaning of the term. When ODEE remarks that the sense 'cattle property' is not appropriate, it means that no 'world' has been discovered which would account both for the literal meaning and for the implied obligation to render service. It is here that the admittedly archaic Celtic world may again suggest a solution. Professor D. Binchey has drawn my attention to the fact that the 'exchange gift' (see on *mūnus* above) is still a living concept in Ireland today. Most significant is that in old Celtic society this gift could take the form of cattle to be pastured on the chief's land which bound the vassal[1] to his lord. It is such a 'world' which would make sense of *fehu-ōd*. We must imagine that far back in Germanic history this term actually meant 'cattle-possession', made by an overlord to a retainer and involving 'feudal' obligation'. The term persisted even when the gift took other forms, and so came to refer to a grant of land. What persisted into historic times was the duty of service which such a grant involved.

Such, then, is the outline picture of Germanic society which is conjured up by etymological analysis. Apart from the king with land of his own, we have the main distinction between the nobles with their *ōpala-* and the common people with their 'shareland'. The retainers of the nobles received a *fehu-ōd-* which they pastured on their lord's land. It need hardly be said that so speculative a suggestion by the etymologizing linguist about the origin of 'feudalism' would need to be followed up by historical research which far surpasses his competence. The example has been worked as an illustration of a structural approach to etymology.

LEXICOSTATISTICS OR GLOTTOCHRONOLOGY

The existence of a Proto-Indo-European community is an incontrovertible conclusion from the facts of relationship, even though the realization in speech of the abstract dialanguage must remain indeterminable. Inevitably the question arises how far back in time this community must be put; and it was no less inevitable that linguists should try to devise a test comparable to Carbon 14 dating in archaeology. Radio-active carbon, as is well known, decays at a constant rate, and this fact is held to be of some limited usefulness in establishing the chronology of prehistoric finds. The equivalent of this in linguistics is the 'decay' of the basic vocabulary. Glottochronology, or lexicostatical dating, rests on the assumption that the stock of certain focal items of the vocabulary wastes away at a uniform rate which can be determined and is valid for all languages. This theory was put forward by the

---

1. This word came to us from Old French *vassal*, but it was of Celtic origin: cf. Welsh *gwas*, Irish *foss* 'servant'.

American scholar M. Swadesh,[1] who devised such a word list based on thirteen languages, and claimed to have established that the wastage was 14·6 per cent per millennium, the causes of such word loss being regarded as irrelevant. Irrelevant also is the renewed accretion of lost items through language mixture, e.g. the Norman influence on English.

The fundamental difficulty is to discover a set of lexical 'items' which are valid for all languages, since the method is supposed to have universal application. The items cannot be 'vocables' since these are by definition unique in a given language. There must, therefore, be such 'meanings', content units, as are essential to any conceivable human society, such as man, woman, father, mother, child, parts of the body, eat, drink, etc. In Swadesh's own terms, they are 'easily identifiable broad concepts, which can be matched with simple terms in most languages'. Yet a 'concept' cannot be talked about unless it is matched with a word in some language or other. At the outset, therefore, we are forced to choose a set of words from a base language and by identification of their 'signal content' undertake translations into other languages. Yet it is a commonplace of linguistics that there are few, if any, exact equivalents or 'synonyms' in any two compared languages. Each human society has its own way of articulating its 'world' to make it amenable to linguistic communication. As U. Weinreich[2] has put it: 'The semantic mapping of the universe by a language is, in general, arbitrary, and the semantic "map" of each language is different from those of all other languages.' Kinship terms are an obvious example of such culture-bound semantic systems.

These difficulties made themselves predictably apparent in the process of devising the basic list, which was made up of relatively stable items, consisting of body parts, numerals, certain objects of nature, and simple universal activities which might reasonably be expected to be culturally neutral. Swadesh's first list comprised in fact some two hundred and fifteen items, and it was apparently largely based on European languages. He ran into difficulties when

---

1. For an account of lexicostatistics, see S. C. Gudschinsky, *Word*, 12, 1956, 175–210; D. H. Hymes, *Current Anthropology*, 1, 1960, 3–44.
2. In *Universals of Language* (ed. J. H. Greenberg), p. 142.

the attempt was made to find equivalents in languages which were the vehicles of communication in cultures far removed from the European. As a result a second list was devised, which contained only one hundred items. This was subjected to a practical application by H. Hoijer,[1] who tried to translate the terms into Navaho and other Athapaskan languages. His conclusion was 'that none of the items of the test list are necessarily "relatively neutral in their cultural implications" . . .'. 'On the contrary, it would appear that any item may be subjected to cultural influences, simply by the fact that it is the product of the total culture, in which language, its structural and semantic patterns must be included . . .' 'Every attempt to translate the test list into a particular language . . . is bound to leave a residue of items for which no single, simple term, meeting all of Swadesh's requirements, can be found.' Since this residue, for obvious reasons connected with the uniqueness of each culture, will not be the same in all languages, it follows that any list, however devised in the first instance, will be whittled down as it undergoes the necessary test of translation into a large number of widely scattered languages. Consequently no list, not merely Swadesh's revised list, can hope to represent one hundred 'easily identifiable broad concepts which can be matched with simple terms in most languages'.

Given these fundamental defects, and the difficulties encountered in choosing satisfactory translation equivalents, it is not surprising that application of the lexicostatistical hypothesis should 'produce percentages of retention and times of separation that are quite illusory'.

The point has been rammed home by J. A. Rea,[2] who has applied the hypothesis to the Romance languages in order to fix a chronology for the Proto-Vulgar Latin from which these languages took their origin. A comparison of Spanish and Portuguese yielded a date A.D. 1586, while Rumanian and Spanish pinpointed A.D. 874. Since there is general agreement among Romance scholars on 'a date around 100 A.D. as the time when there was any remaining phonemic uniformity', and it is likewise generally accepted that

1. 'Lexicostatistics: a Critique', *Language*, 32, 1956, 49–60.
2. 'Concerning the Validity of Lexicostatistics', *IJAL*, 24, 1958, 145–150.

'there was already some divergence in both morphology and VOCABULARY as early as 250 to 200 B.C.', it would follow that the Romance languages have been diverging for over two millennia. Rea concludes '. . . the figure of 1·08 millennia obtained by the use of lexicostatistics is too far from known facts to indicate that this method of dating linguistic splits has any usefulness or validity even for the languages upon which it was based'. This last point reinforces what was said above, namely that the original list was largely based on data from European languages. In fact six of the thirteen languages were Romance.

LANGUAGE AND 'WORLD-PICTURE' (WELTBILD)

It will now be clear that much of a nation's history and culture is embedded in its language. From time to time in the history of linguistics it has been argued that language does not merely reflect a people's attitude to its world but actually shapes and moulds its Weltanschauung ('view of the world'), and its way of coming to grips with its environment. A simple example will make this clear. Let us suppose we came across a language in which there were no general words for number, but only contextually bound numbers like the English *pair*, *couple* and *brace*, but no general word for 'two'. The speakers of such a language, who could not say the equivalent of 'twice two are four', would encounter difficulties in arithmetic, since the concept of pure number had not been evolved. A similar point was made in a recent conference on the relationship between language and culture.[1] The Bororo of South America have only two distinct number words meaning 'one' and 'two' respectively. This does not mean that they cannot count up to more than two, but that for higher numbers they use compound expressions. Common to all speakers are those for 'three', 'four' and 'five' but thereafter much depends on individual ingenuity. F. G. Lounsbury (the speaker in question) commented:[2] 'Now what must a Bororo's mathematics consist of? Not more than a single proposition, one and one makes two, because beyond

---

1. *Language in Culture* (ed. H. Hoijer), p. 129.
2. *Op. cit.*, 129.

that he would be saying that two and one makes two and one, which is not an equation but an identity.'

In the light of these facts and conclusions it will be of interest to consider briefly and simply what part language plays in the formation of general concepts.

In the first chapter we learned how a child comes to understand the meaning of a word. The constant association of an object with a given set of sounds finally results in the sound complex acquiring the power of calling up the object in the mind of the hearer. Now this explains only the most elementary type of speech behaviour. A sound group is associated merely with one particular object. This is borne out by observation of a bilingual child, who once possessed a red rubber doll which was variously called *Puppe* and *dolly*. Her German nurse left, and for a considerable time she heard only English. Meanwhile she acquired several other dolls that were also called *dolly*. What is significant is that the German word *Puppe* was never applied to any other doll but the original red rubber one. It was in fact nothing more than a proper name. Thus we can see that, when first acquired, all names are proper names: that is, they refer to one object and no other. Now let us examine the further progress of the child from this primitive stage. It hears *dolly* applied to various more or less similar objects. At first it may merely mean that there is a collection of objects with the same name, like two boys called Jack. One day, however, someone brings her a present and she utters quite spontaneously the word *dolly*. This is a significant step in her whole intellectual development: she has made a class concept. How does language help in this process?

The attachment of a name to various objects is like sticking a similar label on them. They are picked out from the bewildering chaos of the external world and grouped together. In this way the child is invited to examine them and to discover a similarity. This can be illustrated by analysing the acquisition of so-called common nouns by a child. The child learns the word *bow-wow*. At first this word is applied to any four-footed beast seen on the street. Later the child sees another quadruped, and on uttering the word *bow-wow* hears 'No! That's not a *bow-wow*, it's a *moo-cow*'. This linguistic difference prompts it to still finer observation and analysis. It eventually decides that a cow is a large four-footed beast with horns. Later, when faced with the stuffed head of a stag, it utters the ecstatic cry '*moo-cow*'. Corrected again, it proceeds to still finer observation and analysis; and so the process of intellectual training is continued until its speech usage coincides with that of its environment. Every word-symbol receives a more or less definite mental content, and the world it knows and perceives is grouped and arranged accordingly. This 'understanding' of a word involves a preliminary intellectual effort on the part of the child—a certain articulation and mental shaping of the external world.

The importance that the word-symbol plays in the building up and retention of general concepts has been illuminated by studies of speech disturbances, such as those cases of partial aphasia when the patient forgets the words for colours. In one particular case the patient had been wounded in the war, and as a result of a head injury his memory was impaired. Thus when asked to name an indicated colour, he could remember none of the general words such as *red, blue, yellow*, etc. Even when a series of colour words containing the right term was recited, he could not pick it out. On the other hand he was able to distinguish shades, e.g. of red. If, for instance he were asked to choose from a number of colours the colour of a ripe strawberry, he could perform the task with ease. Furthermore, he was able to match colours perfectly. It was obvious that there was no optical injury or disturbance at the root of the malady. He was able to distinguish different colours in the normal way; it might be cherry-coloured, violet-coloured, salmon-coloured, etc. All his colour perceptions were, in fact, individual and allied to some concrete object; but he had no conception of colour groups, or of any division and articulation of the spectrum.

Let us consider this with the behaviour of the normal person. A child, faced with a certain number of objects, say a flower, a ball, a brick and a ribbon, hears them all characterized as *blue*. That means that its attention is directed to a similarity between these objects; it cannot understand the word *blue* until it has solved the problem of analysis set it and abstracted from these dissimilar objects their common quality. Thus words are, as it were, pieces of string that tie up the world of phenomena in ready-made bundles. Once these word-concepts have been acquired by a child, it means a tremendous lightening of the burden which his memory has to bear. A normal person who is asked to pick out the *green* threads of wool is enabled to do so with the help of his speech knowledge. He does not compare colour with colour, but on each piece of wool which the patient found too dissimilar to be grouped together, he sticks his linguistic label. To return to the above case, it is obvious that there must be some close connexion between the loss of the general colour words and the inability to form colour groups.

The question remains whether the loss of the 'concept' rendered the name unintelligible or whether the loss of the name (symbol) resulted in an intellectual deterioration. We must remember that the child learning his language must form his concepts by an independent mental effort before he can *understand* the name. But we have seen that this intellectual work is prompted and guided by the name, which is just as much a characteristic of an object as its size, shape or smell.[1] H. Head, the aphasia specialist, concluded that in those cases of aphasia where the word is forgotten, the piece of string is, as it were, broken and the world falls apart into a limitless diversity of unrelated colours.[2]

We return now to the example from which our discussion started. The constant use of the speech symbol *two*, which is invariable no matter what the group of objects enumerated may be, concentrates the attention on the common characteristic and thus facilitates the work of the intellect in building up general concepts of number. The child whose language contains no such general symbol is not prompted to the necessary intellectual effort and remains on the level of the patient whose colour terminology was

---

1. So also Stern, *Meaning and Change of Meaning* (Göteborg, 1931), p. 36: 'If some large and heavy cardboard objects are called *gazun*, the being "gazun" is a characteristic of these objects in exactly the same degree as the being large and being heavy.'

2. Cf. Stern, p. 126: 'Not seldom the word is the most substantial part of the mental content, and it is through the word that the fugitive operations of thought receive sufficient impressiveness and power of preservation to survive the moment and to be reproduced.'

impaired. His ideas remain bound up in the concrete world of sense, particularizing and distinguishing rather than classifying, and he is incapable of rising by general concepts to the intellectual heights attained by speakers of more advanced languages.

Symbols form then, as it were, the rungs of the ladder by which thought gradually ascends from the concrete impression to the most abstract juggling with pure ideas such as we find in mathematics. A symbol fixes a thought-content that we have hammered out and provides a firm foothold from which to climb still higher. It may be thus stated as a general proposition that the progress of thought depends on the efficacy of its symbolism. Complicated arithmetical processes that were almost impossible to execute with the clumsy Roman system of numerals were considerably simplified by the introduction of the ingenious Arabic system.

It is not merely in the formation of class-concepts that languages differ. The world may be articulated along fundamentally different lines. As E. A. Nida has written:[1] '... language seems to provide the "grooves of thought" in the same way that cultural patterns constitute the molds for more general modes of behaviour'. He illustrates this by a peculiarity of New Caledonian. This Melanesian language has two possessive systems which are dubbed 'intimate' and 'non-intimate' possession. Among the nouns distinguished by the first are nouns such as *mother*, *liver* and *descendants*, whereas *father*, *heart* and *personal life* belong to the second class. Nida rightly stresses that 'the apparently arbitrary character of the distinction can only be understood if one realizes that New Caledonian society has been traditionally matrilineal, that the liver has been regarded symbolic of the whole person (the liver is used in sacrifices as symbolizing the victim) and that one's descendants have a more intimate continuing relationship to a person than even his own life'. What is important in the present connexion is that the all-pervading opposition intimate/non-intimate has been institutionalized in the language and that the growing child cannot manipulate this piece of grammatical machinery until it has made this 'inner form' its own. The existence of the

---

1. *IJAL*, 24, 1958, 282.

grammatical distinction impels it to articulate the world in the light of this opposition.

The importance of language in the mental formation of the young language learner has been stressed by two American scholars, Edward Sapir and Benjamin Lee Whorf. The thesis has become known as the Sapir–Whorf hypothesis, although the idea that language is a dynamic process (an 'energeia') by means of which man fashions his view of the world and crystallizes it goes back to Wilhelm von Humboldt and was taken up by the philosopher E. Cassirer and the linguists such as Leo Weisgerber and Jost Trier.[1] Sapir insisted,[2] 'It is quite an illusion to imagine that one adjusts to reality essentially without the use of language . . . the "real world" is to a large extent unconsciously built up on the language habits of the group. . . . We see and hear and otherwise experience very largely as we do because the language habits of our community predispose certain choices of interpretation.' This is echoed by Whorf:[3] 'We dissect nature along lines laid down by our native languages. The categories and types that we isolate from the world of phenomena we do not find there because they stare every observer in the face; on the contrary, the world is presented in a kaleidoscopic flux of impressions which has to be organized by our minds—this means largely by the linguistic systems in our minds.' Whorf went further and claimed[4] that 'the Hopi language [an American Indian language studied by him] and culture conceal a metaphysics such as our so-called naïve view of space and time does, or the relativity theory does, yet a different metaphysic from either'. The difficulty about such formulations is their vagueness. As Hockett pointed out,[5] '. . . we all know of low-level correlations: the Eskimos have many terms for different kind of snow . . .; Arabs do not talk about the weather . . . some Australian aborigines cannot count higher than three. . . . It is

---

1. See H. Basilius, 'Neo-Humboldtian Ethnolinguistics', *Word*, 8, 1952, 92–105.
2. *Selected Writings in Language, Culture and Personality* (ed. David Mandelbaum), p. 162.
3. *Collected Papers on Metalinguistics*, 1952, 5.
4. *Op. cit.*, 47.
5. *Language in Culture*, p. 108.

here that we find the most reliable and the dullest correlations between the rest of culture and language.' But the Whorf thesis is at a much higher level of abstraction, which requires the scrutiny of the philosopher. Max Black[1] has noted the difficulties encountered in making the Whorf hypothesis 'sufficiently precise to be tested and criticized: variant formulations of the main points are often inconsistent, there is much exaggeration, and a vaporous mysticism blurs perspectives already sufficiently elusive'. After a searching examination of Whorf's main theses Black concludes: 'Perhaps the best to be said for Whorf's metaphysics is that in all its amateurish crudity it is no worse than some philosophical systems that have had a considerable vogue.'

This is not to deny that there are inextricable connexions of language and culture. If speech is defined as significant vocal sound, it cannot be studied without constant attention to its social setting. It is from their use in social situations that the linguist gathers the meaning of utterances. In this sense the linguist cannot help being an ethnographer. This point was stressed by Hockett in the conference on the Whorf hypothesis:[2] 'I think it is important to get down to this level of more simple, directly observable behavior, and more immediately deducible patterns of behavior, both nonlinguistic and linguistic. . . . If the ethnographer is taking language into account, then he gets the words and patterns of speaking that accompany practices, and if the linguist is studying the vocabulary connected with the particular range of behavior, then he takes note of the practices and objects to which the utterances refer. . . . Ethnography without linguistics is blind. Linguistics without ethnography is sterile.'

It is by ethnography that we elicit the meaning of words and utterances. It has been the main thesis of this book that meaning is relevant at all stages of linguistic analysis. Although speech symbolism to some extent determines and limits the intellectual development of the individual as he grows into society, that does not mean that he is incapable of rising beyond the limitations of his language. It must be borne in mind that language merely records

---

1. *The Philosophical Review*, 68, 1959, 228, 238.
2. *Language in Culture*, p. 225.

and fixes past intellectual achievements. We have already said that the learning of a word does not implant automatically a certain ready-made idea in the mind of the learner. The 'understanding' of a word involves the establishment of a certain relationship between the vocable and its content or signal value; but it is necessary for the individual to work this out by a previous effort of thought. If he is incapable of this effort, he cannot learn the meaning of the word; it can merely prompt and aid his cogitations. These remarks have been made necessary by a certain confusion of thought present in certain works by linguistic sociologists who have been investigating the relations between language and thought.

It has been pointed out that although we can distinguish thousands of varieties of odours, yet science has been unable to establish any such grouping as we have for the colours red, blue, yellow, etc. It has been suggested that the reason for this failure of science in this field is due to the state of our language: the inherited speech terminology brings it about that optical impressions prevail over all other senses. But however true that may be for the modern person learning the language, it does not explain why his ancestors were able to evolve a series of generic terms for colours but not for smells. The existing linguistic state merely testifies that our forefathers experienced the same difficulties in the classification of smells as ourselves. The reason for the difficulty lies in the physiological constitution of the various senses. Colour impressions depend on a limited number of cells, some of which are sensitive to colour and others to light and shade. Light constitutes the sole source of optical impressions, the colour depending on the wavelength. That explains why 'jasmin, lilies-of-the-valley, camphor and milk' have the same colour. The same quality of light is reflected from them. Sensations of smell, on the other hand, are caused by chemical reactions of which there may be endless varieties. I quote Adberhalden, a distinguished physiologist: 'The very way in which we designate particular sensations of smell suggests that the conditions of their reproduction cannot be simple. We usually name smells after the objects from which they proceed. We say this product smells of roses, etc. . . . These remarks are meant to show how far more difficult is the task of bringing the smell impressions into any order or system than is the case with sensations of light or sound.' Conclusive evidence for the correctness of our contention is provided by the investigations of psychologists. They have found out by experiment that animals, which are speechless, have the same basic colours, blue, red, etc., as ourselves. It is therefore obvious that these particular groupings are independent of language.

We may conclude that the relationship of speech and thought represents a problem that has at least two aspects. It is, of course, correct to say that speech has a great influence on the mental development of its speakers. Every language embodies a certain system of ideas that involves a particular articulation and structure of the world. This is what is called the 'inner form' of a language. But it must not be forgotten that the state of a language at any moment represents a stage in the intellectual *development* of its speakers and that this development may be carried further by the efforts of isolated original thinkers who transcend the limits of their linguistic knowledge. A 'world view' is not something static, but constantly developing, as men in society come to grips with their changing environment. In finding ways to talk about these new experiences and attitudes, the language is constantly enriched, and this means that new insights are passed on to the rising generation. Old world-classifications give way to new. An example given by Basilius may be adduced in illustration. In Middle High German and even Modern High German the zoological world was divided up into the categories of fish, fowl, crawling animals and running animals (*fisch*, *vögel*, *gewürm* and *thier*). There was as yet no generic term corresponding to the modern word *Tier* 'animal'. The progress of zoology has radically modified this fourfold 'articulation' of the animal world. The German has not been the helpless prisoner of his language. Not all Germans subscribe to a single metaphysics.

Appendix A

The Indo-European Languages

The application of the comparative method has disclosed the fact that a large group of languages extending from Ireland to northern India and Chinese Turkestan are descended from a common ancestor. English is a member of this group, the chief members of which will now be enumerated.

INDO-IRANIAN

The speakers of this group are commonly called the Aryans.[1] One group of these invaded India from the north and carried their language as far south as the Dekkan. The most archaic record we have of their language is contained in the religious hymns known as the Rig-Veda. A later stage of their language is revealed in the religious prose commentaries, the Brāhmaṇas, and in the great epics, the Mahābhārata and the Rāmāyaṇa, the language of which is called Sanskrit. This Indo-European language, known as Old Indic, was brought into India towards the end of the second millennium. From it many languages of modern India are descended, such as Hindi, the official language of India, and Urdu, that of Pakistan. These languages have an interesting relative which has travelled far from India. This is Romany, the language of the

---

1. On the word *ārya-*, see p. 369f.

nomadic Gypsies, which originated in a Northwest dialect of Indo-Aryan and has been carried across Persia and Armenia as far as western Europe.

A second group of Indo-European invaders, closely related to the invaders of India, entered the country known in modern times as Iran, a name which is derived from the genitive plural of *Ārya-*. Here again the most archaic stage of the language is revealed by religious texts. This is the Avesta, the sacred book of the Zoro-astrian religion, parts of which (the so-called *Gāthās*) do not yield in point of antiquity to the Vedic hymns of India. The next most ancient writings are the inscriptions of Darius (522–486 B.C.);[1] these were written in Old Persian, which differs considerably from the language of the Avestan hymns. In the third century A.D. Iranian appears in a greatly modified form. The western form of this 'Middle Iranian' is called Pahlavi, this being the official language of the Sassanid Church and Empire (226–652 A.D.). Apart from this 'Parthian' dialect, western Middle Iranian is also represented by Middle Persian, which lies in the direct line between Old Persian and Modern Persian. The eastern branch of Middle Iranian comprises Sogdian and Khotanese. Apart from Persian, other modern representatives of the Iranian group are Kurdish and Afghan. The language of the ancient Scythians also belonged to this group.

ANATOLIAN

During the second millennium Asia Minor was occupied by Indo-Europeans speaking languages which form the Anatolian group. The best known is Hittite, the language of the Hittite Empire (1700–1200 B.C.). Numerous tablets written in a cuneiform script were discovered during excavations near the Turkish village of Boğaz Köy during 1905–1907, and the language was identified in 1915 as Indo-European by the Czech scholar Hrozny. The archive

---

1. Apart from a short inscription of Cyrus the Great (560–529 B.C.).

also contained material giving evidence of two other related languages: Luvian, which was used, roughly speaking, in the southern half of Asia Minor, and Palaic in the northern central area. Texts written in a hieroglyphic script (see p. 258) had been known long before the excavation of Boğaz Köy. The decipherment of the script revealed that this 'Hieroglyph Hittite' is virtually identical with the Luvian of the cuneiform texts. A late descendant of Luvian is Lycian, and Lydian is also regarded as belonging to the same group.

ARMENIAN

Today Armenian is spoken in the Soviet Republic of Armenia in the Caucasus and adjoining areas of Turkey and Iran. The earliest extant text is a translation of the Bible dating from the ninth century A.D., but the presence of Armenians is attested in Asia Minor as early as the sixth century B.C. by the mention of *Arminiya*- in the Old Persian inscriptions of Darius. The Armenians were supposed to have originated in northern Greece, and their language has often been connected with Phrygian. But this is exploded, and scholars now connect Phrygian with the language of the Thracians, a people who once lived in the Northern Balkans and along the western coast of the Black Sea and also established themselves in Asia Minor. Little is known of either Thracian or Phrygian.

TOKHARIAN

Before we leave Asia and proceed to catalogue the Indo-European languages of Europe, there remains to mention another language that belongs to the same family. Tokharian, as it has been named, is the language of texts which were discovered in Chinese Turkestan at the beginning of this century. The language in which they were written seems to have been spoken in those regions until the first half of the seventh century of our era, but it is now extinct.

Greek is today spoken chiefly in the southern parts of the Balkan peninsula. It is a language of which we have continuous and unbroken records for nearly 2500 years. The oldest Greek inscriptions to which we can assign a definite date are those written by Greek mercenaries in Egypt in the year 591 B.C., but the most archaic inscription (on an Attic vase) in all probability goes back to the eighth century B.C. From the fifth century onwards an abundance and variety of inscriptions have been brought to light, and from the linguistic material provided by them the following groups of dialects may be distinguished.

The speakers of Attic-Ionic settled in Attica, in parts of the Peloponnese around the Saronic Gulf, and planted colonies on the southern seaboard of Asia Minor. It was in one dialect of this group, the language of the city of Athens, that classical Greek prose literature was chiefly written. Aeolic comprises the dialects of Thessaly, Boeotia and Lesbos, and it was in the last named dialect that Sappho and Alcaeus wrote. Closely related to Aeolic is Arcado-Cypriot, which was spoken in the Late Bronze Age in the Peloponnese, whence colonists were sent to the island of Cyprus. Those who remained in the Peloponnese were isolated in Arcadia by a later wave of invaders, so that in historical times there was a dialect island Arcadia with a language closely related to Cypriot.

The new intruders, the Dorians, seem to have proceeded from northwest of the peninsula and overran the Peloponnese, parts of Thessaly and Boeotia and many Aegean islands. This group of dialects is known as West Greek. It is divided into two main groups: Northwest Greek and Doric. During excavations at the beginning of the century at Knossos in North Central Crete clay tablets were recovered inscribed in the script known as Linear B. From 1939 onwards similar texts were found at Bronze Age ('Mycenaean') sites on the Greek mainland. After the script had been deciphered by Michael Ventris in 1952, it emerged that the texts were written in a form of Greek resembling the reconstructed ancestral 'Arcado-Cypriot'.

ILLYRIAN

The northwest of the Balkan peninsula was occupied in ancient times by speakers of Illyrian. Our knowledge of it is confined to personal names and place-names, although the language of the Messapian inscriptions of Apulia and Calabria is assigned by some scholars to the Illyrian group.

ALBANIAN

Illyrian was long considered to the direct ancestor of modern Albanian, which in fact contains Latin loan words of an early date. Our knowledge of this language does not reach further back than the fifteenth century.

ITALIC

The Italic dialects fall into two groups: Osco-Umbrian and Latin-Faliscan. Umbrian at one time occupied a large territory extending to the north and west of the peninsula, but in historic times it was confined within the narrow limits of Umbria. Our knowledge of this dialect is derived chiefly from the seven bronze tablets found in Gubbio, which are known as the Euguvine tables. They contain the regulations of a brotherhood of priests. Oscan was the language of the Samnites. The chief texts were found in cities like Capua, Abella and Pompeii.

Latin is properly the language of Latium, but in its narrow sense it refers to the dialect of the city of Rome, in which classical Latin literature was written. This is the language that in mediaeval times became the common language in use among European scholars, statesmen and churchmen. In its vulgar form it was carried by Roman legionaries and bureaucrats to all parts of the empire, in many provinces of which it replaced the language of the natives. It became thus the ancestor of the modern Romance languages. The most important of these are Italian, Spanish, Portuguese, French and Rumanian.

CELTIC

Celtic was once spoken over a wide area that included northern Italy, Spain, Gaul and the British Isles. In the time of the Celtic migrations they sacked the city of Rome and sent hordes as far as Greece and even across to Asia Minor, where they founded the kingdom of Galatia. We have, however, practically no ancient records of their language apart from a few meagre inscriptions found in northern Italy and Gaul. These constitute, except for loan-words in Latin and other languages, our sole knowledge of Gaulish or what is known as Continental Celtic. Island Celtic is the name given to the Celtic languages of the British Isles. These are divided into Goedelic and Brythonic (also called Brittonic). The earliest Goedelic texts are the Ogam inscriptions found in Ireland, which date from the fifth century A.D. During the Dark Ages it was in Ireland that the lamp of classical learning was kept alight, and much information about the language is contained in the glosses which Irish scribes wrote on Latin texts. From Ireland Goedelic was carried to Scotland and northwest England. Scots Gaelic, spoken in the western Highlands, and the dialect of the Isle of Man, are the modern descendants of this language.

Brythonic (Brittonic) was the language of Great Britain at the time of the Roman conquest. The Celtic inhabitants, however, were driven to the western regions by the invasion of the Angles and Saxons. Their language is still spoken in Wales, and it sur- vived until the end of the eighteenth century in Cornwall. The Armorican peninsula in the north of France was settled by fugitives from Cornwall in the fifth and sixth centuries A.D. The Celtic language spoken in Brittany today is therefore not a descend- ant of ancient Gaulish, but is closely related to Welsh. Celtic has a number of resemblances to Italic and many scholars have posited a prehistoric 'Italo-Celtic' unity.

GERMANIC

The next great group of Indo-European languages is Germanic, of which English is a member. The earliest text of this language group is a brief inscription on a helmet found in the Austrian province of Styria, and it is dated around the beginning of our era. Germanic falls into three sub-groups: (1) East Germanic, (2) North Germanic, (3) West Germanic. The first two belong more closely together, and a more recent classification contrasts this combined 'North Germanic', with (3), which is renamed 'South Germanic'.

Of East Germanic, Gothic is the only member of which we have any extensive knowledge. The Goths at one time seem to have occupied southern Scandinavia. From there they made their way southeast, and established a kingdom to the north and west of the Black Sea. It was from here that they sent their hordes over the Roman Empire in the fourth century A.D. Our knowledge of their language is chiefly derived from the remnants of the Bible which was translated by their Bishop Wulfila in the fourth century of our era. The Goths who invaded the Roman Empire were soon absorbed in the Romance-speaking population and their language was lost. In the east, however, it survived much longer, and a form of Gothic was still spoken in the Crimean peninsula as late as the year 1560, when a Dutch scholar, Angerius von Busbeck, noted down the last remaining vestiges.

North Germanic comprises the so-called Scandinavian languages, Norwegian, Swedish, Danish and Icelandic. We have some very ancient records of this group in the Runic inscriptions, which date from the fourth century A.D. At the height of their vigour, in the Viking age, these peoples sent out marauders and colonizers in all directions. The Norwegians came to Scotland, Ireland and northwestern England and eventually settled in the northern and eastern parts of the island in the so-called Dane-Law. North Germanic remained virtually undifferentiated until about 800 A.D. Later two dialect groups are distinguishable: West Norse comprises Norwegian and Icelandic; Swedish and Danish together form the East Norse sub-group. Old Icelandic was the vehicle of a rich literature concerned with ancient Germanic myths and legends which dates from the thirteenth century, the so-called Eddas.

The two chief members of West Germanic are English and German. German is divided sharply into two groups, Low German and High German, by the phenomenon known as the High German sound shift. The line of division crosses Germany from east to west. The High German dialects lie south of this line. They fall into three subdivisions: Bavarian is spoken in Austria and Bavaria; Alemannic lies to the west and includes the German dialects of Switzerland, Alsace, Baden and Swabia. Alemannic and Bavarian are grouped together as Upper German (Oberdeutsch). The region of the third group, known as Franconian or Middle German, is roughly the Rhine basin below Worms. The standard High German spoken and written throughout Germany today is the language which was evolved by the Imperial chancellery and was based on the Franconian dialects. This language was also used by Luther in his translation of the Bible, so that it received the weight and authority which led to its acceptance throughout Germany. Low German is spoken in a variety of forms on the north German plain. Its most ancient document is the poem called the Heliand, written in the ninth century. Its language is Old Low German ('Old Saxon'). Closely related to the Low German dialects are Dutch and Flemish. The inhabitants of the Frisian islands speak a language that is perhaps closest to English. Frisian is known from the thirteenth century, while the earliest Old English literature dates from the eighth century. In Old English three dialects are distinguished: Kentish, West Saxon and Anglian, the last being subdivided into Northumbrian and Mercian.

BALTIC

The Baltic languages comprise Lithuanian, Lettish and Old Prussian. The last-named language died out in the seventeenth century, its only documents being a translation of some religious texts and the so-called 'Vocabulary of Elbing'. Lettish is spoken by about a million and a half people on the east coast of the Baltic. Lithuanian is among the most archaic of modern Indo-European languages. Especially notable is the preservation of the pitch accent. The earliest document is of religious origin, the translation of Luther's catechism, dating from the sixteenth century.

SLAVONIC

The Slavonic (also called Slavic) group has many features in common with the languages just discussed. Three varieties are distinguishable: (1) Southern Slavonic, (2) Western Slavonic and (3) Eastern Slavonic. Variety (1) comprises Slovenian, Serbian, Croatian (these two being virtually identical, hence the name Serbo-Croatian) and Bulgarian; they are spoken over an area extending from the Adriatic to the Black Sea. The most ancient Slavonic document belongs to this group. In the ninth century the Bible was translated by the bishops Cyrillus and Methodius into the Slavonic dialect of the region of Salonica. This is the language, known variously as Old Bulgarian and Old Church Slavonic, which has continued to be the religious language of the Slavs of the Orthodox Church down to the present day.

The chief members of the West Slavonic group are Czech, Slovak and Polish. The first two are the languages spoken in the republic of Czechoslovakia. The first textual evidence dates from the thirteenth century.

East Slavonic comprises the various types of Russian. We may distinguish Great Russian, the Muscovite variety of which is the administrative standard language of Russia; White Russian, which is the collective name for a group of dialects in the western part of Russia; and Little Russian or Ruthenian, which is the language of the Ukraine and extends westwards as far as northern Hungary.

Appendix B

Some Indo-European Sounds
A Specimen of the Comparative Method

The application of the comparative method has made it probable that the Indo-European parent language possessed the following series of plosive consonants:

	VOICELESS		VOICED	
	Unaspirated	Aspirated	Unaspirated	Aspirated
Labial	p	ph	b	bh
Dental	t	th	d	dh
Palatal	k	kh	g	gh
Velar	q	qh	g	gh
Labio-Velar	q^w	$q^w h$	g^w	$g^w h$

We shall first illustrate these sounds by adducing the etymological correspondences (see Chapter 9) in the related languages. No example will be quoted from Germanic for the time being since in this group the plosives underwent a series of changes which will be discussed below.

p   Skt. *pitár-* 'father', Gk. *patḗr*, Lat. *pater*, OIr. *athir.*

       Skt. *pad-* 'foot', Gk. *pod-*, Lat. *ped-.*

       Skt. *tápati* 'heats', OCS *teplostĭ* 'warmth', Lat. *tepéo.*

b   This sound was rare in Indo-European
        Lith. *trobà* 'dwelling', Lat. *trabs* 'beam', Osc. *tríibúm* 'house', OIr. *treb*
        'settlement'.

        Skt. *bálam* 'strength', *bálīyān* 'stronger', OCS *boljĭjĭ* 'bigger', Gk.
        beltíōn 'bigger', Lat. *dē-bilis* 'weak'.

bh   Skt. *bhrátar-* 'brother', OCS *bratrŭ, bratŭ*, Gk. *phrátēr*. Lat. *fráter*,
        OIr. *bráthir*.

        Skt. *bhárati* 'he bears', OCS *berǫ*, Gk. *phérō*, Lat. *fero*, OIr. *biru*.

        Skt. *nábhas* 'cloud', OCS *nebo* 'sky', Gk. *néphos*, Lat. *nebula*, Welsh
        nef 'sky'.

t   Skt. *tráyas* 'three', OCS *trĭje*, Gk. *treîs*, Lat. *trēs*, OIr. *trí*.

        Skt. *tanús* 'thin', OCS *tĭnŭkŭ*, Gk. *tanu-*, Lat. *tenuis*, OIr. *tanae*.

        Skt. *śrutás* 'heard', Gk. *klutós*, Lat. *(in)-clutus* 'famous', OIr. *cloth*
        'fame'.

d   Skt. *dáśa* 'ten', OCS *desętĭ*, Gk. *déka*, Lat. *decem*, OIr. *deich*.

        Skt. *ádmi* 'I eat', Lith. *édu*, Gk. *édō*, Lat. *edo*, OIr. *ith*.

        Skt. *sada-* 'sit', OCS *sędǫ*, Gk. *hézomai* 'I sit', *hédos* 'seat', Lat. *sedeo*,
        OIr. *saidid* 'sits'.

dh   Skt. *dhūmá-* 'smoke', OCS *dymŭ*, Gk. *thūmós* 'soul, spirit', Lat. *fūmus*,
        OIr. *dumacha* 'mist'.

        Skt. *vidhávā* 'widow', Gk. *ē-(w)íthe(w)os* 'unmarried youth', Lat.
        vidua, OIr. *fedb*.

        Skt. *mádhu* 'honey', OCS *medŭ*, Gk. *méthu* 'wine', OIr. *mid*.

        Skt. *rudhirá-* 'red', OCS *rudrŭ, rudŭ*, Gk. *eruthrós*. Lat. *ruber*, OIr.
        ruad.

The series of dorsal stops presents complications which have
defied complete explanation up to the present day. It will be
observed that there is a double series of correspondences:

Greek	Latin	Sanskrit
k	k	ś
k	k	k

At first sight it would be tempting to explain the Sanskrit fricative
ś as the product of a palatalization such as is observed in the

change of Latin *centum* to the Italian *cento* [tʃɛntɔ] (see p. 65).
This fails to account for the facts because the fricative occurs
before any sort of vowel. Moreover, this treatment of the Indo-
European dorsal plosives is found in a number of languages. Thus
the word for 'hundred' is found in the following forms:

Skt. *śatám*, Avestan *satəm*, Lith. *šìm̃tas*, OCS *sŭto*, Gk. *he-katón*, Lat.
centum, OIr. *cēt*, Welsh *cant*.

Consequently we are forced to postulate the existence in Indo-
European of two different dorsal series, one palatal and the other
velar. In Celtic, Italic, Germanic, Greek, Hittite and Tokharian
both these sets of stops are represented by a single series of
dorsal stops. Other languages which have preserved the velar
plosives but transformed the palatals into fricatives are called
satem languages from the form which the word for 'hundred'
takes in Iranian. They include Indo-Iranian, Baltic, Slavonic,
Armenian, and Albanian. The opposing group, enumerated above,
are known as *centum* languages.

k　　Skt. *dáśa* 'ten', OCS *desętĭ*, Gk. *déka*, Lat. *decem*, Welsh *deg*.

　　Skt. *śrávas-* 'fame', OCS *slovo* 'word', Gk. *klé(w)os* 'fame', OIr. *clū*.

　　Skt. *śvan-* 'dog', Lith. *šuõ*, Gk. *kúōn*, Lat. *canis*, OIr. *cú*.

　　Skt. *viś-* 'settlement', OCS *vĭsĭ*, Gk. *(w)oîkos* 'house', Lat. *vīcus*.

　　áśva- 'horse', Lith. *ašvà*, Gk. *híppos*, Lat. *equus*, OIr. *ech*.

g　　Skt. *jánas-* 'race', Gk. *génos*, Lat. *genus*, OIr. *in-gen* 'girl'.

　　Skt. *jnātá-* 'known', OCS *znajǫ*, Gk. *gnōtós*, Lat. *(g)nōtus*, OIr. *gnáth*.

　　Skt. *jắnu* 'knee', Gk. *gónu*, Lat. *genū*.

　　Skt. *ájati* 'drives', Gk. *ágō*, Lat. *ago*, Ir. *ad-aig* 'leads'.

gh　Skt. *hima-* 'snow', OCS *zima* 'winter', Gk. *khiṓn*, Lat. *hiems*, OWelsh *gaem*.

　　Skt. *haṁsa-* 'swan', Lith. *žasìs*, Gk. *khḗn*, Lat. *anser*, OIr. *gēiss* 'swan'.

Skt. *váhati* 'carries', OCS *vezǫ*, Gk. *(w)ékhō* 'bear, carry, bring', Lat. *veho*, OIr. *fén* 'carriage'.

q   Skt. *kráviṣ*- 'raw meat', OCS *krŭvĭ* 'blood', Gk. *kré(w)as* 'flesh', Lat. *cruor*, MIr. *crú*.

Skt. *loká*- 'free space', Lith. *laũkas* 'field', Lat. *lūcus* 'grove, sacred wood' (original meaning 'clearing', cf. OHG *lōh*).

g   Skt. *yugá*- 'yoke', OCS *igo*, Gk. *zugón*, Lat. *iugum*, OWelsh *iou*.

Skt. *sthag*- 'cover', OCS *o-stegŭ* 'dress', Gk. *stégō*, Lat. *tego, toga*.

Avest. *aogarə* 'strength', Lith. *augti*, Gk. *aux*- 'increase', Lat. *augeo*.

gh   Skt. *dīrghá*- 'long', OCS *dlŭgŭ*, Gk. *dolikhós*, Hittite *dalugas*.

OCS *lęgǫ* 'lie', Gk. *lékhos* 'bed', Lat. *lectus*, OIr. *lige*.

Skt. *stigh*- 'stride', OCS *stignǫ*, Gk. *steíkhō*, OIr. *tiagu* 'I go'.

LABIO-VELARS

These sounds were velar stops pronounced with protruded lips (see p. 61). In some languages (e.g. Greek and certain dialects of Italic and Celtic) this labial element became predominant. In others, however, it has disappeared; this is the case with the *satem* languages, in which the pure velars and the labio-velars eventually merged. In Attic Greek the labio-velars are represented by labials before back vowels and consonants, and by dentals before front vowels, while in the neighbourhood of *u*-sounds they lose the labialization and become indistinguishable from the pure dorsals. The forms assumed by the root *q^wel*- 'move around, be busied about' provide a good illustration:

> Skt. *cárati*, Lat. *colo*, Gk. *télomai* (functioning in some dialects as a substitute for the verb 'to be'), *ai-pólos* 'goat-herd', *bou-kólos* 'cowherd', *peri-pl-ómenos* (aorist middle participle with zero grade of the root *q^wl*-) 'circling'.

q^w Avest *čiš* (interrogative-indefinite pronoun), OCS *čĭ-to*, Gk. *tís, oú-ki*, Lat. *quis*, OIr. *cid*.

Skt. *kás*, Lith. *kàs*, OCS *kŭto*, Gk. *poû* 'where', *póthen* 'whence', Lat. *quod*, Ir. *cia*, Welsh *pwy*.

396   APPENDIX B

Skt. *pañca*, Lith. *penkì*, Gk. *pénte*, Lat. *quinque*, OIr. *cóic*, Welsh *pump*.

Skt. *sácate* 'follows', Lith. *sekù*, Gk. *hépomai*, Lat. *sequor*, OIr. *sechur*.

Skt. *cáyate* 'avenges', *apa-citi-* 'vengeance', Avest. *kaēnā* 'punishment', Lith. *káina* 'price', Gk. *tísis* 'vengeance' (from *$q^w i$-*, zero grade of *$q^w ei$*), *poinḗ* 'penalty' (from *o*-grade *$q^w oi$-*).

g^w   Skt. *gáus* 'cow', Lett. *gùovs*, Gk. *boûs*, Lat. *bōs* (a borrowing from a dialect with labial representation), OIr. *bó*.

Skt. *gam-* 'come', Lith. *gemì* 'be born', Gk. *baínō*, Lat. *venio*.

Skt. *jáni-* 'woman', OCS *žena*, Gk. *gunḗ*, OIr. *ben*.

Skt. *nagna-* 'naked', OCS *nagŭ*, Lat. *nūdus* (from *$nog^w edos$*), Ir. *nocht*.

g^wh   Skt. *gharmá-* 'heat', OPruss. *gorme*, OCS *gorěti* 'burn', Gk. *thermós* 'hot', Lat. *formus*, MIr. *gor* 'heat'.

Skt. *ghnánti* 'they strike', Lith. *genù* 'I drive', Gk. *theínō* (from *$g^w henjō$*), *phónos* (from *$g^w honos$*), OIr. *gonim* 'I wound, kill'.

Avest. *snaēzāt* (subj.) 'will snow', OCS *sněgŭ*, Gk. *neíphei* (*$sneig^w hei$*) 'it snows', Lat. *nix, niv-* 'snow', *ninguit* 'it snows', Ir. *snigid*.

It is important to notice that in Old Indic the velars alternate with palatals: e.g. *arka-* 'song', *árcati* 'he sings'. It was this phenomenon which revealed to scholars the true character of the Indo-European vowel system. Sanskrit, in common with all the members of the Indo-Iranian group, levelled all the vowels *a*, *e* and *o* of the parent language to *a*. Since Sanskrit at the beginning of Indo-European studies was considered to be the most archaic stage known to us, the Sanskrit vowel system was believed to represent the original vowel system. Scholars noticed, however, that where a velar was palatalized in Sanskrit (e.g. *k* > *c* as in the above example), the *a* following the consonant corresponded to *e* in other languages:

Skt. *sácate*, Gk. *hépetai*, Lat. *sequitur*, all from IE *seq^w-*.

This could only mean that Indo-Iranian must once have possessed the stem-vowel *e*, as in Greek, and that this was responsible for the palatalization of the *k* which developed from the labio-velar *q^w*. It was not until after this palatalization that the levelling of the short vowels took place. Thus there were three stages within the historical development of Indo-Iranian which may be summed up by this example: $*seq^{w}etai >$ (1) *seketai*, (2) *secetai*, (3) *sacate*. This is an example of the so-called Palatal Law, which revealed that it was Greek and not Sanskrit which had best maintained the original Indo-European vowels.

After this survey of the Indo-European plosive consonants we can now proceed to examine their treatment in the Germanic languages. A glance at the etymological correspondences of certain words shows that in Germanic these consonants have been systematically changed:

Lat. pater: Engl. father	Lat. decem: Engl. ten
tenuis thin	trab- thorp
centum hund-red	genus kin

The facts of these changes are summed up in Grimm's Law (see p. 226). This states that (1) the voiced aspirated plosives (*bh*, *dh*, *gh*) became deaspirated (*b*, *d*, *g*); (2) that the unaspirated voiced plosives (*b*, *d*, *g*) became voiceless (*p*, *t*, *k*); and (3) that the voiceless plosives (*p*, *t*, *k*) became voiceless fricatives (*f*, θ, $*\chi$, the last appearing as the aspirate *h*). Further examples are adduced to illustrate the correspondences on which the law is based:

p   Lat. *pater*, Goth. *fadar*, Engl. *father*.

      Lat. *pecus*, Goth. *faihu*, Germ. *Vieh*.

      Lat. *ped-*, Goth. *fotus*, Engl. *foot*.

      Lat. *piscis*, Goth. *fisks*, Engl. *fish*.

t   Lat. *tenuis*, OE *þynne*, Engl. *thin*.

      Lat. *trēs*, OE *þrī*, Engl. *three*.

k   Lat. *centum*, Goth. *hund*, Engl. *hundred*.

      Lat. *cord-*, OE *heorte*, Engl. *heart*.

q^{w} Lat. *quī, quod*, OE *hwā*, Engl. *who, what*.

      Skt. *cakrá-* 'wheel', Gk. *kúklos*, OE *hweol*, Engl. *wheel* (this word is based on a noun formed by means of reduplication from the root $*q^{w}el-$ 'go around', $*q^{w}e-q^{w}los$).

Lat. *linquo, līquī*, Goth. *leilvan* 'lend', OE *līhan*, Germ. *leihen*.

b   Lith. *dubùs*, Goth. *diups*, Engl. *deep*.

Lat. *lūbricus*, Goth. *sliupan*, Engl. *slip*.

d   Lat. *domāre* 'to subdue', Goth. *ga-tamjan*, Engl. *tame*.

Lat. *dent-*, Goth. *tunþus*, Engl. *tooth*.

Lat. *edo*, Goth. *itan*, Engl. *eat*.

Lat. *sedeo*, Goth. *sitan*, Engl. *sit*.

g   Lat. *genus*, Goth. *kuni*, Engl. *kin*.

Lat. *(g)nōsco*, OE *cnāwan*, Engl. *know*.

Lat. *ager*, Goth. *akrs*, Engl. *acre*.

g   Lat. *iugum*, Goth. *juk*, Engl. *yoke*.

Lat. *grūs*, OE *cran*, Engl. *crane*.

Lat. *augeo*, Goth. *aukan*, Engl. *eke*.

g^w *g^wem-* 'come': Goth. *qiman*, OE *cuman*, Engl. *come*.

g^wen- 'woman': Goth. *qino*, OE *cwēn*, Engl. *queen*.

bh   Lat. *fero*, Goth. *bairan*, Engl. *bear*.

Lat. *frāter*, Goth. *broþar*, Engl. *brother*.

Lat. *nebula*, OHG *nebul*, Germ. *Nebel*.

dh   Skt. *vidhavā-*, Goth. *widuwo*, Engl. *widow*.

Gk. *oūthar*, Lat. *ūber*, OE *uder*, Engl. *udder*.

Gk. *thugátēr*, Goth. *dauhtar*, Engl. *daughter*.

Gk. *tharséō* 'I am bold', Goth. *ga-dars*, Engl. *dare, durst*.

gh   Gk. **theîkhos* (> *teîkhos* by Grassmann's Law, see p. 223), Lat. *fingo, figulus*, Goth. *digan*, Engl. *dough*.

Gk. *khĕn*, OHG *gans*, Engl. *goose*.

Gk. *(w)ékhō* 'I bring', *(w)ókhos* 'chariot', Goth. *ga-wigan* 'move, shake', Engl. *waggon, wain*.

gh   OCS *gostĭ*, Lat. *hostis*, Goth. *gasts*, Engl. *guest*.

Gk. *steíkhō* 'pace', Goth. *steigan*, OE *stiȝan* 'climb'.
From the last word are derived Engl. *stile* (OE *stīgel*) and *stirrup* (OE *stig-rāp*, literally 'mounting rope').

gʷh   This sound developed first to CGmc. *w* and thence in different conditions to *w*, ʒ and (*n*)*gw*.

gʷherm- 'hot': Goth. *warms*, Engl. *warm*.

lengʷh- 'light': OE *līht*, Engl. *light*.

sneigʷh-/snoigʷh- 'snow': Goth *snaiws*, OE *snāw*, Engl. snow.

There are a number of Germanic words the development of which seems contrary to Grimm's Law. Thus the Germanic equivalents of the sound **t* varies in the following words (see p. 239);

> Skt. *pitár-*: OE *fæder*.
>
> Skt. *mātár-*: OE *mōdor*.
>
> Skt. *bhrắtar*: OE *brōþor*.

In 1875 Karl Verner showed that these changes depend on the position of the accent in Indo-European, which is reflected in the Sanskrit accentuation of the above words. Verner's Law is briefly this: in Germanic the voiceless fricatives which were the product of the Indo-European voiceless plosives (by Grimm's Law) became voiced between two sonant sounds *unless the immediately preceding syllable bore the accent*. This can be easily remembered if we compare the pronunciation of the medial *s* in the words *póssible* [s] and *posséss* [z]. The resulting voiced fricatives *b̄*, *đ*, ʒ became for the most part voiced stops, *b*, *d*, *g*, the change having taken place partly in prehistoric, and partly in historic times. This explains why in **bhrắter-*, where the accent immediately preceded, we find the voiceless fricative *þ*, which we expect from Grimm's Law, whereas in **patér-* and **mātér-*, the fricatives were first voiced to *đ* and then changed to *d* (the modern English forms present an example of analogical levelling, see above p. 237). Other illustrations of Verner's Law follow.

> Skt. *śrutás* 'heard', Gk. *klutós*, OE *hlud*, Engl. *loud*.
>
> Gk. *makrós* 'long, slender', Lat. *macer*, OHG *magar*, Germ. *mager*.

Finally we may adduce once more the example of the word for 'hundred', which in Indo-European bore the accent on the last syllable: *$kṇtóm$. This developed by Grimm's Law to CGerm. *$\chi unṗám$ and by Verner's Law to *$\chi unđám$, whence Gothic *hund*, OHG *hund*. The corollary to Verner's Law is that the Indo-European accent must still have been preserved in its original position when the law was operating.

Bibliography

The following list contains a selection of important books which, with their bibliographies, will enable the student to find his way further into the subject. A survey of linguistic work appears annually under the title *Bibliographie Linguistique* (Paris) under the auspices of UNESCO.

HISTORIES OF LINGUISTICS

Arens, H., *Sprachwissenschaft: Der Gang ihrer Entwicklung von der Antike bis zur Gegenwart*. Freiburg-Munich: Karl Alber, 1955; 2 te Auflage, 1969.
Lepschy, G. C., *A Survey of Structural Linguistics*. London: Faber & Faber, 1970.
Pedersen, Holger, *Linguistic Science in the Nineteenth Century*, transl. J. W. Spargo. Cambridge (Mass.): Harvard University Press, 1931. (Republished as *The Discovery of Language*, Bloomington (Ind.): Indiana University Press, 1959.)
Robins, R. H., *A Short History of Linguistics*. London: Longmans, 1967.

GENERAL INTRODUCTIONS

Bloch, B. and Trager, G., *Outline of Linguistic Analysis*. Baltimore, Md.: Waverly Press, 1942.

Bloomfield, L., *Language*. New York: Holt, Rinehart, and Winston, 1933; and London: Allen and Unwin, 1935.

Carroll, J. B., *The Study of Language*. Cambridge (Mass.): Harvard University Press, 1953.

Dinneen, F. P., *An Introduction to General Linguistics*. New York: Holt, Rinehart, and Winston, 1967.

Entwistle, W. J., *Aspects of Language*. London: Faber & Faber, 1953.

Gleason, H. A., *An Introduction to Descriptive Linguistics*. 2nd ed. New York: Holt, Rinehart, and Winston, 1961.

Hall, R. A., *Introductory Linguistics*. Philadelphia: Chilton, 1964.

Hockett, C. F., *A Course in Modern Linguistics*. New York: Macmillan, 1958.

Jespersen, O., *Language, Its Nature, Development, and Origin*. London: Allen and Unwin, 1922.

Lyons, J., *Introduction to Theoretical Linguistics*. Cambridge University Press, 1968.

Martinet, A., *Elements of General Linguistics*, 2nd ed. London: Faber & Faber, 1968.

Robins, R. H., *General Linguistics: An Introductory Survey*. London: Longmans, 1964.

Sapir, E., *Language: An Introduction to the Study of Speech*. New York: Harcourt, Brace, and World, 1921.

de Saussure, F., *A Course in General Linguistics*, transl. W. Baskin. New York: Philosophical Library, 1959.

Vendryès, J., *Le langage*. Paris: Albin and Michel, 1923. English transl., *Language*. London: Kegan and Paul; and New York: A. Knopf, 1931.

Wartburg, W. v., *Einführung in Problematik und Methodik der Sprachwissenschaft*. 2nd ed. Tübingen: Niemayer, 1962.

SOURCE BOOKS (ANTHOLOGIES)

Each of the works in this section consists of reprints of important articles or extracts from books representative of a particular approach to linguistic problems.

Fodor, J. A. and Katz, J. J. (eds.), *The Structure of Language:*

Readings in the Philosophy of Language. Englewood Cliffs (N.J.): Prentice-Hall, 1964.

Hamp, E., Householder, F. W. and Austerlitz, R. (eds.), *Readings in Linguistics II.* Chicago and London: Chicago University Press, 1966.

Hymes, D. (ed.), *Language in Culture and Society: A Reader in Linguistics and Anthropology.* New York: Harper and Row, 1964.

Joos, M. (ed.), *Readings in Linguistics.* Washington, D.C.: American Council of Learned Societies, 1957. (Re-published as *Readings in Linguistics I.* Chicago and London: Chicago University Press, 1966.)

Saporta, S. (ed.), *Psycholinguistics: A Book of Readings.* New York: Holt, Rinehart, and Winston, 1961.

Vachek, J. (ed.), *A Prague School Reader in Linguistics: Studies in the History and Theory of Linguistics.* Bloomington (Ind.): Indiana University Press, 1964.

GLOSSARIES OF TECHNICAL TERMS USED BY LINGUISTS

Hamp. E. P., *A Glossary of American Technical Linguistic Usage 1925–1950.* Utrecht, 1958.

Marouzeau, J., *Lexique de la terminologie linguistique.* 3rd ed. Paris: Geuthner, 1951.

Pei, M. A. and Gaynor, F., *Dictionary of Linguistics.* London, 1958.

SURVEYS OF THE LANGUAGES OF THE WORLD

Kieckers, E., *Die Sprachstämme der Erde.* Heidelberg: Winter, 1931.

Meillet, A. and Cohen, M., *Les langues du monde.* 2nd ed. Paris: Centre national de la recherche scientifique, 1952.

Schmidt, W., *Die Sprachfamilien der Erde.* Heidelberg: Winter, 1926.

LANGUAGES AS SYMBOLIC SYSTEMS

Gardiner, A. L., *The Theory of Speech and Language.* Oxford: Clarendon Press, 1932.

Morris, C. W., *Signs, Language, and Behavior*. New York: Prentice-Hall, 1955.
Ogden, C. K. and Richards, I. A., *The Meaning of Meaning*. 8th ed. London: Routledge, Kegan Paul, 1946.
Urban, W. M., *Language and Reality: the Philosophy of Language and the Principles of Symbolism*. New York: Macmillan, 1939.
Wittgenstein, L., *Philosophical Investigations*, transl. G. E. M. Anscombe. 2nd ed. Oxford: Blackwell, 1958.

PHONETICS

Abercrombie, D., *Elements of General Phonetics*. Edinburgh University Press, 1966.
English Phonetic Texts. London: Faber and Faber, 1964.
Fant, G., *Acoustic Theory of Speech Production*. The Hague: Mouton, 1960.
Jones, D., *An Outline of English Phonetics*. 8th ed. Cambridge: Heffer, 1956.
Ladefoged, P., *Elements of Acoustic Phonetics*. University of Edinburgh Press, 1962.
Malmberg, B., *Phonetics*. New York: Dover Publications; and London: Constable, 1963.
—— (ed.), *Manual of Phonetics*. Amsterdam: North Holland Publ. Comp., 1968.
Pike, K., *Phonetics*. Ann Arbor: University of Michigan Press, 1967.
Pulgram, E., *Introduction to the Spectrography of Speech*. The Hague: Mouton, 1959.
The Principles of the International Phonetic Association. Hertford, 1949 and 1961.

PHONOLOGY

In addition to the general works cited above:

Firth, J. R., *Papers in Linguistics, 1934–1951*. London: Oxford University Press, 1951.
Hockett, C. F., *A Manual of Phonology*. Bloomington: Indiana University Press, 1955.

BIBLIOGRAPHY   405

Jakobson, R. and Halle, M., *Fundamentals of Language*. The
Hague: Mouton, 1962.
Jakobson, R., Fant, C. G. and Halle, M., *Preliminaries to Speech
Analysis*. Cambridge: M.I.T. Press, 1952.
Jones, D., *The Phoneme*. 3rd ed. Cambridge: Heffer, 1957.
Martinet, A., *Phonology as Functional Phonetics*. Publications of
the Philological Society, 15. Oxford: Blackwell, 1949.
Pike, K., *Phonemics*. Ann Arbor: University of Michigan Press,
1947.
Trubetzkoy, N. S., *Grundzüge der Phonologie*. Prague: Cercle
Linguistique de Prague, 1939. Engl. trans. *Principles of Phon-
ology*. University of California Press, 1969.
Twaddell, W. F., *On Defining the Phoneme*. Language Mono-
graph, 16, 1935.

MORPHEMICS

Bazell, C. E., *Linguistic Form*. Istanbul Press, 1953.
Harris, Z., *Methods of Structural Linguistics*. Chicago: University
of Chicago Press, 1951.
Hill, A. A., *Introduction to Linguistic Structures: from Sound to
Sentence in English*. New York: Harcourt, Brace, and World,
1958.
Nida, E. A., *Morphology: A Descriptive Analysis of Words*. 2nd ed.
Ann Arbor: University of Michigan Press, 1949.
Robins, R. H., *Ancient and Mediaeval Grammatical Theory in
Europe*. London: Bell, 1951.

SYNTAX

Bach, E., *An Introduction to Transformational Grammars*. New
York: Holt, Rinehart, and Winston, 1964.
Chomsky, N., *Syntactic Structures*. The Hague: Mouton, 1957.
—— *Current Issues in Linguistic Theory*. The Hague: Mouton,
1965.
—— *Aspects of the Theory of Syntax*. Cambridge (Mass.): M.I.T.
Press, 1965.
—— *Topics in the Theory of Generative Grammar*. The Hague:
Mouton, 1966.

Chomsky, N., *Cartesian Linguistics*. New York and London: Harper and Row, 1966.

—— *Language and Mind*. New York: Harcourt, Brace, and World, 1968.

Elson, B. and Pickett, V. B., *An Introduction to Morphology and Syntax*. Santa Ana: Summer Institute of Linguistics, 1962.

Fries, C. C., *The Structure of English: An Introduction to the Construction of English Sentences*. London: Longmans, 1957.

Harris, Z., *String Analysis of Sentence Structure*. The Hague: Mouton, 1962.

Hockett, C. F., *The State of the Art*. The Hague: Mouton, 1968.

Jespersen, O., *The Philosophy of Grammar*. London: Allen and Unwin, 1929.

—— *Analytic Syntax*. Copenhagen: Munksgaard, 1937.

Nida, E. A., *A Synopsis of English Syntax*. The Hague: Mouton, 1966.

Strang, B. M. H., *Modern English Structure*. London: Edward Arnold, 1962.

Tesnière, L., *Eléments de syntaxe structurale*. Paris: Klincksiek, 1959.

SEMANTICS

Bréal, M., *Essai de sémantique*. Paris: Hachette, 1897. Engl. transl., *Semantics: Studies in the Science of Meaning*. New York: Dover Publications, 1964.

Cohen, L. J., *The Diversity of Meaning*. 2nd ed. London: Methuen, 1966.

Guiraud, P., *La sémantique*. Paris: Presses universitaires de France, 1955.

Householder, F. W. and Saporta, S. (eds.), *Problems in Lexicography*. Publications of the Indiana Research Center in Anthropology, Folklore and Linguistics, 21. Baltimore, 1962.

Katz, J. J. and Postal, P. M. *An Integrated Theory of Linguistic Description*. Research Monographs, 26. Cambridge (Mass.): M.I.T. Press, 1964.

Lyons, J., *Structural Semantics*. Publications of the Philological Society, 20. Oxford: Blackwell, 1963.

Matoré, G., *La méthode en lexicologie*. Paris: Didier, 1953.
Nida, E. A., *Towards a Science of Translating*. Leiden: Brill, 1964.
Ogden, C. K. and Richards, I. A., *The Meaning of Meaning*. 8th ed. London: Routledge, and Kegan Paul, 1946.
Stern, G., *Meaning and Change of Meaning*. Göteborg, 1931. Republished Bloomington: Indiana University Press, 1964.
Trier, J., *Der deutsche Wortschatz im Sinnbezirk des Verstandes*. Heidelberg: Winter, 1931.
Ullmann, S., *The Principles of Semantics*. 2nd ed. Glasgow: Jackson; and Oxford: Blackwell, 1957.
—— *Semantics: An Introduction to the Science of Meaning*. Oxford: Blackwell, 1962.
Weinreich, U., *Explorations in Semantic Theory*. In: *Current Trends in Linguistics*, Volume 3 (ed. Sebeok, T.). The Hague: Mouton, 1966.

DIALECTS

Bach, A., *Deutsche Mundartforschung: ihre Wege, Ergebnisse und Aufgaben*. 2nd ed. Heidelberg: Winter, 1950.
Brook, G. L., *English Dialects*. London: André Deutsch, 1963.
Dauzat, A., *La géographie linguistique*. Paris: Flammarion, 1943.
Gamillscheg, E., *Die Sprachgeographie*. Bielefeld-Leipzig, 1928.
Keller, R. E., *The German Dialects*. Manchester University Press, 1961.
McIntosh, A., *An Introduction to a Survey of Scottish Dialects*. Edinburgh: Nelson, 1952.
Pop, S., *La dialectologie*. Louvain: Chez l'auteur, 1950.

PLACE-NAMES

Cameron, K., *English Place Names*. London: Methuen, 1961.
Ekwall, E., *The Concise Oxford Dictionary of English Place-Names*. 4th ed. Oxford, 1960.
Mawer, A., *Problems of Place-Name Study*. Cambridge, 1929.
Smith, A. H., *English Place-Name Elements*. English Place Name Society, Vol. XXV. Cambridge University Press, 1956.

WRITING

Cohen, M., *L'écriture*. Paris: Editions sociales, 1953.
— *La grande invention de l'écriture et son évolution*. Paris: Klinck-sieck, 1958.
Diringer, D., *The Alphabet. A Key to the History of Mankind*. 2nd ed. London: Hutchinson; and New York: Philosophical Library, 1951.
— *Writing*. London: Thames and Hudson, 1962.
Friedrich, J., *Entzifferung verschollener Schriften und Sprachen*. Berlin: Springer, 1954. Engl. transl. *Extinct Languages*. New York: Wisdom Library, 1957.
Gelb, I. J., *A Study of Writing*. 2nd ed. Chicago: The University of Chicago Press, 1963.
Jensen, H., *Sign, Symbol and Script*. 3rd. ed. Translated from the German by George Unwin. London: Allen and Unwin, 1970.
Moorhouse, A. C., *The Triumph of the Alphabet: A History of Writing*. New York: Schuman, 1953.

HISTORICAL AND COMPARATIVE LINGUISTICS

Bloomfield, W. M. and Newmark, L. D., *A Linguistic Introduction to the History of English*. New York: Random House—A. Knopf, 1963.
Brook, G. L., *A History of the English Language*. London: André Deutsch, 1958.
Fourquet, J., *Les mutations consonantiques du germanique*. Paris: 1948.
Hermann, E., *Lautgesetz und Analogie*. Abhandlungen der Gesellschaft der Wissenschaften zu Göttingen, philosophisch-historische Klasse, Neue Folge, 23, 3. Berlin: 1931.
Hoenigswald, H. H., *Language Change and Language Reconstruction*. Chicago: University Press, 1960.
Jespersen, O., *The Growth and Structure of the English Language*. 9th ed. Oxford, 1946.
Lehmann, W. P., *Proto-Indo-European Phonology*. University of Texas Press and Linguistic Society of America, 1952.
—— *Historical Linguistics: An Introduction*. New York and London: Holt, Rinehart, and Winston, 1962.

Martinet, A., *Economie des changements phonétiques*. Berne: Francke, 1955.

Meillet, E., *Introduction à l'étude comparative des langues indo-européennes*. 8th ed., republished by the University of Alabama Press, 1964.

—— *Linguistique historique et linguistique génerale*. Paris: Champion, 1926, 1938.

—— *La méthode comparative en linguistique historique*. Oslo, 1925.

Moore, S., *Historical Outlines of English Sounds and Inflections*. Revised by A. H. Marckwardt. Ann Arbor: George Wahr, 1951.

Paul, H., *Prinzipien der Sprachgeschichte*. 5th ed. Halle: Niemeyer, 1920.

LANGUAGE AND CULTURE

Benveniste, E., *Le vocabulaire des institutions indo-européennes*. Paris: Les éditions de minuit, 1969. Engl. transl. Faber and Faber (in prep.).

Boas, F., *Race, Language and Culture*. New York: Macmillan, 1940.

Henle, Paul (ed.), *Language, Thought, and Culture*. Ann Arbor: University of Michigan Press, 1958.

Hoijer, H. (ed.), *Language in Culture*. Chicago: University of Chicago Press, 1954.

Krahe, H., *Sprache und Vorzeit*. Heidelberg: Quelle und Meyer, 1954.

Sapir, E., *Selected Writings in Language, Culture, and Personality*. Berkeley: University of California Press, 1949.

Weir, R., *Language in the Crib*. The Hague: Mouton, 1962.

Weisgerber, L., *Muttersprache und Geistesbildung*. Göttingen: Vandenhoeck und Ruprecht, 1929. Repr. 1939.

TABLE OF PHONETIC SYMBOLS

CONSONANTS

	Bi-labial	Labio-dental	Dental and Alveolar	Palato-alveolar	Palatal	Velar	Uvular	Glottal
Plosive	p b		t d		c ɟ	k g		ʔ
Nasal	m		n		ɲ	ŋ		
Lateral Non-fricative			l		ʎ			
Rolled			r				ʀ	
Flapped			ɾ				ʀ	
Fricative	ɸ β	f v	θ ð s z ɹ	ʃ ʒ	ç j	x ɣ	χ ʁ	h
Frictionless Continuants and Semi-vowels	w ɥ		ɹ		j		ʁ	

VOWELS

	Front	Central	Back
Close	i y ɪ	ɨ ʉ	ɯ u
Half-close	e ø	ɘ	ɤ o
Half-open	ɛ œ	ɜ	ʌ ɔ
Open	æ a	a	ɑ ɒ

Notes: (1) Affricates are represented either by two separate symbols (tʃ, etc.) or by ligatures (ʧ, etc.); (2) aspirated plosives as ph, th, etc.; (3) vowel length as : ; (4) nasality as ~ ; (5) breath as ₒ (e.g. l̥); syllabic consonants as ˌ (e.g. n̩).

List of Abbreviations

A	adjective
Adj	Adjective
Adv	Adverb
Aux	auxiliary
Avest	Avestan
BPM	Base phrase-marker
C	consonant
CGmc	Common Germanic
Conj	conjugation
CV	consonant vowel
CVC	consonant vowel consonant
Det	determinant
DS	deep structure
Gmc	Germanic
Gk	Greek
Goth	Gothic
GPM	generalized phrase-marker
HCF	highest common factor
IA	Item and arrangement
IC	immediate constituent
IE	Indo-European
IP	Item and process
Lat	Latin
Lett	Lettish

Lith	Lithuanian
M	modal
M	meaning
ME	Middle English
N	noun
NP	noun phrase
Np	noun personal
Npl	noun plural
Npt	noun personal technical
Nt	noun technical
OCS	Old Church Slavonic
ODEE	Oxford Dictionary of English Etymology
OE	Old English
OHG	Old High German
OIr	Old Irish
ON	Old Norse
OS	Old Saxon
PI	phonological interpretation
PM	phrase-marker
PPP	past participle passive
PS	phrase structure
RP	received pronunciation
S	sound
S	sentence
SA	structural analysis
SC	structural change
SD	syntactic description
SI	semantic interpretation
Skt	Sanskrit
S-M	sound-meaning
TG	transformational grammar
U	utterance
V	verb
V	vowel
VC	vowel consonant
VP	verb phrase
WGmc	West Germanic
WP	word and paradigm

OTHER NOTATIONS

[ ]   phonetic transcription
//   morphemic transcription
{ }   moneme
~   signalling relationship
{ // ~ CAPITALS}   expression (keneme) and content (plereme)
        of a moneme
*   precedes a reconstructed form
italics   orthographic form
CAPITALS   'world' element or 'content' element

Addenda

P. 44, Fig. 5. The correlation of the formants is with the size and shape of the cavities in front of and behind the raised part of the tongue, and they are also affected by the parting or spreading of the lips, which alters the shape of the front cavity.

Pp. 49 and 52. X-ray films show that it is the raising and lowering of the whole soft palate, not just the uvula which shuts off and opens up the nasal passage.

P. 60, footnote 2. The intonation pattern (with two falls) given for *green house* is strictly appropriate only to an utterance which treats each word as an isolate. Ordinarily, only the nucleus before the pause would get the fall, the preceding one being level, i.e.
⌐⌐ .

P. 61, Fig. 11. The size of the dots indicates relative loudness, and their position on the vertical scale their relative pitch.

Pp. 85–86. It should be pointed out that whereas the original Jakobson–Halle 'features' were acoustically based, in transformational phonology (e.g. Chomsky and Halle, *The Sound Pattern of English*) the features are now defined in articulatory terms.

P. 88. Our use of the terms 'keneme' and 'plereme' is different from that of Hjelmslev. He meant by 'ceneme' the abstract ultimate elements of 'expression' (corresponding more or less to the Prague School's 'distinctive features'), and by 'plereme' the ultimate units of 'content'. We quote from B. Siertsema, *A Study of Glossematics* (p. 17): 'The study of the elements of thought, directed to the plane of the content (Fr. contenu), is called plerematics, the units it deals with are pleremes (from Gr. πλήρς = full: these units "contain" a "lump" of meaning, so to say).' In our analysis the terms apply at the final stage of the first articulation: each moneme emerges as the combination of a keneme with a plereme.

Pp. 137 and 169; (Chapter 7). Since this was written there has been much debate about the fundamental concepts of transformational grammar. There is a growing approximation to the position taken up in this book, namely that semantics is prior to syntax. It will be evident that no answer can be given to the primary onoma–rhema question until the utterance has been understood and the semantic components and their interrelationships sorted out. Similarly the statement that the passive and active expressions of a given content are identical in deep structure can be understood only with reference to the semantic content of a given pair. In fact the pairing of the two given utterances is determined semantically. There is also a growing tendency to describe deep structure in semantic terms. If this is accepted, then we are in the first place faced with the problem of structuring a semantic phenomenon. Terms like 'deep structure subject', 'deep structure predicate' and 'deep structure object' now come to look very much like our 'functional sites'. It would appear that such concepts and analyses are a necessary preliminary for building a transformational bridge between a semantic 'deep structure' and the more familiar grammatical structure which is now called 'surface structure'.

As for 'competence' and 'performance', we emphasize again that the former is a psychological hypothesis extraneous to linguistics proper. For us 'performance' is the relation between the 'logos', generated by the two-stage procedures of the Way Down, and the utterance. The Way Down culminates in a notation. To perform this successfully a knowledge of certain 'performance rules' is required, e.g. those relating to the selection of allophones. The psycholinguist would presumably have to include a knowledge of these rules in his model of 'competence'.

Index of Authors

Subject Index

A

ablative, 107
Ablaut, 217, 302
Ablaut verbs, 129
accent, 55
accent, Indo–European, 400
acceptability, 95
accusative, 106
acoustic analysis, 82
acrophonic principle, 258, 263
active, 118
active articulators, 62, 74
acute, 59, 73 f.
adequacy, operational, 171
adequation, 318, 321
adjectives, 92
adverbs, 92, 119
Aeolic, 386
affricates, 53
agentive, 143
agglutination, 110
agricultural terms, 313
Albanian, 387, 394
Alemannic, 281, 390
allokens, 105, 110, 130
allomons, 105, 126
allomorph, 104, 126
allophones, 69
alphabet, 34, 256, 262

alveolars, 52
amalgamation, 104, 110
amplitude, 38
analogy, 240, 315
analysability, 126, 143
analytic, 253
anaphora, 112
anaphoric, 89, 148, 159
anaptyxis, 60
Anatolian, 258, 304, 384
ancestral community, 216
ancestral forms, reconstruction of, 22
Anglian, 390
Anglo-Saxon mission, 353, 354
animal husbandry, 363
animal language, 18
antonomy, 201 f.
aphasia, 376
apicals, 74 f.
apico-alveolar, 76
arbitrariness, 15, 18
Arcado-Cypriot, 386
archiphoneme, 78
areal linguistics, 295
Armenian, 385
arrest, 58
article, 92
articulation, 36, 90
articulation of the world, 376, 382

Subject Index

A

ablative, 107
Ablaut, 217, 302
Ablaut verbs, 129
accent, 55
accent, Indo–European, 400
acceptability, 95
accusative, 106
acoustic analysis, 82
acrophonic principle, 258, 263
active, 118
active articulators, 62, 74
acute, 59, 73 f.
adequacy, operational, 171
adequation, 318, 321
adjectives, 92
adverbs, 92, 119
Aeolic, 386
affricates, 53
agentive, 143
agglutination, 110
agricultural terms, 313
Albanian, 387, 394
Alemannic, 281, 390
allokens, 105, 110, 130
allomons, 105, 126
allomorph, 104, 126
allophones, 69
alphabet, 34, 256, 262

alveolars, 52
amalgamation, 104, 110
amplitude, 38
analogy, 240, 315
analysability, 126, 143
analytic, 253
anaphora, 112
anaphoric, 89, 148, 159
anaptyxis, 60
Anatolian, 258, 304, 384
ancestral community, 216
ancestral forms, reconstruction of, 22
Anglian, 390
Anglo-Saxon mission, 353, 354
animal husbandry, 363
animal language, 18
antonomy, 201 f.
aphasia, 376
apicals, 74 f.
apico-alveolar, 76
arbitrariness, 15, 18
Arcado-Cypriot, 386
archiphoneme, 78
areal linguistics, 295
Armenian, 385
arrest, 58
article, 92
articulation, 36, 90
articulation of the world, 376, 382

vowel area, 45
vowel gradation, 217
vowel harmony, 113, 133
vowel quadrilateral, 270
vowels, 41 ff., 54 ff.
vowels, empty, 262

W

wavelength, 38
Way Down, 95, 97, 113, 123, 139, 153
Way Up, 95, 97, 123, 153, 191
'We', inclusive and exclusive, 112
weakening of meaning, 328
Weltanschauung, 374
West Germanic, 301, 389, 390
West Norse, 389
West Saxon, 390
whispered speech, 51
witness words, 196
word, 32, 132
word classes, 94
word concepts, 337
word family, 303

word formation, 303
word, grammatical, 134
word, morphological, 134
word, phonological, 134
word, syntactic, 134
word and paradigm, 124
words and things, 342
word mortality, 331
word stratigraphy, 291
world, 173, 307
world articulation, 379, 382
world orientated, 88
world picture, 374
writing, 255
Wulfila, 389

Y

yodization, 65, 224
Young Grammarians, 236

Z

zero, 35
zero grade, 303